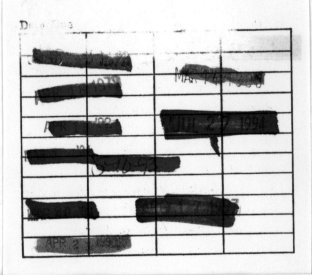

Romanticism in Perspective

ROMANTICISM IN PERSPECTIVE

*A comparative study of aspects of the Romantic
movements in England, France and Germany*

LILIAN R. FURST

HUMANITIES PRESS
New York 1970

First published in the United States of America 1970 by
HUMANITIES PRESS INC.
303 Park Avenue South New York NY

Library of Congress catalog card no. 78–113374

SBN 391–00003–9

Printed in Great Britain by
ROBERT MACLEHOSE AND CO LTD
The University Press, Glasgow

TO EUGÈNE VINAVER

> *O, fear not*
> *What may be done, but what is left undone*
>
> Shelley, *The Cenci*, Act IV, scene iii

Contents

8   *Contents*

Preface

━━◄◄◄◄◄◄ ❈ ►►►►►►━━

THE origins of this book date back to my undergraduate days. After reading some French Romantic poetry at school, I went up to university confident in the knowledge that Romanticism meant a poet weeping over his sorrows, preferably in some suitably wild setting. This notion hardly fitted Wordsworth, who formed part of the first-year course in English and who was casually called a Romantic poet. When, in my second year, I was faced with German Romanticism, my confusion was complete for it struck me as speculative philosophy. With characteristic student logic I decided to avoid examination questions on Romanticism since I was evidently unable to understand it. And there the matter rested, at least for some years, until I began to teach, and saw my students as puzzled as I had been. This gave me the impetus to start work on this book in an attempt to sort things out for myself – and perhaps for others too.

It was not until I had done a good deal of reading that I realized the foolhardiness of my venture. The more material I gathered, the more perplexing it became, but also the more fascinating. One of the cardinal problems was that of presentation : how to organize this stack of observations into a coherent picture. A factual survey (contained in the section entitled 'The Historical Perspective') seemed a necessary start to any process of 'sorting out'. But a mere historical juxtaposition did not appear satisfactory. I preferred to examine in turn certain crucial aspects (i.e. individualism, imagination, feeling) side by side in the three literatures in the hope of finding specific instances of similarity or difference between them. This method has, of course, disadvantages, notably the danger of repetitiveness when certain works are cited as examples first of this and then of that. Nevertheless it is a potentially fruitful approach to the comparative study of literature since it is conducive to a direct confrontation of ideas and texts. I hope that such comparisons will bring the particular character of each country's Romantic movement into truer perspective.

I have confined this study to English, French and German literature of the late eighteenth and early nineteenth centuries. It would be easy enough to argue in favour of extensions, both geographical – to include Italy, Spain, Russia, etc. – and temporal – to embrace the Neo-romanticism of the end of the nineteenth century. But it has not been my aim to compile an encyclopaedic compendium after the manner of van Tieghem's *Le Romantisme dans la littérature européenne*. Rather than range so far and wide, I have sought to probe only certain key aspects in some detail. For this reason also I have kept to what can be called the mainstream Romantics of the period, excluding not only subsidiary figures (e.g. Southey, Clare, Crabbe, Leigh Hunt, Landor, Thomas Moore, Joubert, Desbordes-Valmore, Pixérécourt) but also some major poets marginal to the Romantic movement (e.g. Hölderlin, Kleist, Jean Paul).

Even this relatively limited task was not devoid of difficulties, among them one that is inherent in any comparative study: the language barrier. Ideally I would wish for a reader equally at home in English, French and German; but ideally I myself should like to be able to read Tolstoy, Ibsen, Cervantes and Homer in the original. In deference to our limitations, I have added to the notes translations of all the French and German quotations. I must emphasize that these renderings have no artistic pretensions whatsoever; they are intended merely as a help, and for this reason the verse approximations have been arranged in lines as in the original so as to facilitate their use as a kind of mental crutch. Titles of books I have given in English only where they are familiar (e.g. Schiller's *The Robbers*) or where the actual title is of intrinsic significance (e.g. Bodmer's *Discourse on the Wondrous Element in Poetry*).

I must acknowledge my gratitude to two of my former colleagues at the Queen's University of Belfast : to Professor H. E. Hinderks for the loan – often, indeed, very generous gift – of many rare and stimulating books which I might otherwise not have come across, and to Professor K. Connell for the excellent advice that actually made me put pen to paper. I am also deeply indebted to Miss M. Norquoy of Manchester University for her expert assistance in compiling the index. Finally, I should like to thank my parents for their help with proof-reading, and above all, for having so patiently learned to live with Romanticism.

Manchester, July 1967   L. F.

Introduction: Focus

THE recognition of a certain family likeness among the works of a specific age in different tongues has inspired many comparative literary studies. That appropriate image of 'family likeness' was used by Jacques Barzun in his provocative book *Classic, Romantic and Modern* to characterize the vague resemblances found 'among the works of the Italian Renaissance, among the Elizabethans, and among the Romantics'.[1] Stimulated by the perception of such family likenesses, scholars have in the past sought out the similarities between the literatures of various lands at any particular time: the common traits of the mediaeval romances, of the Renaissance, of the Baroque or Romantic periods. One of the more recent studies of this kind is van Tieghem's *Le Romantisme dans la littérature européenne*,[2] a widely ranging survey of Romanticism in European literature, based on the conviction of its fundamental unity. Always, as in this work, those studies espousing what may be termed the 'family likeness' approach emphasize the underlying similarities between differing national literatures. Thus Wellek maintains that 'we find throughout Europe the same conceptions of poetry: of the workings and nature of poetic imagination, the same conception of nature: its relation to man, and basically the same poetic style, with a use of imagery, symbolism and myth which is clearly distinct from that of eighteenth-century neoclassicism'.[3] That this method has its dangers is well illustrated by an amusing experience of Etiemble:

> comme j'étais chargé de faire à Montpellier un cours sur le *pré-romantisme* en Europe à la fin du XVIIIe siècle, après avoir cueilli dans les manuels de nos historiens tous les thèmes qu'il convenait de cataloguer: la *nature*, le *paysage état d'âme*, l'*amour-passion*,

la *fatalité*, la *sensibilité*, le *temps qui passe*, les *ruines*, enfin : tout, je fis un cours, on ne peut plus conformiste, à la fin duquel j'ajoutai : 'Je tiens à signaler que toutes mes citations sur la naissance du préromantisme en Europe sont prises dans des poètes chinois, entre K'iu Yuan, qui vivait avant l'ère chrétienne, et l'époque des Song.'[4]

Although Etiemble is here actually pleading for a far wider vision in comparative studies to include writing in languages generally beyond the ken of Europeans, his anecdote in fact shows some of the pitfalls of the 'family likeness' approach : the danger not merely of an inevitable simplification, but also of distortion when the similarities between certain features are constantly stressed at the expense of the attendant differences, at the expense indeed of a coherent view of the whole.

Nevertheless, in spite of its inherent dangers, the 'family likeness' approach would seem in the long run more promising of fruitful, worthwhile results than the fragmentary investigation of influences. The German influences on Coleridge,[5] the influence of Goethe[6] and of Schiller[7] in France, German influence in France in the eighteenth and nineteenth centuries,[8] the influence of German literature in England in the nineteenth century,[9] the influence of Wordsworth and the so-called *Lakistes* in France :[10] these are the favourite areas of the influence-hunters in the Romantic period. No doubt some of their findings are both interesting and illuminating, but such work by nature rests on very uncertain foundations. How often can influence really be *proved* with any degree of certainty and how great a part is played by chance or by that coincidence of ideas which Coleridge frequently claimed ? 'If parallel passages are evidence of borrowing,' (IF indeed!) 'then we must conclude that Coleridge borrowed his matter', writes A. C. Dunstan,[11] almost admitting the tenuousness of his own argument. At best the pursuit of alleged influences and parallels is of questionable worth, while at worst it all too easily degenerates into lists of translations available to, and works read by the influenced, no more than boring minutiae. Furthermore, this tendency to concentrate on the external facts of cultural exchange (translations, travellers' reports, reviews, periodicals, etc.) can lead to another very real pitfall: the temptation to deduce from the sheer quantity of such contacts between various literatures the presence of an interaction decisive in quality. But the mere existence of even a considerable number of translations and personal links need not inevitably result in any profound reciprocal effect, as indeed the history of the Romantic movement in Europe illustrates, for in spite of the multiplicity of connections there was in fact little real interdependence.

The supreme advantage of the 'family likeness' approach lies in its width, its expansive view as against the narrowing down forced on the influence-hunter. In this respect, moreover, the image of a 'family likeness' is specially apposite: just as the members of a human family may share certain characteristics, each person, however, displaying only some of those characteristics and only in some degree or variant, likewise the literary works ascribed to any movement can each have some, but by no means necessarily all the traits usually associated with that movement, and as many individual variations are possible as within a human family. Thus the differences between the members of the family would not disqualify from membership; on the contrary, these very differences beneath the resemblances, testifying to the individuality of the person or work, are of particular significance. And it is an idiosyncratic combination of individual and family traits which makes up every person and every literary work too.

From this point of view it is worth taking a new look at that problem family, Romanticism in England, France and Germany. For long the resemblances have been stressed: the imaginative apprehension of experience, the primacy of feeling, the cult of the individual, specially of the artist, the new attitude to nature, the exploration of the unconscious and the fascination of the supernatural, the greater freedom of expression, etc. Undoubtedly all – or at least most of – these elements are manifest in the works of the so-called Romantic period throughout Europe, and by a judicious choice from among the enormous wealth of material some revealing parallels can be drawn : for example the figure of the ill-fated hero in Goethe's *Die Leiden des jungen Werthers*, Chateaubriand's *René*, Musset's *Confession d'un enfant du siècle* and Byron's *Childe Harold's Pilgrimage* or the image of the past in Tieck, Scott and Hugo; the visionary poetry of Novalis and Blake, or the nature poetry of Shelley and Lamartine, and so forth. But even after all these collocations and a thorough study of the similarities between them, a real comparison of the three Romantic movements in England, France and Germany has hardly begun. The paradoxes and incongruities remain : how can Novalis' esoteric delving into the mysterious depths of human experience in the *Hymnen an die Nacht* be related to Wordsworth's sensible account of his development in *The Prelude*? What is the connection between the fervent, rarified rhapsodies on art of Wackenroder's *Herzensergießungen eines kunstliebenden Klosterbruders* and the stormy rebelliousness of Hugo's *Hernani*? Or between Musset's agitated hallucinations in the *Nuits* and Keats' marvellously serene description in the *Ode to Autumn*? Each of these works is recognized and accepted without question in its native land as a product of the Romantic movement; yet the differences between them are patently so vast as to make a comparison appear well-nigh ludicrous. Clearly then any such comparison based solely on an examination of the resemblances between the three Romantic movements will be not only incomplete but distorted, in fact untrue in so far as it ignores the essential differences, which have hitherto been largely overlooked while attention was focused on the common elements. Consequently a much simplified and unsatisfying picture has emerged of almost simultaneous outbursts of a very similar kind of Romanticism in various lands. The real relationship between the Romantic movements in England, France and Germany is infinitely more complex and, unfortunately, fraught with all manner of difficulties.

Foremost among these is the meaning and use of the word 'Romantic' itself. It is surely no exaggeration to claim that no other term of literary criticism has been invested with such a startlingly wide range of meanings. As a sampling of modern usage, Barzun[12] cites the following synonyms: attractive, unselfish, exuberant, ornamental, unreal, realistic, irrational and materialistic, futile, heroic, noteworthy, conservative, mysterious, soulful, bombastic, revolutionary, nordic, picturesque, formless, formalistic, emotional, fanciful, stupid, and this list could quite easily be swelled by further examples of verbal – and mental – imprecision. Not that this multiplicity of meanings stems from any lack of attempts to define the term; on the contrary, definitions abound, but they in turn are so contradictory as to intensify rather than dispel the confusion. The strange assortment of definitions advanced by some recent scholars has been ably and wittily surveyed by A. O. Lovejoy in his excellent article 'On the Discrimination of Romanticisms'.[13] Lovejoy reaches the conclusion that 'the word "romantic" has come to mean so many things that, by itself, it means nothing. It has ceased to perform the function of a verbal sign' [14] so that the wholesale use of the word 'has led to a good deal of unconscious falsification of the history of ideas'.[15] Bringing a welcome measure of sound common sense into the controversy, Lovejoy accordingly pleads for the discrimination of Romanticisms, a process of analysis and clarification to precede the general appraisals and judgements. To illustrate the need for such discrimination, he distinguishes between the Romanticism current before 1790 and the German brand of *circa* 1800: the former was based upon naturalism, associated with primitivism, and showed a preference for simplicity and ingenuous naïvety, believing in the superiority of nature over conscious art, while the latter was founded on elaborate theories, with a liking for diversity, complexity and aesthetic subtlety, and proclaimed the superiority of conscious art over mere nature. That these two groups shared an intense admiration for Shakespeare and an equally passionate conviction of the

B

creative artist's independence of rules hardly justifies the crude application of the epithet 'Romantic' to both alike. This is in fact the weakest link in Lovejoy's argument since the former movement is often already known as 'Pre-romanticism'. Nevertheless he makes his point with some force : that there is a plurality of Romanticisms which must be recognized because the Romanticism of one country and one period may have little enough in common with that of other countries and other periods. This first difficulty thus, far from being merely linguistic, immediately points to far-reaching implications.

It would, however, be unfair to attribute this verbal and conceptual confusion mainly to recent critics, as Lovejoy seems to. Since its introduction into the realm of literary criticism, the term has been a constant source of muddle and misunderstanding. Together with such terms as 'imagination', 'nature', 'truth', the Romantics tended to use the word with little or no indication of its scope or meaning. Nowhere is this more apparent than in the writings of Friedrich Schlegel : in spite of his boast in 1797 to have written some 125 pages in explanation of the word, he does not appear to have arrived at any single definitive meaning. Throughout his theories the connotation of the term fluctuates disconcertingly, not only from work to work, but even within the limits of one and the same work. While his brother August Wilhelm, of a more orderly turn of mind, interpreted *romantisch* fairly consistently in both the *Vorlesungen über schöne Literatur und Kunst* and the *Vorlesungen über dramatische Kunst und Literatur* as denoting 'den eigentümlichen Geist der modernen Kunst, im Gegensatz mit der antiken oder klassischen',[16] Friedrich, in his characteristically unsystematic manner, switched from meaning to meaning to suit the needs of the moment. In his *Gespräch über die Poesie*, though subscribing in broad outline to the antithesis between the Ancient and the Romantic, he promptly qualified it by adding : 'indessen bitte ich Sie doch, nur nicht sogleich anzunehmen, daß mir das Romantische und das Moderne völlig gleich gelte'.[17] For to him 'das Romantische' is 'nicht sowohl eine Gattung als ein

Element der Poesie' [18] and in this sense all poetry, particularly
the novel, is Romantic. In this wider context 'ist eben das
romantisch, was uns einen sentimentalen Stoff in einer phantastischen Form darstellt',[19] which would justify the repeated
epithet 'romantisch' [20] to describe Shakespeare and possibly
even the contention 'Im Orient müssen wir das höchste
Romantische suchen'.[21] If a certain – admittedly somewhat
bizarre – logic is discernible in these various statements, there
is nothing here to foreshadow Friedrich Schlegel's later usage
of the term in his *Geschichte der alten und neuen Literatur*,
written some twelve years later, after his conversion to
Catholicism. The revised version of 1815 shows most plainly
the distorting effect of his new religious beliefs, which lead him
to equate Romantic with Christian when he writes of 'das
eigentlich unterscheidende Merkmal des Romantischen, insofern
wir dieses noch von dem Christlich-Allegorischen unterschei-
den',[22] or: 'Calderon ist . . . unter allen anderen dramatischen
Dichtern . . . der christlichste, und eben darum auch der am
meisten romantische'.[23] Friedrich Schlegel's unpredictability is
that of a weather-vane, blown hither and thither by the wind
of his whims : significantly, 'Willkür' [24] is the word he chooses
to describe the supreme, indeed only law governing the poet.

Although – fortunately – no other writer matches this degree
of instability, the confusion surrounding the term is no less
great in France than in Germany. For Mme de Staël Romantic
is virtually synonymous with Northern, the poetry of Ossian,
as opposed to the Southern, the poetry of Homer. But for Hugo
and Stendhal, as for the majority of their generation the antithesis is between Romantic and Classical, though even in this
context the word is endowed with a number of meanings. To
the rebel of *Cromwell* and *Hernani* it is tantamount to the
free, the picturesque, the characteristic, embracing also the
grotesque, as enunciated in his famous preface to *Cromwell*. To
Stendhal, on the other hand, Romantic signifies quite simply
contemporary, modern, when he declares in *Racine et Shakespeare* : 'Tous les grands écrivains ont été romantiques de leurs

temps',[25] adding: 'les artistes romains furent Romantiques; ils représentèrent ce qui, de leur temps, était vrai, et par conséquent touchant pour leurs compatriotes.'[26] From this definition, that bypasses all the essential problems, Stendhal concludes that

> Le Romantisme est l'art de présenter aux peuples les oeuvres littéraires qui, dans l'état actuel de leurs habitudes et de leurs croyances, sont susceptibles de leur donner le plus de plaisir possible. Le classicisme, au contraire, leur présente la littérature qui donnait le plus grand plaisir possible à leurs arrière-grands-pères.[27]

The theories and counter-theories advanced in the French literary journals of the period, more complex if not more sophisticated than Stendhal's, are also bedevilled by the recurrent question as to the meaning of the word until *Le Globe* tried to settle the argument 'en deux mots' by decreeing that it is 'Le protestantisme dans les lettres et les arts',[28] a formula so glib as to suggest a mounting despair and so outlandish as to be comprehensible only against the background of the specific circumstances of the time.

No wonder then, that those worthy citizens of La-Ferté-sous-Jouarre, Monsieur Dupuis and Monsieur Cotonet, became increasingly perplexed as they diligently read the journals and earnestly endeavoured to grapple with this word, suddenly a favourite of the Parisian intelligentsia, although in the humbler provinces it had hitherto had 'une signification facile à retenir, il est synonyme d'absurde'.[29] At first, they note, the discussion had centred on the grotesque, the picturesque, the description of landscapes in poetry, the revival of the Middle Ages, the use of history. For some two years Dupuis and Cotonet happily cherished the illusion that Romanticism applied only to the theatre to distinguish the Neo-classical drama from the drama that did not observe the unities. They learned that 'le romantisme n'était autre chose que l'alliance du fou et du sérieux, du grotesque et du terrible, du bouffon et de l'horrible, autrement dit, si vous l'aimez mieux, de la comédie et de la tragédie'.[30]

But they discerned the same mingling of the serious and the comic in Aristophanes and likewise that distinctive melancholy, said to be characteristically Romantic, in Sappho, Plato and Priam. They therefore wondered whether 'le classique ne serait-il donc que l'imitation de la poésie grecque et le romantique que l'imitation des poésies allemande, anglaise et espagnole?'[31] or again: 'Ne serait-ce pas, pensâmes-nous, seulement affaire de forme? Ce romantisme indéchiffrable ne consisterait-il pas dans ce vers brisé dont on fait assez de bruit dans le monde?'[32] From 1830 to 1831 they thought it was 'le genre historique'; in 1831 they identified it as 'le genre intime'; from 1832-3 it occurred to them that it might be a philosophical and political system. The whole affair seemed strange, then bizarre, finally almost baroque so that 'pour en finir, nous croyons que le romantisme consiste à employer tous ces adjectifs, et non en autre chose'.[33]

Musset's brilliant satire sheds a glaring light on the confusion that envelops this term like a cocoon. Perhaps the English poets were sufficiently perceptive to foresee the disastrous outcome of the quest for definitions for they gracefully sidestepped the whole issue. It is in fact perfectly feasible to study and characterize the English poetry of the late eighteenth and early nineteenth centuries without ever having recourse to the epithet Romantic. The word rarely occurs in the works of Blake, Wordsworth, Coleridge, Shelley and Keats in contrast to its frequent appearance in German and French theoretical writings. The English critics of the period were not, by and large, pre-occupied with the philosophical basis of the movement as were the Germans, nor was the distinction between Classical and Romantic of any importance, as in France. The strong English preference for concrete, practical, empirical criticism resulted therefore in a paucity of theoretical definitions. Even Coleridge, the most philosophically interested and inclined, based his findings on inductive generalizations rather than laying down absolute *a priori* rules. Thus the very approach to the term Romantic and its interpretation already reveal profound and significant differences between the literary movements of that name in England, France and Germany. In each language the word was endowed with special meanings not acceptable nor even readily comprehensible to the poets of other lands; for instance, Friedrich Schlegel's – and Novalis' – highly personal elaboration of *romantisch* was totally alien to the English and remote from the French too. Since the word had so diverse a connotation for the various protagonists, it is evidently erroneous to compare these Romanticisms as if they were based on an agreed definition, as if they meant the same thing. Yet this is just what many comparative studies have attempted to do, led on by the outer deceptive similarity of the words romantic, *romantique* and *romantisch*.

Moreover, it is false to assume that each country had a single, unified 'Romantic school' with clear national characteristics. Far from it: and herein lies the second obstacle to any comparison. Who would have the temerity to speak of a 'Romantic school' in England after reading the visionary poetry of Blake and the mordant satire of Byron's *Don Juan*? Yet both are generally assigned to the Romantic group, albeit to opposite ends of it, so to speak. Similarly, in surveying the 'Romantic school' in France, the reader of today might well be as perplexed as Dupuis and Cotonet. The Chateaubriand of the *Essai sur les Révolutions* and of the earlier written parts of *Atala* can properly be called a Romantic, and so can the author of the later written parts of the latter work and of the *Génie du Christianisme*, but it is obvious that the word has, in many important respects, a different and even antithetical meaning as applied to the two phases of Chateaubriand's writing. Nor is the Hugo of *Cromwell* and *Hernani*, the rebel-chieftain in the uprising against Neo-classical drama, the same as the poet of the *Odes et Ballades* where he preaches the social and moral responsibility of the genius, the chosen few, 'ces sentinelles laissés par le Seigneur sur les tours de Jérusalem, et qui ne se tairont ni jour ni nuit.' [34] Faced with these shifts and changes, one may well ask whether there is any such thing as the average or typical or representative or even characteristic 'Romantic attitude' in any land. In part perhaps the trouble stems from the Romantics' love of paradox and contradiction in every form, mingled at times with a naive desire to startle, to *épater le bourgeois*. But there were also more serious causes of the constant flux and flow of ideas, such as Friedrich Schlegel's demand, in the celebrated 116th Fragment from the *Athenäum*, that Romantic poetry should always be 'progressive'. He could hardly foresee that in Germany this progression would lead from the so-called *Frühromantik** to the *Hochromantik*, two quite dissimilar groups: the former, often known as the *Jena-Romantik*, essentially philosophical, metaphysical, speculative, introvert in its interests, while the latter, the *Heidelberg-Romantik*, more creative and extrovert, cultivating the heritage of the Germanic past in the folk-song and folk-tale. With this pride in their history, literature and language, the German Romantics tended to become increasingly nationalistic in keeping with the political trend towards unification. On the other hand, the French Romantics grew more and more cosmopolitan as they moved away from the aggressive fervour and isolationism of the Revolutionary period. Since the Romantic age spans at least fifty years, there was ample time for such developments, which further complicate the situation.

Considering these divergences within the Romantic movements of each land, as well as the multiplicity of meanings given to the term itself, it is not surprising that the relationship between the various literatures should at first sight look like one long list of misconceptions. For that which seemed Romantic to the Germans, did not strike the English and French as such; just as what was Romantic in the eyes of the French, was not so to the English or Germans, and so forth. Each seized in the literature of other tongues that which was most nearly consonant with its own notions: hence there arose those misinterpretations that are comprehensible only when seen through

---

* 'Early' or 'Jena Romantics', and 'Later' (literally 'High') or 'Heidelberg Romantics'.

the eyes of the beholder in the foreign group, in terms of *its* conception of Romanticism. For instance, Goethe's *Werther* and *Götz von Berlichingen*, which to the Germans are the symbols of the introvert and the extrovert aspects of the *Sturm und Drang*,* are to the French the very epitome of German Romanticism. Thus when the French critics of the early nineteenth century write about German Romanticism, they are always referring to Goethe, Schiller, Bürger – in fact the *Stürmer und Dränger* – or to Kotzebue, without any mention of Friedrich Schlegel, Novalis, Wackenroder, who appear to have been totally unknown at that time. Likewise Byron was – indeed still is – regarded in Germany and France as the English Romantic poet *par excellence*, whereas in England he is considered a marginal figure, who has some affinities with the Romantics, but stronger links with the earlier, eighteenth-century tradition of Pope. For the English Wordsworth's *Lyrical Ballads*, with its important *Preface*, represent a cornerstone of the Romantic school and every countryman and contemporary of Wordsworth was struck by the novelty of a description such as this :

> Upon the forest-side in Grasmere Vale
> There dwelt a Shepherd, Michael was his name;
> An old man, stout of heart, and strong of limb.
> His bodily frame had been from youth to age
> Of an unusual strength : his mind was keen,
> Intense, and frugal, apt for all affairs,
> And in his shepherd's calling he was prompt
> And watchful more than ordinary men.
> Hence he had learned the meaning of all winds,
> Of blasts of every tone; and, oftentimes,
> When others heeded not, He heard the South
> Make subterraneous music, like the noise
> Of bagpipers on distant Highland hills.
> The Shepherd, at such warning, of his flock
> Bethought him, and he to himself would say,
> 'The winds are now devising work for me!'
> And, truly, at all times, the storm, that drives

---

* Usually rendered by 'Storm and Stress'.

The traveller to a shelter, summoned him
Up the mountains : he had been alone
Amid the heart of many thousand mists,
That came to him, and left him, on the heights.[35]

The German might well perceive in this a fine example of what he would call Poetic Realism, while to the French it seems altogether too realistic, too pedestrian, too didactic, too devoid of fervour to qualify as Romantic at all; Wordsworth describes, analyses, dissects, explains and reasons where his French counterparts enthuse, exclaim, extol, exaggerate and explode.

It should by now be evident that the inter-relationship of the English, French and German Romantic movements is far more complex than is usually realized. In part the difficulties arise from the nature of Romanticism itself, which in turn led to its sporadic outbursts throughout Europe. The scope and breadth of the concept allows a considerable range of variations and possible permutations, all of which are still admissible as Romantic so that there can be, and in fact are, genuine differences between the many groups and schools which comprise the Romantic movement in Europe. These factors combine to make a straightforward comparison on a broad front between the Romantic schools of various lands virtually impossible; attempts at such a comparison must inevitably either lead to a distortion that verges on falsification or to an outcome modified by so many qualifications as to lose most of its worth.

Nevertheless, that 'family likeness' between Romantic works in different tongues does become apparent again and again, almost as if to tempt the reader to a comparison, in spite of the manifold difficulties. Nowhere was the ambivalent character of European Romanticism so vividly illustrated as in the exhibition of European Romantic paintings held at the Tate Gallery in London in the summer of 1959. Even a cursory visit to that exhibition could hardly have failed to produce a twofold impression : on the one hand the awareness of a certain unity, the recurrence of specific motifs and moods, and on the other the startling diversity of the faces of European Romanticism.

And even if there is little hope of a finite definition of Romanticism, certain vital traits are distinguishable within the members of this family, traits not manifest in a like manner or in equal intensity, but nonetheless such as to form a common, unifying element. Surely herein lies a valid basis for comparison : instead of confronting the total sum of a nation's Romantic writers with another in all their respective paradoxicality, it would be less hazardous and more promising to juxtapose a limited number of key characteristics, such as the predominance of individualism, the primacy of the imagination and the emphasis on feeling. These particular strains suggest themselves because they are fundamental to, and inherent in, every interpretation of Romanticism in so far as this represents the free, imaginative expression of individual experience and emotion. A study of the ways in which these strains appear in England, France and Germany could reveal both the similarities and the differences between the three Romantic literatures, thereby producing a more balanced final picture.

As a preliminary to any more detailed analysis of specific aspects, it is worth beginning with a chronological survey. This is a necessary, though apparently elementary first step because Romanticism was not by any means a simultaneous manifestation in a number of countries, as is generally supposed; on the contrary, its spread is characterized by curious time-lags, and unexpected spurts.* In fact the movement's external history already sheds much light on its inner nature. To establish the correct sequence and perspective not only obviates some, at least, of the more common misapprehensions, but also creates a sounder base from which to explore the maze of Romanticisms.

* See Appendix A : Chronological chart.

The Historical Perspective

————— ❖ —————

'UNE crise de la conscience européenne':[1] this is the succinct and telling phrase chosen by van Tieghem to describe the Romantic movement in Europe. The claim that it was far more than just another literary movement is not based primarily on the sheer extent, the expanse of Romanticism, though it is in fact true that no other literary movement has ever evoked such a wide response throughout Europe. The real significance of Romanticism as a 'crise de la conscience européenne' lies not in its mere quantity, but in the *quality* of the changes it implied. For Romanticism brought not just a greater freedom and a new technique; these were only the outer manifestations of a complete and deep-seated reorientation, not to say revolution, in the manners of thought, perception and consequently of expression too. The nature of this revolution has recently been outlined in vivid terms by Isaiah Berlin, who defined it as a 'shift of consciousness' that 'cracked the backbone of European thought'.[2] That backbone had been the belief in the possibility of a rational comprehension of the universe. When the rationalistic approach was applied to the arts as well as to the emergent physical sciences, it resulted in those rigid pronouncements on the immutable 'rules' of literature that were the bane of Neoclassicism. This dogmatism was first cautiously questioned and then vehemently rejected in the course of the eighteenth century, and finally the old standards were ousted by the Romantics' new criteria and values. In place of the Neoclassical ideals of rationalism, traditionalism, formal harmony, the Romantics emphasized individualism, imagination and emotion as their guiding principles. Hence the old 'rules' of 'good taste', regularity and conformity gave way to the unbridled creative urge of the original genius, and the ideal of a smooth beauty was scorned in favour of a dynamic outpouring of feeling. A new mode of imaginative perception gave birth to a whole new vocabulary and new forms of artistic expression: this is the essence of that 'crise de la conscience européenne' which lies at the heart of the Romantic revolution, and this is also perhaps as near an approximation to a definition of Romanticism as is possible. It may not have the neatness of a snappy catch-phrase (such as: 'the return to nature' or 'the cult of the extinct'), but it is sufficiently comprehensive and sufficiently plain to serve as a viable working basis.

This reorientation occurred in varying degrees throughout Europe in the latter part of the eighteenth and the early years of the nineteenth centuries. In this sense Romanticism can rightly be regarded as a European phenomenon that can be appreciated in all its implications only by means of a comparative study. Many of the Romantics themselves were well aware of the supranational character of the movement: the brothers Schlegel consciously cherished the notion of a specifically European Romantic literature as part of their striving for an all-embracing 'universal' poetry, and both Coleridge and Novalis hoped for an eventual European reintegration. Perhaps these cosmopolitan tendencies of the Romantics have encouraged critics to seek out the common denominators of the Romantic movements and to over-emphasize the similarities between the literatures of various countries. The 'family likeness' which certainly meets the eye can be traced back to the communal ancestry of Romanticism throughout Europe, which springs from one and the same momentous spiritual and intellectual reorientation.

To delve into the origins of this revolution is beyond the scope of this study. The first unmistakable signs of impending change manifested themselves before the middle of the eighteenth century, and in this earliest phase – say 1740 to 1770 – it is England that was to the fore. As early as 1742 Young, inspired by personal grief at the death of his daughter and of a friend, published his *Night Thoughts*, which were followed in

1745 by Akenside's *Pleasures of Imagination*. Historically these two works have much in common in that they stand midway between the conventional moralism of the age and a fresh outlook which admits imagination to respectability in poetic practice. Imagination, according to Akenside, 'diffuses its enchantment' and makes the soul

> To that harmonious movement from without
> Responsive[3]

– no very startling claim as yet, but at least a first glimmer of a recognition of the powers of the imagination. The personal melancholy, the funereal cult of the *Night Thoughts* were reiterated in Hervey's *Meditations among the Tombs* (1746) and Gray's *Elegy written in a country churchyard* (1751) with their awareness of the fleetingness and pathos of human life, their preference for darkness, solitude, the evocation of solemn, sombre scenes. The slightly moralizing sensibility of the period is as apparent in these poems as in the novels of Richardson and his imitators. This sensibility was deeply affected by Macpherson's *Fingal* (1762) which, together with Percy's *Reliques* (1765), laid the foundations for the subsequent popularity of supposedly naïve folk-poetry, the natural utterances of primitive, spontaneous genius. Macpherson's concoctions, purporting to be a transcription from the ancient bard Ossian, made a particularly strong impression throughout Europe with their highly coloured intrigues, their gloomy Northern setting, their whole outlandishness and, above all, their rhythmic prose, which seemed so much more poetic than the poetry of the early eighteenth century :

> Star of descending night! fair is thy light in the west! thou liftest thy unshorn head from thy cloud : thy steps are stately on thy hill. What dost thou behold in the plain ? The stormy winds are laid. The murmur of the torrent comes from afar. Roaring waves climb the distant rock. The flies of evening are on their feeble wings; the hum of their course is on the field. What dost thou behold, fair light ? But thou dost smile and depart. The waves

come with joy around thee : they bathe thy lovely hair. Farewell,
thou silent beam! Let the light of Ossian's soul arise![4]

Alongside Ossian, the other decisive document of English
Pre-romanticism, Young's *Conjectures on Original Composition*
(1759), was of far-reaching import as the herald of the new
aesthetics. Some of Young's ideas were, it is true, already
current in England among his contemporaries, notably in the
discourses of Burke, Thomas and Joseph Warton and William
Sharpe. But never before had these ideas been stated as cogently
as in the *Conjectures*; by his clear-sighted distinctions between
imitation and originality, the ancients and the moderns,
learning and genius, the observation of rules (rejected as
'crutches' needful only to the lame) and the energy of the inspired enthusiast, Young was crucial in precipitating the reorientation away from the old accepted notions. Here for the
first time, the superiority of the new ideals was proclaimed
beyond a shadow of doubt :

> An Original may be said to be of a vegetable nature; it rises
> spontaneously from the vital root of genius; it grows, it is not
> made : Imitations are often a sort of manufacture, wrought by
> those mechanics, art and labour, out of pre-existent materials not
> their own.[5]

Or again, take the contrast between a 'genius' and a 'good
understanding' :

> A genius differs from a good understanding, as a magician from a
> good architect; that raises his structure by means invisible; this
> by skilful use of common tools. Hence genius has ever been
> supposed to partake of something divine.[6]

These two brief examples alone suffice to illustrate the incisive
quality of Young's thinking. Many of the key-concepts of
Romanticism are already contained in the *Conjectures*, in the
prominence given to such words as 'original', 'genius', 'grows',
'magician', 'divine'. There is thus some justification for the
contention that 'this vast romantic movement was the European
reverberation of English eighteenth-century romanticism, like

the thunder of Alpine re-echoing to a pistol-shot'.[7] Many of the essential elements of Romanticism were indeed present in England towards the middle of the eighteenth century: some recognition of the role of the imagination, the emphasis on the original composition of the genius, the cult of sensibility, the vague religious feeling, the melancholy reverie, the interest in 'natural' poetry, the discovery of external nature. But it would be premature to call this anything other than Pre-romanticism, for these were merely trends and beginnings with the stress on the natural – no doubt in reaction against the artificial over-refinement of Neo-classicism – whereas the dominant factor in Romanticism proper was the transfiguring imagination, whose true significance was not yet appreciated.

While this reorientation was progressing rapidly in England, France and Germany were far behind during this initial phase. France was still suffering from the backwash of its glorious Neo-classical age, which continued to overshadow creative writing and to a large extent to stifle innovation. A spirit of enlightenment does pervade at least the early criticism of Diderot, such as the prefaces to his plays *Le Fils Naturel* (1757) and *Le Père de Famille* (1758), where he advocates a greater realism; but after this advance towards emotionalism he was, in his later works, to return to the assumptions of the Neo-classical creed. Only Rousseau broke really new ground: his disgust with the social order of the time, based on ownership of land and goods, led him to idealize the primitive state of mankind and to call for the famous return to nature. Important though this was, it was by no means Rousseau's sole contribution to Pre-romanticism; his assimilation of external nature to man's moods in *Les Rêveries du Promeneur Solitaire* (1778) and *La Nouvelle Héloïse* (1761), his musical prose style and his spotlight on his ego in his autobiographical writings all plainly foreshadow certain later developments. Rousseau, however, was not understood, at least not in France, until later; meanwhile his most immediate effect was in Germany through the intermediary of Herder, an enthusiastic disciple of Rousseau's,

who transmitted his admiration for Rousseau to the young
adherents of the *Sturm und Drang* movement.

In the mid-eighteenth century Germany was in the literary
field the most backward of the major European countries;
politically disunited and economically disrupted by internal
strife, Germany had in the latter half of the seventeenth and the
early years of the eighteenth century virtually been lying
fallow. A new era began to dawn in the 1730s with the notorious
quarrel between the doctrinal rationalist Gottsched and the
somewhat less narrow-minded Swiss critics Bodmer and
Breitinger, who realized that poetry could not be made according to a set recipe – like a cake – as Gottsched had assumed.
Bodmer in 1740 published his *Kritische Abhandlung von dem
Wunderbaren in der Poesie* (*Discourse on the Wondrous Element
in Poetry*), the title of which already indicates the progression
towards a more fruitful conception of art. The Enlightenment
found its most vigorous and wise exponent in Lessing, who
savagely attacked the 'frenchified' ('französierend' he contemp-
tuously called it in the seventeenth *Literaturbrief*) mode of
writing favoured by Gottsched. He pleaded instead that German
writers should model themselves on the freer products of the
English, whose spirit was more akin to their own. Lessing was
not the first to turn his gaze towards England; Bodmer and
Breitinger had earlier championed and translated Milton, and
Klopstock's *Messias* (1748) is patently indebted to *Paradise
Lost*. Although Lessing was thus not the first to point towards
England, nevertheless his position in Germany was as crucial
as, and in some respects comparable to, that of Young in
England. For it was Lessing who in his *Literaturbriefe* (1759)
and *Hamburgische Dramaturgie* (1767) presented a reasoned and
compelling case for the decisive reorientation not only from
France to England, but also from imitation to original creation,
extolling Shakespeare as the supreme creative genius. Herder
in his rhapsodic appraisal of Shakespeare and also of Ossian
furthered the cult of genius, stimulated no doubt by the German
translation of Young's *Conjectures* which appeared in 1760. The

vital impetus therefore reached Germany from England, the
fountain-head of European Pre-romanticism.

In the second phase, between about 1770 and 1790, this
position was reversed, for the ascendancy which had been
England's now passed to Germany. Both England and France
were in no haste to accept new notions, perhaps because the
native literary tradition was firmly established; in France it
tended to exercise a retarding influence – the great battle of
Hernani took place only in the year 1830 – while in England
the lack of resistance to innovations paradoxically led to their
comparatively slow infiltration. Germany, on the contrary,
was thirsting for a fresh start after its long period of inertia. So
Germany's very backwardness proved in fact an advantage
when the young writers of the *Sturm und Drang* movement, for
lack of a strong native tradition, eagerly seized on the stimuli
from abroad, and it was they who popularized and propagated
the new attitudes throughout Europe.

The essence of the *Sturm und Drang*, whose name was
derived from Klinger's drama of 1776, lay in rebellion against
finite restriction in any shape or form – literary, political or
social. This self-assertive rebelliousness was more than the
adolescent defiance of a few gifted young men; it arose directly
out of the proud conviction of the limitless rights and powers of
the divinely inspired genius. Thus the theories formulated a
few years earlier by Young were activated by the *Sturm und
Drang* and found living examples in the youthful Goethe and
Schiller. All the favourite ideas of the *Sturm und Drang* pivoted
on the figure of the truly great, exceptional man; it was his
personal experiences and emotions which were to be transformed
into art through the creative power of his unbridled imagination.
No wonder that the *Sturm und Drang* is often and aptly termed
the *Geniezeit*.* Incoherent and supremely arrogant though it
was, the credo of the *Sturm und Drang* foreshadowed very many
of the basic concepts of Romanticism : the belief in the autonomy
of the divinely inspired genius, the release of the imagination

* 'Age of Genius'

from the bondage of 'good taste', the primacy of spontaneous, intuitive feeling, complete freedom of artistic expression, the notion of organic growth and development, from which arose both an interest in the past, particularly the Middle Ages, and a new pantheistic vision of nature as part of a unified cosmos. Nor were these ideas to remain mere theories any longer; in the early works of Goethe and Schiller the new mode of perception and expression burst upon a startled Europe. And how immeasurable is the gulf that separates Goethe's dynamic nature poetry from the pretty lyrics of the preceding generation! Compare the formal, pedestrian description by Brockes in his *Betrachtungen des Mondscheins in einer angenehmen Frühlings-nacht (Considerations on the Moon of a pleasant Spring night)* in the collection *Irdisches Vergnügen in Gott (Earthly Joy in God)* (1721) – (note already the clumsy titles) :

> Kaum hatte sich die Nacht zu zeigen angefangen,
> Die nach der Hitze Last der Kühlung Lust verhieß,
> Als sich ein neuer Tag dem Schein nach sehen ließ :
> Der volle Mond war aus dem grauen Duft,
> Der nach des Tages schwüler Luft
> Mit Purpur untermischt den Horizont bedeckte
> Wie rötlich Gold nur eben aufgegangen,
> Aus dessen wandelbarem Kreise,
> Der alles in der Nacht mit Licht und Schimmer füllt,
> Mehr Anmut noch als Licht und Schimmer quillt.[8]

– compare these mundane lines with the intensely imaginative, mysteriously intuitive perception of the same scene in Goethe's bewitching *An den Mond (To the Moon)* :

> Füllest wieder Busch und Tal
> Still mit Nebelglanz,
> Lösest endlich auch einmal
> Meine Seele ganz ;
> Breitest über mein Gefild
> Lindernd deinen Blick,
> Wie des Freundes Auge mild
> Über mein Geschick.[9]

In face of these two texts, further verbal comment on the

revolution wrought by the *Sturm und Drang* becomes superfluous.

It was at this time too, in the early 1770s, that the great Romantic proto-types were delineated in the melancholy hero Werther and the insatiable seeker Faust, figures that were to haunt Europe. The impact of *Werther* (1774) is, of course, notorious; Goethe became the idol of Europe. The success of Schiller's *Die Räuber* (*The Robbers*) (1781) was even more immediate and widespread: in England as well as in France Schiller was acclaimed with such wild enthusiasm as to trigger off a veritable mania for the German theatre, admittedly excessive and short-lived. Nevertheless Goethe and Schiller remained in the eyes of both the English and the French the typical representatives of German Romanticism, and strange though this misconception may at first seem, it is in fact not without some justification. For in the *Sturm und Drang*, the culmination of Pre-romanticism, the first significant breakthrough was achieved, and in this Goethe and Schiller were largely instrumental. With the publication of Kant's three major works, the *Kritik der reinen Vernunft* (*Critique of pure Reason*) in 1781, the *Kritik der praktischen Vernunft* (*Critique of practical Reason*) in 1788 and the *Kritik der Urteilskraft* (*Critique of Judgement*) in 1790, the mortal blows were struck at the old rationalist system. F. Schlegel was justified in his proud claim that the springs of the new age were rising in Germany. To suggest, however, that Romanticism should really be called 'Germanticism' on account of its essentially Germanic roots and spirit[10] is an exaggeration, not to say a distortion in view of its early sources in England, although it is not without some element of (albeit poetic) truth, and the high incidence of German words used in connection with Romanticism (*Sehnsucht, Weltschmerz, europamüde, Dies- und Jenseitigkeit*) in itself indicates its deep entrenchment in Germany.

Thenceforth the overall picture of European Romanticism becomes increasingly complex as the new creed slowly spread from country to country. For a time yet Germany was to remain

in the ascendancy so that this third phase was again largely
overshadowed by Germany. This was her most glorious age
for the 1790s witnessed not only the elaboration of Romanticism
but also the heyday of her Neo-classical period. These were the
momentous years of the Goethe–Schiller friendship when the
former wrote *Reineke Fuchs* (1794), *Römische Elegien* (1795),
Wilhelm Meisters Lehrjahre (1795), *Venezianische Epigramme*
(1797), *Hermann und Dorothea* (1798) and many of his best-
known ballads, while Schiller's work included *Über Anmut und
Würde* (1793), *Über naive und sentimentalische Dichtung* (1795),
Briefe über die ästhetische Erziehung des Menschen (1795), *Das
Ideal und das Leben* (1795), *Wallenstein* (1798–9), *Das Lied
von der Glocke* (1799) and other ballads, as well as the *Xenien*
(1796) on which the two friends collaborated. In order to
realise fully the extent to which Romantic and Neo-classical
strains were contemporaneous in Germany – a fact that is often
forgotten or overlooked – it is perhaps worth enumerating
briefly some of the other works which appeared during this
period : in 1794 Fichte's *Wissenschaftslehre*; in 1797, the great
ballad-year of Goethe and Schiller, Schelling's *Ideen zu einer
Philosophie der Natur*, Tieck's *Volksmärchen*, Wackenroder's
Herzensergießungen eines kunstliebenden Klosterbruders, A. W.
Schlegel's first translations from Shakespeare; in 1798 the
journal of the Jena Romantic group, the *Athenäum*; in 1799
Schleiermacher's *Reden über die Religion* and F. Schlegel's
Lucinde; and the new century opened with Novalis' *Hymnen an
die Nacht*. In these works the writers of the Jena Romantic
group expounded their own *Weltanschauung* which was in many
essential points a development of the earlier ideas of the *Sturm
und Drang*, although these had never been fashioned into a
coherent aesthetic system. Like their predecessors, the Jena
group founded their whole system on the unquestioned primacy
of the subjective imagination of the original creative genius, a
doctrine which had been strengthened by the powerful support
of Fichte's philosophy, so that this subjective imagination now
became literally the alpha and omega of the universe. The notion

of organic growth and development and the consequent interest
in history and in living nature, the arrogation of complete
artistic freedom as the birthright of the autonomous divine
genius, the trust in spontaneous emotion and instinct: all these
were inherited from the *Sturm und Drang*, although German
Romanticism was not a mere continuation of the earlier movement and there were vital shifts of emphasis and mood which
reveal the distinct character of the Jena school. The later group
was more complex than the relatively straightforward rebels of
the *Sturm und Drang* who sought to live and create solely
according to the dictates of feeling, while the Romantic strives
also for knowledge, consciousness, a mastery of those feelings
which in turn produced a certain self-detachment, the key to that
curious Romantic concept of irony. As its name implies, the
Sturm und Drang had been youthful, forward-looking, vigorous,
realistic in its rebellion against an irksome reality, whereas
with the Jena school an introvert, transcendental longing came
to the fore as the Romantic looked beyond this world in his
quest for an intangible, unattainable ideal in a dream sphere
of his own creation. To the revolutionary naturalism of Rousseau
and the melancholy pietism of English Pre-romanticism was
now added the transcendentalism of the German philosophers.
For the Jena Romantic group, speculative rather than creative
by nature, was responsible for the major body of German
Romantic philosophy and it was at this point that German
Romanticism assumed its characteristic hue. An all-embracing
expansiveness, coloured by a pervasive mysticism is its hall-
mark so that it is a way of living and perceiving rather than
merely of writing which was expounded in the theories of the
brothers Schlegel, Schelling, Schleiermacher and Wackenroder.
The spread in scope and breadth is vast. As poetry turns into
'eine progressive Universalpoesie',[11] it tends not only to mingle
the various genres and media, but also more and more to lose
its specific meaning and to become confused and amalgamated
with philosophy, religion, history, philology, science and
politics. This cosmic extension of the meaning of poetry was

to be of the utmost importance for the whole of the nineteenth
century and beyond too.

So rapidly had the European balance changed that in these
years it was the turn of England and France to be comparatively
backward. In France the Revolution blotted all else from men's
minds and the Reign of Terror virtually silenced creative
writing for a time. As Mme de Staël reported :

> Les Français, depuis vingt années, sont tellement préoccupés par
> les événements politiques, que toutes leurs études en littérature
> ont été suspendues.[12]

or again :

> Depuis quelque temps on ne lit guère en France que des
> mémoires ou des romans; et ce n'est pas tout à fait par frivolité
> qu'on est devenu moins capable de lectures plus sérieuses, c'est
> parce que les événements de la Révolution ont accoutumé à ne
> mettre de prix qu'à la connaissance des faits et des hommes.[13]

From the welter of arguments as to whether the Revolution
impeded the advance of Romanticism or fostered it by breaking
down the old authoritarian order in the social sphere, only one
fact emerges with any certainty : namely, the dearth of creative
writing during the Revolutionary period. Hence that curious
hiatus in French literary development in the years 1790 to 1820.
The few works which did appear were mainly in the Rousseauistic tradition, such as the exotic novels of Bernardin de Saint-
Pierre whose *Paul et Virginie* (1787) and *La Chaumière Indienne*
(1791) both illustrate the so-called return to nature. Chateaubriand's *Atala* (1801) and *René* (1805) are also indebted to the
ideas of Rousseau, and none of these, no more than the *Génie
du Christianisme* (1802), was regarded by contemporaries as a
serious menace to the Neo-classical tradition which still reigned
unchallenged. French Romanticism, when it did finally assert
itself, was to be above all a revolt against this firmly entrenched
and ossified Neo-classicism and it is significant that the earliest
glimmerings of the new orientation first insinuated themselves
into the stronghold of Neo-classicism in prose, the genre least
subject to the dictates and rules of the Neo-classical creed.

There were no such hindrances to overcome in England, which was gradually awakening to the new tendencies. In Blake's *Songs of Innocence* (1787) and *Songs of Experience* (1794), imagery was used in a manner totally different to its eighteenth-century decorative function, and this was a vital break-through of the new type of poetic expression. The mid-1790s also witnessed the growing popularity of tales of horror with Mrs Radcliffe's *Mysteries of Udolpho* in 1794 and *The Monk* by Lewis in 1796. It was in 1798, the year of the *Lyrical Ballads*, that Wordsworth accompanied Coleridge to Germany. Ironically England was now to receive its stimulus from Germany, from ideas which had in fact originated on her shores and had been elaborated abroad while they were more or less ignored at home. That home-coming began in the 1790s with the spread of knowledge about German literature which had previously been dismissed, in spite of the success of *Werther*, as revolutionary, sensationalist, extravagantly sentimental and not quite respectable. The term 'German novel', for instance, was for long a self-explanatory expression of opprobrium, a stigma stemming from the many worthless *Schauerromane*, stories that send a shudder down the reader's spine, which had been translated into English to satisfy the thirst for horror-stories. A number of original English Gothic novels of dubious quality were at that time passed off as renderings from German, thus bringing German literature into further disrepute. Gradually a truer picture was to emerge, dating from Henry Mackenzie's paper on German drama read before the Royal Society of Edinburgh in 1788 and published in 1790. Here Schiller was mentioned for the first time in Britain in a startling eulogy of *Die Räuber*, the tremendous appeal of which lay in the novelty of its subject, the atmosphere of horror and the unbridled expression of emotional crises. It made a vehement impression on Coleridge when he read it in 1794, arousing the curiosity about German literature that was to take him and Wordsworth to Germany in 1798.

While France was in the throes of the Revolution and England only gradually assimilating the new tendencies, Germany still remained the home of Romanticism. The Heidelberg group of the years 1805–15 differed from the earlier, more closely-knit Jena circle in that it was far less philosophically inclined. Forsaking the metaphysical speculations of the Jena theorists, the Heidelberg poets created many of the works for which German Romanticism earned its fame abroad, such as the tales of Hoffmann, Chamisso, Fouqué, the poems of Uhland, Körner, Brentano, Arnim. More extrovert than their immediate predecessors, these Heidelberg poets exploited the Jena theories for practical creative purposes: so the demand for a spontaneous expression of emotion led to a glorious blossoming of lyric poetry; the probing of the irrational aspects of life – the so-called 'nocturnal sides of nature' – was now precipitated into a host of supernatural and fantastic stories, such as those of Tieck and Hoffmann, and finally the interest in history, formerly part of a composite belief in organic growth and development, now also assumed more specific forms either in scholarly research into the past, as exemplified by the philological enquiries of the brothers Grimm, or in the newly emergent national consciousness and pride which evoked, under the threat of the Napoleonic wars, lyric cycles with such titles as the *Geharnischte Sonette* (*Sonnets in Armour*) by Rückert (1814), Körner's *Leyer und Schwert* (*Lyre and Sword*) of the same year and Arndt's *Lieder für Teutsche* (*Songs for Germans*) of 1813. This was the climate which fostered Arnim's and Brentano's *Des Knaben Wunderhorn* (1806–8) and like collections of folk-tales in Görres' *Die teutschen Volksbücher* (*Germanic Folk-tales*) (1807) and Grimm's *Märchen* (1812). In these patriotic nationalistic endeavours the writers of the Heidelberg group foreshadowed the more directly political and social aims of the *Jung-Deutschland** movement of the 'thirties and 'forties of the nineteenth century. It is at this point that the time-lag in European Romanticism is at its most blatant; for while Romanticism has hardly stirred in France as yet and is

* 'Young-Germany'

only about to unfold fully in England, in Germany it is already past its zenith and moving steadily towards the more sober social preoccupations of the subsequent period. In the face of these discrepancies alone, who would dare to envisage European Romanticism as one unified and consistent entity?

In this interregnum there appeared a work that was of extraordinary importance in the history of Romanticism in Europe: Mme de Staël's *De l'Allemagne* (1813). During her exile from France Mme de Staël travelled fairly extensively in Germany where she met among others Goethe, Schiller and A. W. Schlegel who became her son's tutor. In contrast to his volatile and inventive brother Friedrich, August Wilhelm Schlegel was the most perceptive and orderly of the Jena group, so that his elegantly clear formulations of German Romantic thought were more comprehensible and accessible to foreigners than the perhaps profounder, transcendental thinking of Friedrich Schlegel, Schelling or Schleiermacher; with the translation of his *Vorlesungen über dramatische Kunst und Literatur* (*Lectures on Dramatic Art and Literature*) (1809) into French in 1813 and into English in 1815, A. W. Schlegel truly became the 'Herold oder Dolmetscher' [14] of Romantic thought. In A. W. Schlegel Mme de Staël thus met a man well able to fan her enthusiasm for Germany. The external history of *De l'Allemagne* – the hindrances to publication, the role of political considerations etc. – are irrelevant in the present context except in so far as this opposition in itself indicates the French reluctance, indeed fear, to import foreign ideas which seemed an insult and a menace to French cultural dominance. In spite, or perhaps partly because, of the violent resistance to its publication, *De l'Allemagne* became the standard source of knowledge on Germany, and beyond that a manifesto of the new cosmopolitanism, a decisive step in the renewal of French literature after its long subservience to the tenets of an emasculated Neo-classicism. In this work Mme de Staël sought to delineate the concept of a poetry different from the great native tradition of France, for she fully realized the need for a transfusion of new blood. In

introducing contemporary German writing to France she
constantly contrasted its originality, vitality and imagination
with the sterile rigidity, 'le genre maniéré' [15] of moribund
French Neo-classicism. Much valid criticism can be levelled
against Mme de Staël : she saw Germany in the literary as well
as in the social and moral sense as the country of *Hermann und
Dorothea*, thereby nurturing the strangely persistent French
picture of Germany as 'une région fabuleuse, où les hommes
gazouillent et chantent comme les oiseaux'.[16] Moreover, she
had little acquaintance with the work of the Jena group (there
is, for instance, no mention whatsoever of Novalis) and regarded
Goethe, Schiller, Bürger and Tieck as the representative
German Romantic poets; nor had she much head for abstract
philosophy and no more than a superficial comprehension of
Romanticism, distinguishing between Classical and Romantic
poetry as 'celle qui a précédé l'établissement du christianisme et
celle qui l'a suivi'.[17] All her judgements are formed from a
plainly French standpoint so that she regards German and
English literature as one unit, the literature of the Romantic
North, as against the Classical literature of France and Southern
Europe. Nevertheless, in spite of her undeniable weaknesses
and failings, Mme de Staël was an astute, perspicacious arbiter,
whose observations are often acute and who grasped the
essence of the new orientation of German literature. In some
respects Mme de Staël's position is reminiscent of that of
Lessing : though more emotional and fanciful in manner than
the sensible exponent of the Enlightenment, basically she
advocates the same emancipation from the traditional rules in
favour of a poetry fathered by the enthusiasm of genius. In fact
De l'Allemagne presents an admirable survey of the *Sturm und
Drang* phase of German literature, that is of Pre-romanticism,
rather than of the Romantic groups themselves. This is a
crucial factor for the comprehension of European Romanticism
since the opinions expressed by Mme de Staël and, perhaps even
more important, her omissions, for long not only determined
the French (and to a lesser extent the English) view of German

literature, but also shaped the course and nature of the French Romantic movement. So the preference for Schiller, the conception of Goethe as 'le chef de l'école mélancolique',[18] the appraisal of *Faust* as the supreme Romantic masterpiece, the emphasis on the picturesque element in poetry and the belief that German literature is characterized primarily by fantasy and liberty: all these curious notions stem from *De l'Allemagne*. And Mme de Staël's view of German literature was persistent as well as potent; till after 1830 the French continued to believe that German literature consisted solely of Goethe, Schiller, Bürger, Tieck and Jean Paul. No good history of German literature was available in French and while a few works, notably *Werther*, *Faust*, *Die Räuber*, and later, the dramas of Werner were read with respect and devotion, poets such as Novalis, Brentano and Arnim were virtually unknown to the French Romantic poets, very few of whom, incidentally, had any knowledge of German. The belief that French Romanticism was directly influenced by German Romanticism, one of the principal and most common misapprehensions about the history of Romanticism in Europe, is therefore contravened by the undeniable evidence of chronological fact. The true relationship is rather between the German *Sturm und Drang* and French Romanticism. Once this correct historical perspective is established, the striking differences between the faces of Romanticism in Germany and France become somewhat less puzzling.

De l'Allemagne, which was originally published in England, also served in some degree as a mediator between Germany and England. In the early years of the nineteenth century, because of the political situation – the opposition to Napoleon – the English tended to turn more to Germany than to France and many links were forged between the two lands through both travellers and translations.[19] These links were remarkable rather for their large number than for their depth, there being little to suggest any very decisive significance. As in France, so in England too actual knowledge about Germany was fairly scant; the Carlyle image of a land of poets and thinkers succeeded the earlier one of a realm of the picturesque and fantastic. As for German literature, it was again the *Sturm und Drang* which made the only real impression through the early works of Goethe and Schiller, as well as the dramas of Kotzebue, whose popularity turned into an absolute furor. The writings of the Jena group, on the other hand, gained little or no hearing until well into the nineteenth century; Carlyle was the first to write about Novalis in 1829 and even then Novalis was interpreted as a disciple of Kant and Fichte without any appreciation of his poetry. In her relationship with her European neighbours England showed that same sturdy independence that characterizes her own Romantic movement. England had indeed no need to be instructed in Romantic thought and feeling by other nations for in Shakespeare, Milton, Young, Macpherson, Percy and Richardson she exported far more than she imported in Schiller, Goethe and Rousseau.

The great flowering of English Romanticism occurred about the middle of the second decade of the nineteenth century when for some ten years England became the focus of European Romanticism. By then the Romantic impetus had slackened in Germany and was gradually being diluted by the beginnings of the sober realism of the mid-nineteenth century. Meanwhile France, apparently still stunned by the consequences of the Revolution, was taking stock in social and political affairs with thinkers such as Saint-Simon, Cousin and Thierry, while artistic creativity was relegated to the background. England with a galaxy of fine poets in Blake, Wordsworth, Coleridge, Shelley, Keats and Byron assumed the primacy which had been Germany's. Not that there was ever a Romantic 'school' in England as there had been in Germany; there was no conscious, homogeneous programme, few manifestoes or literary discussions compared with Germany and with the violent controversies that were to sway France. Wordsworth's famous *Preface to the 'Lyrical Ballads'* (1798) was written chiefly to counter criticism and to forestall further attacks. The second generation of English Romantic poets were even less concerned than the first with questions of poetic technique; Keats indeed was outspoken in his rejection of abstract theorizing, which he branded as 'the whims of an Egotist'. In a letter to J. H. Reynolds (3 February 1818) he wrote:

> Every man has his speculations, but every man does not brood and peacock over them till he makes a false coinage and deceives himself. . . . Poetry should be great and unobtrusive, a thing which enters into one's soul, and does not startle it or amaze it with itself, but with its subject. – How beautiful are the retired flowers! how would they lose their beauty were they to throng into the highway crying out, 'admire me I am a violet! – dote upon me I am a primrose!' [20]

Informal in character, English Romanticism remained less systematic, less dogmatic, less self-conscious than its Continental counterparts, of an independent approach consonant with the innate individualism of the Briton. Although Jeffrey, the most vehement opponent of the Lake Poets, accused them in the *Edinburgh Review* of 1802 of being 'dissenters from the established systems in poetry', who had borrowed their doctrines from the Germans and from 'the great apostle of Geneva', this charge was far from true. For the Romantic movement in England was above all of evolutionary, not revolutionary origin; a sense of belonging to and restoring the native tradition distinguishes the Romantic poets in England, where there was no incisive break in continuity, as in Germany and France. The English Pre-romantics and Romantics looked back with approval on Shakespeare and the Pre-Restoration poets, nor did the Augustans rouse opposition comparable to the rejection of convention by the *Stürmer und Dränger* or the French onslaught on their tyrannical literary establishment. In contrast to the necessity imposed on the French and Germans to find some way out of a kind of *cul-de-sac*, the English were cast in a historically more fortunate position. Whereas the Germans and the French Romantics had to follow and in some way to outdo their glorious immediate predecessors, the English Romantics were strongly conscious of representing a new beginning and upsurge, not a reaction as in France or an over-refinement as in Germany. From this perhaps English Romanticism derives its special quality of freshness, freedom, flexibility and grace.

With the deaths of Keats in 1821, Shelley in 1822 and Byron in 1824 the period of English ascendancy came to an abrupt and untimely end. Now it was the turn of France in the 1820s and 1830s. But how different was the face and spirit of Romanticism in France from what it had been in England! Whereas the English Romantic movement had evolved slowly and organically out of the native tradition, French Romanticism was essentially a revolt against the native tradition, an ousting of the firmly rooted Neo-classical attitudes and forms by alien lines of thought and feeling. Hence the violence and bitterness of the quarrels attendant on the emergence of Romanticism in France, hence also the stubbornness and vehemence of the opposition. For this was far more than a literary debate; all manner of political and national considerations were implicated too in the complex web of this 'querelle nationale'.[21] The Revolution, though it had halted literary development for many years, can also be evaluated as an indirectly positive factor, for with the fall of the absolute monarchy the Neo-classical dogmatism that had been associated with it was severely undermined : 'à société nouvelle, littérature nouvelle' became the popular slogan. Moreover, the revolutionary era with its free spectacle of the guillotine created a new theatre audience avid for rapid action, melodrama and sharp contrasts. On the other hand, Napoleon's Empire tended to have a reactionary effect not only through its strict censorship but also through its revival of Neo-classical taste as exemplified by Corneille's heroic characters who were regarded as the apotheosis of martial glory. Romanticism was, therefore, feared as a tendency associated with revolution, violence and foreign domination, a threat to the national heritage of Greco–Latin origin. Even in 1825 *Le Globe* still reported that 'on se sert aujourd'hui en France du mot "romantique" pour désigner toute composition contraire au système suivi en France depuis

Louis XIV'.[22] This fear of the Romantic as tantamount to the revolutionary explains, in part at least, Constant's extraordinarily cautious attitude in his preface to *Wallstein* (1809), where he compared the German and French dramatic systems. He deliberately avoided the word Romantic altogether and repeatedly stressed his support of the native tradition, which was to be strengthened and refreshed, not ousted, by innovations from abroad. A similar revival of the French heritage was advocated in Sainte-Beuve's *Tableau de la Poésie au seizième siècle* (1827) which was of vital importance in the history of Romanticism in France; here Sainte-Beuve rehabilitated the hitherto neglected French poets of the sixteenth century, thereby pointing to the existence of a native tradition anterior and different to the Neo-classical one.

Considering the strength of this Neo-classical canon of clarity, harmony and 'good taste', as well as the complexity of the political and social background, it is little wonder that the new Romantic orientation was so slow to infiltrate into France. The French Romantics had begun to emerge as a shadowy force in opposition to the Neo-classicists towards the middle of the 1810s, stimulated by *De l'Allemagne* and also by the translation in 1813 of A. W. Schlegel's *Vorlesungen über dramatische Kunst und Literatur*. During the years 1814–22 an outburst of anglomania swept through France following the isolation during the Napoleonic wars; lively interest was focused on the conqueror, on the workings of the Constitutional monarchy and parliamentary government, the industrial revolution, new economic doctrines and of course new writing, although unfortunately there was no outstanding personality to do for England what Mme de Staël had done for Germany. Nevertheless the technique of the Lake poets, their use of imagery, the music and innovations of their verse and their note of mystery aroused curiosity. In fact Scott, Byron and Shakespeare as well as Goethe and Schiller were already known in France, but their real vogue came only in about 1820 onwards, when Byron in particular became the object of an idolatrous enthusiasm. This growing appreciation of English and German poets coincided with the formation of a number of Romantic groups centered either on a literary journal such as the *Muse française* (1823–4) or the famous *Le Globe* (1824–32) or in the French tradition of a *salon* such as that of Deschamps (1820), the *Société des Bonnes-Lettres* (1821), Charles Nodier (1823) and finally the *Cénacle* of Hugo and Sainte-Beuve (1827). The French Romantics were thus unlike the English and more like the Germans in their preference for groups, and the dates of these various groups and journals help to site the real break-through of Romanticism in France. Opposition was, however, far from silenced by the early 1820s; the traditionalists continued to attack Romanticism as an alien, dangerous element, branding it as a 'romantisme bâtard', to quote the phrase coined in 1924 by Auger, the director of the *Académie française*, in spite of the efforts of the movement's defenders, such as Charles Nodier, who sought to distinguish between *le frénétique* (vampirism, mere sensationalism) and the genuinely *romantique*.

Long after Romanticism had become more or less acceptable in lyric poetry through the works of Lamartine, Hugo and Vigny in the years 1822–6, the final and most acrimonious battle was fought in the field of drama, the 'dernière forteresse', the 'bastille littéraire' [23] of the Neo-classical tradition. Several earlier attempts to storm this bastion had failed; a performance in 1807 of Lemercier's *Christophe Colomb*, sub-titled a 'comédie shakespearienne', proved an utter fiasco, and in his rendering of Schiller's *Wallenstein* trilogy, which dates from 1809, Constant cautiously felt the need to respect the rules of French drama, as he put it, by reducing the number of acts to five and the characters to twelve. In the winter of 1827–8 a company of English actors made a deep impression in Paris and it was during that winter, when enthusiasm for Shakespeare was at its zenith, that Hugo wrote *Cromwell* with its epoch-making preface. Not that Hugo's ideas in themselves were of startling originality; sensational though it was in its historical context, Hugo's attack on the three unities is in fact forestalled by Lessing's arguments in the *Hamburgische Dramaturgie*. Indeed the whole tone and spirit of the polemics in France in the 1820s recalls the mood of the German *Sturm und Drang* of the 1770s. Thus *Le Globe* defines its doctrine as 'la liberté', 'l'imitation directe de la nature', 'l'originalité',[24] while the concept 'romantique' is equated with 'vie, activité, mouvement en avant',[25] that is in terms which clearly echo the dynamism of the *Sturm und Drang*. There is therefore ample justification for Goethe's perspicacious comment:

> Was die Franzosen bei ihrer jetzigen literarischen Richtung für etwas Neues halten, ist im Grunde weiter nichts als der Widerschein desjenigen, was die deutsche Literatur seit fünfzig Jahren gewollt and geworden.[26]

Goethe's estimate of fifty years as the time-lag between Germany and France is well judged for it was only with the noisy victory of *Hernani* in 1830 that French drama achieved the freedom attained in Germany in the 1770s by *Götz von Berlichingen* and *Die Räuber*. Moreover, while the French Romantics were related to the German *Stürmer und Dränger*, the true heirs of the German Romanticism of 1800–15 were the French Symbolist poets of the latter half of the nineteenth century. Baudelaire, Nerval, Mallarmé and Rimbaud subscribed to a new conception of art and the artist, which was closely akin to the theories of the German Jena Romantic group: poetic experience was envisaged as essentially different from ordinary experience, a magic form of intuitive spiritual activity, a mysterious expansion into the transcendental in which the visionary poet adventured into a dream realm to explore the hidden sources and 'correspondences 'of life.

The battle for *Hernani* in the year 1830 marks the last great milestone in the Romantic conquest of Europe. Although Romanticism was to reign in France for some ten more years, other currents were increasingly in evidence. By the mid-1830s already Hugo was advancing a more utilitarian conception of art, urging the artist to an awareness of his serious duty to

D

further the progress of mankind. In this change of outlook Hugo was anticipating a trend characteristic of the mid-nineteenth century throughout Europe. In England and Germany the springs of Romanticism had dried up much earlier than in that late starter France, and in both countries by the mid-1830s only a diluted, rather sentimentalized form of Romanticism survived alongside some witty satire directed against Romantic attitudes, such as Peacock's *Crotchet Castle* (1831), Carlyle's *Sartor Resartus* (1833–4), Heine's *Romantische Schule* (1833) and Immermann's *Die Epigonen* (1836) with its significant title, as well as his comic *Münchhausen* (1839). Romanticism was increasingly out of tune with the spirit of the age as the century advanced; the new sober mood and materialistic aims of the industrial era had little sympathy for obscure flights of individual imagination and no use whatsoever for an art that 'bakes no bread' to quote a pertinent American proverb. The artist was called to cease his selfish exploration of his private realm, to come out of his ivory tower and to assume his share of social responsibility. The disciplined objectivity of Realism came to replace – at least for a time – the autonomous imagination of Romanticism.

This chronological survey should dispel a number of common misconceptions regarding Romanticism. Foremost among these is the misapprehension that European Romanticism is a clearly defined entity, a unified school which manifested itself in several countries simultaneously and which shared certain ideals and predilections. Almost equally prevalent and mistaken is the belief that the origins of Romanticism are to be found in Germany and that both the English and the French Romantic poets were directly and decisively influenced by the German theories. Such notions are more than gross over-simplifications; they are false premises that can only breed further error. A historical analysis of the course of Romanticism in Europe reveals a far more complicated picture, for the Romantic manner of perception and expression appeared in various literatures at different times and in different guises. Its emergence is an uneven, straggling process of long duration, punctuated by curious time-lags as the ascendancy passed from one land to another. Moreover, since the spread of new ideas was largely dependent on the chance reports of travellers in an age when communications were still relatively poor and further disrupted by war, information on contemporary developments even in neighbouring countries was often scant and belated so that many assumptions of influence must be discounted. The outstanding example of such slow and fragmentary infiltration of ideas is to be found in *De l'Allemagne* : though written by a perspicacious and widely-travelled critic, it contains in 1810 very few of the ideas of the Jena Romantics which were to reach France only some half a century later.

The outer history of European Romanticism, its successive waves, its new upsurge in one country after another suggests both the vehemence of its impetus and the complexity of its nature. Though part of that fundamental reorientation of values that took place throughout Europe at the turn of the eighteenth to the nineteenth century, it was not a single, but a multiple movement; indeed it comprised a whole series of movements from the *Sturm und Drang* onwards, each separate and distinct in character, yet all involved in a profound 'crise de la conscience' as individualistic, imaginative, subjective attitudes replaced the old rationalistic approach. The timing and form of this crisis differed from land to land because it was in each case determined by the literary background as well as by social and political factors. Hence the bewildering variety of the faces and products of Romanticism : it is not just a matter of genre, with the English excelling at lyric poetry, the French concentrating on drama in their battle against the stronghold of the Neo-classical theatre, while the transcendental yearnings of the Germans find their most appropriate vehicle in the dream-like narrative. This in itself is only a symptom of far deeper divergences. German Romanticism, for instance, is not only the most

radical and thoroughgoing, embracing all the arts and philosophy, politics, religion, science and history too, but also
distinguished from its English and French counterparts at first
by a strong bias towards the metaphysical and later by its
patriotic colouring. French Romanticism resembles the German
brand in its preference for organization in groups and in its
dynamic thrust; on the other hand it differs from the German
movement (and is herein closer to the English) in remaining
almost entirely in the domain of art, and it is characterized
above all by its violent revolt against the stifling dominance of
the native Neo-classical tradition. In contrast, English Romanticism is the freshest and freest, the least self-conscious and codified
because it evolved not against, but organically out of the native
tradition.

In view of the confusion surrounding the term and the concept
of Romanticism, there is surely a strong case for an honest
recognition of these differences – of the fact that there have been
a number of Romantic movements in Europe. It is only in the
light of the correct historical perspective that a new approach
can then be made to the Romantic movements in England,
France and Germany in an attempt to appreciate the particular
character of each and at the same time to understand their inter-
relationship. This is the aim of the following three main sections
of this book in which the significance of certain key-concepts
will be examined in order to discern the similarities and differences between the three Romantic movements.

Individualism

Individualism as a Creed

———— ❋⊗❋ ————

INDIVIDUALISM is defined in the Oxford Dictionary as the 'tendency to regard oneself as the paramount interest in one's life; egoism; social doctrine which emphasizes the rights of individuals rather than those of society and of the State as a whole'. Such individualism lies at the core of the European 'crise de conscience' of the late eighteenth century and forms the basis for the development of the specifically Romantic outlook. The affirmation of the overriding importance of the individual represents indeed the crucial turning-point in the history of society as well as of literature. From this belief in the rights of individuals sprang the ideals of liberty, fraternity and equality that inspired the French Revolution. So long as an established, universally recognized social order persisted, as for example in the feudal system of the Middle Ages, men had to strive for integration into that hierarchy so that the desires of the individual were subordinate to the wider aims of the group whose code of behaviour required a high degree of conformity. For the surrender of his personal claims the individual was rewarded by a sense of belonging, the protection vouchsafed by the position, however lowly, allocated to him within an organized community. In return for his acceptance of certain conditions and standards, he was himself accepted. The growth of individualism ran counter to the older ideal of integration, which rested on a subjective attitude of humility, whereas individualism is essentially arrogant in its assertion of personal rights without any regard for the common weal. Individualism therefore tends to undermine and eventually to destroy the fabric of society when a code of behaviour equally valid and binding for all is replaced by the individual's demand for self-determination. As a penalty for this freedom he has seized, the individual forfeits the security derived from adherence to the group and the eagerly sought privilege of personal decision may well become a frightening burden. In its extreme consequences individualism can result in the uncertainty, the moral relativism, the anxious soul-searching typical of the age of *Angst*. It is surely a significant comment on this development that the brand of satire so popular nowadays, instead of pillorying an eccentric victim against the background of an ordered society, in the manner of Pope and Keller, is aimed at a whole way of life. The firm standards and absolute criteria of the past have been replaced by the characteristically vacillating, evasive attitude summed up in that favourite catch-phrase 'it all depends'; – but on what?

Once the external frame of reference, the concept of a fixed order is abandoned, man is driven to seek a point of certainty within himself. This was the position of the Romantic poets, who sought a principle of order established not in terms of the outer world and an appeal to reason, but in terms of the inner world of the individual and an appeal to imagination. Hence they whole-heartedly espoused the nascent individualism of their time; so much so that the championship of individualism is one of the distinctive hallmarks of the Romantic attitude as against the tendency to conformism implicit in any Classicism. When Novalis wrote: 'Das Individuum interessiert nur, daher ist alles Klassische nicht individuell',[1] his logic may have been somewhat wayward but his intention is clear enough: he was virtually equating the 'individual' not only with the 'interesting' but also with the 'romantic' by the implied contrast with the classical preference for the non-individual, the characteristic. Henceforth it is man in the singular – in both senses of that word – who holds the centre of the stage, not mankind in general. This new curiosity about the exceptional individual is evident in the spate of confessions and autobiographies which begin to appear during the Romatic period, all of which testify to the cult of the egocentric. Following in the tracks of Rousseau's *Confessions*

came De Quincey's *Confessions of an English Opium Eater* and
Musset's *Confession d'un enfant du siècle*, not to mention the
stream, later to become a torrent, of partially veiled self-
portrayals, which continue unabated even today, each springing
from that narcissistic pride in one's otherness so blatantly
proclaimed in the opening words of Rousseau's *Confessions* :

> Je forme une entreprise qui n'eut jamais d'exemple, et qui n'aura
> point d'imitateur. Je veux montrer à mes semblables un homme
> dans toute la vérité de la nature; et cet homme, ce sera moi. Moi
> seul. Je sens mon coeur, et je connois les hommes. Je ne suis
> fait comme aucun de ceux que j'ai vus, j'ose croire n'être fait
> comme aucun de ceux qui existent. Si je ne vaux pas mieux, au
> moins je suis autre.[2]

Rousseau was perhaps the first to surrender unequivocally to
'la douceur de converser avec mon âme',[3] as he put it in *Les
Rêveries du Promeneur Solitaire*, where he portrays an individual
totally 'enlacé de moi-même',[4] seeking 'toute sa pâture au-dedans
de moi'[5] in the hope of answering the question : 'que suis-je
moi-même ?'.[6] This summarizes one effect of individualism : the
new attitude of the individual towards himself, his interest in
himself, which seduces him to that introspective analysis of his
thoughts, reactions and feelings that was in turn to produce and
to characterize the Romantic hero.

But individualism was of deeper import to the Romantics
than this cult of the interesting personality, which alone would
not suffice to distinguish them from their immediate predecessors. For the Pre-romantics had already focused attention on the
exceptional individual either by exploring the intricacies of
personal emotion as in Rousseau's *La Nouvelle Héloïse* and
Young's *Night Thoughts* or by depicting the relationship of the
great man with his milieu, as Goethe intended in his fragments
about Caesar, Socrates and Mohammed as well as in *Faust*.
Indeed in *Werther* Goethe sketched the prototype of the
Romantic hero as early as 1774 so that in their cult of the
individual the Romantics were elaborating a theme previously
enunciated. But whereas the Pre-romantics showed a spon-

taneous and sporadic interest in the individual, it was the real
innovation of the Romantics to turn individualism into a whole
Weltanschauung, to systematize it – in so far as their irrationalism permitted any logical ordering of ideas into a cohesive
philosophy. For their thought consists of a wealth of highly
suggestive, though sometimes contradictory notions rather than
a well-made jigsaw in which all the pieces fit neatly into an
appropriate place. (This characteristic, incidentally, accounts
for much of the difficulty encountered in any attempt to analyse
Romantic theories.) The basic – and perhaps only – unifying
factor underlying all these disparate ideas is just their very
individuality, by which is meant not so much their idiosyncrasy
as their essential subjectivity. It is a fundamental trait of the
Romantic that he invariably apprehends the outer world through
the mirror of his ego as against the objective approach of the
Realist. What matters to the Romantic is not what *is* but how it
seems to him. Hence the profound importance of the imagination
as the medium of perception.

The ego thus forms the centre and pivot of the Romantic's
universe : 'For all we see, hear, feel and touch the substance is
and must be in ourselves.' [7] Instead of starting by positing the
existence of an external objective reality, as Cartesian rationalism sought to do, the Romantic follows Fichte's advice to turn
his gaze inward :

> Merke auf dich selbst : kehre deinen Blick von allem, was dich
> umgibt, ab und in dein Inneres; ist die erste Forderung, welche
> die Philosophie an ihren Lehrling tut. Es ist von nichts, was
> außer dir ist, die Rede, sondern lediglich von dir selbst. [8]

Through this choice of the inner being as the point of departure
Romanticism becomes a form of egoism in the most literal sense
of the word : self-centredness. The earlier interest in the
individual is transformed here into a veritable creed with
strange and far-reaching implications. For this new sensitivity
to the individual phenomenon, to individual uniqueness is
comparable to a fire, alarmingly rapid in its spread and capable

of devouring all before it, not only men's lives, but also poetry and art and later even weightier substances like the state. It is worth examining the basic assumptions in some detail since even this individualism, fundamental to every Romantic, manifests itself in a different guise in England, Germany and France.

* * *

That there is so little mention of individualism in the writings of the English poets and critics of the Romantic period is striking and at first puzzling. They tended on the whole to show more concern for particular problems : Wordsworth investigated specific questions of artistic technique and expression, while Coleridge probed the nature of imagination and Shelley the function of poetry in society. In all these deliberations there is a certain undertone of common-sense which precludes lengthy excursions into abstract theorizing. The discussions centre on special crucial areas of controversy without opening out into philosophical speculation about the primary issues of human existence. Hence there is no exposition of any favoured philosophy of life, such as characterizes the German *Frühromantik* circle, and consequently no overt championship of individualism. Coleridge indeed, in spite of his supposedly German sympathies, went so far as to draw an adverse comparison between the 'poet of the present age' who strives to express the 'specific and individual' in 'new and striking IMAGES' and the artists of the fifteenth and sixteenth centuries among whom 'novelty of subject was avoided' and 'superior excellence in the manner of treating the same subjects was the trial and test of the artist's merit'.[9] In this respect he declared :

> I adopt with full faith the principle of Aristotle, that poetry as poetry is essentially ideal, that it avoids and excludes all accident; that its apparent individualities of rank, character, or occupation must be representative of a class; and that the persons of poetry must be clothed with generic attributes, with the common attributes of the class.[10]

and in a footnote to this statement, to make his meaning more
plain, he added that Aristotle 'required of the poet an involution
of the universal in the individual'. The same scepticism concerning personal poetry is implied in his praise of Shakespeare's
early works as revealing 'promise of genius' in 'the choice of
subjects very remote from the private interests and circumstances of the writer himself'.[11] This suggests that Coleridge
was not so much opposed in principle to individualism as such,
but rather to its excessive intrusion into poetry in the form of
personal emotion. He was in fact voicing that reticence and
reserve characteristic of English Romantic poetry. Thus in
contrast to Rousseau's somewhat theatrical display of his ego,
Wordsworth felt that it was a thing unprecedented in literary
history, and by implication, daring, even unseemly, that a man
should talk so much about himself as he does in *The Prelude*.
For to Wordsworth the poet is not a frenzied enthusiast, a
vessel for the divine afflatus, set apart in lordly magnificence;
he is rather a man speaking to men, differing from them not in
kind but only in degree, endowed with a livelier sensibility, an
uncommon imagination and a greater articulateness. Here
Romantic individualism is tempered by democratic leanings and
an inborn modesty.

This strange lack of explicit emphasis on individualism among
the English Romantics can perhaps be explained by reference to
their heritage, which was so very different to that of their
German and French counterparts. In England there was no need
to make a special plea for individualism for the simple reason
that it was so much taken for granted as part of the British
tradition of liberty and independence in personal opinion, of
radicalism and local autonomy in politics and of Protestantism
in religion. The Englishman of the late eighteenth and early
nineteenth centuries enjoyed a far greater measure of freedom
than his French or German contemporary. France, for all its
idealistic proclamation of liberty, fraternity and equality was
hardly a haven of liberalism during the Reign of Terror nor
under the rule of Napoleon. And Germany, parcelled out

among many often despotic, petty princelings, frightened by the goings-on across the Rhine, rapidly became more and more reactionary; this was a time of sobriety and austerity, exemplified by the *Biedermeier* style in architecture, a time when the humdrum was preferable to the progressive that might turn into the revolutionary, when men were discouraged from active political participation, even from suspect social criticism so that their ideas could safely range unimpeded only in the realms of metaphysics and aesthetics. The Englishman, possessing greater liberty in every respect, had less need to seek a safety-valve through which to express his individuality in literary and philosophical revolutions. English Romantic poetry could thus evolve organically out of the native tradition, finding a fertile soil for its development in the primitivism of Warton, the naturalism of Spenser, the melancholy of Gray and the realism of Burns. With such antecedents there was no need for the English Romantics to assert themselves in rebellion. Poetry was, as a matter of course, regarded as the expression of the special experience of a rare individual, valuable because in it there is truth of insight.

In spite of its lack of emphasis on individualism in its theories, the English Romantic movement is in practice most profoundly individualistic. The very absence of a coherent body of theory, the reluctance to form specific groups, the whole unorganized and rather haphazard growth of the movement: all these testify to its sturdy inner independence. Even Keats' opposition to poetic theory can be seen as part of that innate individualism. Hence the difficulty encountered in trying to discern the common denominators of English Romantic poetry; for each poet associated with the movement followed his own bent so completely that the writings of the English Romantics embrace an exceptionally wide range of approaches and styles, none of which can glibly be labelled as typical. Each poet has his pronounced flavour: the visionary ecstasy of Blake, at once simple and complex, the realism of Wordsworth, the imaginative surrealism of Coleridge, the sensuous richness of Keats, the so-called etherealism of Shelley, the satirical wit of Byron.

These differences in character are best illustrated by a comparison of the treatment of the same theme, the description of a bird. Shelley's famous *To A Skylark* opens with the greeting :

> Hail to thee, blithe Spirit!
>   Bird thou never wert,
> That from heaven or near it
>   Pourest thy full heart
> In profuse strains of unpremeditated art.
>
> Higher still and higher
>   From the earth thou springest,
> Like a cloud of fire,
>   The blue deep thou wingest,
> And singing still dost soar, and soaring
>   ever singest.

The movement here is always upwards, away from the earth towards heaven, to which the creature seems to belong, and the short lines, as if by their weightlessness, facilitate the soaring flight they describe. Shelley's bird exists only for song and flight, truly an ethereal being, a sky-born form sequestered from the brutal contact of insensitive mediocrity, a lonely seeker after the ideal, like his creator. Wordsworth's linnet in *The Green Linnet* is a good deal more terrestrial :

> Beneath these fruit-tree boughs that shed
> Their snow-white blossoms on my head,
> With brightest sunshine round me spread
>   Of Spring's unclouded weather,
> In this sequester'd nook how sweet
> To sit upon my orchard-seat :
> And flowers and birds once more to greet,
>   My last year's friends together.
>
> One have I mark'd, the happiest guest
> In all this cover of the blest :
> Hail to Thee, far above the rest
>   In joy of voice and pinion!
> Thou Linnet! in thy green array
> Presiding Spirit here to-day

Dost lead the revels of the May,
And this is thy dominion.

While birds, and butterflies, and flowers,
Make all one band of paramours,
Thou, ranging up and down the bowers,
Art sole in thy employment;
A Life, a Presence like the air,
Scattering thy gladness without care,
Too blest with any one to pair;
Thyself thy own enjoyment.

While Shelley's skylark is a solo virtuoso performer, Wordsworth's linnet is seen in a social setting. His return every year is as regular as the verse in which it is described and the bird fulfils his function as 'presiding Spirit' in the 'revels of the May' as punctiliously as the poet carries out his task of observing and recording. In contrast to the ranging freedom of Shelley's songster, Wordsworth's bird fits into an orderly Utopia. Very different again is Keats' *Ode to a Nightingale*:

My heart aches, and a drowsy numbness pains
My sense, as though of hemlock I had drunk,
Or emptied some dull opiate to the drains
One minute past, and Lethe-wards had sunk:
'Tis not through envy of thy happy lot,
But being too happy in thine happiness, –
That thou, light-wingéd Dryad of the trees,
In some melodious plot
Of beechen green, and shadows numberless,
Singest for summer in full-throated ease.

Here it is the personal element, with which the poem opens, that predominates and that gives the stanza its sombre colouring as the poet's misery is contrasted with the bird's carefree happiness. In the first half of the stanza, with its preponderance of long dark vowels, the verse moves slowly to convey the poet's heaviness as against the 'light-wingéd' nightingale who sings with 'ease' in pleasant nooks. In the rich imagery a subtle web is woven between the poet and the bird. These three poems then, through their differing approaches to the same theme, reveal already the diversity of English Romantic poetry.

In England, where individualism was an innate, natural part of the native tradition, there was not only least need to emphasize it but also least tendency to exaggeration, least distortion into a blatant egoism. So in England are found the fewest examples of this type of individualism in the figure of the Romantic hero. Only Byron among the English Romantics was interested in the Romantic hero and Byron was in fact something of an exception : perhaps not as gifted as he would have wished as a poet and innovator, he sought an outlet for his frustration both in personal publicity and in projecting his feelings on to his heroes. While an inventive poet such as Blake demanded unimpeded freedom in the exercise of his imagination, Byron, with his passionate belief in individual liberty, arrogated a similar freedom for his self and sought to fulfil himself without the constraints of convention, which he hated. It is, moreover, significant that the Byronic explosion of individualism occurred just at the time when the fabric of tradition had begun to disintegrate. Whereas the earlier generation of Romantic poets had been able to identify themselves with the spiritual movement of their age in a hopeful search for balance and order, Byron's background was one of reaction. The real meaning of the French Revolution was slowly dawning on men as they recognized its implications and witnessed the break-down of the equilibrium on which the civilization of the eighteenth century had rested. The new social climate of doubt and questioning fostered a new type of man, well represented by Byron with his rejection of established ties, his cult of the self, his love of adventure and his ironical distrust of his own emotions and beliefs. But Byron remained the exception among English Romantic poets, whose merit lies not least in their ability to channel their individualism directly into their poetry without need of preliminary discussions or personal revolt. Their individualism remains healthy because it is precipitated into their works.

Compared to the English, the Germans are infinitely more

self-conscious and explicit in their interpretation of individualism. Under the strong influence of Fichte and his imperative to turn one's gaze always inwards, the *Frühromantiker* perfected a system of subjectivism, in which the existence of the whole universe depended solely on the individual's vision. Hence they believed in the artist's power to transform, to 'poeticize' the world in so far as it was a product of his perception. In such a system the individual obviously became the focus and pivot of all activity and it is in this context that the *Frühromantiker* extolled the importance of individuality: 'Gerade die Individualität ist das Ursprüngliche und Ewige im Menschen', wrote F. Schlegel; and he went on: 'Die Bildung und Entwicklung dieser Individualität als höchsten Beruf zu treiben, wäre ein göttlicher Egoismus.' [12] This call to the individual to develop his potentialities to the full seems at first sight akin to Goethe's notion of *Bildung*;* but whereas Goethe's ideal of *Bildung* furthered also the social side of the personality, leading to a peaceful integration of the mature human being into society, as in *Wilhelm Meister*, the Romantic cult of individuality is essentially centripetal, resulting, as F. Schlegel indeed conceded, in a kind of divine egoism. Seen from this angle, Novalis' avowed intent to write an anti-*Wilhelm Meister* novel assumes a new significance. Novalis concurred with F. Schlegel when he maintained: 'Die höchste Aufgabe der Bildung ist, sich seines transzendentalen Selbst zu bemächtigen, das Ich seines Ichs zugleich zu sein.' [13] This is an expression in metaphysical terms of the necessity to attain total self-knowledge, to penetrate to the very core of the individual's being. The *Hymnen an die Nacht* could be interpreted in this sense as an attempt on the poet's part to plumb the hidden recesses of his subconscious, and it is characteristic of Novalis and of the *Frühromantiker* that 'nach Innen geht der geheimnisvolle Weg', [14] always inwards. This is the path also of Heinrich von Ofterdingen; his real aim throughout

---

* A term difficult to translate because it has changed in meaning and is nowadays used freely to denote 'culture'. To Goethe, however, it meant the full development of a person's possibilities, the attainment of his ideal self.

E

his journey might be defined in the poet's own words in the *Blütenstaub* fragment just quoted : to take possession of one's transcendental self ('das Ich seines Ichs zugleich zu sein'). Heinrich's picaresque experiences of war, nature, history, love and poetry do not serve to teach him anything new about the outside world, in fact all that he sees strikes him as already vaguely familiar, *déjà vu* in some mysterious manner. The outer adventures only act as stimuli, opening the hitherto shut doors and windows of his soul so that Heinrich gradually comes to take possession of his latent potentialities, to find his own individuality.

This cult of the individual penetrated every aspect of German Romantic thought. Religion, based on the mysticism of Jacob Böhme, became with the growth of Pietism a matter of personal belief. Where the soul was the focal point, the emphasis was on individual devotion, individual experience of God rather than any organized spiritual exercise. This championship of individual faith reached its climax in Schleiermacher's *Reden über die Religion* which reject the objective validity of Christian authority in favour of a personal approach through feeling. In psychology too interest centred on all that was individual, extra-ordinary and inward : hence the research into such twilight states as somnambulism, automatism and magnetism as well as the fascination of the unconscious, of dreams, of schizophrenia in the motif of the Jekyll and Hyde dual-figure (*Doppelgänger*), explored particularly by E. T. A. Hoffmann, and so ably analysed by R. Tymms in *Doubles in Literary Psychology* (Cambridge 1949). Paradoxically, the importance attached to the individual leads also to a new cultivation of social life, of that *Geselligkeit** which was so prominent a feature of German Romanticism with its group individualism in a collective ivory tower, that finds such curious expression in all those terms coined with the Greek prefix *syn* meaning together : *Synexistenz, Symphilosophieren, Sympoesie, Synenthusiasmus.* For each person, inspired by a belief in the worth of individuality,

* togetherness

should endeavour in friendship to appreciate the individuality of others. According to Schleiermacher, 'Freundschaft ist Annäherung zur Individualität ins Unendliche, und daher selbst ins Unendliche teilbar und perfektibel, und nur Annäherung zu sich selbst.' [15] Thus friendship too was systematized into a theory in the *Versuch einer Theorie des geselligen Betragens* and it too was subordinated to the overriding cult of the individual.

At the summit of this mountain of individualism stands the artist, as far above other men as they are above the creatures of the earth: 'Was die Menschen unter den andern Bildungen der Erde, das sind die Künstler unter den Menschen',[16] or, to use Novalis' image, the artist rests on humanity as the statue does on its pedestal. A kind of super-individualist, the artist even more than his fellow-men has his true centre of gravity within himself: 'Ein Künstler ist, wer sein Zentrum in sich hat.' [17] Through his special powers of perception and his more intense capacity for experience, the artist has a profounder insight into the workings of the universe than ordinary mortals, more direct contact with the infinite forces of transcendental reality. Thus he is better able to guess ('erraten' is Novalis' word) the meaning of life and it is his prime function to act as mediator, to transmit his visionary perceptions to others: 'jeder Künstler ist Mittler für alle übrigen'.[18] With this conception of his nature and task the artist is immediately exalted to the position of leader, *vates*, high-priest of the new religion of art. The religious aura surrounding him is deliberately fostered: 'Wir sind auf einer Mission: zur Bildung der Erde sind wir berufen.' [19] How far removed this is from the commonsensical attitude of the English, who had no need or use for such hero-worship. To the Germans, however, the artist was more than a hero; he was virtually a divinity, endowed like God himself with the power of creation, for all art is, according to Schelling, a direct reflection of the absolute act of creation and consequently an absolute self-affirmation. This is an extension of the Promethean strand of the *Sturm und Drang* which had already admired the man who defied the gods in his attempt to mould his own creatures.

Now this legacy of the 'Age of Genius' was elaborated by the Romantics, who elevated the artist from an exceptional individual into a veritable divinity, invested with the rights and privileges of a godhead, above all with unbounded freedom. While the *Sturm und Drang* had sought the release of the imagination from the bondage of Gottsched's stifling rules, and the English Romantics wanted liberty of self-expression, the Germans demanded nothing less than a total autonomy. Again F. Schlegel acted as spokesman when he wrote that Romantic poetry 'allein ist unendlich, wie sie allein frei ist und das als ihr erstes Gesetz anerkennt, daß die Willkür des Dichters kein Gesetz über sich leide'.[20]

This refusal to accept any aesthetic discipline, this literary libertinage was to prove highly detrimental to Romantic poetry. Instead of becoming the ideal poetry of poetry, as F. Schlegel called it, the starting-point of the new Utopia, poetry was subject to the caprice of the super-artist, who felt justified in giving free rein to his every whim. The quest for novelty tended to replace the older ideal of harmonious beauty as Romantic poetry seemed the more interesting and individual, the more it was a poetry of the strange, a poetry of discovery and exploration, of new experiences and new regions. With his customary astuteness A. W. Schlegel characterized the Romantic spirit as that attitude of mind which strives at any cost for 'eine um die klassischen Muster unbekümmerte Originalität'.[21] In their undue emphasis on originality the Romantic thinkers once more took to its extreme a notion inherited from the *Sturm und Drang*. Furthermore, when the caprice of the moment is allowed to reign supreme, there is a danger of concentrating on arresting detail at the expense of the design and structure of the whole. It is therefore no mere coincidence that so many of the works, particularly of the *Frühromantik*, should have remained fragments; indeed the fragment as such became a recognized literary genre. Even some of those works that are complete suffer from a certain disjointedness and lack of inner unity that must be attributed to an excess of the poet's caprice, as, for instance, F. Schlegel's *Lucinde* or Tieck's *Franz Sternbalds Wanderungen*. On the whole, in fact, the German Romantics are at their best in shorter works such as the lyric and the *Märchen*,* which demand less of a sustained effort, or in longer works that are held together by a web of symbols, as in the case of *Heinrich von Ofterdingen*, or are made up of separate entities united by a certain mood, like the *Herzensergießungen eines kunstliebenden Klosterbruders*, rather than the product of any intellectual organization. The far-reaching effects of this extreme individualism are well summarized by Korff when he describes the essence of the Romantic revolution as the 'entscheidende Wendung . . . von einer Orientierung der modernen Dichtung nach dem Schönheitsideal der Antike zur selbstbewußten Behauptung ihrer selbst'.[22] An arrogant, well-nigh megalomanic self-assertiveness is a dominant feature of German Romanticism in the extraordinary lengths to which it takes its individualism.

The phrase 'selbstbewußte Behauptung ihrer selbst' † can be used to describe the attitude of the French too, for their individualism was also self-assertive, although in a different manner and above all with different objectives to that of their neighbours. The Romantic movement in France was determined by two factors, peculiar to that country alone, which distinguish it from the parallel movements in England and Germany : firstly the coincidence of the literary with the political Revolution, and secondly the stranglehold exercised by the Neoclassical tradition with its rigid rules, particularly those governing the structure of drama. Of these two factors, the second was by far the more potent. Contrary perhaps to expectation, the political Revolution seemed to retard rather than further the literary renewal while men's energies were concentrated on social, economic and bellicose matters at the turn of the eighteenth century; and later, under the Empire and the Restora-

---

* Another awkward term because it means so much more than its English dictionary equivalent : 'fairy-tale'. Not necessarily a tale about fairies, the *Märchen* essentially transcends the limits of reality and is enacted in a dream-world.

† 'confident self-assertion'

tion, a reaction set in which discouraged and even banned anything suspiciously novel. Nevertheless the iconoclasm of the political Revolution was soon enough manifest in literature too :

> Et sur les bataillons d'alexandrins carrés,
> Je fis souffler un vent révolutionnaire.
> Je mis un bonnet rouge au vieux dictionnaire.

or again, echoing closely the call to battle of the *Marseillaise* :

> Aux armes, prose et vers! formez vos bataillons! [23]

These utterances are characteristic of the aggressiveness of French Romantic individualism, which had to fight for its rights, to storm the Bastille of 'good taste' and rules. Herein lies the salient difference between French Romanticism on the one hand and English and German on the other : whereas the latter both already enjoyed an ample measure of freedom, the Germans having won it in the *Sturm und Drang* and the English as heirs to a long-established tradition, the French had to begin their Romantic reorientation with a protracted and tempestuous battle. Hence contemporary French critics insisted again and again that the essence of the new doctrine was nothing other than a quest for liberty. Duvicquet wrote in *Le Globe* in 1825 :

> Ce qui caractérise la nouvelle doctrine, ce qui la distingue surtout du classicisme, c'est un vif mépris pour toutes les idées adoptées de confiance, pour les théories apprises par cœur, pour les traditions qui n'ont pas passé au creuset de la raison; c'est enfin une méfiance de l'autorité, et un amour pour la liberté tout à fait séditieux.[24]

Similar ideas were expressed still more trenchantly by his colleague Duvergier de Hauranne in the same journal : 'Quelle est la Jérusalem qu'ils' (les romantiques) 'veulent conquérir, l'ennemi qu'ils s'attachent à combattre? cet ennemi c'est la routine, cette Jérusalem, c'est la liberté'.[25] A few pages later he sums up as follows : 'En un mot, asservissement aux lois de la grammaire, indépendance pour tout le reste, telle doit être la double devise du parti romantique.' [26] Hugo too, in his prefaces to both *Cromwell* and *Hernani* placed the demand for liberty in first place in the creed of French Romanticism : 'Le romantisme, tant de fois mal défini, n'est, à tout prendre, et c'est là sa définition réelle, si l'on ne l'envisage que de son côté militant, que le libéralisme en littérature.' [27] This militant quality of French Romanticism was invariably directed against the conventional rules, specially the three unities of the Neo-classical theatre : 'contre le despotisme des systèmes, des codes et des règles',[28] to use Hugo's words once more. On this point also there was universal agreement among the theoreticians of the time : 'Le romantisme pratique est une coalition animée d'intérêts divers, mais qui a un but commun, la guerre aux règles, aux règles de convention' [29] wrote Vitet in *Le Globe*, and Deschamps voiced the same opinion in an appendix to his *Préface des Études françaises et étrangères* : 'Ce qui constitue le romantisme c'est bien moins l'époque et la littérature où l'on prend son sujet, que la tendance de quelques auteurs à s'affranchir des règles de l'art.' [30]

All these pleas for liberty and the rejection of any rules are surely strongly reminiscent of the German *Sturm und Drang*. As in the German literary theories of the mid-eighteenth century, so in the French writings of the early nineteenth century the same key-words recur: 'liberty', 'originality', 'genius', 'nature', 'truth' are concepts as common in Hugo as in Herder. Moreover, the tone and atmosphere are similar, not only as regards the aggressive individualism, but also that frenzy, fury, vehemence typical of adolescent rebelliousness. Both the German *Stürmer und Dränger* and the French Romantic wanted to 'burn the paper' with his inspirations, not to 'recollect emotion in tranquillity'. Both have an absolute belief in the individual genius; so much so that the term 'Age of Genius' could almost equally be applied to French Romanticism, which, like its German predecessor, sought to replace the old system of rules by the new standards of the autonomous genius, subject to no discipline other than the dictates of his genius. 'Tous les systèmes sont faux; le génie seul est vrai' [31] is a significant remark attributed to Hugo, who was certainly in the forefront of the assault on Boileau's 'good taste'. Mme de Staël had already championed genius when she wrote in *De la Littérature* :

> Si l'on demande ce qui vaut mieux d'un ouvrage avec de grands
> défauts et de grandes beautés, ou d'un ouvrage médiocre et cor-
> rect, je répondrai, sans hésiter, qu'il faut préférer l'ouvrage où
> il existe, ne fût-ce qu'un seul trait de génie.[32]

– although she does compromise by adding that in practice 'good
taste' never demands the actual sacrifice of genius. Hugo, bolder
than Mme de Staël and writing at a time when the Romantic
revolution was on the point of victory, could go much further.
In the preface to *Les Orientales*, starting from the assertion that
the sole criterion of criticism is : 'l'ouvrage est-il bon ou est-il
mauvais ?', he goes on to posit the poet's undisputed right to
utter liberty, not restricted in any way by 'les limites de l'art',
by the 'géographie précise du monde intellectuel', the 'cartes
routières de l'art avec les frontières du possible et de l'impossible tracées en rouge et en bleu.' [33] Here the emphasis is on the
negative aspect, the opposition to the rules and limitations
accepted hitherto. In the preface to *Cromwell*, Hugo outlined the
new doctrine which was to supersede the old one now rejected :

> Il n'y a ni règles ni modèles; ou plutôt il n'y a d'autres règles
> que les lois générales de la nature, qui planent sur l'art entier,
> et les lois spéciales qui, pour chaque composition, résultent des
> conditions propres à chaque sujet . . . Le poète, insistons sur ce
> point, ne doit donc prendre conseil que de la nature, de la vérité
> et de l'inspiration.[34]

The parallel between the programme of French Romanticism
and that of the *Sturm und Drang* could hardly be made plainer
than in these words. The individualism of the French, con-
ditioned by their historical and literary position, is thus of an
extrovert, barn-storming type, very different from that of the
English or the German Romantics.

In its literary outcome too it diverges radically from its
English and German counterparts, once more determined by the
lasting dominance of a firmly entrenched Neo-classical tradition
such as existed in no other European country. Since it was

primarily iconoclastic, the weakness of French Romantic doctrine lay in the fact that it made too few positive suggestions to replace what it rejected. French Romanticism tended to share with other Romantic movements mainly the negative aspects: the anti-rationalism, anti-classicism, aversion to aesthetic discipline, but in its quest for new sources of inspiration and new forms of art it suffered from a lack of really original thinkers. Perhaps the French were unconsciously too indoctrinated by the very Classicism that they were attacking to branch out in any significantly new direction instead of merely proceeding always by opposition. Both Vigny and Stendhal accused their fellow-countrymen of an innate conservatism: the former called 'la Routine' the 'mal qui souvent afflige notre pays' leading to an undiscriminating repetition of the 'mêmes idées, mêmes expressions, mêmes sons'.[35] Stendhal with his curious combination of an instinct for clarity and a fierce liberalism and cult of passion was very much more vehemently outspoken: he regarded the adherence to the old rules as a bad habit, 'une habitude française, habitude profondément enracinée'[36] and he urged the French to acquire a modicum of 'courage civil'[37] since 'il faut du courage pour être romantique, car it faut hasarder'.[38] It is no coincidence that France produced at this time few philosophical or aesthetic ideas such as abounded in Germany; France indeed laboured under a dearth of that kind of lofty idealism which through its excessiveness was to prove baneful in Germany. While the Germans all too easily lost themselves in clouds of metaphysical speculation, the French, rational even in their anti-rationalism, remained soberly close to the ground, concentrating their attention chiefly on problems of literary technique such as the form of the drama and the shape of the Alexandrine. In this respect also French Romanticism stands under the shadow of the great era of Neo-classicism, of which the drama remained 'la dernière forteresse'.[39] So French Romantic criticism is devoted almost entirely to the drama, particularly the Neo-classical genre, the tragedy, which was to be demolished; the novel, not a prominent form of the Neo-classical period, was virtually

ignored in contrast to the marked German preference for the
Roman, which was extolled as the Romantic vehicle *par excellence* in so far as it permitted the freest mingling of moods and
thus the nearest approach to a universal work of art. As against
the tendency to abstraction that characterizes the German
theoreticians, the French critics are realistically down-to-earth
in their discussions of the future of drama, ever aware of the
outline of the Neo-classical drama in the background and
therefore preferring to examine details of execution rather
than to expand the problem into the infinite, as the Germans
frequently did. As a representative sample of the tone of
French Romantic criticism Vigny's *Lettre à Lord* * * * could be
cited :

> Une simple question est à résoudre. La voici : La scène française
> s'ouvrira-t-elle, ou non, à une tragédie moderne produisant :
> – Dans sa conception, un tableau large de la vie, au lieu du tableau
> resserré de la catastrophe d'une intrigue ; – Dans sa composition,
> des caractères, non des rôles, des scènes paisibles sans drame,
> mêlées à des scènes comiques et tragiques ; – Dans son exécution,
> un style familier, comique, tragique et parfois épique ?[40]

This is clear, concise, level-headed, yet always envisaging the
new in comparison or rivalry with the old established. For all
its outbursts of aggressive self-assertion, French Romantic
individualism was never really free in that it was constantly and
anxiously measuring itself up against the past.

This failure to achieve an inner emancipation from the burden
of an overwhelming past probably accounts both for the clamour
for individual liberty and the demand for naturalness in the
theatre. Since the Neo-classical drama was hedged in on all
sides by a fairly rigid set of rules and conventions so that it was,
as A. W. Schlegel put it, totally unnatural,[41] Romantic drama as
a reaction had necessarily to be as unforced as possible. This is
another point of contact between French Romanticism and the
German *Sturm und Drang* : the latter, in its revolt against the
dogmatism of Gottsched's recipe for making a good play, also
sought a completely free and natural form and opted for the

prose drama unrestricted by the unities, as the French were to do. Again like that of the *Sturm und Drang*, the new French theatre was to be modelled on the English, with Shakespeare as its guiding influence. In the same way as Lessing had pointed the way for the Germans, so Mme de Staël directed French attention towards the English dramatic tradition which showed 'les héros peints avec leur faiblesses, les vertus avec leurs inconséquences, les circonstances vulgaires à côté des situations les plus élevées', with characters drawn 'de la vie humaine' not just 'du beau idéal'.[42] Here already is implicit that ideal of naturalness which was to be elaborated by later theoreticians. Vigny for instance not only hoped that the 'grâces de convention' would be replaced by 'plus de beautés naturelles',[43] but even hinted at a kind of realism when he sketched the method of the dramatist of the future :

> D'abord il prendra dans sa large main beaucoup de temps, et y fera mouvoir des existences entières; il créera l'homme, non comme espèce, mais comme individu; il laissera ses créatures vivre de leur propre vie, et jettera seulement dans leurs cœurs ces germes de passion par où se préparent les grands événements; puis, lorsque l'heure en sera venue et seulement alors, il montrera la déstinée enveloppant ses victimes dans des nœuds inextricables et multipliés. Alors, bien loin de trouver des personnages trop petits pour l'espace, il gémira, il s'écriera qu'ils manquent d'air et d'espace, car l'art sera tout semblable à la vie.[44]

Apart from outlining a more vigorous and individualistic type of play, Vigny also reveals his awareness of the expansive tendencies of Romantic drama. Infinite digression through the lure of the picturesque is the pitfall that mars German Romantic drama, which has been compared to a picture, framed on three sides, but continuously in the process of improvement on the fourth! The French are on the whole less prone to fall prey to this danger because their attention is usually firmly riveted on concrete details, on questions of dramatic technique. The cultivation of local colour, so prominent a feature of French Romanticism, is an outcome both of the interest in the individual and the particular – as against the general that attracted the Neo-classicists – and of the insistence on truth, for 'la couleur locale est la base de toute vérité'.[45] The general brief for truthfulness and naturalness becomes a specific plea for freedom in speech and verse as part of the rebellion against the artificial decorum of noble, poetic diction in the Neo-classical drama. In the preface to *Cromwell*, itself a document couched in a clear vivid style, full of illuminating metaphor, Hugo advocated 'un vers libre, franc, loyal, osant tout dire sans pruderie, tout exprimer sans recherche; passant d'une naturelle allure de la comédie à la tragédie, du sublime au grotesque'.[46] Similarly Vigny declared himself 'en faveur du mot vrai, moderne',[47] for a style that 'dans l'art comme dans la vie, passera de la simplicité habituelle à l'exaltation passionnée'.[48] Indeed Vigny in his rejection of the old limited and standardized vocabulary went so far as to foreshadow the realism of the later Naturalists, who were to imitate personal peculiarities of speech with a pedantic punctiliousness :

> Un drame ne présentera jamais aux peuples que des personnages réunis pour se parler de leurs affaires; ils doivent donc parler. . . . Chaque homme, dans sa conversation habituelle, n'a-t-il pas ses formules favorites, ses mots coutumiers nés de son éducation, de sa profession, de ses goûts ? n'a-t-il pas des comparaisons de prédilection et tout un vocabulaire journalier ? Faut-il donc toujours que chaque personnage se serve des mêmes mots, des mêmes images, que tous les autres emploient aussi ? Non, il doit être concis ou diffus, négligé ou calculé, prodigue ou avare d'ornements selon son caractère, son âge, ses penchants.[49]

After these enlightened ideas it is disappointing to come upon Vigny's *Chatterton*, a *drame* in three acts under the Shakespearean devise 'Despair and die'. This play is a curious mixture of old and new : though written in prose, it still observes the unities, and while there are exact stage directions, including characterization before the opening, and plenty of local colour in the descriptions of the characters' appearance and clothing, the play fails because of the feebleness of its plot. Vigny, like F. Schlegel with his *Lucinde*, could not put his theories into practice. In this Hugo was far more successful; in *Hernani* he created the prototype of French Romantic drama with a play that not only revelled in realistic speech and a free verse-form after banishing the unities, but was also spectacular and melodramatic, full of appeal to eye and ear in its violent, startling happenings. How right Deschamps was when he foresaw that 'tout sera decidé en une soirée' – with the battle and triumph of *Hernani* – and how perspicacious his recognition

> que la question n'est pas dans la coupe matérielle des scènes et des actes, dans les passages subits d'une forêt à un château, et d'une province à un autre, mais qu'elle est réellement dans la peinture individualisée des caractères, dans le remplacement continuel du récit par l'action, dans la naïveté du langage ou le coloris poétique, dans un style enfin tout moderne.[50]

The long struggle surrounding the emergence of Romantic drama in France was in fact not so much a matter of literary techniques and forms as an assertion of the new creed of individualism against the old doctrine that 'the ego is hateful'.

The Effects of this Individualism

THE fundamental individualism of every Romantic, however disparate its origins, determines in a decisive manner both the form of his art and his attitude towards the world around him. In spite of the differences just discerned between the flavour of English, German and French individualism, in its effects there are often similarities. These surface likenesses have perhaps concealed the underlying divergences, thereby helping to foster the concept of a single European Romanticism.

A. On Form

Starting from the outer shape, let us first consider some of the effects of individualism on form. The whole conception of the origin, nature and function of the work of art underwent a radical change in the course of that reorientation that is an essential part of Romanticism. Whereas previously art had been regarded as a skill, a proficiency in the manipulation of certain exacting rules, albeit not without an element of invention, it now became an experience surrounded by a kind of mystique because it sprang from a very special sensitivity, the artist's inspiration. This change obviously stems from the new vision of the artist, no longer a propagator of knowledge, one who *does*, but a poetic soul, one who *is*. What matters, in other words, is the artist's individuality, of which the work of art is a direct expression, without the intervention of any conventions whatsoever. It is thus in individualism that the Romantic cult of spontaneity is rooted.

Spontaneity is, for one reason or another, the object of many

Romantics. The French, as we have seen, directly and explicitly pursue the ideal of naturalness as part of their campaign for the liberty of the individual. But for very different motives the German *Hochromantiker* also aimed at naturalness, or at least at a semblance of naturalness in their *Lieder** and *Märchen*. The junior group, the Heidelberg poets, turned away from the metaphysical complexities and excessive sophistication of the *Frühromantik* theoreticians, and with the growth of patriotic nationalism became increasingly immersed in the glories of their German heritage (just when the French were trying to rid themselves of their past). The earlier interest in naive folk-poetry, already nurtured during the *Sturm und Drang* period by Herder's anthology *Stimmen der Völker* (*The Peoples' Voices*) (1778) as well as by the poems of Ossian, was at this time re-kindled and received fresh stimulus through such collections as *Des Knaben Wunderhorn*, Görres' *Die teutschen Volksbücher* and the *Kinder- und Hausmärchen* gathered by the brothers Grimm. Inspired by these models, the *Hochromantiker* began to create their own *Lieder* and *Märchen* : these in fact are the works for which German Romanticism achieved its lasting fame, such as the poems of Eichendorff, Heine, Mörike or tales like Brentano's *Geschichte vom braven Kasperl und dem schönen Annerl*, Fouqué's *Undine*, Chamisso's *Peter Schlemihl*. These were not true *Volkslieder* or *Volksmärchen* in that they were the products of conscious artists and therefore at best *Kunstvolkslieder* or *Kunstmärchen*,† imitations of traditional folk-art, which aimed at a creative renewal of poetry through the use of certain favourite themes, figures and genres, and above all through the adoption of a particular style and manner, dependent on deliberate simplification. This was an art so polished and so finely controlled as to appear quite artless; in other words, a return through sophistication to the ideal of naturalness held by the *Stürmer und Dränger* and by the French Romantics,

* literally 'songs'; often means 'poems'
† *Volkslied* : folk-song; *Volksmärchen* : folk-tale. The prefix *Kunst-*, meaning literally 'art', conveys conscious creation.

although for both these latter groups naturalness was the spontaneous outcome of a robust individualism, whereas with the *Hochromantik* it became the object of a conscious quest. Incidentally, naturalness of a rather different kind is of course a prominent characteristic of some English Romantic poetry, notably Wordsworth; this naturalness, however, does not arise from individualism but from other factors to be discussed later.

Another perhaps even stranger *rapprochement* may be drawn between the consequences of the German demand for artistic autonomy and the French programme of naturalness in that ultimately the effect of F. Schlegel's championship of the artist's caprice was similar to that of Hugo's doctrine of the grotesque. Remote from each other though they are in origin, in their practical results these two notions prove extraordinarily alike. Hugo's theory of the grotesque was derived from his belief that art should portray truth so that, like nature, it must show 'pas le beau, mais le caractéristique'.[51] It was, moreover, in the choice of the characteristic rather than the beautiful that Hugo saw the essential difference between Romantic and Classical art :

> La muse moderne sentira que tout dans la création n'est pas humainement beau, que le laid y existe à côté du beau, le difforme près du gracieux, le grotesque au revers du sublime, le mal avec le bien, l'ombre avec la lumière. Elle se mettra à faire comme la nature, à mêler dans ses créations, sans pourtant les confondre, l'ombre à la lumière, le grotesque au sublime.[52]

This admission of the grotesque and even the ugly into art as part of the liberalizing programme of the French Romantics led as surely to a widening of the horizon as F. Schlegel's inclusion of the strange and monstrous, justified in his opinion by originality, and also as one stage in the progress towards universality :

> Aus dem romantischen Gesichtspunkt haben auch die Abarten der Poesie, selbst die exzentrischen und monströsen, ihren Wert, als Materialien und Vorübungen der Universalität, wenn nur irgend etwas drin ist, wenn sie nur original sind.[53]

This apologia for literary monstrosities stems from the individual's arrogation of a boundless freedom and from the artist's demand for absolute autonomy. Since the caprice of the genius was to brook no check, monstrosities were permissible. In effect, therefore, this theory was akin to Hugo's welcome of the grotesque : the possibilities of artistic expression were immensely expanded, but the inevitable result was a marked dissolution of the traditional forms. This is particularly evident among the German Romantics, for whom the notion of the so-called *Mischgedicht** was a key principle. In the words of F. Schlegel's authoritative 116th Fragment :

Die romantische Poesie ist eine progressive Universalpoesie. Ihre Bestimmung ist nicht bloß, alle getrennten Gattungen der Poesie wieder zu vereinigen und die Poesie mit der Philosophie und Rhetorik in Berührung zu setzen. Sie will und soll auch Poesie und Prosa, Genialität und Kritik, Kunstpoesie und Naturpoesie bald mischen, bald verschmelzen, die Poesie lebendig und gesellig und das Leben und die Gesellschaft poetisch machen, den Witz poetisieren und die Formen der Kunst mit gediegnem Bildungsstoff jeder Art anfüllen und sättigen und durch die Schwingungen des Humors beseelen. Sie umfaßt alles, was nur poetisch ist, vom größten wieder mehrere Systeme in sich enthaltenden Systeme der Kunst bis zu dem Seufzer, dem Kuß, den das dichtende Kind aushaucht in kunstlosen Gesang.[54]

With that tendency to fanciful extremism that characterizes German Romanticism, F. Schlegel here claims and hopes for very much more than Hugo. whose desire to mingle the comic and the tragic, prose and verse is comparable to the freedoms sought by the *Stürmer und Dränger*. The *Frühromantiker*, never modest or finite in their aims, conceived this mingling in the widest possible terms, as F. Schlegel's words show. Even the orderly and sensible A. W. Schlegel not only subscribed to the *Mischgedicht*, in his aphorisms and his *Vorlesungen über dramatische Kunst und Literatur*, but even went so far as to define Romantic art in words reminiscent of his brother's :

* Literally 'mixed poem', i.e. a work of art that mingles tragedy and comedy lyrical, dramatic and narrative styles.

F

Die antike Kunst und Poesie geht auf strenge Sonderung des Ungleichartigen, die romantische gefällt sich in unauflöslichen Mischungen; alle Entgegengesetzten : Natur und Kunst, Poesie und Prosa, Ernst und Scherz, Erinnerung und Ahndung, Geistigkeit und Sinnlichkeit, das Irdische und Göttliche, Leben und Tod verschmelzt sie auf das innigste mit einander.[55]

The members of the Jena circle repeatedly avowed their allegiance to this basic principle of their *ars poetica*; Tieck for example declared :

Ich halte dafür, daß alles nebeneinander bestehen könne und müsse, und daß nichts eine so engherzige Verleumdung der Kunst und Hoheit ist, als wenn man zu früh scharfe Linien und Grenzen zwischen den Gebieten der Kunst zieht.[56]

Even so consummate an artist as Novalis ranged himself on the side of 'die Verworrenen' who eventually achieve much more than 'die Geordneten'.[57] No wonder therefore that German Romanticism abounds in works such as F. Schlegel's *Lucinde*, Brentano's *Godwi*, Tieck's *Der gestiefelte Kater* or *Die verkehrte Welt*, wild potpourris in which the author's caprice has run riot in a crazy mixture of the most diverse elements. Many of Tieck's dramas outstrip by far any of Hugo's plays in their grotesqueness, their deliberate *reductio ad absurdum* of all theatrical conventions. Thus *Der gestiefelte Kater* is not a mere re-telling of the story of Puss-in-Boots, but a performance of a performance within an elaborate framework, in which the real subject is the reaction of the audience who constantly interrupt and comment in a ribald manner.

This tendency to dissolve the traditional forms is a consistent characteristic of Romantic art, equally evident in some of the music of the period, say Schumann's cello concerto and his fourth symphony. Just as the French deliberately broke the bounds of their Neo-classical drama, so the Germans expanded their favourite genre, the novel, well beyond its customary range. Indeed it is only with some reservations that the term 'novel' can be applied to F. Schlegel's *Lucinde* or even to Novalis' *Heinrich von Ofterdingen*, which its author called a *Märchen-*

roman and which so freely mingles prose and verse, interspersing the narrative with lyrical and dramatic interludes that it gradually glides away from the world of reality into a dream realm of its own : 'Die Welt wird Traum, der Traum wird Welt' [58] is its appropriate motto. More perplexing still is Wackenroder's *Herzensergießungen eines kunstliebenden Klosterbruders,* a work of so strange an individuality as to defy classification into any recognized category. The English Romantics too tended to produce great formless poems, but whereas with the Germans and the French this defect was the direct outcome of their programme, with the English it must rather be called accidental, a side-effect of their interest in collecting, exploring and recording esoteric mental experiences – Coleridge's 'facts of mind' – which superseded and overshadowed their wish to create form.

In its effect on literary form individualism therefore proves an ambivalent factor. Concomitant to the new freedom which it brings are certain dangers, that increase in proportion to the licence arrogated by the Romantic poet. The effect on form is accordingly more far-reaching where individualism is at its most extreme – in Germany – than in England where it is tempered by a certain traditionalism.

B. *On the relationship to nature*

In his relationship to the world around him, more specifically the world of nature, the Romantic poet could be deeply and directly influenced by his innate individualism.

This, of course, is the area where Romantic poetry has achieved its greatest fame. Rightly or wrongly, the notion of Romantic poetry is for many people virtually synonymous with nature poetry, particularly in English-speaking countries, where it is often claimed that the Romantic movement's 'chief glory lay, without doubt, in the extraordinarily various, intimate, and subtle interpretation of the world of "external

Nature" '.[59] The word 'interpretation' here provides a clue to
the novelty of the Romantics' approach to nature, which stemmed
from a reorientation as radical as the new affirmation of the
individual. For the old rationalistic, predominantly Cartesian
conception of nature as a machine, which had been set in motion
at the creation of the universe and henceforth continued to work
automatically according to certain pre-ordained, immutable
laws, was rejected in favour of a dynamic, organic view. The
former static picture of a mechanistic, dead nature was replaced
by the revelation of an ever changing, growing nature, a
creature with a life and soul of its own. This revolution in the
conception of nature, an inestimable gain for poetry, cannot be
ascribed wholly to the Romantics for it had already been
perceived intuitively by many writers of the latter half of the
eighteenth century, such as Herder, Goethe, Rousseau. The
scientific discoveries of the period, however, added the backing
of scholarship to this new vision of a dynamic nature, and it is
worth noting that the research of Lavoisier, Galvani and
Mesmer shows a fascination with the hidden movement of
natural forces. Nature was therefore envisaged no longer as a
passive object, but as an animate being; animals, trees, plants,
even stones and stars are as much active inhabitants of the
universe as man himself.

> Gehören Tiere, Pflanzen und Steine, Gestirne und Lüfte nicht
> auch zur Menschheit und ist sie nicht ein bloßer Nervenknoten in
> dem unendlich verschieden laufende Fäden sich kreuzen? Läßt
> sie sich ohne die Natur begreifen und ist sie denn so sehr anders
> als die übrigen Naturgeschlechter?[60]

asked Novalis, whose work is full of examples to illustrate his
belief: in *Hyazinth und Rosenblütchen* (the *Märchen* interpolated
in *Die Lehrlinge zu Saïs*) the flowers, the stones and the stream
take a tender, smiling interest in Hyazinth's quest, while from
the sketches for the second part of *Heinrich von Ofterdingen* it
seems that Heinrich was to become part of the natural world not
merely through speech but by actually turning into a stone,
flower, tree, animal in order to divine the real meaning of the

universe. This was to be part of the poet's task: to learn to understand nature, to feel his way into her innermost being, to read her code, and the Romantic artist, with his heightened sensibility, thought himself particularly well suited to this new role.

This image of the Romantic poet as a man with a specially intimate relationship to nature has been all too readily accepted. Looking dispassionately at the evidence of Romantic nature poetry, one is surely led to question the truth of the proposition. Did the Romantics really have an arcane insight into, and appreciation of, nature? Were they sufficiently self-detached and sympathetic to other existences to be able to feel their way into the soul of nature, as they maintained? Or did not their peculiar individualism, i.e. their tendency to regard self as the paramount interest in life, interfere by directing their gaze always inwards? To these questions there is no single or simple answer since the attitude of the Romantic poets to nature varies very widely, though it is perhaps possible to distinguish certain broad avenues of approach.

The implied criticism – that the Romantics' egoism impeded their relationship to the outer world – is certainly not appropriate to all the Romantic poets as a group. There are remarkable exceptions. Keats, for instance, was as unsentimental in his attitude to nature as to himself. Just as his letters reveal an ability for self-analysis of a detached, almost clinical sort without prejudice, touchiness or self-love, so his poetry testifies to his scrupulous fidelity to the object of his attention. The very word 'object' is in itself significant: the outer world remained to Keats an object never swamped by his own emotions. Being one of 'those who delight in Sensation', as he told Bailey in a letter on 22 November 1817, he could derive an intense pleasure from nature:

> To one who has been long in city pent,
> 'Tis very sweet to look into the fair
> And open face of heaven, – to breathe a prayer
> Full in the smile of the blue firmament.[61]

In his superb *Ode to Autumn*, he is able to conjure up the mood of autumn, that blend of satiety and wistfulness, as though the 'season of mists and mellow fruitfulness' were itself speaking through his mouth. He does indeed, in his sonnet *The Human Seasons*, perceive the parallels between the natural and the human sphere, but here too there is a characteristic uprightness in facing reality that precludes any sentimentality. Far from expecting the participation of nature in human suffering, Keats recognized and accepted her 'happy insensibility'.

Wordsworth too was able to look at nature with detachment so as to observe and describe her as she really is. His is not some vast, vague, infinite nature; he wrote from experience of the scenes he knew, choosing concrete images and precise adjectives. When he portrays Simon Lee :

> And still the centre of his cheek
> Is red as ripe cherry

this is no mere embellishment; we can actually visualize the old huntsman, the *centre* of whose cheek is red as a *ripe* cherry : the circumscribing details make the picture both real and vivid. Similarly England is

> a fen
> Of stagnant waters[62]

and the deserted heart is

> left more desolate, more dreary cold
> Than a forsaken bird's nest fill'd with snow
> 'Mid its own bush of leafless eglantine[63]

Yet this clarity of vision is allied to a potent mystical sense of the strong bond between nature and human life : it is this unique combination of realism and intuition which gives Wordsworth's poetry its unmistakable flavour. Poems such as *Michael, The Simplon Pass, The Education of Nature* express man's communion with nature in language of extraordinary directness. In a moving passage in the *Lines composed a few miles above Tintern Abbey* Wordsworth traced the change in the significance of nature to him from his early naïve, sensuous

delight in its appearance to a calmer, deeper appreciation of its
meaning :

> For nature then
> (The coarser pleasures of my boyish days,
> And their glad animal movements all gone by)
> To me was all in all. – I cannot paint
> What then I was. The sounding cataract
> Haunted me like a passion : the tall rock,
> The mountain, and the deep and gloomy wood,
> Their colours and their forms, were then to me
> An appetite : a feeling and a love,
> That had no need of a remoter charm,
> By thought supplied, nor any interest
> Unborrowed from the eye. – That time is past,
> And all its aching joys are now no more,
> And all its dizzy raptures. Nor for this
> Faint I, nor mourn nor murmur; other gifts
> Have followed; for such loss, I would believe,
> Abundant recompense. For I have learned
> To look on nature, not as in the hour
> Of thoughtless youth; but hearing oftentimes
> The still, sad music of humanity,
> Nor harsh nor grating, though of ample power
> To chasten and subdue. And I have felt
> A presence that disturbs me with the joy
> Of elevated thoughts; a sense sublime
> Of something far more deeply interfused,
> Whose dwelling is the light of setting suns,
> And the round ocean and the living air,
> And the blue sky, and in the mind of man;
> A motion and a spirit, that impels
> All thinking things, all objects of all thought,
> And rolls through all things. Therefore am I still
> A lover of the meadows and the woods,
> And mountains; and of all that we behold
> From this green earth; of all the mighty world
> Of eye, and ear, – both what they half create,
> And what perceive; well pleased to recognize
> In nature and the language of the sense
> The anchor of my purest thoughts, the nurse,
> The guide, the guardian of my heart, and soul
> Of all my moral being.

Wordsworth is here describing how he gradually came to perceive the immanence of the spiritual in nature, although he never actually mentions God other than indirectly in the term 'a presence'. This pantheism Wordsworth had in common with Shelley and Coleridge, who saw and heard in nature

> The lovely shapes and sounds intelligible
> Of that eternal language, which thy God
> Utters, who from eternity doth teach
> Himself in all, and all things in himself.[64]

But whereas Coleridge was so conscious of the symbolical substratum of nature that the physical surface appearances 'vanish from my thought',[65] Wordsworth always remained

> A lover of the meadows and the woods

observing with eye and ear the realities of nature as well as divining their significance.

Such a degree of objectivity is, however, rare among the Romantic poets, most of whom tend to consider nature primarily in relationship to man, and more specifically to themselves. In their approach to nature they were not so much looking at extraneous objects with a life of their own as seeking a symbolical counterpart to something within themselves. Hence it is a feature of Romantic nature poetry that meanings are read into the landscape, or to borrow Hazlitt's vivid and scathing phrase from his discourse on Wordsworth's *Excursion* in *The Round Table*, a puddle is filled with preternatural faces. To Wordsworth

> the meanest flower that blows can give
> Thoughts that do often lie too deep for tears.[66]

while Coleridge too can

> trace in leaves and flowers that round me lie
> Lessons of love and earnest piety.[67]

Thus the spiritual is discovered, often in the more intangible and mysterious aspects of nature, such as the wind, a recurrent image to convey the animation of nature.[68] This idea of a consonance between man and nature was by no means a novel one : it already permeated the nature-poetry of the *Sturm und Drang*, particularly Goethe's lyrics of the Strasbourg period; it was likewise implicit in the illuminist and occultist traditions current in France in the eighteenth century, and refurbished by Mme de Staël in the seventh chapter of the fourth part of *De l'Allemagne*, where she writes 'Des philosophes religieux appelés Théosophes'. Furthermore in many of the descriptions in Rousseau's *Nouvelle Héloïse*, as well as in the famous *paysages état d'âme** in *Les Rêveries du Promeneur Solitaire*, the correspondence between man and nature is adumbrated :

> c'est une impression générale qu'éprouvent tous les hommes, quoiqu'ils ne l'observent pas tous, que sur les hautes montagnes où l'air est pur et subtil, on se sent plus de facilité dans la respiration, plus de légèreté dans le corps, plus de sérénité dans l'esprit, les plaisirs y sont moins ardens, les passions plus modérées. Les méditations y prennent je ne sais quel caractère grand et sublime, proportionné aux objets qui nous frappent, je ne sais quelle volupté tranquille qui n'a rien d'acre et de sensuel. Il semble qu'en s'élevant au dessus du séjour des hommes on y laisse tous les sentimens bas et terrestres, et qu'à mesure qu'on approche des régions éthérées l'âme contracte quelque chose de leur inaltérable pureté.[69]

This parallelism between man and nature was developed to its logical conclusion by the Romantics, who nurtured a quasi-religious belief in the total fusion of man with nature. Coleridge, in criticizing Bowles' 'dim analogies', maintained that 'a Poet's Heart and Intellect should be *combined, intimately* combined and *unified* with the great appearances in Nature – and not merely held in solution and loose mixture with them, in the shape of formal Similes.'[70] This ideal of an intuitive fusion between man and nature, even if it amounted to what has since been termed 'pathetic fallacy', is a cardinal feature of Romantic poetry. Nature is everywhere in sympathy with the poet, sharing his joys and, more often, his sorrows. Only occasionally

* landscape descriptions that reflect a state of mind

was it represented as a sinister, even hostile force, as in Tieck's *Der Runenberg*, Hoffmann's *Bergwerke zu Falun* and Vigny's *La Maison du Berger*. Generally the Romantics insisted on the intimate bond between man and nature, to which they gave expression in some of their finest writing.

All too often in this partnership, however, the one element becomes dominant to the detriment of the other when the poet's ego so absorbs his attention that nature is no longer seen as an independent object, but is reduced to the role of a mirror that serves to reflect the poet's emotions. This is the point where an introverted individualism interfered with the poet's relationship to the outer world, as all the fine feeling for nature was submerged in mere feeling for self, a self-seeking sympathy in nature. 'In solitude or in that deserted state when we are surrounded by human beings, and yet they sympathize not with us, we love the flowers, the grass and the waters, and the sky. In the motion of the very leaves of spring, in the blue air, there is then found a secret correspondence within our heart.' [71] Shelley believed that nature was not just an outward world but rather a spirit that suffered in unison with man. He therefore sought in nature the image of his own mood and situation and repeatedly called on nature to participate in his woe. In the 'rough wind', the 'sad storm' he hears 'a dirge', a 'wail for the world's wrong'. The same image recurs in the *Ode to the West Wind*, the first three verses of which, all ending in 'Oh hear!', are an invocation to the wild wind, while the last two express the poem's theme:

> If I were a dead leaf thou mightest bear;
> If I were a swift cloud to fly with thee;
> A wave to part beneath thy power – .

The longing for identification with the wind finally culminates in the cry

> Be thou, Spirit fierce,
> My spirit!

where the enjambement reinforces the impression of a surging power. In nature Shelley was certain of finding that response so disappointingly lacking in his fellow-men. Hence it is

> Away, away, from men and towns,
> To the wild wood and the downs –
> To the silent wilderness
> Where the soul need not repress
> Its music, lest it should not find
> An echo in another's mind,
> While the touch of Nature's art
> Harmonizes heart to heart.[72]

The characteristic movement of Shelley's poems is thus always inwards, away from the physical appearance towards the recondite meaning of what he sees in nature. The *Stanzas written in Dejection near Naples*, for instance, open with a description of the outer scene only to draw the parallel between the mood of nature and his own :

> Yet now despair itself is mild
> Even as the winds and the waters are.

A similar progression inwards takes place in *To a Skylark*, where the image of the bird is attached to the poet. So Shelley, instead of exploring reality in his nature images, in fact flies away from it in a centripetal drive that is the opposite of Wordsworth's gaze, which tends outwards, as indeed do his poems. In contrast to Shelley's musings *To A Skylark*, Wordsworth's *The Green Linnet* is concerned with the bird itself and even a reflective poem such as *To a Distant Friend* expands from its personal core in the fine, precise nature image adduced to illuminate the human predicament. Shelley aptly defined his own relationship to the world around him when he wrote

> I felt the centre of
> The magic circle.[73]

For Shelley, as for Musset, the whole universe radiated from his ego. No wonder that he had little interest in the details of a real nature, seeing rather the 'visionary flowers' [74] projected by his mind's eye. His is a very generalized impression of nature, conveyed in vague plurals and in deliberately non-specific adjectives. The same indeed is true of Lamartine : again a hazy picture of nature, without precise details, a blurred amalgam of 'fleuves, rochers, forêts',[75] 'terre, soleil, vallons',[76] that hardly seems observed from reality. Lamartine in fact shows scant appreciation of nature as an independent object; for him nature exists solely for the poet's benefit, to provide first a suitable setting for the drama of his love and later consolation in his misery. In the song of the nightingale[77] Lamartine hears only the message addressed to the poet : this is characteristic of an attitude that interprets nature exclusively in relation to the self, using it as a 'mirror seeking of itself'.[78] Nature was a reflection of personal feelings to the young Hugo too; vying with Lamartine, he regards nature as a background and an echo of his reverie. He hardly cares to see nature for all attention is focused on the poet, who can enter into himself in the stillness of the forest.

Such self-absorption can become so thorough-going that the Romantic's gaze is completely averted from the world around him when he follows the instructions with which Fichte began his *Wissenschaftslehre* : to avert his gaze from all about him in order to look only into himself ('Merke auf dich selbst : kehre deinen Blick von allem, was dich umgibt, ab und in dein Inneres'). This outright rejection of the physical world of appearances is characteristic of the visionary poets Novalis and Blake, who look, in the latter's words, not with, but *through* the corporeal eye towards the representations of the imagination. Since Blake categorically stated : 'I do not behold the outward creation',[79] it is not surprising that no extended nature descriptions are found in his poetry. Coleridge too, the metaphysician fed on honey-dew and the milk of Paradise, is tempted in *Kubla Khan* to conjure up his own enchanted inner landscape, far removed from the realities observed by Wordsworth. Likewise the later Hugo, partly no doubt under the influence of his interest in the occult, sought to decipher in nature the mysterious depths of an invisible world.

The lure of the individual's inner vision was at its strongest among the German *Frühromantiker*, who ignored the surface of nature in order to look through and beyond it, like Blake, in search of its ultimate meaning. 'Tief ins Gemüt der weiten Welt zu schauen':[80] this, the avowed aim of Novalis and his circle, surely accounts for the dearth of nature poetry in the usual sense among the *Frühromantiker*, who produced instead a philosophy of nature, a mass of theory without parallel either in France or England. Briefly, the essence of this philosophy of nature lay in the identification of nature with the realm of the spirit as expounded by Schelling in his *Ideen zu einer Philosophie der Natur*: 'Die Natur soll der sichtbare Geist, der Geist die unsichtbare Natur sein.' [81] Schelling insisted on the absolute identity of spirit within us and nature without, i.e. the instinctive harmony between the soul of man and the wondrous inner processes of nature which man may apprehend by intuition. This mystical approach to nature was, curiously enough, accepted even by the scientists of the group, including the physicist Ritter. Nature was thus transformed into an abstract, theoretical concept: the symbol of man's harmony with the infinite cosmos. While Shelley and Lamartine read a personal meaning into the vaguely perceived reality of nature, the *Frühromantiker* could see nature only as through a veil, the veil of their ideology, which turned nature into a focus of their subjective longings and thereby blinded them to the actual phenomena of her existence. In other words, their concentration on their own individuality precluded appreciation of nature's individuality. This indifference to the physical appearance of nature is borne out by the marked preference for the nocturnal aspects of nature: not only Tieck's 'mondbeglänzte Zaubernacht' * and Novalis' yearning for the apparitions of night, but also the blackness of the mine held a special fascination. The visible reality is in these instances shrouded by darkness as by a veil, a peculiarly appropriate image in this context, which recurs throughout Novalis' *Die Lehrlinge zu Saïs* and *Heinrich*

* 'enchantment of the moon-lit night'

von Ofterdingen, in both of which the landscapes have a strange, stylized quality, as in a dream :

Hyazinth lief nun was er konnte, durch Täler und Wildnisse, über Berge und Ströme, dem geheimnisvollen Lande zu. Er fragte überall nach der heiligen Göttin (Isis) Menschen und Tiere, Felsen und Bäume. Manche lachten, manche schwiegen, nirgends erhielt er Bescheid. Im Anfange kam er durch rauhes, wildes Land, Nebel und Wolken warfen sich ihm in den Weg, es stürmte immerfort; dann fand er unabsehliche Sandwüsten, glühenden Staub, und wie er wandelte, so veränderte sich auch sein Gemüt, die Zeit wurde ihm lang und die innere Unruhe legte sich, er wurde sanfter und das gewaltige Treiben in ihm allgemach zu einem leisen, aber starken Zuge, in den sein Gemüt sich auflöste. Es lag wie viele Jahre hinter ihm. Nun wurde die Gegend auch wieder reicher und mannigfalter, die Luft lau und blau, der Weg ebener, grüne Büsche lockten ihn mit anmutigem Schatten, aber er verstand ihre Sprache nicht, sie schienen auch nicht zu sprechen, und doch erfüllten sie auch sein Herz mit grünen Farben und kühlem, stillem Wesen. Immer höher wuchs jene süße Sehnsucht in ihm, und immer breiter und saftiger wurden die Blätter, immer lauter und lustiger die Vögel und Tiere, balsamischer die Früchte, dunkler der Himmel, wärmer die Luft, und heißer seine Liebe, die Zeit ging immer schneller, als sähe sie sich nahe am Ziele.[82]

The intent of this description is primarily symbolical so that nature serves as an emotional accompaniment, an indicator of mood and atmosphere, as in Eichendorff's works. Even among the later German Romantics, notwithstanding their tacit abdication from transcendentalism in favour of an increasingly realistic nationalism, the natural scene remained a curiously stereotyped landscape of forests, rivers (the great German Rhine), birds and buds that change not so much according to their own laws as in reflection of the poet's state of mind. The more subjective feelings predominate, the more nature was reduced to the role of a mere adjunct.

Furthermore, the German Romantics' tendency to an introversion so complete as virtually to exclude the outer reality could and did at times lead to a rejection of existing physical nature in favour of some inner hidden scene. This was generally represented as a subterranean world, most commonly in the depths of a mine, but this obviously is a mere fiction to permit an imaginative evocation of a dream-nature, which is preferable to the real. This is already evident in the fifth chapter of *Heinrich von Ofterdingen* when Heinrich explores the mine : as he descends, in his outer journey, into 'ein unterirdisches seltsames Reich',[83] he is in fact, in his inner pilgrimage, groping his way to his 'in sich gekehrte Traumwelt',[84] just as Novalis himself in his *Hymnen an die Nacht* discovered his true milieu in night after paying a brief preliminary tribute to daylight. This same inversion occurs in Tieck's *Der Runenberg*, characteristically in a less metaphysical and more tangible form. In Christian's eyes, outer nature is at best bare and unfriendly :

> Er kam in Gegenden, in denen er nie gewesen war, die Felsen wurden steiler, das Grün verlor sich, die kahlen Wände riefen ihn wie mit zürnenden Stimmen an, und ein einsam klagender Wind jagte ihn vor sich her.[85]

He comes to dread

> die Seufzer und Klagen, die allenthalben in der ganzen Natur vernehmbar sind, wenn man nur darauf hören will; in den Pflanzen, Kräutern, Blumen und Bäumen regt und bewegt sich schmerzhaft nur eine große Wunde, sie sind der Leichnam vormaliger herrlicher Steinwelten, sie bieten unserm Auge die schrecklichste Verwesung dar.[86]

Christian flees from this groaning, suffering, dying corpus of outer nature into the recesses of the Runenberg, where he glimpses splendours in direct contrast to the misery without. Similarly in E. T. A. Hoffmann's *Die Bergwerke zu Falun*, the visible surface of the landscape is devastated and even uncanny :

> Kein Baum, kein Grashalm sproßt in dem kahlen zerbröckelten Steingeklüft und in wunderlichen Gebilden, manchmal riesenhaften versteinerten Tieren, manchmal menschlichen Kolossen ähnlich, ragen die zackigen Felsenmassen ringsumher empor. Im Abgrunde liegen in wilder Zerstörung durcheinander Steine, Schlacken – ausgebranntes Erz, und ein ewiger betäubender

Schwefeldunst steigt aus der Tiefe, als würde unten der Höllensud gekocht, dessen Dämpfe alle grüne Luft der Natur vergiften. Man sollte glauben, hier sei Dante herabgestiegen und habe den Inferno geschaut mit all seiner trostlosen Qual, mit all seinem Entsetzen.[87]

Underneath this, however, Elis Fröbom finds subterranean wonders as he ventures into the shafts of the mine which are significantly likened to 'die Gänge eines Zaubergartens'.[88] His imagination, first in a dream and subsequently in what must be interpreted as an attack of schizophrenia, transforms the gloom of the mine into a glittering new vision of an enchanted nature :

Er blickte in die paradiesischen Gefilde der herrlichsten Metall- bäume und Pflanzen, an denen wie Früchte, Blüten und Blumen feuerstrahlende Steine hingen.[89]

This artificial garden foreshadows that conjured up by Stefan George in *Algabal* and all the other *paradis artificiels* of the Symbolists and Neo-romantics at the end of the nineteenth century. How utterly remote such a synthetic Elysium is from the fresh air and realism, of, say, Wordsworth's nature poetry!

The wide variations in the Romantic poets' relationship to nature should reinforce the plea that Romanticism in Europe is far from a single or simple phenomenon. Even the national differences are somewhat less clear-cut than in many other fields, although the main lines of distinction are plain enough. Once more it is the Germans who espouse the most extreme attitude with their predilection for abstract theory as well as their very marked introversion. Among the English poets there is the least national uniformity : Blake's visionary gaze and to a much lesser extent Coleridge's metaphysical turn of mind lead to a certain affinity with the German *Frühromantiker*. Shelley's approach on the other hand is more akin to the emotionalism of the French poets, while Wordsworth and Keats show the great- est measure of realistic objectivity. Yet beneath these blurred contours too the separate quality of each Romantic movement is perceptible : the English nonconformist freedom, the German preference for the esoteric and the French vehemence.

The Individualism
of the Romantic Hero

BESIDES determining the attitudes of the Romantic poets, individualism often also forms the subject of their works. Most commonly the social and psychological problems attendant on extreme individualism are portrayed in the predicaments of the so-called Romantic hero, a popular figure of the period throughout Europe.

The family likeness between these various heroes is striking, and hardly surprising since they are, almost without exception, descended from Goethe's Werther, the prototype of a long line of unfortunates who condemn themselves to a life sentence within the prison of their own egocentricity. Werther admits, 'Ich könnte das beste, glücklichste Leben führen, wenn ich nicht ein Tor wäre',[90] born as he is to a life of ease and endowed with considerable personal charm and many talents. But his temperament prevents him from enjoying these gifts; he retreats from his friends into the country where he withdraws more and more deeply into himself; his unhappy love for Lotte, already betrothed to another man, and his consequent feeling of having been rejected by the world intensify his gloomy self-hatred until his failure to cope with reality eventually drives him to suicide. This inability to adapt the ego to the demands of the outer environment, the dissonance and tension between the ideal and the real is the essence of Wertherism, *Weltschmerz, mal du siècle*, Byronism, all related, if not identical syndromes, whatever the name. While such *Weltschmerz* can be cosmic (as with some adolescents nowadays in their anxiety over 'the Bomb'), more usually it is, as with the Romantics, personal, rooted in an

G

awareness of dissatisfaction that stems from the individual's mis-relationship to his surroundings. Such a mis-relationship can arise when the claims of the ego assume a disproportionate importance, to which all else is subordinated. If his desires are thwarted, the individual then withdraws into himself to nurse a sense of grievance – hence the sorrows of young Werther – a *Weltschmerz* which is in fact really a form of egoistic *Ichschmerz*.* Once in this psychic state, the victim tends increasingly to lose a sense of perspective through constant self-observation, self-analysis and self-pity, so that he sinks deeper and deeper into the quagmire of his egocentricity.

It is this self-centredness which blights the Romantic hero's life, although he would be the last to realize it and often enough wonders, like Childe Harold

> what secret woe
> I bear, corroding joy and youth? [91]

The true source of the mysterious sufferings of this 'gloomy wanderer' [92] lies within himself, just as it does with Werther and with Chateaubriand's René, who regards himself as ill-fated without acknowledging that his fate is, at least in some measure, in his own hands. René is finally told the truth by old Souël, who sizes up his character correctly and offers him little sympathy :

> Je vois un jeune homme entêté de chimères, à qui tout déplaît, et qui s'est soustrait aux charges de la société pour se livrer à d'inutiles rêveries. . . . Que faites-vous seul au fond des forêts où vous consumez vos jours, négligeant tous vos devoirs ? Jeune présomptueux, qui avez cru que l'homme se peut suffire à lui-même. . . .[93]

With the wisdom of his long experience, old Souël here indicates to René a way of escape from the *mal du siècle* afflicting him : by casting aside his own reflections and resuming his position in

* literally 'ego-suffering'

society to take up his duties to his fellow-men – in other words, by forgetting himself and giving of himself instead of remaining in the splendid isolation of his egocentricity. The deliberate withdrawal from society, in the case of Werther and of René, like Octave's obsessive attachment to his independence (in Musset's *Confession d'un enfant du siècle*) are not only symptomatic of a self-centredness that is already beyond the norm, but in turn foster the unhappy hero's tendency to introspection by blocking the normal flow of emotion between human beings. Werther, René, Octave, and Byron's Manfred are everywhere as much 'the cold stranger' [94] as Childe Harold of the hard heart whom 'none did love'.[95] Nor, for that matter, was he able to bestow love on anyone because he was not capable of stepping out of the magic but vicious circle of his self-centredness. This is the crux of the Romantic hero's tragedy : his egotism is such as to pervert all his feelings inwards on to himself till everything and everyone is evaluated only in relationship to that precious self, the focus of his entire energy. In such circumstances no genuine, let alone altruistic love is possible : 'Ah! malheureux! malheureux! tu ne saurais jamais aimer!' [96] is the reproach addressed to Musset's 'enfant du siècle', and equally appropriate to all these extreme individualists. Nor is this child of his age even perturbed by so serious an accusation; he accepts it philosophically enough in the reply : 'Eh bien! peut-être, oui, je le crois; mais, devant Dieu! je sais souffrir.' Suffering, a veritable enjoyment of his ill-fate thus represents the egocentric's substitute for normal human ties. In this context it is surely significant that a spontaneous, sincere gesture of love breaks the spell of the curse in Coleridge's *Ancient Mariner* :

> O happy living things! no tongue
> Their beauty might declare :
> A spring of love gushed from my heart,
> And I blessed them unaware :
> Sure my kind saint took pity on me,
> And I blessed them unaware.

The selfsame moment I could pray;
And from my neck so free
The Albatross fell off, and sank
Like lead into the sea.[97]

This disinterested appreciation of other creatures, even if they
are as lowly as the water-snakes blessed by the Mariner, marks
a turning-point in the whole poem : the one involuntary movement of love occasions his release from the burden of the
albatross, from the prison of his guilty selfishness.

The Ancient Mariner is an exception; none of the other
Romantic heroes was able to cure himself of this 'fever at the
core',[98] this malady which manifested itself in a number of
different symptoms common throughout European literature.
Among the milder of these symptoms are restlessness and 'un
penchant mélancolique',[99] the source of which, while a mystery
to the victim, can undoubtedly be traced to his exclusive pre-
occupation with his self. Shunning all duties which might divert
his attention from his own problems the idle Romantic hero
is soon 'more restless than the swallow in the skies'[100] sometimes seeking refuge, like Childe Harold, in perpetual movement, activity, that is tantamount to flight, from 'the fullness of
satiety',[101] the terrible boredom and emptiness of an egocentric
existence. The same 'profond sentiment d'ennui'[102] besets
René too, and Musset's 'enfant du siècle', in his 'combat
terrible de ma jeunesse avec mon ennui'[103] even tries for a
short while to assume his father's old daily routine as if he had
a dim inkling that his 'sentiment de malaise inexplicable'[104]
stemmed from his aimless drifting. De Quincey resorted to a
more drastic remedy which he described in *The Confessions of an
English Opium Eater*, where he called opium a counter-agent
'to the formidable curse of *taedium vitae*'.[105]

More often, however, the Romantic hero is unable to find any
such means of escape and suffers (albeit not in silence!) from his
'goûts inconstants',[106] from a characteristic alternation of the
manic and the depressive, in which the latter tends to predomin-

ate. Laments about his emotional instability re-echo in almost uniform fashion throughout Romantic literature from Goethe's Werther :

> denn so ungleich, so unstät hast du nichts gesehn, als dieses Herz. Lieber! brauch ich dir das zu sagen, der du so oft die Last getragen hast, mich vom Kummer zur Ausschweifung und von süßer Melancholie zur verderblichen Leidenschaft übergehn zu sehn ? [107]

to René :

> Mon humeur était impétueuse, mon caractère inégal. Tour à tour bruyant et joyeux, silencieux et triste.[108]

to the more extrovert form of Musset's 'enfant du siècle' :

> Toutes ces souffrances m'inspiraient comme une sorte de rage; tantôt j'avais envie de faire comme les moines, et de me meurtrir pour vaincre mes sens; tantôt j'avais envie d'aller dans la rue, dans la campagne, je ne sais où de me jeter aux pieds de la première femme que je rencontrais, et de lui jurer un amour éternel.[109]

This combination of sentimentality and cynicism is typical of a hero who is in tears on every page and meanwhile seeks comfort in the pleasures of a libertine, like Childe Harold who also

> spent his days in riot most uncouth,
> And vex'd with mirth the drowsy ear of Night.
> Ah me! in sooth he was a shameless wight,
> Sore given to revel and ungodly glee;
> Few earthly things found favour in his sight
> Save concubines and carnal companie,
> And flaunting wassailers of high and low degree.[110]

although – or perhaps because – he too is 'sore sick at heart',[111] laughing and carousing in order to drown his melancholy, for, as Octave says, 'dès que je ne raillais plus, je pleurais'.[112] Yet never in this alternation of sentimental tears and desperate laughter does the Romantic hero dare to look 'réellement en face de moi-même',[113] for fear of having to admit to himself what Byron recognized : that it is in his own heart that hell lies. For all the Romantic hero's introspection is characterized by a deep-

seated refusal to see things as they are, above all to see himself
as he really is. Shrouded in a protective self-delusion, he
continues to seek his salvation outside himself in the typically
Romantic pursuit of vague longings :

> hélas! je cherche seulement un bien inconnu dont l'instinct me
> poursuit. Est-ce ma faute si je trouve partout des bornes, si ce qui
> est fini n'a pour moi aucune valeur ? [114]

The same inevitable disappointment of the Romantic's infinite
longings in a finite world was expressed by Novalis in the first
of the *Blütenstaub* fragments, where he conceded : 'Wir suchen
überall das Unbedingte, und finden immer nur Dinge.' [115] All
these varied manifestations of ego-suffering were admirably
summarized by Rousseau in his *Confessions*, when he described
his own state of mind in adolescence :

> J'atteignis ainsi ma seizième année, inquiet, mécontent de tout et
> de moi, sans goût de mon état, sans plaisirs de mon âge, dévoré
> de désirs dont j'ignorais l'objet, pleurant sans sujet de larmes,
> soupirant sans savoir de quoi, enfin caressant tendrement mes
> chimères faute de rien voir autour de moi qui les valût.[116]

So an egocentric individualism with its exaggerated self-aware-
ness leads to introspection, melancholy, restlessness, emotional
instability, discontent with present reality and flight into vague
dreams and longings.

Since his temperament disbars him from finding a normal
human happiness, the Romantic hero determines at least to
savour his 'delightful gloom' [117] to the full. Childe Harold's
longing for woe, René's desire to experience a misfortune and
Octave's cult of sorrow are a kind of occupation, a means of
filling the emptiness of their days and of their souls. There is,
however, more in this than a mere thirst for a real emotion;
surely such enjoyment of grief suggests a streak of perversity :

> Je trouvai même une sorte de satisfaction inattendue dans la
> plénitude de mon chagrin, et je m'aperçus, avec un secret mouve-
> ment de joie, que la douleur n'est pas une affection qu'on épuise
> comme le plaisir.[118]

Octave's attitude appears even more pathological, specially as the use of the imperfect tense makes it plain that this is a repeated, habitual action : 'Je descendais jusqu'au fond de mon cœur, pour le sentir se tordre et se serrer.' [119] Gratuitous though this masochism may seem at first sight, it is in fact deliberately nurtured by the Romantic hero as a salient part of that innate differentness which distinguishes him from ordinary men and in which he takes a particular pride. 'As night to stars, woe lustre gives to man' [120] and so the devise of that 'chosen band', the 'wretched' is ' "That my heart has bled" '.[121] Thus the Romantic hero, in his individualistic urge to apartness at any cost, welcomes even exceptional sorrow or dramatic misfortune if it will serve to foster the image he cherishes of himself as a creature singled out for the special attention of fate. 'On jouit de ce qui n'est pas commun,' maintains René, 'même quand cette chose est un malheur.' [122] Such an inversion of the normal values is not without parallel in other works of the period. Young in his *Night Thoughts* had already described the fascination of oblivion in death as a means of escape from his grief at the loss of his daughter, and Novalis, in his despair at the death of his Sophie, came to reject the life of daylight in favour of the intense visions brought by the darkness of night, which he celebrates in the *Hymnen an die Nacht* as the only truly valid experiences. But whereas these inversions are, so to speak, genuine, in so far as they arise out of an actual grief and reflect the writer's sincere conviction, the Romantic hero's cult of sorrow is largely a matter of pretence, part of his self-dramatizing pose. That mysterious curse under which so many of Byron's figures labour is nothing other than the equivalent of what would, in contemporary jargon, be called a status symbol, like the 'demon' that possesses René. This demon, moreover, is an expression of the Romantic hero's subconscious drive to self-destruction. The mortality among the victims of *mal du siècle*, real as well as fictional, must have been exceptionally high, judging by the spate of suicides that followed the publication of *Werther*. But few were sufficiently astute to recognize that the inextinguish-

able fire that consumes the victim is fed from within. For the
Romantic hero is essentially 'la proie d'une imagination',[123] as
René is told, of his own egocentric imagination, that drives him
to his doom. It is not outer fate that constitutes his demon, as he
would fondly believe, but his own temperament, marred by a
fundamental tragic flaw which can be summarized as a blindly
exclusive individualism.

   The heroes of the Romantic period throughout Europe share
so many characteristics that it is easy to overlook the differences
that do nevertheless exist beneath the strong family likeness.
The notorious *mal du siècle* is neither evenly distributed nor
entirely uniform in its symptoms in the various lands. It is
striking that there is no English term equivalent to *mal du
siècle* or *Weltschmerz*, probably because the malady itself seems
at this time to have been less acute in England than on the
Continent. Perhaps the traditional English admiration for sound
common sense and abhorrence of any extremism and exhibitionism discouraged its spread. Perhaps also the very fact that
'spleen', as it was called on the Continent, was endemic in
England prevented an outbreak of epidemic proportions such
as occurred in France. Byron alone suffered from it violently
and portrayed it, and he is in this respect too the most un-
English of the Romantic poets. How alien this state of mind
was to the English is well illustrated by *The Confessions of an
English Opium Eater*, whose title would lead one to expect the
customary sentimental and melodramatic outpourings. Instead
De Quincey gives a lively account of the adventures and travels
of his youth. In the preface he does refer to opium as a counter-
agent to the *taedium vitae*, but the actual experiences of this
vigorous young man show little sign of boredom and certainly
none of any *mal du siècle*. Nor was it in fact prominent in
Germany during the Romantic period. There *Weltschmerz* as a
phenomenon belongs more to the Pre-romantic *Sturm und Drang*
with its typically adolescent rebelliousness. So in his study of
the syndrome, W. Rose[124] draws all his examples from the
adherents of the *Sturm und Drang* or the *Göttinger Dichterbund*

or from Pre-romantics such as Hippel, Jung-Stilling, Heinse,
Hölty, Matthison, K. P. Moritz. During the actual Romantic
period, *Weltschmerz* tended to disappear because its fundamental
problem, the dissonance between the real and the ideal, had no
meaning for the German Romantic who unhesitatingly jettisoned
banal reality wholesale in favour of some higher transcendental
realm. He was always concerned with the quest for that elusive
blue flower of his imagination after the manner of Heinrich
von Ofterdingen, not with the delicate balance between longings
and realities that obsesses a Werther. Werther in fact had
the most numerous and ardent following not among his fellow
countrymen but in France, where an immense 'littérature
werthérienne'[125] appeared in the closing years of the eighteenth
century and the beginning of the nineteenth. The French, far
from regarding Werther as a failure, the first anti-hero, unable
to cope with the demands of his life, rather saw in him a model
to be imitated, the prototype of the *homme fatal* who was to
become a stock literary figure in France. In spite of this idealized
interpretation of Werther, it is curious that the deepest and most
lasting impression was nevertheless made by his melancholy.
This emphasis on melancholy as the characteristic sentiment of
the modern age was in keeping with Hugo's view in the preface
to *Cromwell* that 'le christianisme fit la mélancolie',[126] by re-
placing heathen hedonism with pessimism. In its high incidence
of *mal du siècle* the French romantic movement again reveals a
distinct similarity to the German *Sturm und Drang*.

In the presentation and portrayal of this malady there are
also some significant variations. The external set-up itself
differs from work to work in an interesting manner. The most
discreet is that of *Werther*, whose sufferings are introduced to
the reader by his faithful friend Wilhelm, to whom the letters
of the first part of the novel are addressed, while the second part
consists of further letters, some to Lotte, entries from the diary
found after his death and two brief reports from Wilhelm, one
depicting Werther's despair and the other describing the scene
of his suicide. Thus Werther himself never speaks directly to

the reader; his feelings were poured only into private documents and it was Wilhelm who decided to publish them for the benefit of others. Werther's gaze remained always turned inward, with no thought of a possible public. In Chateaubriand's *René* the framework is slightly different, though once again it is René's friends who ask him to reveal his past in order to explain his mysterious sadness. In this case the narrative is by word of mouth, and inevitably the physical presence of two listeners affects the tone and style. Werther's silent rhapsodies are therefore succeeded by a spoken account. A decisive change occurs with Musset's *Confession d'un enfant du siècle*, where Octave decides quite spontaneously, without prompting from others, to record his own story. He does indeed purport to write for the instruction of others like himself, but he seems to have little to teach in his pseudo-cautionary tale, which proves a mere vehicle for the display of his ego. The trend towards increasing exhibitionism and with it towards a greater externalizing is obvious. Yet the effectiveness of *Werther* lies partly in its very atmosphere of secrecy, in the reader's impression that he is enjoying the privilege of being admitted – by Wilhelm – into the hidden recesses of Werther's tormented soul. It is a curious paradox that the malady of introspection should become more and more the subject of a blatantly extrovert exhibitionism. An illuminating example of development in this direction is Byron's *Childe Harold's Pilgrimage*. In the preface to the First and Second Cantos, Byron still categorically denies the work's autobiographical origin, firmly maintaining that Harold is 'the child of imagination'. In subsequent Cantos, however, the figure of Harold rapidly recedes into the background as the word 'I' becomes more frequent and prominent, so much so that by the Fourth Canto already Harold is hardly mentioned, although he is supposed to be the hero. Eventually, in a new preface Byron has to admit that 'it was in vain that I asserted, and imagined that I had drawn, a distinction between the author and the pilgrim. . . . I determined to abandon it altogether . . . and have done so.'[127] Henceforth the poem turns unashamedly into a description of Byron's own journeyings, interspersed with a display of his own sentiments.

Moreover these differences of presentation are not merely external; they are paralleled by considerable divergences in the attitudes of the characters. The basic similarity, the family likeness remains in that all are victims of their own temperament, yet within this framework their maladjustment takes varying form. Again, as in the narrative technique, *Werther* is by far the most introverted. At the very beginning of the novel, before his encounter with Lotte, Werther writes to Wilhelm: 'Ich kehre in mich selbst zurück und finde eine Welt! Wieder mehr in Ahnung und dunkler Begier, als in Darstellung und lebendiger Kraft. Und da schwimmt alles vor meinen Sinnen, und ich lächle dann so träumend weiter in die Welt.' [128] These are clearly the words of a dreamer, who flees from reality into the realm of his own imagination. Werther's is an artistic temperament, given to sudden excitement and to bouts of speculation, and perhaps his tragedy lies partly in the fact that, while endowed with an artist's sensitivity, he lacks the power of self-expression, of transforming and objectifying his perceptions in a work of art, as Goethe himself was able to do. Werther can only pour out his experiences into his letters and diaries, thereby revealing his inner need to share, indeed his unconscious quest for comfort and support. 'Werther, Sie sind sehr krank': [129] this verdict of Lotte's is fully justified by Werther's neurasthenic reactions, his manic-depressive instability, his inability to meet the inevitable vicissitudes of human existence. His unhappy love for Lotte is not the prime cause of his misery or of his suicide; rather it is the occasion for the virulent outbreak of the disease already dormant within him. In this sense Werther can be called the innocent victim of his temperament since he is driven to destruction in spite of himself. He does in fact make an effort to conquer 'meine Krankheit', [130] to overcome the physical lassitude and emotional paralysis besetting him when, for a while, he takes up a post in a small court and tries to integrate himself into society. The failure of this attempt, however, only intensifies his malady, which he now faces with complete honesty: 'ich kann mir selbst nicht helfen',[131] he confesses to Wilhelm. His lack of illusions about himself reaches its climax when he acknowledges: 'Ich fühle zu wahr, daß an mir allein alle Schuld liegt, – nicht Schuld! – Genug, daß in mir die Quelle alles Elends verborgen ist, wie ehemals die Quelle aller Seligkeiten.' [132] – an admission that requires more than a little courage as well as insight. There is no answer to Lotte's rhetorical question: 'Oh, warum mußten Sie mit dieser Heftigkeit, dieser unbezwinglich haftenden Leidenschaft für alles, was Sie einmal anfassen, geboren werden!' [133] As Lotte recognizes, Werther's vehemence is constitutional, a manifestation of that extremism that leads to his despair and suicide. In *Die Leiden des jungen Werthers*, to give it its full and significant title, Goethe has portrayed a pathological state of mind with a moving authenticity that stems alike from the genuineness of the sentiments and the discretion of the narrative.

Chateaubriand's René, too, suffers from 'des maux qu'il se fait à lui-même',[134] but as that phrase seems to imply, he is as much the cause as the victim of his sorrows. He is both more and less active than Werther: more active in that he contributes to his unhappiness by his deliberate cult of a loneliness and a sadness that appear to have scant foundation either in his circumstances or in his disposition. There is nothing in the account of his childhood and adolescence to suggest that he was by nature melancholy. His salient trait then and throughout his career is a petulant instability that throws him, always dissatisfied, from one project to another until the physical movement of travel alleviates his restlessness. On the other hand, René is less active than Werther in that he makes no real attempt to escape from his predicament: 'Je luttai quelque temps contre mon mal, mais avec indifférence et sans avoir la ferme résolution de le vaincre.' [135] In contrast to Werther's agonized struggles, this sounds suspiciously like the voice of self-indulgence. No wonder that René welcomes the mystery of his bizarre relationship to his sister Amélie as a way of filling the emptiness of his life.

The idea of some meaningful occupation never occurs to him; he turns all his thoughts inwards to his private sorrow without ever realizing that the true source of his unhappiness does not lie in Amélie's surprising confession, a gratuitous blow, but in his own self-pitying egocentricity. The gulf between *Werther* and *René*, in sentiment and manner, is perhaps best illustrated by the juxtaposition of two descriptions of autumn. Werther evokes the desolation of autumn in nature and in his own heart in words touching for their simplicity, directness and musical cadence :

> Wie die Natur sich zum Herbste neigt, wird es Herbst in mir und um mich her. Meine Blätter werden gelb, und schon sind die Blätter der benachbarten Bäume abgefallen.[136]

The bareness of the stripped trees and of Werther's stricken heart seems to echo through these stark sentences. René's much longer description of autumn is more complex :

> L'automne me surprit au milieu de ces incertitudes : j'entrai avec ravissement dans les mois des tempêtes. Tantôt j'aurais voulu être un de ces guerriers errant au milieu des vents, des nuages et des fantômes, tantôt j'enviais jusqu'au sort du pâtre que je voyais réchauffer ses mains à l'humble feu de broussailles qu'il avait allumé au coin d'un bois. J'écoutais ses chants mélancoliques, qui me rappelaient que dans tout pays le chant naturel de l'homme est triste, lors même qu'il exprime le bonheur. Notre coeur est un instrument imcomplet, une lyre où il manque des cordes et où nous sommes forcés de rendre les accents de la joie sur le ton consacré aux soupirs.[137]

In this oratorical outburst René quickly loses sight of his starting-point, autumn, and lets himself drift into an exalted speculation. Autumn is for him a stirring season ('les mois des tempêtes') and he dramatizes himself too by visualizing himself in the various roles to which he is fleetingly attracted. Before long, however, he returns to his favourite theme, the prevalence of melancholy, which gives him scope for another flow of grandiloquence. The prose has the harmoniousness for which Chateaubriand was famed, but this poetic quality seems in places deliberately sought, thereby betraying an artificiality that corresponds to René's posing. It is typical that he should perceive autumn solely in relation to himself for, though less truly introverted than Werther, René is undoubtedly more self-centred.

With Musset's *Confession d'un enfant du siècle* the gradual move away from the morbid introspection of Werther towards an increasing exhibitionism reaches a decisive point. Octave can still be called a victim of his own temperament, but there is an even stronger streak of wilfulness in him than in René. The honesty as well as the tenderness of Werther have given way to self-deception and to a self-indulgence that is counterbalanced by cruelty to others; whereas Werther tortured himself with his pathological masochism, Octave's behaviour often seems inspired by sadism. In his tentative excuses ('ce sont mes sens qui agissent; mon coeur n'est pour rien là-dedans'),[138] he only in fact accuses himself by revealing his true character as a sensualist, hedonist, cynic, almost a pervert at times. In spite of his frequent tears, he is so totally self-centred, so 'renfermé dans ma solitude' [139] that he is quite incapable of any real feeling towards other people and in this sense he becomes a victim of his own character, when his inability to give love, his cruelty, his capriciousness, his cynicism, his suspiciousness bring nothing but unhappiness. No wonder that Musset's novel closes with the phrase 'il ne restât qu'un malheureux', a rather melodramatic ending, in keeping with the oratorical style of the whole work and in contrast to the simple, abrupt sentences that record Werther's funeral:

> Um zwölfe mittags starb er. Die Gegenwart des Amtmannes und seine Anstalten tuschten einen Auflauf. Nachts gegen elfe ließ er ihn an die Stätte begraben, die er sich erwählt hatte. Der Alte folgte der Leiche und die Söhne. Albert vermocht's nicht. Man fürchtete für Lottens Leben. Handwerker trugen ihn. Kein Geistlicher hat ihn begleitet.[140]

There is more pathos in this unadorned, dry report than in Musset's phrases that are so laden with overt emotion.

This process, that could be termed the externalization of the Romantic hero's problems, is carried furthest by Byron. Childe Harold has many of the familiar characteristics: he is restless, always disatisfied, weary, gloomy, blasé, blighted by some unspecified grief, glad even of a genuine sorrow, ever seeking pleasures or at least new ventures to deaden the pain of living, incapable of genuine love, the prisoner of his own egocentricity. Likewise Manfred, the central figure of the strange *dramatic poem* of that name, labours under a mysterious curse that generates a sense of doom till he seeks at best 'oblivion, self-oblivion' [141] as the only escape from the web of narcissism in which he is caught. Significantly, both these pseudo-heroes are negative in their attitude in so far as they lack aspirations towards any ideal; devoid of those vague golden longings that are so typically Romantic, they are impelled only by the sterile urge to flight from themselves. Thus *Childe Harold's Pilgrimage*, and even more *Don Juan*, tend to turn into picaresque stories, in which the hero becomes a mere peg on which to hang descriptions of places and happenings. Byron concentrates more and more on the external adventures at the expense of character analysis; his change to the personal narrative in the latter part of *Childe Harold's Pilgrimage* is indicative also of this loss of interest in his hero. For while Byron still invests his figures with the outer trappings of the Romantic hero, he shows no desire to explore their psychology in depth. Hence it is the adventures, not the complexes of the characters that are in the foreground. Childe Harold seems no more than a spoilt child compared to the psychopath Werther, whose outer life is by and large uneventful because attention remains focused on his inner dilemma. The difference between the two sorts of individualism exemplified by Werther and Childe Harold could hardly be greater. Whereas Werther's is inescapably thrust upon him by his whole disposition, Childe Harold's is an individualism deliberately cultivated by choice, part of the endeavour to turn the spotlight always on to the self. René's wayward self-dramatization and Octave's wilful capriciousness mark the intermediate stages in this evolution.

A postscript and at the same time a new element is added in *Don Juan* which turns 'what was once romantic to burlesque'.[142] The dominant tone throughout this long epic satire is a mocking note, in keeping with the underlying disillusionment, cynicism and rebelliousness of its author, who feels 'born for opposition'.[143] Don Juan himself, a picaresque hero with many adventures, appears more like a satire on the great lover, specially at the outset where his youthful ignorance is such that it is he who is seduced by Julia. Like Fielding's Tom Jones, he is a natural man, acting according to impulse, in contrast to the hypocrite who is always careful to comply with convention. Later, with increasing experience, he does grow more into his traditional role but there is never any abatement of the self-mockery that distinguishes Byron's approach. Aware of the 'nothingness of life' [144] which is, in his debunking, admittedly theatrical phrase, 'not worth a potato',[145] Byron makes an outspoken protest:

> When we know what all are, we must bewail us,
>   But ne'ertheless I hope it is no crime
> To laugh at *all* things – for I wish to know
>   *What*, after *all*, are *all* things – but a *show*?

> They accuse me – *Me* – the present writer of
>   The present poem – of – I know not what –
> A tendency to under-rate and scoff
>   At human power and virtue, and all that;[146]

The accusation is in substance justified, for Byron does in *Don Juan* scoff, deflate and debunk as he pricks the bubble of hypocrisy and pretentiousness with sustained zest and vitality. Where tenderness occurs, as in the Fourth Canto following the death of Haidée, it is quickly dispelled by the play of Byron's wit that is in such amusing evidence in the cleverly aimed parting shots with which many of the stanzas end.

> In thoughts like these true Wisdom may discern
>   Longings sublime, and aspirations high,
> Which some are born with, but the most part learn
>   To plague themselves withal, they know not why :
> 'T was strange that one so young should thus concern
>   His brain about the action of the sky;
> If *you* think 't was Philosophy that this did,
> I can't help thinking puberty assisted.
>
> He pored upon the leaves, and on the flowers,
>   And heard a voice in all the winds; and then
> He thought of wood-nymphs and immortal bowers,
>   And how the goddesses came down to men :
> He missed the pathway, he forgot the hours,
>   And when he looked upon his watch again,
> He found how much old Time had been a winner –
> He also found that he had lost his dinner.[147]

In both these stanzas the lofty thoughts conveyed in the grandiloquent flow of the verse are sharply interrupted by Byron's down-to-earth common-sense, a quality hardly associated with a Romantic poet. Often that deliberately bathetic drop to reality occurs through the startling juxtaposition of the ideal and the banal as for example in the stanza that closes thus :

> Well – Juan, after bathing in the sea,
> Came always back to coffee and Haidée.[148]

(Notice incidentally that the 'coffee' precedes 'Haidée' as an attraction!) With a careless ease, a variety of tone and a rhythmic energy derived from his appreciation of the spoken word, Byron again and again deliberately breaks the dramatic illusion so that the reader is rudely jolted when he comes upon such lines as

> Let us have Wine and Woman, Mirth and Laughter,
> Sermons and soda-water the day after.[149]

Byron's cynical mockery grows from a sober perception of reality that is far removed from the Romantic's tendency to idealize. Indeed Byron's lack of illusions about human relationships leads him to a view of life diametrically opposed to that of

H

the Romantic, who by nature will always elevate what Byron reduces :

> Think you, if Laura had been Petrarch's wife,
> He would have written sonnets all his life? [150]

The question is rhetorical; Byron's answer is in no doubt. This is an individualism turned against itself, inverted into the satirical humour that links Byron with Pope and the English tradition of colloquial poetry.

*   *   *

After this analysis of only one of the three proposed themes, it should be evident that any glib generalizations about either the similarities or the differences between the Romantic movements in England, France and Germany are bound to be misleading. Nevertheless, it is possible to discern areas of congruence and of divergence between the brands of Romanticism that evolved in the three lands. The affirmation of individualism was central to the Romantic creed in all three literatures, although the interpretation given to this principle varied considerably both in emphasis and in scope from one country to another, determined in large measure by the native background : the tradition of freedom in England meant that individualism was more or less taken for granted whereas in France it had to be demanded vociferously in violent opposition to Neo-classical conformism, while in Germany the Romantics were tempted to exaggeration in a bid to outdo their predecesssors. In its effects individualism is strangely variegated, but even if the picture that emerges from the comparison is far from wholly consistent, it does begin to indicate the distinctive characteristics of the three Romanticisms. Among the English the prevalent spirit was one of independence, revealed in Wordsworth's and Keats' approach to nature, Byron's treatment of the figure of the hero and above all in the strongly individualized note of each poet. In contrast to this robust self-reliance, the Germans were extremists in their ideology as well as in their practice : the grotesque distortion of form in F. Schlegel's *Lucinde* and Tieck's plays, the subjective relationship to the external world and the *non plus ultra* of introversion exemplified by Werther all testify to the urge to carry everything to its logical conclusion, however unreasonable. This the French did not do in spite of the vehemence of their arguments; in practice their dominant trait is just that note of passion, heard repeatedly in their theoretical plans for reform, in the voice of René, and of Lamartine and Musset in their poetry.

Imagination

———◆———

The Role of Imagination

Just as the individual is the pivot of the Romantic universe, so within the individual the focal point is his imagination, his power to perceive and recreate the world according to his own inner vision. This primacy of the imagination (as well as the cultivation of personal feeling usually associated with Romanticism) is a direct consequence of the supremacy of the individual, the key tenet of the Romantic *Weltanschauung*. For in a cosmos literally centred on the individual's ego, it is necessarily the perceptions, reactions and feelings of that ego which alone matter. The organ of the ego's perceptions is the imagination, and as such it is the supreme faculty of the Romantic, distinguishing him immediately from those who approach objects empirically through sense impressions. For the Romantic the object is always of immeasurably lesser importance than his own ego, by means of which he endeavours to control the outer universe, to re-shape it through his imagination. As Blake wrote:

> I assert for My Self that I do not behold the outward Creation and that to me it is a hindrance and not Action; it is as the dirt upon my feet, No part of Me. 'What', it will be Question'd, 'When the Sun rises, do you not see a round disc of fire somewhat like a Guinea?' O no, no. I see an Innumerable company of the Heavenly host crying, 'Holy, Holy, Holy is the Lord God Almighty'. I question not my Corporeal or Vegetative Eye any more than I would Question a Window concerning a Sight. I look through it and not with it.[1]

There can be no clearer statement of the Romantic evaluation of imagination than this absolute assertion of the validity of the inner vision at the expense of outer reality. To the true

Romantic of any age or land, the objects of this world are, as for Blake, no more than an uninteresting frame to be 'seen through' on the path towards the only meaningful perception, that presented by the imagination. It is this characteristic of Romantic writing, often either overlooked or not fully grasped, which causes so many difficulties of access to the literature of this period. Coleridge's *Kubla Khan*, Novalis' *Hymnen an die Nacht* and Musset's *Nuits*, to cite but three random examples, cannot be understood unless the primacy of the imagination is accepted without reserve.

That the vital role of imagination tends to be underestimated is all the more surprising in view of the repeated and explicit emphasis on imagination in the theoretical writings of the period. For Blake, of course, the supremacy of imagination was self-evident:

> This world of Imagination is the world of Eternity; it is the divine bosom into which we shall all go after the death of the Vegetated body. This World of Imagination is Infinite and Eternal, whereas the world of Generation, or Vegetation, is Finite and Temporal. There Exist in that Eternal world the Permanent Realities of Every Thing which we see reflected in this Vegetable Glass of Nature.[2]

Even more radical is Coleridge's definition:

> The primary IMAGINATION I hold to be the living Power and prime Agent of all human Perception, and as a repetition in the finite mind of the eternal act of creation in the infinite I AM.[3]

The mind is here invested with that power to create the world that Blake exercised when he saw the sun as the heavenly host. The imagination is the means for a fresh perception and consequently it is the cardinal quality of the poet, indeed the very 'Soul' of poetry according to Coleridge. On this point there was widespread agreement: Wordsworth referred to all serious writing as 'works of imagination and sentiment',[4] while Shelley not only endowed the poet with 'the most delicate sensibility and the most enlarged imagination' [5] but went so far as to define poetry as ' "the expression of the imagination" '. [6] Keats too subscribed to the same principle, putting it in the first person when he characterized the poetic process in the succinct phrase : 'I describe what I imagine', [7] therein reaffirming his earlier belief in 'the truth of Imagination'. [8] The only dissident voice among the English Romantic poets in their hymn to imagination was that of Byron, the deliberate rebel who would miss no chance to air his wit. 'It is the fashion of the day,' he wrote in a letter on Bowles's *Strictures on Pope*, 'to lay great stress upon what they call 'imagination' and 'invention', the two commonest of qualities : an Irish peasant with a little whiskey in his head will imagine and invent more than would furnish forth a modern poem.' [9] Byron stood, however, very much on the fringe of the English Romantic movement so that this exception in no way detracts from the vital importance of the imagination to the English Romantic poets.

They were indeed far more vociferous in their stress on imagination than their counterparts on the Continent. This very articulate championship of imagination on the part of a group otherwise more inclined to reticence in aesthetics was possibly still a protest against the rationalism of the Augustan Age. As recently as 1732 Pope had proclaimed in his *Essay on Man* 'that REASON alone countervails all human faculties'. It sounds almost like a reply to this contention when Shelley wrote : 'Reason is to the imagination as the instrument to the agent, as the body to the spirit, as the shadow to the substance.' [10] The historical context is important in this instance to explain an apparent paradox : that the English Romantics were so much more insistent on the primacy of imagination than the Germans, usually in the forefront of theoretical discussion. In the Germany of the emergent Romantic movement there was, however, as little need to campaign for imagination as there was in England for individualism. The *Sturm und Drang* of the 1770s had made a clean sweep of the rationalism of Gottsched and his contemporaries and had truly effected what is aptly known as 'the

release of the imagination'. So much so that imagination had
rather tended to run wild for a time, even in the early works –
and especially in the uncompleted fragments – of Goethe. In
this respect, therefore, the way had already been thoroughly
prepared for the Romantics, who inherited from their predecessors the established autonomy of the imagination. Not that this
led them to take it for granted. Schleiermacher was careful to
point out 'daß Phantasie das Höchste und Ursprünglichste ist im
Menschen',[11] and the concept featured most prominently in F.
Schlegel's famous definition of the term romantic: 'Nach meiner
Ansicht und nach meinem Sprachgebrauch ist eben das romantisch, was uns einen sentimentalen Stoff in einer phantastischen
Form darstellt.'[12] Though the Germans were less militant than
the English in this point, it would be a serious mistake to assume
that imagination was of slighter importance to them. On the
contrary, probably never before or since in the history of
aesthetics has imagination been exalted as highly as by the
Frühromantiker. It was their avowed intent to poeticize the
world, that is to say, to transform the real existing world into
the Utopia of their esoteric vision; and this transformation was
to be achieved through the magic power of the imagination.
Perhaps this programme of poeticization may be interpreted as a
symptom of a collective megalomania; nonetheless, it indicates
most cogently the key role assigned to imagination in the fabric
of German Romantic thought. While Blake did still register the
sun as a golden disc of fire, that is, he remained aware of,
though uninterested in the reality of appearances, the *Frühromantiker* tended to dismiss the world of objects out of hand
as a mere dull shroud that conceals beneath its surface the true
image of the universe:

> Was wir Natur nennen, ist ein Gedicht, das in geheimer, wunder-
> barer Form verschlossen liegt. Doch könnte das Rätsel sich ent-
> hüllen, würden wir die Odyssee des Geistes darin erkennen, der
> wunderbar getäuscht, sich selber suchend, sich selber flieht
> denn durch die Sinnenwelt blickt, wie durch Worte der Sinn, nur
> wie durch halbdurchsichtigen Nebel das Land der Phantasie, nach
> dem wir trachten.[13]

The work from which this quotation is taken bears the appropriate title *System des transzendentalen Idealismus*. Like Blake, Schelling used the image of 'seeing through' reality, but he went further than Blake in investing only the realm of imagination with genuine significance by comparing it to the meaning beneath the words. It is then the 'Land der Phantasie' towards which the German Romantic always directed his course and which formed the source and object of his unquenchable longing. The pilgrimage to this land of imagination is the theme of probably the greatest, certainly the most representative work of the *Frühromantik* : *Heinrich von Ofterdingen*, in which Novalis traces the poet's gradual progression from the world of reality into that realm of the imagination that is shaped by his own visions and dreams. So 'the world becomes dream and the dream becomes world', ('Die Welt wird Traum, der Traum wird Welt'), to use the motto of the second part of the novel, where Heinrich was to go through the same encounters and experiences as in the first part, but translated now into a higher plane. The world also becomes dream and the dream world, though in a decidedly insidious manner, for Anselmus, the hero of E. T. A. Hoffmann's *Der goldene Topf*, who is troubled by a kind of dual vision, a constant oscillation between a realistic and an imaginative perception of the persons and things around him. The rustling of the leaves is at the same time the seductive whisper of enchanting snakes and a man in a bright dressing-gown is also a brilliantly coloured exotic bush. Imagination has gained the upper hand.

This was not so in France : herein lies one of the fundamental differences between the Romantic movement in France and those across the Rhine or the Channel. For the great majority of French Romantics imagination was far from having the significance and the prominence it enjoyed in the eyes of their contemporaries in other lands. True, for Vigny imagination was 'une puissance toute créatrice' [14] which totally possesses the genuine poet (as opposed to the mere man of letters). But Vigny was an exception; a more typical view was that of

Lamartine, who in the first preface to his *Méditations* relegated
imagination to a secondary place when he listed it *after* sensibility among the qualities essential to a poet. Lamartine in fact
expressed an attitude that is startingly unexpected from a
Romantic poet: 'la vie est la vie', he propounded, and in the
scheme of things art comes only 'avant et après le travail
sérieux et quotidien' for 'chanter n'est pas vivre : c'est se
délasser ou se consoler par sa propre voix.' [15] This is directly
antithetical to the belief of the German *Frühromantiker* in the
sacred value of art as against the despicable worthlessness of a
Philistine life. Perhaps though, any Frenchman who had gone
through the Revolution and the Reign of Terror must have
become forcibly aware of the deadly seriousness of the business
of living at a time when the problems of art necessarily paled
beside the urge for sheer physical survival. Nevertheless the
conception of imagination current during the Romantic period
in France is nearer to that of their predecessors than to that of
their German and English counterparts. This has been admirably analysed by M. Gilman in her history of *The Idea of Poetry
in France* where she concludes that

> in the romantic period we encounter all the conceptions of the
> imagination we had met in the eighteenth century; it is seen as a
> picture-making faculty, as identical or closely allied with
> memory, as a combining and arranging faculty, and as a purveyor
> of poetic images. It is not surprising that there should be also
> frequent echoes of the eighteenth century discussion as to
> whether imagination 'creates'. ... One may note too that
> 'create' and 'creative' are applied more frequently to art and to
> poetry, to the genius and to the poet, than to imagination.[16]

The affinity to the German *Sturm und Drang* is obvious; there
too imagination was linked to enthusiasm, the cult of feeling,
truth and naturalness in reaction against the restrictions of
rationalism. Whereas in Germany, however, imagination was
to come more and more into the forefront, in France it was
overshadowed by the allied notions. For none of the French
Romantic poets, with the possible exception of Vigny, did

imagination have the star part in poetic creation, and even Vigny conceded that 'l'art, c'est la vérité choisie'.[17] This repeated emphasis on truthfulness (*vérité*) and naturalness (*nature*), the imitation of living nature in all its variety, including the grotesque, as outlined in the preface to *Cromwell*, limited the scope of imagination. Again and again, throughout French Romantic criticism, the demand was for realism, probability, truth to life, particularly in drama. 'Le caractère du drame est le réel',[18] Hugo posited, as did Stendhal. This curious paradox that French Romantic drama should be founded on a plea for greater realism is of course explicable as a protest against the highly stylized, stilted dramatic conventions of the Neo-classical age. Nevertheless it resulted in a certain – not unjustified – distrust of imagination as a dangerous bedfellow for *vérité*. Instead of the flights of imagination in which German theoreticians indulged, the French preferred to tackle concrete problems, the main debating points being the technicalities of dramatic construction. Their aesthetic writings, such as Vigny's *Lettre à Lord* *** and Stendhal's *Racine et Shakespeare*, were of a sober, reasonable, practical character, concerned with specific difficulties and entirely devoid of metaphysical questionings. The Romantic movement in France thus represents an essentially *artistic* crisis rather than the total *existentialist revaluation* attempted in Germany and, to a somewhat lesser degree, in England. For this reason French Romanticism seems 'bien pédestre dans ses élans, bien sage écolière',[19] conceding only a brief excursion into reverie as against the rich, sustained visions of a Blake, a Novalis, a Coleridge or a Hoffmann.

Not that the French themselves were blind to their own limitations; Soumet warned them in 1814 already :

On ne saurait trop répéter aux Français qu'ils marchent avec trop de crainte dans les champs de l'imagination; ils ne font point entrer assez d'idéal dans leur manière de considérer les beaux-arts; ils veulent en ramener toutes les productions à des imitations positives; et cependant le talent poétique, ce luxe de notre âme, a quelquefois besoin de dédaigner la beauté des objets réels, pour arriver à cette sorte de sublime dont il ne trouve de modèle que dans sa propre inspiration.[20]

But the French continued to be suspicious of imagination, perhaps fearing the excesses recently witnessed during the Revolution. Moreover, their need for caution seems to be borne out by the exaggerations of some of the apostles of Romanticism. As I. Babbitt has pointed out, 'in outer and visible freakishness the French romanticists of 1830 probably bore away the palm, though in inner and spiritual remoteness from normal experience they can scarcely vie with the German romanticists.' [21] This extrovert exhibitionism forms a strange contrast to, perhaps in effect a partial compensation for the inner timidity of the French Romantics. Yet there can be little doubt that the former helped to increase the latter by fostering the image of Romanticism as a dangerous poison. And this impression remained paramount in France in spite of the attempts to distinguish between serious Romanticism and the so-called *goût frénétique*.* It is surely no coincidence that the current term for 'imagination' during the Romantic period was *fantaisie*, implying as it does caprice, fancy, fantasies, even bizarre whims. Baudelaire later referred to 'les monstres de ma fantaisie' in contrast to 'la reine des facultés',[22] namely imagination. It was in fact only with Baudelaire and the Symbolists that imagination was finally enthroned in France as a divine faculty that can perceive directly secret and intimate relationships, 'correspondences', between things.

There are thus considerable, far-reaching differences in the evaluation of imagination in the various national movements. In France, under the guise of fantasy it was eyed with some distrust and subordinated to the pursuit of truth and naturalness. In England imagination was widely acclaimed as the fountain-head of poetry, the means for a fresh, creative perception of reality. The German estimate of imagination was in essence similar to this, except that English moderation was cast aside

* the frenzied manner

in the boundless exaltation practised by the Germans, who conceived imagination as the tool with which to transform the whole world.

* * *

What then did the Romantics understand by this term 'imagination'? Certainly not what it meant to their predecessors in the eighteenth century, except possibly in France. Throughout Europe Cartesian mechanism still remained the dominant force in the eighteenth century, and with its emphasis on logic, clarity and regularity it was bound to engender a mental climate cold for the imagination. So imagination had long been a secondary quality of the poet, whose principal task had been to arrange the material received through the sense impressions. Gottsched, for instance, in his *Kritische Dichtkunst* of 1730 laid great stress on the careful ordering and regular division of the substance from which a play was to be 'made'. The poet was a mere recorder, whose imagination was only 'a sort of decaying memory' in Hobbes' vivid phrase; it is therefore not surprising that he was fond of comparing what he called 'fancy' to a spaniel in so far as both needed a good nose, a quick scent and an aptitude for ranging over the fields of memory in quest of the appropriate quarry. This sporting metaphor was readily adopted by Dryden when he likened fancy to a good hound. For Locke, with his emphasis on sensation, imagination had a slightly wider significance: as the receiver of sensory ideas, it was, however, a physical rather than an intellectual experience, tantamount in fact to a power of observation. The limitations of the conception become fully apparent when we read Addison's definition:

> By the pleasures of the imagination or fancy . . . I here mean such as arise from visible objects, either when we actually have them in view, or when we call up their ideas into our minds by paintings, statues, descriptions, or any the like occasion. We cannot indeed have a single image in the fancy that did not make its first entrance through the sight.[23]

At best, in an age of rationalism, imagination might provide adornment, adding wit to the expression of truths already known. So Gray, giving advice as to how a flat piece of prose could be turned into a poem, suggested that the aspiring poet should 'twirl it a little into an apophthegm, stick a flower in it, gild it with a costly expression' for it was accepted that there must be 'florid additions' 'if it would appear in rhyme'.[24] In this way the role of the imagination was reduced to a very minor one.

Seen against this background, the Romantic evaluation of imagination was nothing short of a revolution. Instead of serving as a mere device of memory or ornamentation, imagination now played an integral, essential part in any work of art. F. Schlegel insisted that art was nothing 'anders als ein hieroglyphischer Ausdruck der umgebenden Natur in dieser Verklärung von Phantasie'.[25] This neatly pinpoints the change from the earlier peripheral to the new primary function of imagination as a means both of perception and of artistic expression in the 'hieroglyph', the symbol. The nature of this change has been graphically summarized by M. H. Abrams in his penetrating study *The Mirror and The Lamp* (O.U.P. 1953), in which he uses this pair of images borrowed from Yeats. He shows that in traditional criticism from Plato until the eighteenth century the mind had been a mirror, a reflector of external objects, whereas for the Romantics it became a lamp, a radiant projector. Abrams rightly regards this shift from a mimetic to an expressive conception as a decisive break in the continuity of critical theory. It is no exaggeration to claim that this revolutionary evaluation of imagination represents the greatest single advance made by the Romantic movement as a whole, its most valuable contribution to the development of criticism; indeed, no modern aesthetic is conceivable without some such notion of a creative imagination as one of its corner-stones. For the first time a clear distinction was drawn between the two aspects of imagination: on the one hand, the power of *recalling* to mind, and reproducing in more or less detail experiences already undergone in the past, and on the other hand, the power of *creating*, constructing mental images of things not previously experienced, but merely suggested or hinted at. It is in this latter sense that the Romantics interpreted imagination; to them it was not so much the faculty of forming images of reality as the gift for forming images which go *beyond* reality, images that are conjured up by the inner eye and that transform existential reality into some higher reality in song or dream.

A dim awareness of the powers of the imagination had, in fact, already been creeping in since the middle of the eighteenth century. In reaction to Cartesian logic there was a mounting wave of speculation on such topics as instinct and intuition as well as imagination in the writings of Joseph Warton, William Sharpe, William Duff, Alexander Gérard, and, of course, Addison and Hume in England, and Bodmer and Lessing in Germany. For instance, the dual capacity of imagination was well appreciated :

> Aber diese Einbildungskraft ist nicht nur die Schatzmeisterin der Seele, bei welcher die Sinnen ihre gesammelten Bilder in sichere Verwahrung legen, wo sie dieselben zu ihrem Gebrauch abfordern kann, sondern sie besitzet daneben auch ein eigenes Gebiete, welches sich unendlich weiter erstrecket als die Herrschaft der Sinnen. . . . Diese '(Einbildungskraft)' übertrifft alle Zauberer der Welt; sie stellet uns nicht alleine das Würkliche in einem lebhaften Gemälde vor Augen und macht die entferntesten Sachen gegenwärtig, sondern sie zieht auch mit einer mehr als zauberischen Kraft das, so nicht ist, aus dem Stande der Möglichkeit hervor, teilet ihm dem Scheine nach eine Würklichkeit mit und machet, daß wir diese neuen Geschöpfe gleichsam sehen, hören und empfinden.[26]

That was written in 1741 by the otherwise cautious Bodmer, one of Gottsched's adversaries, and in spite of the tortuousness of its language, it does convey a realization of the two-fold possibilities of the imagination. Bodmer's choice of the word *Einbildungskraft* to denote imagination, in place of the *Phantasie* previously customary, is significant in that here too he foreshadowed the usage of Lessing, Kant and Fichte. This is more

I

than a philological reflection since the preference for the new word is symptomatic of the fundamental change in the conception of imagination from a play of fancy to an active *creative* principle : a power that shapes (*-bildungskraft*). Most of these early speculations, however, tend to show up the innate limitations of the Enlightenment. For Addison and even for Hume the imagination was still tied to the senses and credited with creating only by mixing and compounding, without ever exceeding the original stock of ideas as it does for the Romantics. The tameness of these would-be innovators, attached as yet to the accepted critical tenets, only serves to bring out the boldness of the Romantic revaluation.

The crux of the Romantic revolution in the evaluation of imagination lies in the distinction between its memorative and its creative capacities. Whereas the former leads to a reproductive, representational type of art, the latter is conducive to an original illumination in the light of the inner image, a new vision of the world based on a highly individual perception. The new activist, vitalist function of the imagination was envisaged as similar to God's creative act. This novel conception grew equally out of an organic theory of life and out of the affirmation of individualism. For only with the establishment of the individual's absolute autonomy, was his imagination too freed from its rationalistic confinement. The prisoner's shackles were in fact replaced by a mystical halo, never since shed.

Henceforth the emphasis was always squarely on the creative faculty of the imagination : in this respect there is a large measure of agreement between the English and the Germans. The reproductive ability, if mentioned at all, was promptly relegated to a subordinate position :

> The functions of the poetical faculty are two-fold; by one it creates new materials for knowledge, and power and pleasure; by the other it engenders in the mind a desire to reproduce and arrange them according to a certain rhythm and order which may be called the beautiful and the good.[27]

Soon Shelley was by far to exceed this modest claim when he

wrote towards the climax of his eloquent *Defence of Poetry* that

> All things exist as they are perceived; at least in relation to the percipient. 'The mind is its own place, and of itself can make a Heaven of Hell, a Hell of Heaven.' But poetry defeats the curse which binds us to be subjected to the accident of surrounding impressions. And whether it spreads its own figured curtain, or withdraws life's dark veil from before the scene of things, it equally creates for us a being within our being. It makes us the inhabitants of a world to which the familiar world is a chaos. It reproduces the common Universe of which we are portions and percipients, and it purges from our inward sight the film of familiarity which obscures from us the wonder of our being. It compels us to feel that which we perceive, and to imagine that which we know. It creates anew the universe.[28]

In this brilliantly compact and subtle passage, Shelley has delineated the main strands of the Romantic view of imagination: the dependence of so-called reality on the subjective perception of the individual imagination, its power to release us from an earth-bound existence, to create a new world within, into which we are projected so that our own vision may be renewed. In short, the poetic imagination brings into being an entirely new kingdom, distinct from the outer physical realm, a 'dear image' projected by 'the mind's too faithful eye' in the words of his poem *The Recollection*. For Blake it was this inner sphere alone that had any validity:

> Mental Things are alone Real; what is call'd Corporeal, Nobody knows of its Dwelling Place: it is in Fallacy, its Existence an Imposture. Where is the Existence Out of Mind or Thought? Where is it but in the Mind of a Fool?[29]

Rejecting outright the sense impressions of the empiricists, Blake regarded the creative imagination as the primary, indeed sole reality. God and imagination were to him one and the same principle, God manifesting himself as the creative, spiritual power in man: 'Man is All Imagination. God is Man and exists in us and we in him. Imagination is the Divine Body in Every Man.'[30] The precise logic of this contention may not be very clear, but the intent of Blake's argument is evident enough : an exaltation of the creative imagination surely without parallel in England. Not that Coleridge was all that far removed from Blake when he defined the Primary Imagination as 'the living Power and prime Agent of all human Perception, and as a repetition in the finite mind of the eternal act of creation in the infinite I AM'.[30] Coleridge regarded the imagination as an essentially creative force, through which the mind in the common everyday acts of perception makes its own world. This conception was diametrically opposed to the old tradition of Hartley and Locke, who considered the individual as a passive onlooker of a mechanistic process : it is, on the other hand, akin to the subjectivism of Fichte and the *Frühromantiker*, who believed that the world hangs on our active perception.

At this point of confluence, however, a difference begins to become manifest. Coleridge diverged from his German contemporaries in his refusal to grant the imagination complete autonomy. There was for him no separation of intellect and imagination; on the contrary, it was the artist's task to achieve a perfectly balanced fusion of the two :

> The artist must first eloign himself from nature in order to return to her with full effect. Why this? Because if he were to begin by mere painful copying, he would produce masks only, not forms breathing life. He must out of his own mind create forms according to the severe laws of the intellect, in order to generate in himself that co-ordination of freedom and law, that involution of obedience in the prescript, and of the prescript in the impulse to obey, which assimilates him to nature, and enables him to understand her.[31]

The emphasis here is still on the creative function of imagination : 'forms breathing life' not 'masks only', the result of a purely reproductive approach, 'mere painful copying'. But the imagination has to be in consonance with the intellect, 'he must create forms according to the severe laws of the intellect,' not the bizarre monstrosities which F. Schlegel was prepared to admit as the price for the freedom of the artist to exercise his every whim. The difference lies in the fact that whereas the German Romantics tended to gaze exclusively into the transcendental regions of their longings, the English endeavoured above all to come to terms with reality. Imagination, far from being an escape into illusion, was for them a path of access to the truth, a means of ordering the chaos facing them. So each poet, in his writings on imagination, sought to establish a valid order of priorities. This is true even of Blake although he reached the extremist conclusion that the world of physical reality held nothing for him so that he would devote himself to the exploration of the realm of imagination. Shelley's position is more delicate for he was at some pains to delineate the role and function of imagination within the framework of human life. Finally, Coleridge, while subscribing to the primacy of the creative imagination, wished to combine it with the workings of the intellect to reach a new understanding of the universe. His method, like that of Shelley, is an ordering process.

The German Romantics on the contrary aimed to transform reality through imagination. Like Coleridge, the *Frühromantiker* compared, even equated the act of artistic creation with the original Divine Creation. Schelling's theory that all art is a direct imitation of what he called 'absolute production', runs parallel to Coleridge's view of the Primary Imagination 'as a repetition in the finite mind of the eternal act of creation'. The German Romantics moreover, again carrying an idea to its logical extreme, elevated 'die produktive Einbildungskraft zum Weltprinzip' [32] when they preached in all earnestness that the world could – and would – be transformed, poeticized by means of the imagination. Exactly what was planned for this transformation does not emerge very clearly from the wealth of F. Schlegel's words. In practice, of course, the world could not be transformed magically into a Utopia on earth and the Romantic poets had perforce to exercise their imagination only in the inner sphere of their own visions. In this sense their poetry 'ist die der Sehnsucht', oscillating 'zwischen Erinnerung und Ahndung', as opposed to that of the ancient Greeks whose art was 'die des Besitzes', firmly rooted in the reality of the present.[33] With great perspicacity A. W. Schlegel has caught in these brief phrases the essential introversion of German Romantic writing. To some degree all the German Romantics were like Don Quixote, whom Tieck extolled in his early essay on *Shakespeares Behandlung des Wunderbaren* 'weil seine Phantasie sich allenthalben die Personen und Begebenheiten erschafft, die er sucht; er verwandelt Hütten in Paläste, Windmühlen in Riesen etc.' [34] Unkind though the comment may be, this was in fact the tendency of the Romantic, particularly of the German Romantic, who found the world of imagination within himself. 'Die Phantasie', Novalis observed,

> setzt die künftige Welt entweder in die Höhe, oder in die Tiefe, oder in der Metempsychose zu uns. Wir träumen von Reisen durch das Weltall : ist denn das Weltall nicht in uns? Die Tiefen unseres Geistes kennen wir nicht. – Nach Innen geht der geheimnisvolle Weg. In uns, oder nirgends ist die Ewigkeit mit ihren Welten, die Vergangenheit und Zukunft. Die Außenwelt ist die Schattenwelt, sie wirft ihren Schatten in das Lichtreich.[35]

In that last sentence Novalis used one of his favourite images, light and darkness, as in the *Hymnen an die Nacht*, where he reverses the normal values in the same way as in this fragment, envisaging the outer world of daylight as a region of shadows compared to the brilliance of the inner realm. Through this image he conveys most strikingly his conception of the creative imagination as an illumination from within. This introversion is the dominant trait of the German Romantics' conception of imagination. It has been attributed by A. W. Schlegel to the effect of Christianity :

> In der christlichen Ansicht hat sich alles umgekehrt: die Anschauung des Unedlichen hat das Endliche vernichtet; das Leben ist zur Schattenwelt und zur Nacht geworden, und erst jenseits geht der ewige Tag des wesentlichen Daseyns auf.[36]

A more immediate impetus was given by Fichte's command in the opening words of his *Wissenschaftslehre* : 'avert your gaze from all about you in order to look only into yourself' ('Merke

auf dich selbst : kehre deinen Blick von allem, was dich umgibt,
ab und in dein Inneres'). This the *Frühromantiker* certainly
carried out to the full, and so the imagination became the chief
tool for the exploration and illumination of the inner world.
Herein they differed from their predecessors, the *Stürmer und
Dränger*, who fought for the release of the imagination from the
bondage of rationalistic restrictions and demanded freedom for
the imagination to roam at will. Their strain of Wertherian
introversion was counter-balanced by strong extrovert interests,
whereas the more complex Romantics disdained the outer world
in favour of the wonders of the supra-natural, as is shown by their
predilection for the artificial garden, the product of the
imagination.

So the difference between the roles assigned to imagination
by the English and the Germans begins to emerge in broad
outline. While the two shared a basic belief in the essentially
creative task of the imagination, they differed in their use of this
force. The Germans, with their desire to transform the universe,
harnessed the imagination as a means to this end by conjuring
up their inmost visions. The English meanwhile endeavoured
somehow to fit the imagination into the framework of the known
world. Neither as distrustful of imagination as the French nor en-
trusting themselves to its sway as wholeheartedly as the Germans, they steered an admittedly precarious middle course. The
pattern is one of differences within similarities, such as recurs
too throughout the specific powers attributed to imagination.

The Powers of Imagination

━━━━ ❖ ━━━━

A. The 'Esemplastic' Power

THIS outlandish word 'esemplastic' was coined by Coleridge to describe one facet of the powers of imagination. In chapter X of *Biographia Literaria* he explains that the word is not found in Johnson or anywhere else because he himself had constructed it in the belief that a new term would best convey the new sense he had in mind. The Oxford English Dictionary traces a hybrid derivation: though originally derived from a Greek word signifying 'to mould', it is in fact an irregular formation after the German *Ineinsbildung*, 'forming into one'; its meaning is 'moulding into a unity, unifying'. This was the new sense of the word to Coleridge who understood by it 'bringing into one', 'combining'; he intended to denote by it his conception of the imagination as an instrument to achieve unity within the universe, to bring disparate elements together into a coherent shape. The same idea was expressed by Shelley in a more readily comprehensible manner when he called imagination 'the power of association', contrasting it with reason which 'respects the differences' whereas imagination discerns 'the similitude of things'.[37] Fortunately Coleridge's theory is not invalidated by the ludicrous mistake inherent in it: it seems that he owed the word 'esemplastic' to an erroneous rendering of the term *Einbildungskraft** which he took quite literally as 'the unifying power'. This mis-translation casts more than a little doubt on the thoroughness of his study of German (and even Gothic!) in Göttingen. Nevertheless it proves a curiously apposite error

---

* Imagination

since th_____ endow imagination with
a combi__
 The _____ t stress on the ideal of
harmon_____ tings and in their own
lives. They endeavoured to put their ideal into practice through
the cultivation of *Geselligkeit*, a sort of high-minded togetherness.
Again it was left to A. W. Schlegel to grasp the source and the
real import of this longing for harmony :

> Das griechische Ideal der Menschheit war vollkommene
> Eintracht und Ebenmaß aller Krafte, natuürliche Harmonie. Die
> Neueren hingegen sind zum Bewußtsein der inneren Entzweiung
> gekommen, welche ein solches Ideal unmöglich macht; daher ist
> das Streben ihrer Poesie, diese beiden Welten, zwischen denen
> wir uns geteilt fühlen, die geistige und die sinnliche, miteinander
> auszusöhnen und unauflöslich zu verschmelzen.[38]

A. W. Schlegel interpreted the quest for harmony against the
backcloth of his age as an escape from the painful consciousness
of a profound dualism and discord. This approach sheds light on
the German Romantics' desire to partake in all fields of human
activity, in social philosophy as well as in poetry, in science as
well as in religion, as an expression of their attempt at a kind
of reintegration. Their apparently naïve Utopianism, like
Southey's project for a Pantisocratic society, assumes a new
significance in this context too. In the past which they idealized
and in the future for which they held such high hopes, the
Romantics saw images of that harmoniousness for which they
so ardently yearned. Hazlitt was not mistaken when, in his
Spirit of the Age, he interpreted 'Romantic' to mean in quest of
serenity. Schleiermacher's definition of friendship as 'Annäherung zur Individualität ins Unendliche, und daher selbst ins
Unendliche teilbar und perfektibel, und nur Annäherung zu sich
selbst' [39] is not just a sophisticated, rather opaque play on words,
nor is F. Schlegel's attack on marriage as a mere concubinage
and his plea for a true union of kindred spirits in any way
frivolous. Both may in fact be considered an outcome of the
revolt against the old Cartesian dualism of body and mind,

which the Romantics rejected with the utmost vehemence. This led them to protest against the scientific neutralization of nature and its attendant isolation as a purely mechanistic phenomenon. In this 'protest of the imaginative consciousness' throughout the Romantic movement in Europe, B. Willey has rightly seen 'one of the deepest meanings of romanticism'.[40] In Germany the protest was voiced most cogently by A. W. Schlegel when he refuted the old view of the world as a dead, static mass of products and posited in its stead a living dynamic force, constantly in the process of evolution. Schelling too, in his *Ideen zu einer Philosophie der Natur*, was convinced of the animation of nature as an extension of the human spirit. And even a scientist such as Ritter grew lyrical in his rhapsody on the organic unity of the universe :

> Wer in der unendlichen Natur nichts als *ein* Ganzes nur, *ein* vollendetes Gedicht findet, wo in jedem Wort, in jeder Silbe, die Harmonie des Ganzen wiedertönt, und nichts sie stört, der hat den Preis errungen, der unter allen der höchste, und das ausschließliche Geschenk der Liebe ist.[41]

Ritter's fellow physicist Franz von Baader was equally pressing in his insistence on this basic unity of all phenomena, which we must come to perceive if the world is to have any meaning :

> Liebe ist das allgemeine Band, das alle Wesen im Universum an- und ineinander bindet und verwebt. Man nenne es nun allgemeine Schwere, Attraktion, Kohäsion, Affinität, Ätzbarkeit etc., lauter Wörter, wenn man will, die freilich alle nichts erklären; aber wie könnten sie je auch das ? – Genug, das allgemeine Streben aller Teile der Materie gegeneinander zur Vereinigung ist (und wirkt sichtbar unter und über unserm Monde). Attraktion, Bindung ist hiemit unantastbares Faktum, Phänomen, das vielleicht keine weitere Erklärung verträgt, aber also solches auch keiner bedarf. Ohne Affinität ist kein Ganzes, keine Welt, nicht einmal gedenkbar; unser Erdball ein wüstes ewig totes Chaos, ein Brei ohne Gestaltung und Form, hiemit ein wahres Unding.[42]

This excerpt, taken from Baader's dissertation *Vom Wärmestoff*, dates from 1786, when Baader was still a medical student, long before he became immersed in mysticism. Although this dissertation is concerned with the chemical process of burning, it is as much a document of the Romantic philosophy of nature as a piece of scientific research. Philosophy and science coalesce at this point, and this is exactly what Baader sought in his opposition to purely rationalistic, quantitative physics and his advocacy of a more intuitive qualitative approach. This suggests a new perspective to the Romantics' interest in science, which springs not from any desire to explore natural phenomena *per se*, but rather from the urge to perceive the recondite laws of the universe, to comprehend and seize the flux and flow, the inner hidden unity of the universe. The scientific studies of the *Frühromantiker* therefore represent yet another expression of their longing for harmony. So does their conception of religion : under the strong influence of Pietism, religion became essentially a matter of personal communion with the Divine through the heart, the intuition, the imagination. Religious fervour opened the gateway to some yonder realm, in which the individual might be at one with the whole of creation. Once more, as in the sciences, the goal was a mysterious apprehension of the underlying unity of the universe and in both cases the Romantics believed that this could be achieved only through the exercise of the creative imagination.

It was, however, above all in art that the German Romantics invested their highest hopes. Through religion or the contemplation of nature they might make a temporary escape from the dualism of reality; in art, on the other hand, a new realm of harmony was to be established for ever. 'Durch Poesie', wrote Novalis, 'entsteht die höchste Sympathie und Koaktivität, die innigste Gemeinschaft des Endlichen und Unendlichen' [43] or again in *Blütenstaub* : 'Die Menschenwelt ist das gemeinschaftliche Organ der Götter. Poesie vereinigt sie, wie uns.' [44] In accordance with this belief Novalis intended to show in *Heinrich von Ofterdingen* how the tensions and discords inherent in the first part are dissolved in the second, after the world has been poeticized. This transformation was to be achieved in the final marriage of the seasons, symbolical of the suspension of ordinary time and the dawn of a new era of eternal harmony. This is a striking instance of the fluidity of the time concept in the Romantic mind, constantly in search of a unity transcending time. So the experiences of the past irrupt into the present while the present in turn foreshadows the future. This happens not only in *Heinrich von Ofterdingen*; Wordsworth's *Prelude*, turning as it does on the theme of time, is inspired by an awareness of the interdependence of things, of what De Quincey called 'connections', which later aestheticians were to term 'correspondences'. For Novalis, as for Schelling, entry into that realm of art signified a wondrous revelation, similar to, but more lasting than, a religious revelation. That indeed is the central experience recorded in the *Hymnen an die Nacht* :

> Und mit einem Male riß das Band der Geburt, des Lichtes Fessel – Hin floh die irdische Herrlichkeit und meine Trauer mit ihr. Zusammen floß die Wehmut in eine neue unergründliche Welt – Du Nachtbegeisterung, Schlummer des Himmels kamst über mich.[45]

Novalis here evokes in language of mystical colouring a kind of leap into the dark, into an inner transcendental sphere where the antitheses of the outer world are suspended through the esemplastic power of the imagination. A belief in this power is implicit in F. Schlegel's definition of the function of poetry as

> nicht bloß, alle getrennte Gattungen der Poesie wieder zu vereinigen, und die Poesie mit der Philosophie und Rhetorik in Berührung zu bringen. Sie will, und soll auch Poesie und Prosa, Genialität und Kritik, Kunstpoesie und Naturpoesie bald mischen, bald verschmelzen, die Poesie lebendig und gesellig, und das Leben und die Gesellschaft poetisch machen.[46]

Through its central unifying force the imagination of the Romantic poet was to embrace every facet of human life, shaping and transforming it into one harmonious, beautiful entity. This, I believe, was what F. Schlegel had in mind when he called Romantic poetry 'a progressive universal poetry' and when he wrote of the poeticization of the world. And this main task of Romantic poetry was to be carried out by the creative, specifically unifying power of the imagination.

This aim was, predictably, to prove beyond realization. F. Schlegel, in the section of the *Gespräch über die Poesie* entitled 'Brief über den Roman', may have been able, with an elegant fluency, to outline the scope of what he pleased to call a *Roman*:* it could present a comprehensive view of the world in a single work, it could effect the reunion of all faculties, trends and functions, the fusion of beauty, truth, goodness, sociability, absolute individuality and absolute universality, poetry and science, thereby creating a new mythology. It was, in other words, the perfect vehicle for the esemplastic power of the imagination. That at least was the theory. In practice F. Schlegel's attempt at the genre in *Lucinde* is made up of a bizarre hotchpotch of diverse elements, that are certainly not moulded into a coherent whole, let alone poeticized in his sense of the word. Nor was this simply an isolated failure on the part of one writer, who lacked a sufficient measure of plastic creative imagination. Neither Tieck nor Novalis could be criticized on that score, as F. Schlegel can, yet *William Lovell* and *Franz Sternbalds Wanderungen* come nowhere near the realization of the grandiose plans made for the *Roman*, and even *Heinrich von Ofterdingen*, probably the nearest approach to F. Schlegel's ideal, was destined to remain incomplete. And so the Romantics gradually had a subterfuge forced on to them: the distinction between art as an absolute principle, and its actuality in the concrete work of art, which was excused as no more than a mere approximation, one stage in the progression towards the radiant ideal. Of necessity this distinction crept in quite early in the evolution of the Romantic movement when, for instance, Schleiermacher referred in 1799 to 'die Kunst und ihre Werke'.[47] In a contribution by Tieck to Wackenroder's *Phantasien über die Kunst* the dichotomy between art as a meta-

---

* Usually means 'novel', but F. Schlegel so expanded the term as to embrace even Shakespeare's plays.

physical entity and its temporal manifestations became even
more evident :

> Gemälde verbleichen, Gedichte verklingen, – aber Verse und
> Farben waren es auch nicht, die ihnen ihr Dasein schufen. In sich
> selbst trägt die Gegenwart der Kunst ihre Ewigkeit, und bedarf
> der Zukunft nicht, denn Ewigkeit bezeichnet ihre Vollendung.[48]

The success – or failure – of the individual work of art was
thus carefully separated from the total effect of art. This
dissociation between the metaphysical principle and the actual
works is nowhere as sharp as in Germany. When Lamartine
lamented that 'les vers que j'ai publiés ne sont que des ébauches
mutilées, des fragments brisés de ce poème de mon âme',[49]
he was primarily worried by a problem of literary expression :
how to find words adequate to voice the inner poetry of his
soul. This is very different to the practice of the Germans who
were driven to a split that ran counter not only to their avowed
convictions, but to their innermost nature, their longing for
harmony. Yet it was, paradoxically, also their nature that
indirectly forced this split on them. For the whole tendency
of their theory was so expansive that it overstepped the bounds
of possibility. The claims advanced for the esemplastic power
of the imagination were so extreme and so abstract as to pre-
clude realization, and, by an ironical twist, the Germans were
cast back into that dualism which they had thereby sought to
overcome.

In contrast to the vastness of F. Schlegel's theories,
Coleridge's interpretation of the esemplastic power was considerably more restrained and circumspect, and consequently
of greater practical import. While Coleridge's aesthetic ideas
may seem high-flown in the context of English pragmatical
empiricism, compared to the dizzying remoteness of the
Frühromantiker, on the other hand, they are quite firmly rooted
in reality. Yet, curiously enough, Coleridge himself appears to
have shared some of the traits of his German contemporaries : a
startling mental energy, agility and initiative, a versatility that
led to a lively interest in scientific as well as literary problems

(he took part in some of Davy's and Beddoes' early experiments with nitrous oxide at the Bristol Pneumatic Institution, and was able to discuss with Thomas Poole topics as diverse as the processes of tanning and agricultural economics). Again like the Germans, he was not a systematic philosopher for he thrived above all on the dynamic of contraries and contradictions. Herein in fact lay Coleridge's strength as a thinker; whereas F. Schlegel's metaphysical bent too readily tempted him into clouds of transcendental speculation, Coleridge's more acute sense of reality made of him an invaluably provocative questioner, who, moreover, not only raised controversial problems, but offered answers too. He was enabled to do this by a most precious and rare quality of his mind, which Kathleen Coburn has so aptly called his 'sense of the links, of the complexity of interdependent interrelations, not merely among ideas, the products of thought, but in the very process of knowing'.[50] It was this ability to perceive, as it were intuitively, a secret web of connections within the universe that led Wordsworth to the conclusion that to Coleridge the unity of all had been revealed. Certainly a sense of the whole as a living unity was the original impulse that inspired his critical principles, which constantly start from and return to the conviction of a fundamental oneness. So he began his *Principles of Genial Criticism* with the pronouncement that

> All the fine arts are different species of poetry. The same spirit speaks to the mind through different senses by manifestations of itself, appropriate to each. They admit therefore of a natural division into poetry of language; poetry of the ear, or music; and poetry of the eye, which is again subdivided into plastic poetry, or statuary, and graphic poetry, or painting.[51]

It was in unity, interpreted as harmony, that Coleridge also discerned the criterion of beauty : 'The BEAUTIFUL, contemplated in its essentials, that is, in kind and not in degree, is that in which the many, still seen as many, becomes one.' [52] This was subsequently shortened into : 'The most general definition of beauty, therefore, is Multeïty in Unity,' and even more succinctly : 'Beauty is harmony.' And this coalescence of many into one, which results in the harmonious multeïty in unity of beauty, is achieved through the esemplastic power of the imagination. In the famous distinction between fancy and imagination Coleridge conceived the latter as the supreme integrating force, a living creative power, organic in its function, as against the lifeless mechanism of fancy which merely reassembles fixities and definites. The eighteenth-century view of poetry as judicious arrangement of ready-made images culled from the memory would have been dismissed by Coleridge as the work of fancy. The task of imagination, on the other hand, was a radical reshaping : as the coadunating, esemplastic power its essence lay in the fusion of all things into one harmonious entity without losing sight of the validity of each individual element.

That Coleridge's distinction between fancy and imagination has an affinity with A. W. Schlegel's opposition of mechanical and organic form has, of course, not escaped notice. In 1809, in his *Vorlesungen über dramatische Kunst und Literatur*, A. W. Schlegel had said :

Mechanisch ist die Form, wenn sie durch äußre Entwicklung irgend einem Stoffe bloß als zufällige Zuthat, ohne Beziehung auf dessen Beschaffenheit ertheilt wird, wie man z.B. einer weichen Masse eine beliebige Gestalt giebt, damit sie solche nach der Erhärtung beyhalte. Die organische Form hingegen ist einge-bohren, sie bildet von innen heraus, und erreicht ihre Bestimmt-heit zugleich mit der vollständigen Entwickelung des Keimes. Solche Formen entdecken wir in der Natur überall, wo sich lebendige Kräfte regen, von der Krystallisation der Salze und Mineralien an bis zur Pflanze und Blume und von dieser bis zur menschlichen Gesichtsbildung hinauf. Auch in der schönen Kunst wie im Gebiete der Natur, der höchsten Künstlerin, sind alle ächten Formen organisch, d.h. durch den Gehalt des Kunst-werkes bestimmt.[53]

This is by no means an isolated instance of a correspondence of ideas between Coleridge and A. W. Schlegel. The thorny problem of Coleridge's relationship to German thought has indeed fascinated critics ever since Henry Crabb Robinson's comment that Coleridge 'was much more German than English'.[54] Lengthy accounts have been given of Coleridge's travels in Germany and inconclusive reports of his encounters with German notables. The closer scrutiny of J. Shawcross in his enlightening introduction to the *Biographia Literaria* has revealed that the real kinship was between Coleridge and Schiller, in so far as both based their aesthetic theories on Kant who attracted Coleridge far more than F. Schlegel whom he regarded as 'the culminating expression of the anarchy of revolt'.[55] That Kantian idealism was a potent factor in Coleridge's evolution is confirmed by his tribute to Fichte's *Wissenschaftslehre*, which 'was to add the keystone of the arch' [56] — that arch itself being built of Kantian idealism. Coleridge went on to mention Schelling in whose ' "NATUR-PHILOSOPHIE" and the "SYSTEM DES TRANSCENDENTALEN IDEALISMUS" I first found a genial coincidence with much that I had toiled out for myself, and a powerful assistance in what I had yet to do.' [57] Such was the repeated tenor of Coleridge's self-defence, namely that he found in the German philosophers insights at which he had himself already arrived independently. The indebtedness is then reduced to a mere matter of formulations, a certain style and manner of expression which had, so to speak, rubbed off on to Coleridge, and which made him seem in English eyes much more Germanic than he really was. What Lamb termed the 'twist Allemain' [58] of Coleridge's mind was counterbalanced by a strong streak of traditional English empirical practicality, such as emerges from this pertinent comment in one of his notebooks :

> Generally indeed I complain of the German Philosophers — of the Post-Kantians at least — for the precipitance with which they pass to their own determinations of what the thing is, without having first enquired what the word means when it is used appropriately. Instead of asking, *Was Schönheit sey?* I would enquire what *schön** properly meant — i.e. what men mean when

---

* What is Beauty?; beautiful

they use the word *schön* in preference to any other epithet. A rose
is a pleasing sight: and so to a hungry man is a Hogspudding.
But a Rose is beautiful – ergo, beautiful means something else or
something more than pleasing. The difference is not in the
d e g r e e – for add to a keen appetite a long involuntary abstinence
from animal food, and a particular predilection, the Hogspudding
will become tenfold more pleasing without advancing a single
step towards Beauty.[59]

What better example could there be of Coleridge's insistence
on desynonymization, which underlies his distinction between
fancy and imagination and which is striking evidence of a
fundamental realism in his approach to philosophical questions.
His was the 'inquiring spirit'[60] of a 'semasiologist'[61] and he
himself rightly defined his own method as obedience to 'the
dictate of common sense.' [62] Only to a man who himself partook
of it could the notion of 'good sense' assume as vital an importance as it did to Coleridge, to whom it represented 'the
BODY of poetic genius', second only to 'IMAGINATION the SOUL
that is everywhere'.[63] In his analysis of the soul, i.e. imagination, Coleridge never lost sight of the body: good sense, his
sheet-anchor in reality.

It is this that distinguishes him from the *Frühromantiker*,
and nowhere is the difference more evident than in the interpretation of the esemplastic power of the imagination. To Coleridge,
with his intuitive sense of the organic links within the universe,
the esemplastic power of the imagination signified the unifying
principle of the work of art, the force that combines many
diverse elements into a beautiful whole. Coleridge's theory
appears strangely sober and finite beside the transcendentalism
of the *Frühromantiker*. Their conception of the esemplastic
power was bound to be different because they started from a
premise other than Coleridge's firm conviction of the wholeness
of the universe. Their basic drive was an incessant quest for
harmony which is manifest in every aspect of their thought.
Since they despaired of finding it in the present, which they
rejected, they had perforce to project it into a Utopian future,

some higher, better realm beyond the here and now. In this new dimension the imagination would reign unchallenged and its esemplastic power would act as the unifying principle of the entire Romantic kingdom of art. This conception is no doubt infinitely more grandiose than that of Coleridge, but for that reason it is also incomparably less effective as an aesthetic guide. So much so indeed that it had soon to be abandoned and another dualism arose in the split between the admittedly imperfect individual work of art and the ideal realm of art, where the esemplastic power of the imagination would operate.

The analysis of this one facet of imagination therefore reveals both similarity and divergence between the English and German Romantics : similarity in their common conviction of the esemplastic power of the imagination, but contrast between the moderation of English good sense and the extremism of German transcendentalism in the interpretation of this force.

B. *The Mediating Power*

The mediating power of the imagination is, in a sense, an extension of its esemplastic power in that the latter combines diverse elements into a coherent, harmonious whole, while the function of the mediating power is to serve as a link between the known universe and the transcendental realm. Thus both the esemplastic and the mediating power are aspects of the overall unifying effect of the imagination, although the second is by nature more mysterious in its workings. The entire notion of a mediating power stems from a specifically Romantic conception of the imagination as a means of apprehending a superior reality. At this point the Romantics are furthest removed from their predecessors' rationalistic use of imagination as a tool for ornamentation; the revaluation of the imagination is complete when it becomes the organ for a spiritual perception of absolute validity. The tinge of mysticism

is undeniable, and equally undeniable is the fact that on this
point the Romantic poets demand an unquestioning belief,
which is often a stumbling-block for the reader of a more
practical turn of mind. During the Romantic period, artistic
creativity became nothing short of a sacred activity, an esoteric
communion with a divine fountainhead. To this the artist was
thought to have access because he partook of the creative
power of the Divinity. The medium of his participation was his
imagination, through which he gained an intuitive insight, to
which other men, devoid of imagination, were blind. It was
therefore the function of the artist to communicate the special
knowledge accorded to him. His role was that of a mediator,
while the imagination was endowed with a mediating power.

The belief in such a mediating power was widespread and
strong among the English Romantic poets who held that 'the
creative imagination is closely connected with a peculiar
insight into an unseen order behind visible things'.[64] 'Instinct
and intuition' are, according to Shelley, the essence of 'the
poetical faculty',[65] and through the exercise of this intuition
the poet apprehends imaginatively the only true knowledge.
Blake expressed much the same idea, though in more dramatic
terms when he pronounced in his dogmatic fashion that 'Vision,
or Imagination, is a Representation of what Eternally Exists
Really, and Unchangeably'.[66] Blake, it might however be argued,
was more interested in the realm of his visions for its – and for
his – own sake rather than for any revelation that he might
bring back to his fellow-men. Shelley, on the other hand, based
his spirited *Defence of Poetry* on the thesis that : 'To be a poet is
to apprehend the true and the beautiful.' [67] Again and again he
returned to this central theme, the value of the mediating
power of the imagination, clothing it in a variety of elegant
formulations : 'A poem is the very image of life expressed in its
eternal truth'[68] or : 'Poetry lifts the veil from the hidden beauty
of the world, and makes familiar objects be as if they were not
familiar'.[69] As for the poet, his role as mediator was clearly
delineated by Shelley : 'A poet participates in the eternal, the

infinite and the one' through his 'partial apprehension of the agencies of the invisible world'.[70] His effect is compared, in a memorable image, to that of a 'nightingale, who sits in darkness and sings to cheer its own solitude with sweet sounds; his auditors are as men entranced by the melody of an unseen musician, who feel that they are moved and softened, yet know not whence or why'.[71] Thus Shelley arrived at his famous concluding words, often quoted and almost as often uncomprehended:

> Poets are the hierophants of an unapprehended inspiration; the mirrors of the gigantic shadows which futurity casts upon the present; the words which express what they understand not; the trumpets which sing to battle, and feel not what they inspire; the influence which is moved not, but moves. Poets are the unacknowledged legislators of the world.[72]

These words convey brilliantly the picture of the poet as a vessel, a mediator of insights that he perceives and passes on without being able to explain them, almost as if he himself had become a mere medium for his own divine imagination. Coleridge too believed that the poet's

> gifted ken can see
> Phantoms of sublimity

as he wrote in *Apologia pro Vita sua*. As a minister's son, nurtured on the Bible, the interior imaginative life was from an early age more important to him than the sad existential world. So, to borrow his vivid image from chapter XIII of *Biographia Literaria*, he began to look beyond that first range of hills that encircle the scanty vale of human life and form the horizon of most of its inhabitants. He was one of the few who had the courage and curiosity to scale the heights often hidden by mists and clouds, knowing intuitively through an 'ascertaining vision' that the rivers of the vale must have their sources 'far higher and far inward'. Thus imagination became for Coleridge both a form of knowledge and a form of action, a process whereby the essences of things might be seized and transmuted into valid insights.

Seen in this light, as a method of perception, imagination could also become an organ of philosophy, a link between poetry and philosophy. For the object of poetry, as of philosophy, was for Coleridge, Wordsworth, Shelley and Keats truth : not a concrete truth deduced by the reasoning of the intellect, but that transcendental truth that springs from an inspired imaginative insight into the nature of things, a vision of what Wordsworth, in book VI of *The Prelude*, called 'the types and symbols of Eternity'. To Wordsworth its object is truth, not individual and local, but general, and operative; 'not standing upon external testimony, but carried alive into the heart by passion'.[73] This is surely the kind of truth that Keats had in mind when he wrote in the *Ode on a Grecian Urn* that 'Beauty is truth, truth beauty'. The meaning of this statement is illumined by several comments scattered throughout Keats' letter. In November 1817 already, in the important letter to Benjamin Bailey, Keats wrote : 'What the imagination seizes as Beauty must be truth',[74] thus expressing his trust in the insights of imagination to mediate permanent valid truths. The following year Keats admitted : 'I can never feel certain of any truth but from a clear perception of its Beauty', adding very modestly : 'and I find myself very young minded even in that perceptive power – which I hope will increase.'[75] It was this 'perceptive power' that was for Keats the core of the artistic process. When he cried : 'O for a Life of Sensations rather than of Thoughts!'[76] he was rejecting rational speculation in preference for the direct approach through sense impressions because he so passionately believed in the intuitive perception of truth by means of the imagination. Despairing of the rational approach ('I have never yet been able to perceive how any thing can be known for truth, by consequitive reasoning'[76]), he was led to extol the imagination as the supreme, indeed to him, the sole method of perception and he therefore compared it to Adam's dream, recorded in *Paradise Lost* : 'he awoke and found it truth'.[76] These confessions in the *Letters* make it clear that Keats shared Shelley's conviction of the mediating power as the central role of the poet's imagination. The poet 'strips the veil of familiarity from the world, and lays bare the naked and sleeping beauty which is the spirit of its forms'.[77] This image of the poet stripping or lifting the veil off the world to see beyond surface appearances is particularly apposite to convey the mediating power of the imagination and it is significant that it recurs throughout the Romantic period, in the writings of Novalis (e.g. *Die Lehrlinge zu Saïs* and in the interpolated story *Hyazinth und Rosenblütchen*) as well as of the English poets.

In outline there is a closer resemblance between the English and the German Romantics here than elsewhere. In fact, the ideas of Blake, Coleridge and Novalis stemmed in important respects from a common source: the hermetic thought of the sixteenth and seventeenth centuries, which maintained that truth was independent of sensible reality and could therefore only be perceived through mystical intuition. From this arose the notion of a literature in special sympathy with the infinite, such as F. Schlegel's 'poetry of poetry' and De Quincey's 'literature of power' (as against the ordinary didactic 'literature of knowledge'). This is the point at which the English Romantics, without losing their moderation, went somewhat beyond the standards of good sense. In their reaction against the limitations of materialism they came to value also the more obscure workings of the mind and through the mediating power of the imagination they envisaged the possibility of a *rapprochement* between the real and the ideal, the finite and the infinite, the familiar and the unknown. They thereby exalted the poetic imagination as the means for transcendental perception and the poet as the medium for special insight in a manner not unlike that of the *Frühromantiker*.

Beneath this similarity there are, however, certain differences both of degree and of emphasis. For the Germans were not only more given to the abstraction and extremism characteristic of their theories; they also laid far greater stress on the mystical, quasi-religious aspect of the mediating power of the imagination than did the English, to whom it remained essentially an aesthetic faculty. So Coleridge called art

> the mediatress between, and reconciler of, nature and man. It is the power of humanizing nature, of infusing the thoughts and passions of man into every thing which is the object of his contemplation; color, form, motion, and sound are the elements which it combines, and it stamps them into unity in the mould of a moral idea.[78]

whereas Schelling claimed that art razed the invisible wall dividing the real and the ideal world. Although the fundamental idea of mediation is common to Coleridge and Schelling, the difference is more than one of formulation: to the English poets the exercise of the imagination was a method of perception, of apprehending certain truths not accessible to the intellect, while to the Germans it was an esoteric activity, concerned not with the portrayal of transfigured physical experience ('colour, form, notion and sound are the elements which it combines') but with the revelation of metaphysical perceptions. The processes of the imagination were thus given a religious colouring in keeping with the view that, notwithstanding its imperfections, Romantic art 'ist dem Geheimnis des Weltalls näher'.[79] Imagination was therefore, in F. Schlegel's words, man's organ for the divine and for art, 'indem sie den sterblichen Schleier lüftet, läßt sie uns das Geheimnis der unsichtbaren Welt in dem Spiegel einer tief sehenden Fantasie erblicken'.[80] Here imagination again lifts the veil to reveal not only 'the naked and sleeping beauty which is the spirit of its forms',[69] the harmonious pattern beneath the surface appearance, but to lay bare its innermost secret. It is only from a vantage-point behind the veil, to continue the metaphor, *sub specie* of the transcendental, that life has any genuine significance according to Novalis. The imagination's power of mediation thus assumed a central importance in the theory of the *Frühromantiker*. Hence A. W. Schlegel defined beauty as the symbolic representation of the infinite. This was more than the unspecified truth sought by Keats, Shelley and Coleridge, and it gave art a totally new dimension as the vehicle of divine revelation.

Art, moreover, offered another — possibly the best — means to satisfy the Romantics' inherent longing for harmony for 'in jedem vollendeten Kunstwerke fühlen wir durchaus unseren innigsten Zusammenhang mit dem Universum'.[81] This mystical conception of art is admirably brought out by Novalis :

> Der Sinn für Poesie hat viel mit dem Sinn für Mystizismus gemein. Er ist der Sinn für das Eigentümliche, Personelle, Unbekannte, Geheimnisvolle, zu Offenbarende, das Notwendig-Zufällige. Er stellt das Undarstellbare dar. Er sieht das Unsichtbare. fühlt das Unfühlbare. . . . Der Sinn für Poesie hat nahe Verwandtschaft mit dem Sinn der Weissagung und dem religiösen, dem Sehersinn überhaupt.[82]

This is a 'take it or leave it' definition of poetry rather than a 'defence' in Shelley's sense, for which the German Romantics felt no need whatsoever. They not only equated art with revelation, but logically went on to elevate the artist to the role of high-priest. This helps to explain F. Schlegel's puzzling dictum that only he who has a personal religion, an original view of the infinite can be an artist. What was meant, and what was demanded of the artist, was that he should possess that mysterious insight, that visionary power which is the gift of imagination, which also enables him to understand nature better than the scholar with his rational approach. So the artist was frequently described as a priest by Novalis and by Schleiermacher, who began his considerations on religion by conceding that art is the house-god of the age, and consequently the artist is cast as

> 'ein wahrer Priester des Höchsten, indem er ihn' (Gott) 'denjenigen näher bringt, die nur das Endliche und Geringe zu fassen gewohnt sind, er stellet ihnen das Himmlische und Ewige dar als einen Gegenstand des Genusses und der Vereinigung.[83]

The mediating function of the artist could hardly be more clearly stated than in this lofty ideal, which again underlines the intense fervour with which the *Frühromantiker* treated this subject.

Nowhere does this ecstatic quality become as apparent as in the rhapsodies of Wackenroder, in the *Herzensergießungen eines kunstliebenden Klosterbruders* and the *Phantasien über die Kunst*, both of which were completed by Tieck on his friend's premature death. Wackenroder believed that art represented the summit of human achievement, the point of catharsis, and that the artist, of nobler clay than his fellow-men, was supreme among mortals. Beyond this he had, even more strongly than the theologian Schleiermacher, a profound faith – and faith is the operative word – in the transcendental nature of art. To pass through the gateway of the 'Zauberschloß der Kunst' [84] was to enter a new realm, a paradise of unclouded bliss, where all that is lofty, great and divine is opened up before us, as if by magic. The image of the enchanted castle is, of course, reminiscent of *The Magic Flute* and runs true to the pattern of the *Märchen*, in which the hero reaches some castle of happiness after a series of trials and set-backs. For Wackenroder, however, that enchanted castle was not in some distant land of make-believe; it had become real to him in 'die göttliche Erhabenheit der Kunst' [85] and was accessible to us too through the contemplation of great pictures, as if in prayer, or through surrender to a sea of sound. So the holy-man of his Oriental tale in the *Phantasien über die Kunst* was released from his evil spell by the magic of music. This may well appear naïve, but it does reflect Wackenroder's absolute conviction of 'die tiefgegründete, unwandelbare Heiligkeit', [86] 'die Göttlichkeit der Kunst', [87] his unqualified fusion of art and religion. Perhaps even more important than Wackenroder's actual beliefs is the way in which he expressed them, the ecstatic adoration that pulses through his rhapsodic phraseology:

> Aber jetzt wandelt mein trauernder Geist auf der geweihten Stätte vor deinen Mauern, Nürnberg; auf dem Gottesacker, wo die Gebeine Albrecht Dürers ruhen, der einst die Zierde von Deutschland, ja von Europa war. Sie ruhen, von wenigen besucht, unter

zahllosen Grabsteinen, deren jeder mit einem ehernen Bildwerk, als dem Gepräge der alten Kunst, bezeichnet ist, und zwischen denen sich hohe Sonnenblumen in Menge erheben, welche den Gottesacker zu einem lieblichen Garten machen. So ruhen die vergessenen Gebeine unsers alten Albrecht Dürers, um dessentwillen es mir lieb ist, daß ich ein Deutscher bin.

Wenigen muß es gegeben sein, die Seele in deinen Bildern so zu verstehen, und das Eigene und Besondere darin mit solcher Innigkeit zu genießen, als der Himmel es mir vor vielen andern vergönnt zu haben scheint; denn ich sehe mich um, und finde wenige, die mit so herzlicher Liebe, mit solcher Verehrung vor dir verweilten, als ich.[88]

It is well-nigh inconceivable that such emotional prose could have come from the pen of any English Romantic poet (save Byron, half in parody). Yet even the otherwise sober A. W. Schlegel waxed lyrical when extolling poetry as the 'Dolmetscherin jener himmlischen Offenbarung, eine Sprache der Götter'.[89] Given this atmosphere of turbid fervour, it is none too surprising that the *Frühromantiker* should have come to regard this religion of art not only as a means of personal salvation but as the nucleus of a new creed. F. Schlegel, in the *Gespräch über die Poesie*, made an impassioned plea for a new mythology; no doubt he hoped to fashion it himself for he wrote to Novalis in 1798 that he intended to tread in Mohammed's and Luther's footsteps by writing a new Bible. This bizarre avowal is startling evidence of the degree to which the German Romantics carried their belief in the mediating power of the artist's imagination.

Paradoxical though it may seem, the German Romantics were at one and the same time both more literal and more mystical than the English in the interpretation of this facet of the imagination. More literal in that they took their ideas to logical extremes, as was their wont; and more mystical in their readiness to equate the visions of the imagination with divine revelations. Their confidence in their transcendental idealism was absolute, never dimmed by the sort of doubts that Shelley must have harboured when he exhorted the reader of his *Sonnet*:

'Lift not the painted veil', for behind it there lurks Fear as
well as Hope, and Shelley recognized that the 'truth' so
ardently sought may not always be found. It is characteristic
that an English poet, even one as essentially an aesthete as
Shelley, should have been able to face the limitations of the
imagination. For the English Romantic poets took care to keep
at least one toe on the ground while the Germans tended to
fly off into the clouds. This divergence is reflected in the
difference between the stylistic expression of poetic theory in
Germany and England. There is no need to underline the lure of
abstraction for the German :

> Es gibt eine Poesie, deren eins und alles das Verhältnis des
> Idealen und des Realen ist, und die also nach der Analogie der
> philosophischen Kunstsprache Transzendentalpoesie heißen
> müßte. Sie beginnt als Satire mit der absoluten Verschiedenheit des
> Idealen und Realen, schwebt als Elegie in der Mitte, und endigt
> als Idylle mit der absoluten Identität beider. So wie man aber
> wenig Wert auf eine Transzendentalphilosophie legen würde,
> die nicht kritisch wäre, nicht auch das Produzierende mit dem
> Produkt darstellte, und im System der transzendentalen Gedanken
> zugleich eine Charakteristik des transzendentalen Denkens
> enthielte : so sollte wohl auch jene Poesie die in modernen
> Dichtern nicht selten transzendentalen Materialien und Vor-
> übungen zu einer poetischen Theorie des Dichtungsvermögens
> mit der künstlerischen Reflexion und schönen Selbstbespiegelung,
> die sich im Pindar, den lyrischen Fragmenten der Griechen,
> und der alten Elegie, unter den Neuern aber in Goethe findet,
> vereinigen, und in jeder ihrer Darstellungen sich selbst mit
> darstellen, und überall zugleich Poesie und Poesie der Poesie
> sein.[90]

Surely such convoluted pseudo-philosophical terminology is,
more than any other single factor, responsible for the neglect
of German Romanticism throughout Europe even today. It is
difficult enough for a native German, let alone for an Englishman or a Frenchman, to pierce the barrier of this jargon in
order to consider the meaning in this maelstrom of words.
Moreover, the expansive tendencies of the German theoreticians further increase the problem of comprehension in that

ideas are often presented, as in this instance, in their philosophical and historical (Pindar, Goethe) context. For comparison turn then to Shelley's formulation :

> All high poetry is infinite; it is as the first acorn, which con-
> tained all oaks potentially. Veil after veil may be undrawn and
> the inmost naked beauty of the meaning never exposed. A great
> poem is a fountain for ever overflowing with the waters of
> wisdom and delight.[91]

In substance this has a marked affinity with F. Schlegel's
panegyric of poetry. But how far removed from the metaphysical complexities of the German are Shelley's elegant,
marvellously vivid phrases. A wealth of ideas is compressed
into a whole series of plastic images : poetry as an acorn from
which oak-trees grow, as a beautiful dancer stripping one veil
after another, and as an inexhaustible fountain of delight.
Shelley is able to visualize poetry in concrete pictures, as
against F. Schlegel's purely theoretical ruminations. The contrast aptly illustrates the gulf separating the English and the
German Romantics.

Nevertheless, in spite of these differences, the similarities
between the English and the Germans are not insignificant,
particularly when compared to the attitude of the French
Romantic poets, who paid no more than lip-service to the
mediating power of the imagination. Closest to the Anglo-
Saxons, in theory at least, was Hugo, whose subsequent
development was, in fact, to bring his innate leaning towards
the mystical much to the fore. In view of his later attachment
to the occult, it is not unexpected to find him writing in the 1822
preface to the *Odes et Ballades* :

> Le domaine de la poésie est illimité. Sous le monde réel, il existe
> un monde idéal, qui se montre resplendissant à l'oeil de ceux que
> des méditations graves ont accoutumés à voir dans les choses
> plus que les choses.[92]

Although this view seems to approach that of the *Frühromantiker* and of Blake and Shelley, Hugo did make certain

reservations, evident already in the sobriety of his statement as against the fervour of say, Wackenroder and Blake. To Hugo 'le but de l'art est presque divin' :[93] it is only *nearly* divine, a qualification that modifies the basic idea quite radically and that would not have been accepted by either F. Schlegel or Coleridge. Yet this sort of hesitation is typical of the whole French approach to imagination : the somewhat grudging concession of its power followed by a timid withdrawal. So the poet, to use an image from Vigny's *Chatterton*, may act as pilot in the ship of life : 'Il lit dans les astres la route que nous montre le doigt du Seigneur' ;[94] in other words, he may serve as interpreter of the divine will, but he steers along a prescribed course, not according to the free choice of his own will. A similar ambivalance becomes apparent in *Des Destinées de la Poésie*, in which Lamartine expressed an amazing gamut of opinions, beginning with an impressive panegyric of poetry in words more grandiose than meaningful :

> C'est l'incarnation de ce que l'homme a de plus intime dans le coeur et de plus divin dans la pensée, de ce que la nature visible a de plus magnifique dans les images et de plus melodieux dans les sons! C'est à la fois sentiment et sensation, esprit et matière; et voilà pourquoi c'est la langue complète, la langue par excellence qui saisit l'homme par son humanité tout entière, idée pour l'esprit, sentiment pour l'âme, image pour l'imagination, et musique pour l'oreille! [95]

Starting from this lofty, though woolly conception of poetry, Lamartine went on to voice his 'conviction ferme et inébranlable que les philosophies, les religions, les poésies n'étaient que des manifestations plus ou moins complètes de nos rapports avec l'Être infini'.[96] Lamartine here voiced the belief that poetry, by means of the imagination, could establish a link between man and God, but the claim loses some of its importance when poetry is classed together with religions and philosophies, instead of being placed at the summit as the supreme human activity that it certainly was to the Germans; furthermore, that qualifying 'only', familiar already from Hugo, crops up here too ('les poésies n'étaient que . . .') to weaken the force of the argument. And it eventually emerges that this mediating power was indeed just one of the many 'destinées de la poésie' in Lamartine's eyes. For the poetry of the future was to fulfil primarily a social function, by elevating and encouraging man in his progress towards an earthly Utopia, and even becoming directly involved in the struggle :

> A côté de cette destinée philosophique, rationelle, politique, sociale de la poésie à venir, elle a une destinée nouvelle à accomplir : elle doit suivre la pente des institutions et de la presse; elle doit se faire peuple, et devenir populaire.[97]

It would surely be hard to conceive an attitude more diametrically opposed to that of the *Frühromantiker* than Lamartine's advocacy of the popular role of poetry in *following* ('suivre') the climate of opinion. Once more it becomes plain that the attitude of the French Romantics to imagination was so much at variance to that of their English and German counterparts as to offer little basis for fruitful comparison. The poet, for instance, far from being a mediator of transcendental truth revealed by his imagination, as he was to the English and Germans, was cast in France as the leader of a down-to-earth literary revolt. And embroiled as they were in the exciting cut and thrust of their duel with Neoclassicism, the French Romantic poets had, understandably, hardly any of that heightened sense of mystery that inspired the English and German faith in the mediating power of the imagination.

C. The 'Modifying' Power

This adjective too, like 'esemplastic', was brought into currency by Coleridge to denote yet another aspect of the power of imagination. On 15 January 1804 in a letter to Richard Sharp he wrote of the 'imagination or the modifying power in that highest sense of the word in which I have ventured to oppose it to Fancy, or the aggregating power'. In these two words, 'modifying' and 'aggregating' Coleridge has restated his fundamental distinction between imagination and fancy in its essentials. Fancy is an 'aggregating' power in that it may, by a process of association, juxtapose ready-made elements so as to assemble them in a new pattern, as when iron-filings are re-arranged. Imagination, on the other hand, exercises a 'modifying' power because it is a creative force that not only unifies but, over and above that, can transform qualitatively to shape a new compound, as when water freezes to become ice. Transposed into literary terms Coleridge's antithesis is between what he calls 'painting', straightforward rational description, and 'creation', the imaginative transfiguration of 'the inanimate cold world' according to the poet's vision. This transfiguration was for Coleridge the vital function of the imagination, which he characterized in the twelfth chapter of *Biographia Literaria*, in words quoted from Wordsworth, as 'THE VISION AND THE FACULTY DIVINE'. Moreover it was this power of modifying reality in the light of the divine inner vision to which he was referring in the *Dejection* ode when he wrote :

> Ah! from the soul itself must issue forth
> A light, a glory, a fair luminous cloud.

Coleridge never ceased to stress that 'the poet should paint to the imagination, not to the fancy' :[98] that poetic imagination is a modifying power.

Coleridge's contemporaries by and large concurred with this conception of the imagination although none could equal his incisiveness in defining it. What he may have lacked in precision Shelley certainly more than made good by the moving beauty of the words in which he extolled the transforming power of the imagination in the *Defence of Poetry* :

> Poetry turns all things to loveliness; it exalts the beauty of that which is most beautiful, and it adds beauty to that which is most deformed; it marries exaltation and horror, grief and pleasure, eternity and change; it subdues to union under its light yoke all irreconcilable things. It transmutes all that it touches, and every

form moving within the radiance of its presence is changed by
wondrous sympathy to an incarnation of the spirit which it
breathes; its secret alchemy turns to potable gold the poisonous
waters which flow from death through life.[99]

What a profusion of images Shelley was able to conjure up to
convey most vividly the effects of both the esemplastic and the
modifying powers of the imagination. (It is interesting to note
that one of those images was used by Tieck too when he
described the play of imagination as 'diese große Alchymie,
durch die alles, was er berührte, in Gold verwandelt war').[100]
Wordsworth was a good deal more matter-of-fact, as Coleridge
put it, than Shelley, but in outline he too subscribed to the idea
that poetry presents an image of reality transfigured by the
poet's perception. In the *Essay supplementary to the Preface to the
'Lyrical Ballads'* he defined 'the appropriate business of poetry'
in these terms :

> her appropriate employment, her privilege and her *duty*, is to
> treat of things not as they *are*, but as they *appear*; not as they
> exist in themselves, but as they *seem* to exist to the *senses* and to
> the *passions*.[101]

In choosing to emphasize certain key-words, Wordsworth left
no doubt as to the purport of his statement, which rejects
straightforward description ('not as they *are*', 'not as they
exist in themselves'), i.e. Coleridge's 'painting' in favour
of the appearance ('as they *appear*', 'as they *seem* to exist'),
modified by the poet's imaginative vision. Compared to Shelley
and Coleridge, not to mention Blake, Wordsworth did, however,
remain peculiarly cautious. His view of the imagination as 'a
word of higher import, denoting operations of the mind . . .
and processes of creation or of composition' [102] is curiously
dry and muted, and this restraint is evident even where he
conceded its function in poetry : 'to throw over them' (i.e.
'incidents and situations from common life') 'a certain colouring
of imagination, whereby ordinary things should be presented
to the mind in an unusual aspect.'[103] The fact is that for
Wordsworth the 'ordinary things', which formed the material

L

of his poetry, continued to have a far greater importance than for any other Romantic poet. Although these 'ordinary things' were to be presented 'in an unusual aspect' with 'a certain colouring of imagination', fundamentally it was the 'common life' that interested the realist in Wordsworth more passionately than any imaginative vision. So in the ode *Intimations of Immortality*, in spite of his regrets that 'The things which I have seen I now can see no more,' he could nevertheless still find solace in the contemplation of nature because it continued to have an existence outside of himself that was an untarried source of delight :

> What though the radiance which was once so bright
> Be now for ever taken from my sight,
>   Though nothing can bring back the hour
> Of splendour in the grass, of glory in the flower;
>   We will grieve not, rather find
>   Strength in what remains behind;
>   In the primal sympathy
>   Which having been must ever be;
>   In the soothing thoughts that spring
>   Out of human suffering;
>   In the faith that looks through death,
> In years that bring the philosophic mind.
>
> And O, ye Fountains, Meadows, Hills and Groves,
> Forebode not any severing of our loves!
> Yet in my heart of hearts I feel your might;
> I only have relinquished one delight
> To live beneath your more habitual sway.

Compare this with Coleridge's *Dejection*, which arose from a similar spiritual crisis as Wordsworth's poem, when both poets had become conscious of a waning of their creative ability. How different is Coleridge's black despair from Wordsworth's stoical calm :

> O Lady! we receive but what we give,
> And in our life alone does Nature live :

Ours is her wedding garment, ours her shroud!
   And would we aught behold, of higher worth,
Than that inanimate cold world allowed
To the poor loveless ever-anxious crowd,
   Ah! from the soul itself must issue forth
A light, a glory, a fair luminous cloud
   Enveloping the Earth –
And from the soul itself must there be sent
   A sweet and potent voice, of its own birth,
Of all sweet sounds the life and element!

That voice that alone could animate the world for Coleridge was, as he says in a subsequent stanza, 'My shaping spirit of Imagination', and when it appeared to be failing, Coleridge felt that the whole world had become devoid of meaning. It was characteristic of Coleridge that without the exaltation of the imagination there was nothing for him but a gnawing awareness of spiritual privation, because he was so dependent on that inner vision, whereas Wordsworth was not only more modest and flexible, readier to accept compromise, but above all, more interested in the external impressions of the senses. The contrast between the two poets is that between the true Romantic with his absolute reliance on the imagination as the sole organ of perception and the Realist to whom outer phenomena have an independent validity. No wonder that Coleridge accused Wordsworth of matter-of-factness, and that Blake, in his *Annotations to 'Poems' by Wordsworth*, amended the latter's remark that 'the powers requisite for the production of poetry are, first, those of observation and description and secondly, Sensibility' by this emphatic dictum: 'One Power alone makes a Poet: Imagination, The Divine Vision.' [104]

Nor did Blake approve of Wordsworth's cult of the natural; his marginal comment on this point reads: 'Imagination is the Divine Vision not of the World, or of Man, nor from Man as he is a Natural Man, but only as he is a Spiritual Man.' [105] Blake indeed focused his attention exclusively on the spiritual, the transcendental, what he called the Divine Vision which was the product of the transforming imagination. Again it was Coleridge who found the right words to describe him when he wrote on 6 February 1818 to the Rev. H. F. Cary :

> Blake. He is a man of Genius – and I apprehend, a Swedenborgian – certainly, a mystic *emphatically*. You perhaps smile at *my* calling another Poet a *Mystic*; but verily I am in the very mire of common-place common-place compared with Mr Blake, apo- or rather anacalyptic Poet, and Painter!

This judgement was confirmed by the portrait sketched by Henry Crabb Robinson :

> He is not so much a disciple of Jacob Böhme and Swedenborg as a fellow visionary. He lives as they did in the world of his own. Enjoying constant intercourse with a world of spirits, he receives visits from Shakespeare, Milton, Dante, Voltaire and co. and has given me repeatedly their very words in their conversations. His paintings are copies of what he sees in his visions. His books are dictated from the Spirits.[106]

Here then was an artist who, according to the testimony of his contemporaries as well as of his works, was totally immersed in the realm of his imaginings. Throughout his review of paintings in the *Descriptive Catalogue* he repeatedly contrasted the work of art based on nature with that inspired by imagination :

> Men think they can Copy Nature as Correctly as I copy Imagination; this they will find Impossible, and all the Copies or Pretended Copiers of Nature, from Rembrandt to Reynolds, Prove that Nature becomes to its Victim nothing but Blots and Blurs. Why are Copiers of Nature Incorrect, while Copiers of Imagination are Correct?[107]

The answer seemed self-evident to Blake because he was so utterly certain that the imagination alone mattered. Seeing only with his visionary (as against the 'corporeal') eye, Blake had an intense belief in the transforming power of the imagination which is the basis of the 'Divine Vision'. Because he looked through reality he was able

To see a World in a grain of sand,
And Heaven in a wild flower,
Hold Infinity in the palm of your hand,
And Eternity in an hour.[108]

This is at once the most uncompromising expression of faith in the modifying power of the imagination and also the prototype of that transfiguration of reality that characterizes Romantic art.

The belief in the transforming power of the imagination was extremely potent in Germany, where it assumed a strange form paradoxically compounded of concrete as well as speculative thinking. The transformation of the world of reality (*Realität*) into a higher spiritual order of being (*Wirklichkeit*) was of course the primary aim of the *Frühromantik* programme, a transformation that was to be achieved through the 'shaping spirit of Imagination'. This project no doubt had its origin in the prevailing mood of longing for something more harmonious than the familiar world torn by all manner of schisms. Moreover, the German Romantics had genuine cause for dissatisfaction with the present reality for – let it not be forgotten – theirs was the age of the French Revolution and the Napoleonic Wars, a period not only of danger but of reaction and suppression of freedom in Germany. Hence their yearning for a better future was as much concrete as metaphysical in origin, and this is reflected in the plans they made, such as the scheme for the revival of the mediaeval guilds of artists, which would bring together like-minded men. Yet however practical the details, the overall project always kept that lofty, grandiose quality typical of the German Romantic movement. In contrast to the limited objectives of the French, who sought reform in literature, and specifically in the theatre, the Germans confidently set themselves to transform the whole world by a process of progressive poeticization. This accounts for the curious crusading tone of many of the utterances of the *Frühromantiker* on this subject, almost as though these were political slogans – as indeed they were to their authors. 'Wir sind auf einer Mission:

zur Bildung der Erde sind wir berufen',[109] Novalis proclaimed,
or again: 'Die Welt muß romantisiert werden.' [110] In his own
commentary on that statement Novalis explained the nature of
the transformation which the Romantics envisaged in that term
'romantisieren':

> Indem ich dem Gemeinen einen hohen Sinn, dem Gewöhnlichen
> ein geheimnisvolles Ansehn, dem Bekannten die Würde des
> Unbekannten, dem Endlichen einen unendlichen Schein gebe, so
> romantisiere ich es.[110]

Reality was to be transfigured by means of the imagination
through a confrontation with the infinite, which the poet perceived in the special insights bestowed by his 'Offenbarungs-
fähigkeit'.[111] Here again the German Romantics were interpret-
ing the powers of the imagination in a more literal and more
sweeping fashion than their English contemporaries. The latter
sought only a momentary transfiguration of reality in the work
of art or, at most, the creation of a private heaven after the
manner of Blake. The Germans, on the other hand, were
sincerely convinced of the possibility of a kind of public heaven,
a lasting Utopia to be achieved by the transformation of the
world into a superior state. The work of art represented for
them only a foretaste, a first step in the poeticization of the
universe which was their avowed intent. Once more, as in the
case of the esemplastic power of the imagination, what was to
the English an aesthetic principle was expanded and systematized by the Germans into a metaphysical concept.

One outcome of the belief in the transforming power of the
imagination was a strange streak of Utopianism that ran
through Romantic writing. The German Romantics, while
looking nostalgically back into the glorious – needless to say,
idealized – past, simultaneously hankered for a like revival of
harmony in the future. 'Und sollte nicht die Zukunft den alten
Zustand der Dinge wieder herbeiführen?' [112] asked Novalis,
whose survey of the past in his essay *Die Christenheit oder
Europa* ends with the confident prophecy: 'sie muß kommen, die

heilige Zeit des ewigen Friedens'.[113] This poet, who was dying of tuberculosis, described the coming Utopia in a medical image as the restoration of transcendental health. This positive note is even more striking in the utterances of F. Schlegel, whose hopes of paradise sprang from his faith in the trans-figuring impetus of true poetry. Thus he predicted the approach of the new era emerging 'aus dem reinen Lichte der ewigen Hoffnung, als die in Glauben und Liebe verklärte Fantasie wie der Regenbogen nach dem Ungewitter . . . oder wie die Morgenröte aus der Nacht'.[114]

Only Blake among the English poets felt fairly sure of finding his 'Golden Age' : 'The Nature of my Work is Visionary or Imaginative; it is an Endeavour to Restore what the Ancients call'd the Golden Age'.[115] But even Blake with his supreme trust in the 'Divine Vision' significantly used the word 'Endeavour' which suggests a certain tentativeness as against the blind optimism of F. Schlegel. Shelley's reservations were more deep-seated in spite of his pronouncedly transcendental conception of poetry as the vision of an ideal spiritual reality, 'the interpenetration of a diviner nature through our own.' [116] Nonetheless in the Dedication of *The Cenci* he regretted that 'those writings which I have hitherto published, have been little else than visions which impersonate my own apprehensions of the beautiful and the just.' [117] Shelley recognized the limita-tions of the transforming power of the imagination and did not dare to hope for the material realization of the vision. Indeed he lamented that the actual words of a poem are but a feeble shadow of the original brilliant vision for

> the mind in creation is a fading coal, which some invisible influence, like an inconstant wind, awakens to transitory bright-ness : this power arises from within, like the colour of a flower which fades and changes as it is developed.[118]

It seems paradoxical that just Shelley, with his extraordinary ability for conveying an insight in a plastic image, as is shown again by these phrases, should have questioned the possibility of translating vision into reality. The realism of Wordsworth, on the other hand, is more straightforward, without the scepticism that beset Shelley. Holding the didactic view that every great poet should be a teacher, Wordsworth wished to see

> Poesy thus courteously employed
> In framing models to improve the scheme
> Of Man's existence, and recast the world.[119]

Thus the Utopianism of the English tended to be of a more practical kind, even though the Pantisocratic schemes of Coleridge and Southey came to nothing. The English sought to bring at least something of their 'Divine Vision' back into reality in the hope of elevating and improving it. This is more like the socialist method, in contrast to the idealistic approach of the Germans who set out to assimilate reality into their vision.

There is little evidence of either of these strains in France, partly no doubt because the recent practical attempt at reform of society had had such disastrous results. The French Romantics were therefore more inclined to continue the escapism popularized by their predecessors, who had believed with Rousseau that the evils of the present stemmed from civilization and who had accordingly returned to nature in the backwoods of America, like the youthful Chateaubriand, or on some remote island, like Bernardin de Saint-Pierre, in their quest for the Garden of Eden. The simple-life syndrome instituted by Rousseau became a down-to-earth, but apolitical form of Utopianism with the search for Arcadia in a foreign land and society, after the manner of Gauguin. And it was, after all, logical that the French Romantics should seek salvation on earth, albeit in the more exotic regions, since they distrusted the higher reaches of the imagination.

*   *   *

From this analysis of the theories of imagination, a fairly consistent picture emerges of the differences of attitude between the three Romantic movements. What is more, the divergences that become evident here are remarkably like those noted in the examination of their individualism so that a total pattern begins to take shape. Repeatedly it is the French who are in one way or another the outsiders. The arrested development of their Romantic movement through the intervention of the Revolution, its peculiarly rebellious character in opposition to the strong Neo-classical tradition, its emphasis on freedom and realism and its consequent distrust of imagination: all these are in marked contrast to the Romanticisms of England and Germany. Between these two the affinities are considerable: in both the accepted basis of Romanticism was individualism, and in both the central role was assigned to the imagination, whose manifold powers were conceived on a vast scale. Yet within this common framework of individualism and imagination, the differences between England and Germany are still profound. English Romanticism was constantly tempered by a native realism, good sense, moderation and spirit of independence, which protected the movement from the excesses into which the Germans lapsed through their tendency to abstraction and their totalitarian extremism.

The Imagination at Work

GIVEN this pattern of resemblances and divergencies in the English, French and German Romantics' conception of the function of imagination, it is pertinent to ask in what ways these differences in theory are reflected in their works. How are the various powers attributed to imagination put into operation? And can significant distinctions be drawn between the writings of one land and another that may be traced back to variations in their respective notions of imagination? Such questions must be posed although the answers might well fill several fair-sized volumes. However, the vastness of the subject is no valid excuse for evading it in view of its cardinal importance to the comparative study of European Romanticisms. On the other hand, the limits and limitations of this brief sub-section of a monograph must be made clear. I am *not* trying to *interpret* the symbols of Romantic poetry nor to seek after sources. A great many eminent critics have already expounded their ideas – some enlightening, some merely eccentric – on this subject. I need only mention such well-known works as G. W. Knight's *The Starlit Dome* (Oxford 1941), J. L. Lowes' *The Road to Xanadu* (London 1930), H. Bloom's studies of *The Visionary Company* (New York 1961) and of *Shelley's Mythmaking* (New Haven 1959), the whole host of books on the meaning of Blake's writings, J. Barrère's three tomes on *La Fantaisie de Victor Hugo* (Paris 1949–1960), etc. (Rather surprisingly there appears to be a gap here in German literary criticism, which has devoted its whole attention to theories of imagination and apparently none to the actual practices with the exception of B. Haywood's recent analysis of Novalis in *The Veil of Imagery* (The Hague 1959) and K. Negus examination of E. T. A.

Hoffmann's myths in *Hoffmann's Other World* (Pennsylvania U.P. 1965). To this wealth of interpretative criticism I would and could not add. My prime aim being comparative, I shall in the following pages endeavour to juxtapose the characteristic *methods* of certain Romantic poets. These uses of the imagination have in many cases already been fully analysed in detailed individual studies. I offer no more than a sample of certain dominant methods for the sake of comparing the practices of Romantic poets in England, France and Germany.

In the works of the Romantics the imagination acts first and foremost as an image-making force : this is one fundamental generalization that applies almost without reservation throughout Europe. If it be argued that image-making had invariably been the task of the poetic imagination, then it becomes the more imperative to examine the special practices of the Romantics. For their image-making is as sharply distinguished from that of their predecessors as their conception of the creative imagination was revolutionary in the history of aesthetics. The eighteenth century had regarded the image primarily as a form of decoration, a rhetorical figure added to a poem as an extraneous ornament, like a bauble on a Christmas tree : detachable and playful. The image was the calculated product of a kind of wit (see Gray's advice on turning a flat piece of prose into a poem, p. 128). Nothing could be further removed from this type of image-making than the Romantics' use of images. With the Romantic re-orientation the image assumed a central position in the creative process as the tangible expression of unconscious impulses and therefore as the chief carrier of meaning. It is deeply embedded in the total structure of the work, not mechanically superimposed, almost as an after-thought, as it had hitherto been. It is, therefore, true to say that the Romantics wrote not so much *about* winds and waves as *by means* of them. This use of images is indeed as much a hallmark of Romantic art as its individualism, its cult of feeling and its emphasis on imagination from which the profusion of images springs. The new evaluation of imagery is, moreover, directly connected with the substitution of organicist for the earlier mechanistic modes of thinking. Whereas the eighteenth-century decorative image had been compounded of the juxtaposition of dead, fixed objects, the symbolical image of the Romantics grows out of a vitalistic interplay of body and soul. Only in this context could the image become the visual incorporation of an idea, as it did first for the Romantics and subsequently for the Symbolists, who based their aesthetic system on the perception of the latent 'correspondences' between the physical and the transcendental. This view of the universe as one living unity explains also the Romantic preference for so-called organicist analogies. Both Coleridge and A. W. Schlegel habitually compared the work of art to a tree, and Coleridge in particular chose terms that are metaphorical for art and literal for plants when he wrote throughout *Biographia Literaria* of 'assimilation', 'generation' and 'production of a form of its own'. Thus the ideal of a complete interpenetration of matter and form evolved as the artistic counterpart of the organic conception of the world. In the symbolical image this could be achieved in varying degrees. The full realization of the ideal, the total fusion of subject and expression, each inherent in and saturating the other, occurs in music, hence the supreme art for many Romantics. Coleridge believed that music was the direct representation of transcendents (just as Pater later thought all arts aspired to the condition of music and Wagner extolled the music drama as the prototype of an integrated art-form); and Novalis carried the concept of such harmony of idea and expression into literary criticism when he called for the musical organization of poetry which to him, as indeed to most Romantics, meant emblematic image-making.

'Emblematic' and 'symbolical': these are the adjectives that most aptly characterize the images that the Romantics created. For they showed a marked preference for certain types of imagery, favouring for instance the metaphor as against the simile. The reason for this choice is fairly obvious: while the simile is no more than a juxtaposition, the metaphor makes an identification, a correspondence, such as the Romantics sought in order to satisfy their longing for harmony. The Greek verb from which the term 'symbol' is derived means to throw together, which pre-supposes a unifying act of imagination. The esemplastic image, – how useful Coleridge's word proves! – invoked originally as a metaphor, may be raised into a symbol or may even become part of a symbolical, mythic system. This kind of symbolical figure image is eminently suited to the role that the image plays in Romantic poetry as the carrier of meaning, and it therefore has precedence over the representational image, which is more in consonance with a Realistic art. This alienation from the representational form perhaps accounts in part for the Romantics' comparative neglect of the drama, the most objective of the literary genres. There are, moreover, few examples in Romantic writing of imagery used in the Miltonic manner to draw an explicit parallel; the best known is probably Musset's famous pelican image in the *Nuit de Mai*, which is left uncomfortably straddled between simile and metaphor when Musset, after a vivid allegorical description of the scene, points out the moral –

Poète, c'est ainsi que font les grands poètes[120]

– thereby reducing his potential symbol to a mere comparison because he disturbs the process of fusion between pelican and poet.

Considering their evident lack of interest in the representational image, in the projection of a picture of external reality the Romantics' reputed success in the historical novel seems paradoxical. Yet the historical novel has been hailed as the 'création du romantisme',[121] while absorption in the past, specially the Middle Ages, is often accepted as one of the salient traits of the Romantic movement. There must clearly be a fallacy somewhere, and it is not hard to fathom. Admittedly the Romantic poets did write a good many historcial novels, but did they in fact make any genuine attempt to relive the past, to portray it as it truly was, i.e. to paint a representational image? Are not, on the contrary, their portrayals of the past for the most part highly fanciful, inspired by a freely ranging creative imagination rather than by the precise memorative faculty that can recall and reproduce in more or less detail things as they really were? As regards the German Romantics, the answer is beyond doubt: their so-called historical novels are not at all concerned with the reality of the past, only with its significance as experienced by the Romantic poet. So Wackenroder perceived the past as a Utopian haven of artistic culture. Likewise Novalis looked back nostalgically to a Golden Age, which provides a suitably mysterious background to the poetic theme of *Heinrich von Ofterdingen*. Tieck too joined in the idealization of the Middle Ages as 'die eigentliche Blütezeit der romantischen Poesie. Liebe, Religion, Rittertum und Zauberei verweben sich in ein großes, wunderbares Gedicht.'[122] It is the vague Olde Times of ballad and romance that are a shadowy backcloth to the adventures of Franz Sternbald and to the eerie happenings of *Der blonde Eckbert*. For the *Hochromantiker*, on the other hand, the motivation of the historical setting was patriotic, a whip to national fervour; history was again being used – in the drama and the ballad as well as in the novel – as the vehicle of an ulterior purpose (e.g. Arnim's *Die Kronenwächter*, Fouqué's *Der Held des Nordens*, the ballads of Uhland, Rückert etc.).

Even when a historical novel does offer a fairly faithful period reconstruction, it may still be the product of an image-making, not a representational imagination. This is the case of Hugo's *Notre-Dame de Paris*, which introduces the historical background of fifteenth-century Paris, that Hugo had studied with care, for the sake of the picturesque local colour beloved by its author. The novel is accordingly interspersed with lengthy evocations of the setting, such as the chapter entitled *La place de Grève*, which depicts the vagabonds' milieu, or the whole of the third book, devoted to descriptions of the cathedral and the city from a bird's-eye view. The sombre grotesque frescoes of the cathedral's sculptures dominate the melodramatic scenes enacted around them. Nevertheless, 'le livre n'a aucune prétension historique',[123] Hugo wrote to his editor, and indeed this soon becomes apparent as the period representation, in spite of the novel's title, recedes behind the increasingly bizarre plot in the shape of a frantic love-dance round the will-o'-the-wisp Esmeralda. At least Hugo had the honesty to recognize, 'ce n'est pas là' (in the historical representation) 'ce qui importe dans le livre. S'il a un merite, c'est d'être oeuvre d'imagination, de caprice, de fantaisie' [124] – but, it might be added, of an excessive, a Gothic fantasy, that is epitomized in the monstrosity of Quasimodo. As in *Han d'Islande*, the interest of the novel centres on the fantastic superstructure of invention imposed on a historical foundation, which dwindles in importance as the tale progresses. The descriptions of buildings and scenes spring from a desire for local colour, and their surface realism is at odds with the dominant fancifulness of the story.

The very opposite is true of Scott, the only writer of the Romantic period who re-created the past with an authentic historical sense. His best novels, the Scottish ones, differ in every respect from the historical tales of his contemporaries. In the first place, instead of the remote Middle Ages in which the German and French Romantics revelled, Scott chose to write of the recent past, still familiar to the preceding generation and known to him through hearsay : *Sixty Years Since*, to quote the sub-title of *Waverley*. Far from playing the part of the belated minstrel sentimentally eulogizing bygone days, Scott had the clear-sightedness to recognize the disruption of the country through the strife of the Jacobean rebellions; in praising the progress made since then, he was fully aware and shrewdly approving of the newly emergent middle-class society, that gets on with the business of living without clinging to the false glamour of the past. As an historian Scott was never anything other than realistic in spite of his potentially Romantic material, which is often treated with more than a hint of irony at the heroic climaxes. Scott made his attitude clear in the 'Postscript which should have been a preface' to *Waverley* : he insists that his novel has 'a foundation in fact', that it is 'drawn from the general habits of the period (of which I have witnessed some remnants in my younger days)' and that it has 'the purpose of preserving some idea of the ancient manners of which I have witnessed the almost total extinction'. With this aim in mind and with that first-hand knowledge of the period that he repeatedly emphasizes, Scott was able to give a true representation of the Scotland of the 1745 Rebellion. All Scott's best historical novels are thus rooted in the solid ground of an intense local feeling totally different from Hugo's local colour that is artificially contrived. To Scott the past was no repertory of wonders, but the present gone by – and good riddance, he would surely often have added. So the whole theme of *Waverley* runs counter to the Romantic trend in that it depicts the development of Waverley from his early illusions, the product of a dreamy temperament and too much fanciful reading, to a level-headed maturity through the discipline of hard experience. His evolution is the antithesis of Heinrich von Ofterdingen's, who moves further and further away from reality into dream, and more akin to the lessons learnt by the heroes of the nineteenth century novel, who have to come to terms with the world around them. It is in consequence of his essentially objective outlook that Scott excelled at the representational form, which throve on his sober detachment, his ability to face fact. Only on such ground can the representational image as the projection of reality prosper; herein lies the reason for its rarity during the Romantic period. With the exception of Scott (whom I consider as much a Realist as a Romantic), the writers of historical novels are infinitely more concerned with *their own view* of the past than with the past as it was, and generally the historical element is of subsidiary importance as background only. Here again certain differences between the three movements are discernible in the contrast between Scott's English – or rather Scottish! – common-sense and the sequestered aestheticism of the German *Frühromantiker* or the wild excursions of Hugo's Gothic fantasy.

*   *   *

While the representational image is orientated to outer reality, the symbolical image is fed by inner sources. As the product of the creative imagination, it is also the perfect expression of the Romantics' particular conception of that force, and in its formation the esemplastic, mediating and modifying powers of the imagination can be fully exercised. The image is firstly esemplastic in that it points to an analogy, thereby bringing together two or more often very diverse factors. This in turn leads to that density so characteristic of Romantic poetry because its images have the effect of drawing disparate elements together towards an organic whole. When that analogy is between the physical and the transcendental, as is frequently the case in Romantic writing, the resultant image not only unites, but also mediates by a clearer revelation of the imperceptible. In such *rapprochement* or even reconciliation of opposites lies the highest imaginative triumph of the symbolical image. Finally it can also transform by presenting an entirely new vision of the universe, as in the marriage of the seasons at the end of *Heinrich von Ofterdingen* or in *Kubla Khan*, to cite but two examples.

The Romantics themselves were not slow to grasp the appropriateness of the symbolical image to their purposes so that its possibilities are already well documented in their theoretical works. For once the artist had by his esoteric insight perceived the truth, his problem was a technical one : how to express the inward by the outward, the abstract by the concrete. To this question A. W. Schlegel offered an answer : 'Wie kann nun das Unendliche auf die Oberfläche zur Erscheinung gebracht werden? Nur symbolisch, in Bildern und Zeichen.'[125] So he demanded the interaction of what he called the sensuous and the spiritual :

> Die sinnlichen Eindrücke sollen durch ihr geheimnisvolles Bündnis mit höheren Gefühlen gleichsam geheiligt werden, der Geist hingegen will seine Ahndungen oder unnennbaren Anschauungen vom Unendlichen in der sinnlichen Erscheinung sinnlich niederlegen.[126]

M

In the *Vorlesungen über schöne Kunst und Literatur* the same idea was clothed in slightly different words when Schlegel wrote that 'wir suchen entweder für etwas Geistiges eine äußere Hülle, oder wir beziehen ein Äußeres auf ein unsichtbares Innres' and this activity was to him the essence of artistic creation: 'Dichten (im weitesten Sinne für das Poetische allen Künsten zum Grunde Liegende genommen) ist nichts anders als ein ewiges Symbolisieren.' [127] There can be no plainer formulation than this of the central function of the symbolic image in Romantic aesthetics. A. W. Schlegel's famous definition of the beautiful as 'eine symbolische Darstellung des Unendlichen' [128] makes sense only if the crucial role of the symbol is fully understood. This was a cardinal tenet of the *Frühromantiker*, that re-echoes throughout their writings. Novalis for instance saw the origin of all art in hieroglyphics, the signs or symbols of what the primitive artist sought to convey. The same phrase 'Hieroglyphenschrift' [129] occurs in Wackenroder's *Herzensergießungen eines kunstliebenden Klosterbruders*, where he too stressed the fusion of the spiritual and the sensuous worlds in the symbol coined by the God-like artist. Coleridge's thought ran parallel to that of the Germans, though tinged with a Neo-Platonism that is very evident in the poem *The Destiny of Nations* with its reference to Plato's allegory of the cave:

> For all that meets the bodily sight I deem
> Symbolical, one mighty alphabet
> For infant minds; and we in this low world
> Placed with our backs to bright Reality,
> That we may learn with young unwounded ken
> The substance from its shadow.

Coleridge, like A. W. Schlegel, welcomed the symbol as the instrument of the poetic vision, the means of projecting by an outward, visible sign the inner visionary meaning. 'The artist', he wrote in the essay *On Poesy or Art*, 'must imitate that which is within the thing, that which is active through form and figure, and discourses to us by symbols.' [130] With his passion for accurate terminology and subtle distinctions, Coleridge inevitably went on to define the symbol as 'characterized by a translucence of the special in the individual, or of the general in the special, or of the universal in the general; above all by the translucence of the eternal through and in the temporal'.[131] This is another way of saying that the symbol acts as a window, to be opened by the poet, so as to permit a glimpse of the infinity beyond. So, Coleridge concluded, symbolical images 'are the living educts of the Imagination; of that reconciling and mediatory power, which . . . gives birth to a system of symbols, harmonious in themselves, and consubstantial with the truths of which they are the conductors'.[132] Here again Coleridge's thought coincides with that of A. W. Schlegel, who also saw in the poetic symbol the infallible utterance of intuited truth. This indeed became one of the common beliefs of both English and German Romantic writers: that ultimate truths could be conveyed only through symbols, through hieroglyphic suggestion. In France it came into currency later with Baudelaire's championship of the image as the vehicle of a truth to be found in the depths of the human soul.

The star role of the symbolical image in the aesthetics of the Romantics therefore fits in with their conception of the function of the imagination, of art and the artist. The image is perceived and shaped by the divinely inspired artist through his special visionary powers, and this magical ability to create images turns him into something of a sorcerer, as in primitive folklore. Moreover, as Kermode has recently pointed out,

> The work of art itself is a symbol, 'aesthetic monad'; utterly original and not in the old sense 'imitated'; 'concrete', yet fluid and suggestive; a means to truth, a truth unrelated to, and more exalted than, that of positivist science, or any observation depending upon the discursive reason; out of the flux of life, and therefore, under one aspect, dead; yet uniquely alive because of its participation in a higher order of existence, and because it is analogous not to a machine but to an organism;[133]

Since the Romantic work of art is in its totality itself a symbol, it has a particular intensity, which is a heightened form of that density derived from the fabric of images. This intensity accounts, at least in part, for the compelling quality of Romantic poetry. On the other hand, in the source of its spell resides also a cause of its inaccessibility: for much Romantic poetry is a condensed cypher of symbolic images, signifying little to those who do not hold the key. The meaning is expressed, as it were, in a shorthand when the poet invests a symbol – such as Novalis' blue flower or Coleridge's albatross – with a complex content, often stratified in several layers. It is the task of the reader to try to enter into this forest of symbols.

The symbolic image is governed by what T. S. Eliot has called the 'logic of the imagination' which differs radically in object and intent from the everyday logic of the understanding. Whereas the latter might well scoff at, say, *The Ancient Mariner* for making so much ado about a mere bird, or at Heinrich von Ofterdingen for pursuing his peculiar quest for a blue flower, the 'logic of the imagination' knows how to look beyond the surface fable for its underlying, symbolic significance. So every Romantic poem, in so far as it expresses its innermost meaning in symbolic images, demands of the reader a certain imaginative effort, a readiness to see things on *its* terms and not only through the literal-minded eyes of reason. For Romantic poetry, springing as it does from the imagination of the individual, is inevitably under the aegis of the 'logic of the imagination', to borrow once more the neat phrase coined by T. S. Eliot in his preface to his translation of St.-John Perse's *Anabasis* (London 1930). With his customary acuity, Eliot was able, in a few lines, to summarize the salient characteristics not only of St.-John Perse's work, but of any poem written under this constellation: the 'logic of the imagination', as he pointed out, leads to a sequence of images and ideas, a web of symbols in which the links in the chain, the explanatory and connecting matter, are suppressed so that the succession of images coincides and concentrates into one intense impression. This formulation brings out both the dense concentration of the symbolic image, which distinguishes it from the two-dimensional allegory with its static system of point to point equivalents, and also the inner coherence of the symbolic pattern, wayward though it may appear. In such symbolic images, the creative imagination of the Romantic poet is at work; by examining the ways in which they are used, we may be able to see how the differing evaluations of imagination of the English, French and Germans affected their actual writings. For there is a distinct relationship between the theory of imagination and the practices – the incidence and uses of the image – in each land.

That English Romantic poetry is extraordinarily rich in imagery hardly needs to be repeated; indeed, certain poets, notably Shelley and Blake, have been criticized for the overwhelming flood of their images. The habit of arguing through images is much in evidence throughout English Romantic prose too. This abundance of imagery is clearly in consonance with the strong emphasis on the creative imagination as the organ for the intuition of the ultimate truths of human existence. So pervasive is emblematic imagery in English Romantic poetry that certain recurrent figures have, like leitmotifs, become associated with particular poets or ideas. Thus the harp caressed by the breeze is the consistent image of the poetic process throughout Coleridge's *The Aeolian Harp, Fears in Sonnet to the Autumnal Moon*, as the 'mother of wildly-working two poems, and in *The Wanderings of Cain, Kubla Khan, Christabel*, and *The Ancient Mariner*, the moon is seen, as in the *Sonnet to the Autumnal Moon*, as the 'mother of wildly-working visions'. Similarly, the central images of Keats' odes are the moon and sleep, the temple and the nightingale, a series of symbolic pictures by means of which the poet expresses his thought. In Shelley's poem the recurrent images are numerous : the eagle and the serpent, temples and towers, the boat, the stream, the cave, the veil. Shelley shares with Coleridge, Wordsworth and Byron the characteristic Romantic image of 'the correspondent breeze', which has been so ably analysed by M. H. Abrams[134] as the emblem of the activism of the free spirit, a persistent material symbol for a psychological condition.

Other such recurrent images include Prometheus as a symbol of power, childhood as the state of innocence, the rose as a type of beauty, mountains as emblems of aspiration and light as spiritual illumination.[135]

It would, however, be wrong to deduce from the popularity of certain favoured images that English Romantic poetry tended to uniformity in this respect. On the contrary, its image-making bears the imprint of the same individualism that marks the English Romantic school as a whole; the methods of image-making in fact show a wide gamut of variants ranging from Wordsworth to Blake. Wordsworth's approach was a curious compound of realistic perception and imaginative transformation as the visual became visionary and the natural apocalyptic. His habitual point of departure was the outer physical world, which he always endeavoured to scrutinize steadily for he believed that only through accurate notation of appearances could one arrive at a visionary intuition of truths. Far from inventing his symbolic images, Wordsworth found the initial impetus for them in real experience, often a sight or an encounter of some sort, and in his poems he was able to recreate vividly the actual situation that was to lead to the idea. The examples of this technique are too manifold and too familiar to need enumeration: the Highland lass in *The Solitary Reaper*, the leech-gatherer in *Resolution and Independence*, the daffodils in *I wandered lonely as a cloud*, the old huntsman in *Simon Lee*: these are some of the most obvious. The way in which these realities are turned into poetic images can in Wordsworth's case be traced with unusual precision for his sister would record in her journal the experiences from which the poems later grew, often indeed considerably later. On 15 April 1802, for instance, Dorothy Wordsworth made the following entry into *The Grasmere Journal*:

> When we were in the woods beyond Gowbarrow park we saw a few daffodils close to the water-side. We fancied that the lake had floated the seeds ashore, and that the little colony had so sprung up. But as we went along there were more and yet more;

and at last, under the boughs of the trees, we saw that there was
a long belt of them along the shore, about the breadth of a
country turnpike road. I never saw daffodils so beautiful. They
grew among the mossy stones about and about them: some
rested their heads upon these stones as on a pillow for weariness;
and the rest tossed and reeled and danced, and seemed as if they
verily laughed with the wind, that blew upon them over the lake;
they looked so gay, ever glancing, ever changing. This wind blew
directly over the lake to them. There was here and there a little
knot, and a few stragglers a few yards higher up; but they were so
few as not to disturb the simplicity, unity, and life of that one
busy highway.

There can be no doubt that this was the sight that inspired
Wordsworth's poem written more than two years later:

> I wandered lonely as a cloud
> That floats on high o'er vales and hills,
> When all at once I saw a crowd,
> A host, of golden daffodils;
> Beside the lake, beneath the trees,
> Fluttering and dancing in the breeze.
>
> Continuous as the stars that shine
> And twinkle on the milky way,
> They stretched in never-ending line
> Along the margin of a bay:
> Ten thousand saw I at a glance,
> Tossing their heads in sprightly dance.
>
> The waves beside them danced, but they
> Out-did the sparkling waves in glee:
> A poet could not but be gay,
> In such a jocund company:
> I gazed – and gazed – but little thought
> What wealth the show to me had brought:
>
> For oft, when on my couch I lie,
> In vacant or in pensive mood,
> They flash upon that inward eye
> Which is the bliss of solitude;
> And then my heart with pleasure fills,
> And dances with the daffodils.

The passage from Dorothy's journal gives a precise description ('a long belt of them along the shore, about the breadth of a country turnpike road' etc.); the topography is fixed at the outset, and although the daffodils are personified ('a few stragglers', 'danced', 'rested their heads'), it is the visual impression that is dominant, nurtured by her extraordinary powers of observation. In the poem William drew certain elements straight from his sister's record: 'along the shore' becomes 'beside the lake', 'under the boughs of the trees' is abbreviated to 'beneath the trees', 'dance' and 'laugh', the breeze and the waves are all there again. But the poem puts less emphasis on the real daffodils than on their after-effect: the theme of the poem is the memory of the daffodils, the daffodils in their relationship to the poet, and for this reason it begins with 'I', and concentrates on the vision of the 'inner eye' in the last verse. As the visual recedes, the daffodils are raised to a symbolic image of spontaneous joy. A similar process occurred with the leech-gatherer. Here is another excerpt from Dorothy's *Grasmere Journal* of 3 October 1800:

> When William and I returned from accompanying Jones, we met an old man almost double. He had on a coat, thrown over his shoulders, above his waist-coat and coat. Under this he carried a bundle, and had an apron on and a night-cap. His face was interesting. He had dark eyes and a long nose. John, who after-wards met him at Wythburn, took him for a Jew. He was of Scotch parents, but had been born in the army. He had had a wife, 'a good woman and it pleased God to bless us with ten children.' All of these were dead but one, of whom he had not heard for many years, a sailor. His trade was to gather leeches, but now leeches are scarce, and he had not strength for it. He lived by begging, and was making his way to Carlisle, where he should buy a few godly books to sell. He said leeches were very scarce, partly owing to this dry season, but many years they have been scarce – he supposed it owing to their being much sought after, that they did not breed fast, and were of slow growth. Leeches were formerly 2/6 per 100; they are now 30/-. He had been hurt in driving a cart, his leg broke, his body driven over, his skull fractured. He felt no pain till he recovered from his first

insensibility. It was then late in the evening, when the light was just going down.

This rather rambling evocation of the old man concentrates on outer details and mundane facts, whereas William's poem of some eighteen months later already indicates the shift from the physical to the moral in the change of title from the original *The Leech-Gatherer* to the more abstract *Resolution and Independence*. From his sister William took several concrete details : the man's advanced age, his fiery eyes, his bent posture; but then he departed from the model to endow the character with a greater nobility. The beggar, who had already given up gathering leeches, became a symbolic image of resolution and independence :

> And the whole body of the Man did seem
> Like one whom I had met with in a dream;
> Or like a man from some far region sent,
> To give me human strength, by apt admonishment.

As in *Simon Lee* and *Ruth, or the Influences of Nature*, Wordsworth here read a symbolic meaning into an actual encounter, thereby distilling a symbolic image from reality. This is surely what Coleridge had in mind when he praised Wordsworth's poetry for its 'fine balance of truth in observing, with the imaginative faculty in modifying the objects observed'.[136] Wordsworth's image-making, in keeping with his restrained view of imagination, is that of a poetic realist.

At the opposite pole to Wordsworth stands Blake, that 'literalist of the imagination', as Yeats so brilliantly called him. For him only the visions inspired by the imagination had any validity: 'Imagination is My World; this world of Dross is beneath my Notice.' [137] Consequently, in contrast to Wordsworth, Blake turned his back on outer reality in order to dwell entirely among the private visions vouchsafed by his inner eye. Indeed he even maintained that 'Natural Objects always did and now do weaken, deaden and obliterate Imagination in me' [138] so that he sought his true world within himself. For this

reason there are few similes in his poetry because a simile
implies separation in the comparison of two distinct entities,
whereas the symbol expresses a true identification, springing
from the recognition of a hidden relationship. Blake's poetry is
the most profusely and deeply symbolic not only among the
Romantics but probably in the whole of English literature, for
the symbolic image represented the sole means of conveying his
imaginative intuitions. At times, particularly in the earlier
poetry, the symbols are of a traditional connotation, such as the
Biblical figures of the lamb and the good shepherd in the *Songs
of Innocence* and the cycle of seasonal poems in the *Poetical
Sketches* in which spring denotes morning and betrothal, summer
high noon and consummation, autumn evening and fruition, and
winter night and death. From the *Songs of Experience* onwards,
however, the symbols are increasingly of his own making and
are not infrequently elusive in meaning in spite of many
scholarly, often ingenious attempts at interpretation. Not that
the symbols are either vague or chaotic. Blake asserted that all
his imaginings appeared to him 'infinitely more perfect and
more minutely organized than any thing seen by his mortal
eye'.[139] And this is borne out by the elaborate web of dramatic
symbols which are interrelated to form a dominant pattern. Far
from being mere static emblems, Blake's symbols are the dynamic carriers of his thought, used to present an argument in, for
instance, *A Song of Liberty* and *America*. Likewise the dual
view of the world contained in the *Songs of Innocence* and the
Songs of Experience is embodied to perfection in the counterpoint of the imagery. *The Blossom* of the earlier cycle :

> Merry, merry sparrow!
> Under leaves so green.
> A happy blossom
> Sees you, swift as arrow,
> Seek your cradle narrow
> Near my bosom.
>
> Pretty, pretty robin!
> Under leaves so green,

> A happy blossom
> Hears you sobbing, sobbing,
> Pretty, pretty robin
> Near my bosom.

is partnered by the horrifying *Sick Rose* in the *Songs of Experience*:

> O Rose, thou art sick!
> The invisible worm,
> That flies in the night,
> In the howling storm,
>
> Has found out thy bed
> Of crimson joy;
> And his dark secret love
> Does thy life destroy.

Blake's poetry is at its most brilliant when, as in these two poems, he distilled complex and pregnant ideas into such marvellously telling symbolic images. *The Blossom* shows the unity of all nature in the time of innocence, when bird and man and foliage were at one and when the universe was open and spontaneous in joy as in sorrow, that is absorbed in compassion. In contrast to the wild vegetation of Innocence, Experience has only cultivated flowers, grown in a confined setting, isolated in a city garden, roses that are cankered with blight and prickly with the thorns of separation. So the sick rose, attacked by the self-seeking worm in the darkness of night with its ferocious storms expresses destruction and decay more vividly and cogently than any explicit moralizing. The tension between the two conditions that Blake called 'Innocence' and 'Experience' is made apparent throughout the two collections, without need for direct comment, by similar pairs of complementary poems: *Infant Joy* and *Infant Sorrow*, the two *Nurse's Song*s, the two *Holy Thursday*s, the two *Chimney-Sweeper*s, *The Lamb* and *The Tiger*, *A Dream* and *The Angel* etc.. The symbolism is well integrated and dramatically active, and through it Blake projects the Utopian and apocalyptic visions of his imagination.

Esoteric though his symbolic images may be in meaning, they nevertheless make strangely potent poetry.

None of the other English Romantic poets equalled either Blake's exuberance or Wordsworth's sobriety in the theory and practice of imagination. Shelley with his superabundance of images was probably closest to Blake; certainly his gifts as a sheer image-maker are second to none :

> O wild West Wind, thou breath of autumn's being,
> Thou, from whose unseen presence the leaves dead
> Are driven, like ghosts from an enchanter fleeing,
> Yellow, and black, and pale, and hectic red,
> Pestilence-stricken multitudes! O thou
> Who chariotest to their dark wintry bed
> The wingèd seeds, where they lie cold and low,
> Each like a corpse within its grave, until
> Thine azure sister of the Spring shall blow
> Her clarion o'er the dreaming earth, and fill
> (Driving sweet buds like flocks to feed in air)
> With living hues and odours plain and hill :
> Wild Spirit, which art moving everywhere;
> Destroyer and Preserver; Hear, oh hear!

This is the opening of the *Ode to the West Wind* which Stephen Spender has called the most symphonic poem in the English language. The images are scattered forth, often one within another, and in such rapid succession as to leave a breathless impression of fleetingness. Shelley did not develop his images systematically after the manner of Blake; they run parallel to his thought, whereas in Blake's poetry the symbol conveys the thought. There is a similar dualism in much of Coleridge's poetry, although at his best he did achieve 'a relatively high degree of expressive integration', to quote Robert Penn Warren's phrase from his compelling analysis of *The Ancient Mariner* as a symbolic 'work of such pure imagination'.[140] Here and in some of his other poems, notably *Kubla Khan* and *Christabel*, Coleridge's practice is in accord with his theory in that the symbols are the carriers of meaning. But not always, unfortunately, is the imaginative transfiguration thorough-

going. Even *Kubla Khan* and *Christabel* were left unfinished, and
T. S. Eliot's objection to the exaggerated repute of the sur-
realist *Kubla Khan* is not unjustified. Moreover, the customary
criticism of Coleridge as a cerebral poet would seem to be
borne out by those poems such as *This Lime-tree Bower my
Prison* or *The Pains of Sleep*, which tend more towards a direct
statement than an imaginative presentation of a personal
dilemma. (Pehaps this accounts for the continuing interest in
the sources of Coleridge's poetry, examined in J. L. Lowes'
The Road to Xanadu). Keats' poetry too is uneven, though in a
different way, which could be attributed to his poetic immaturity
since he was during his brief career as a poet markedly less
successful in longer poems, which the symbolical structure
could not adequately support. On the other hand, the *Ode to
Autumn* with its consistent personification of the season is a
superb cluster of dense imagery and so is the ballad-like
narrative poem *The Eve of St Agnes*, built of tightly inter-
locking motifs as the counterpoint of the cold outside and the
warmth inside is grouped around the central theme of the
special day, St Agnes' Eve.

All these poets – Blake, Shelley, Keats, Coleridge and
Wordsworth – exalted the powers of the creative imagination,
albeit in varying degrees; likewise, in the works of them all the
'logic of the imagination' is active in their image-making,
though again differences are manifest in extent, intensity and
organization. The sole exception is Byron, the only one
among the English Romantics who did not join in the general
acclaim of imagination and significantly also the only one whose
poetry tends to suffer through lack of it, even though his brain
may at times have become

> In its own eddy boiling and o'erwrought,
> A whirling gulf of phantasy and flame.[141]

Childe Harold, for instance, so little comes to life that it is not
surprising when this cardboard puppet is superseded by the
poet's ego in the later cantos. Similarly Prometheus remains no

more than an abstraction; Byron called the protagonist 'a symbol and a sign', but he was in fact not able to transfigure him into a valid symbol :

> Thy Godlike crime was to be kind,
>   To render with thy precepts less
>   The sum of human wretchedness,
> And strengthen Man with his own mind;
> But baffled as thou wert from high,
>   Still in thy patient energy,
>   In the endurance, and repulse
>   Of thine impenetrable Spirit,
> Which Earth and Heaven could not convulse,
>   A mighty lesson we inherit :
> Thou art a symbol and a sign
>   To Mortals of their fate and force;
> Like thee, Man is in part divine,
>   A troubled stream from a pure source;
> And Man in portions can foresee
> His own funereal destiny;
> His wretchedness, and his resistance,
> And his unallied existence :
> To which his Spirit may oppose
> Itself – and equal to all woes,
>   And a firm will, and a deep sense,
> Which even in torture can descry
>   Its own concenter'd recompense,
> Triumphant where it dares defy,
> And making Death a Victory.

The weakness of Byron's Augustan abstraction becomes all the more apparent when his description of Prometheus is placed besides Keats' evocation of Apollo, with which the *Hymn to Apollo* opens :

> God of the golden bow,
>   And of the golden lyre,
>   And of the golden hair,
>   And of the golden fire,
>   Charioteer
>   Of the patient year.

How few words Keats needed to conjure up an image of Apollo that is both living and symbolical.

An even more revealing comparison can be made between Keats' *Ode to a Nightingale* and Lamartine's *Au Rossignol*. These two poems are alike in theme, not only in that both are addressed to the same bird, but also in so far as both concern the relationship between the nightingale and the poet. The treatment is, however, very different. The English poem, undeniably one of Keats' masterpieces, shows a total integration of idea and expression. The bird's song is the background and the stimulus to the poet's reverie, which dwells on the contrast between his own melancholy and the bird's happiness. The presentation is in concrete images throughout; for instance, Keats' familiarity with death is admirably brought out in the line

> Call'd him soft names in many a musèd rhyme.

Or take the concise picture of Ruth, the symbol of nostalgia :

> Perhaps the self-same song that found a path
>   Through the sad heart of Ruth, when, sick for home,
>   She stood in tears amid the alien corn;

We can actually *see* Ruth and at the same time perceive the meaning of the picture, just as we can feel the poet's desire to escape and visualize the scene of his yearning when we read :

> O, for a draught of vintage! that hath been
>   Cool'd a long age in the deep-delvèd earth,
> Tasting of Flora and the country green,
>   Dance, and Provençal song, and sunburnt mirth!
> O for a beaker full of the warm South,
>   Full of the true, the blushful Hippocrene,
>   With beaded bubbles winking at the brim,
>   And purple-stainèd mouth;
> That I might drink, and leave the world unseen,
>   And with thee fade away into the forest dim.

From this wealth of images Keats' poem derives not just its characteristic density and richness but its very meaning, for the

images embody its vital atmosphere, the dream-like suspension
between the real and the imaginary. Without comment or
moralizing, the poet evokes and records his experience. What
Keats puts into images, Lamartine puts into words. His poem,
as his footnote explains, grew, like many of Wordsworth's, out
of a real experience; nevertheless it lacks poetic truth, partly
because its language is vague and rhetorical, studded with
repetitions and deliberately sought effects. As against the
condensation of Keats' thought in his multitude of images,
Lamartine's description tends to be extensive :

> Ah! ta voix touchante ou sublime
> Est trop pure pour ce bas lieu :
> Cette musique qui t'anime
> Est un instinct qui monte à Dieu!

> Tes gazouillements, ton murmure,
> Sont un mélange harmonieux
> Des plus doux bruits de la nature,
> Des plus vagues soupirs des cieux.

> Ta voix, qui peut-être s'ignore,
> Est la voix du bleu firmament,
> De l'arbre, de l'antre sonore,
> Du vallon sous l'ombre dormant.

> Tu prends les sons que tu recueilles
> Dans les gazouillements des flots,
> Dans les frémissements des feuilles,
> Dans les bruits mourants des échos.

> Dans l'eau qui filtre goutte à goutte
> Du rocher nu dans le bassin,
> Et qui résonne sous sa voûte
> En ridant l'azur de son sein,

> Dans les voluptueuses plaintes
> Qui sortent la nuit des rameaux,
> Dans les voix des vagues éteintes
> Sur le sable ou dans les roseaux ;

Et de ces doux sons, où se mêle
L'instinct céleste qui t'instruit,
Dieu fit ta voix, ô Philomèle,
Et tu fais ton hymne à la nuit.[142]

Compare this digressive, precious panegyric of the nightingale
with Keats' sketch :

That thou, light-wingèd Dryad of the trees,
In some melodious plot
Of beechen green, and shadows numberless,
Singest of summer in full-throated ease.

From the outset Keats sees the nightingale as a symbol of
effortless happiness ('singest of summer in full-throated ease'),
a foil to the poet's 'drowsy numbness'; whereas Lamartine
continues right through to his rather sentimental conclusion
with his explicit presentation :

Oh! mêle ta voix à la mienne!
La même oreille nous entend;
Mais ta prière aérienne
Monte mieux au ciel qui l'attend.[143]

Dangerous though it is to generalize on the basis of a
comparison of just two poems, the difference in manner between
Keats' *Ode to a Nightingale* and Lamartine's *Au Rossignol* does
nevertheless indicate the divergence between the English and
the French Romantics in their use of images, which in turn
reflects the gulf that separates their respective evaluations of
imagination. In antithesis to the English – and German –
exaltation of the creative imagination, the French distrusted the
imagination as a potential menace to the naturalness at which
they aimed. Moreover, in reaction against the Neo-classical
tradition with its emphasis on the general, the French Romantic
poets made a veritable cult of the personal and the particular.
These two factors, the distrust of the imagination and the cult
of the personal, combined to throw the symbolic image into
disfavour. Poetry was to be natural and spontaneous, not
symbolical, and it was to express personal emotion, rather than

N

any remote transcendental truths. This attitude accounts for the
perplexing otherness of the French Romantic lyric compared to
its counterparts in England and Germany. Where the spotlight
falls on to personal emotion, the imagination is bound to retire
into the shadows. This is very evident in much of Lamartine's
poetry, which sometimes even retreats from the symbolic
image, as in *Le Crucifix* and *Le Lac*, both of which explore the
personal background of the symbols with which they open.
Musset too always concentrated on the personal; even when he
created a consistent image, as in his *Nuits*, where he presents
his dilemma in a series of dialogues between himself and his
muse, it is in order to dramatize his ego and not to convey any
higher vision. Even Hugo in his early poetry (that of the
Romantic period) is surprisingly restrained in his use of
imagery. Many of the *Odes et Ballades* are dedicated and
addressed to specific persons or open with an invocation to
his 'friends' in general. In such poems Hugo is intent on putting
a certain message over to his listeners and the image becomes
the carrier of meaning in a precise and limited sense. The
emphasis, however, is always on the message itself so that the
image is no more than a poetic means to an end, i.e. the means
of conveying the message. As such the image tends to stand
beside the meaning, explaining and embodying the message,
but not actually *standing for* the meaning, as it does with Blake
and the Symbolists, for whom the symbolical image was a
transubstantiation of a reality that was thereby obliterated.
Whereas in Hugo's poetry of the 1820's the images serve as
illustrations of ideas :

> Voilà l'image de la gloire :
> D'abord un prisme éblouissant,
> Puis un miroir expiatoire,
> Où le pourpre paraît du sang ! [144]

or in the ode *A la Colonne de la Place Vendôme* :

> O monument vengeur ! Trophée indélébile !
> Bronze qui, tournoyant sur ta base immobile,

Sembles porter au ciel ta gloire et ton néant;
Et, de tout ce qu'a fait une main colossale,
Seul es resté debout; – ruine triomphale
    De l'édifice du géant!

Débris du Grand Empire et de la Grande Armée,
Colonne, d'où si haut parle la renommée!
Je t'aime: l'étranger t'admire avec effroi.[145]

again in *Promenade*:

Vois, – c'est un météore! il éclate et s'éteint.
Plus d'un grand homme aussi, d'un mal secret atteint,
    Rayonne et descend dans la tombe.
Le vulgaire l'ignore et suit le tourbillon;
Au laboureur courbé le soir sur le sillon,
    Qu'importe l'étoile qui tombe! [146]

What is striking in all these instances is that Hugo's imagery
is so transparent and explicit, partly because the connection
between the object and the image is made perfectly plain, and
partly because the chosen images are, so to speak, public ones,
in contrast to the personal, esoterically involuted symbols of
Blake and Novalis.

The same sort of clarity characterizes the imagery of Vigny,
who made more extensive use of symbols to present his ideas
than any of his contemporaries. But then Vigny was also less
grudging than his contemporaries in his appreciation of the
powers of the imagination. In a manner similar to that of Hugo,
Vigny gravitated towards public images, being less a creator of
new symbols than an interpreter of traditional ones, which he
often invested with a novel, personal meaning. So he vented his
own doubts about womanhood after his break with Marie
Dorval in *La Colère de Samson*, just as he embodied the loneliness of the man of genius in his portrayal of Moses. When he
invented a symbol, it tended to be fairly conventional: the bottle
with a message in the sea, the death of the wolf. For Vigny, as
for Wordsworth, the symbol was in fact a means to an end, and
his method was not unlike that of Wordsworth. Vigny too
generally took as his point of departure a real happening (*La*

Mort du Loup) or a scene (*La Bouteille à la Mer*) or a character (*Moïse*); these are graphically described with the frequent introduction of direct speech that again is reminiscent of Wordsworth. From the real Vigny extracts the symbol: the wolf is the emblem of stoical bearing of suffering, the bottle in the sea of science and progress, Moses of the solitary genius; finally from the meaning of the symbol the moral message is drawn. It is a significant comment on the relative importance of the symbolic image in French and in English Romantic poetry that the method of the French poet who makes most use of the symbolic image should approximate to that of the most matter-of-fact English poet. In this respect too the evolution of French poetry lagged behind English and German; for genuine appreciation of the powers of the imagination and of the function of the symbolic image was to come in France considerably later in the nineteenth century with the later works of Hugo – a glance at the drawings he executed in Guernsey reveals the trend from observation to visions symbolically represented – and, of course, with the writings of Baudelaire, Nerval, Mallarmé and Rimbaud. Then, of course, the French more than made up for their earlier backwardness when they in turn became the leaders of the Symbolism that was to fertilize poetry throughout Europe as well as America.

Such systematic symbolizing occurred in Germany with the Romantic poets already, when they broadened – or, as they would say, universalized – their image-making into a world-making activity. This 'world-making' was entirely different, indeed diametrically opposed to what might be called the 'world-reproduction' in the social novel of the mid-nineteenth century. Whereas the worlds portrayed by Balzac, Dickens and Fontane are firmly founded in a scrupulously detailed observation of reality, the worlds conjured up by the Romantics, on the contrary, grow solely out of the imagination. Despising and rejecting reality as vehemently as they did, poets such as Novalis, Tieck and Brentano naturally eschewed any representational portrayal. Instead they drew on their inner vision for the prototype of a subjective, often fantastic reordering of the universe, which is implicit in their works. So they both poeticized reality (i.e. transformed it through the imagination) and shaped the new mythology for which F. Schlegel had campaigned. Novalis' *Hymnen an die Nacht* and *Heinrich von Ofterdingen*, the tales of Tieck, Hoffmann and Brentano are all fundamentally projections of a realm, a remaking of the world according to a personal vision. It is this quality which makes the products of German Romanticism peculiarly inaccessible unless the reader is prepared to enter without demur into the domain of the imagination. Here once again, in this use of imagination to create new worlds, the German Romantics prove more extreme and thoroughgoing than their counterparts in other lands. In France, it is true, this world-making had its parallels in such works as Rimbaud's *Une Saison en Enfer*, Nerval's *Les Filles du Feu* and Baudelaire's *Fleurs du Mal*. But these appeared considerably later, after the middle of the century, testifying again to that strange delay that was to make the Symbolist poets heirs to the heritage of German Romanticism. There were also some attempts by the English Romantic poets at a sustained exploitation of images. Shelley, for instance, aspired to create a new myth of the redemption of the earth in *Prometheus Unbound* by a very free use of Classical materials. Keats was trying to gather experiences into a coherent whole through a consistent reinterpretation of traditional images in his longer poems *Endymion* and *Hyperion*, neither of which was, however, entirely successful : *Endymion*, written in the summer of 1817 as a testing of his poetic capacity, still shows signs of immaturity, above all in the diffuse, elaborate decoration, while both versions of *Hyperion* remained unfinished, although the second, dating from the autumn of 1819, when Keats was at the height of his power, is tauter and denser in its web of symbolic significances than any of his other long poems. Coleridge too created his own worlds, particularly in the three major poems, *The Ancient Mariner*, *Christabel* and *Kubla Khan*, which have prompted numerous mythological interpretations, many of which are

more ingenious than convincing. But Coleridge's world-making
is distinguished from that of his German contemporaries by a
quality that might be characterized as casualness: for it is
chance and intermittent, occasioned perhaps by opium-dreams,
rather than the outcome of any deliberate quest for a new
cosmology. Only Blake attempted this, standing in this respect
also closer to the German than to the English tradition. In the
visionary works of his later years such as *Jerusalem* (1804), he
tried to give both a cosmogony and an apocalypse in terms of a
mythology neither Classical nor Christian, essentially original
in its incorporation of Biblical, Miltonic and Celtic elements. No
wonder that it requires a considerable effort to penetrate
Blake's private world in spite of the proliferation of learned
explanations. But even this world-making of Blake's, the
nearest approximation to that of the German Romantic poets,
appears curiously self-conscious and stilted beside their ingenuous re-creation of the world through the powers of the
imagination.

This indeed is the great forte of the German Romantics,
particularly of the *Frühromantiker*, who excelled at conjuring up
entire new realms, the products of their image-making faculty
(*Einbildungskraft*), the capacity to project pictures out of an
inner vision. Such a re-creation of the world was, of course,
fully in accordance with their avowed theories. In this context
F. Schlegel's repeated insistence on the progressive nature of
Romantic poetry acquires a specific meaning: 'Die romantische
Dichtart ist noch im Werden, ja das ist ihr eigentliches Wesen,
daß sie ewig nur werden, nie vollendet sein kann',[147] ever
evolving – in contrast to the completed, closed form of Classical
literature – in so far as it was still constantly creating its own
world. This new superior realm was to be characterized first
and foremost by an ideal state of harmony, the wish-fulfilment
of the Romantics' yearning for unity in antithesis to the jarring
dualisms of their physical surroundings. In this sense the
imaginative creation of new worlds was a form of escapism.
Here again there is a noteworthy difference between the three

Romantic movements. The English were, as ever, very inconsistent: Blake's refuge was in his 'Divine Vision'; Coleridge and Southey nurtured concrete plans for an earthly Utopia in their Pantisocratic scheme; Wordsworth found solace in nature around him; while Byron, in spite of his heroes' pilgrimages and picaresque adventures throughout the wide world, really fled into mockery. The French, on the other hand, inspired in part by Rousseau, sought their haven in distant, exotic lands, as in Chateaubriand's *Atala* and *René* and Bernardin de Saint-Pierre's *Paul et Virginie*, just as the *Stürmer und Dränger* demanded first outer freedom in their rebellion against a conventional society and literature. Having won their liberty as early as the 1770s, by the turn of the century, at the dawn of Romanticism, the Germans were so disillusioned with the fleshpots of this world as to experience a total revulsion. So the German Romantic poets believed that the only genuine salvation lay in removal from reality, in the creation of their own new and better worlds. This instinctive introversion was, moreover, further reinforced by the swing of interest from the paganism of ancient Greece to the Christian heritage of Western Europe. Against this background and with the assumption of absolute autonomy, the imagination was free to make its own image of the world.

In the *Märchen* the *Frühromantiker* discovered the perfect vehicle for their original visions of the world, and in this form – together with the lyric – German Romanticism both attained its highest summit and made its most important contribution to European literature. The lack of a satisfactory equivalent for this term in either English or French is in itself significant of the German dominance in this genre. A *Märchen* is far from being a mere fairy-story in the accepted English sense, nor is it primarily a fantastic tale in the customary superficial usage of that word. This latter conception of the *Märchen* derives from the popularization of Tieck and was eventually spread in France by the vogue for Hoffmann, but the fantastic tale of horror, after the manner of Poe, is in fact

indebted chiefly to the Gothic tradition of Pre-romanticism. To
the *Frühromantiker*, however, the *Märchen* was above all an
expression of the imagination, the very opposite of rationalistic
representation, and therefore the epitome of Romanticism.
Novalis certainly understood the appellation *Romantiker* as
denoting a writer of romances and, more specifically, *Märchen*,
for to him, as to his companions in the early Romantic group,
the *Märchen* was the very canon of poetry, the incarnation of the
loftiest ideal of poetry. Its domain was diametrically opposed to
the sphere of historical truth and its estrangement from the
familiar world of reason, its emancipation from traditional
perspectives made it eminently suitable for the prophetic
evocation of new regions. Hence Novalis referred to the writer
of *Märchen* as a seer into the future, that future being the Golden
Age that was to come through the progressive poeticization of
the universe. In this task of transformation the *Märchen* had a
central function to fulfil: in it we are released from the bonds of
the commonplace and transported into a different world where
the wondrous becomes ordinary and natural, to use Tieck's
phrase ('Das Wunderbare wird uns jetzt gewöhnlich und
natürlich').[148] In the *Märchen* then the world is actually being
transformed, re-created according to the imagination's inner
vision, and so this is the literary form most in consonance with
the theory of the *Frühromantiker* that 'Poesie ist Darstellung des
Gemüts – der innern Welt in ihrer Gesamtheit'.[149] The words
themselves are merely the outer manifestation of the inner
vision, while the structure of the *Märchen* is, again according to
Novalis, entirely musical in that it is shaped by its own organic
laws. Thus the *Märchen*, more than any other genre, may be
said to create its own world, and for this reason it became the
favourite form of the German Romantic poets, the ideal – indeed
the *only* apposite – projection of their inwardness.

Moreover, they underlined the gulf between the Philistine
everyday world and their realm of the imagination by frequent
use of the framework technique. Again and again throughout
German Romantic literature a story is told within a story: in

Novalis' *Die Lehrlinge zu Saïs*, the *Märchen* of Hyazinth and Rosenblüte is interpolated into the narrative; similarly *Heinrich von Ofterdingen* is studded with the tales of the merchants and of Klingsohr; Tieck's *Der blonde Eckbert* contains the story of Bertha's adventures within the main story, and in Brentano's *Geschichte vom braven Kasperl und dem schönen Annerl* too, the fate of the two central characters is recounted to the narrator by Kasperl's grandmother. The most complex plural frame-works are found in the *Herzensergießungen eines kunstliebenden Klosterbruders*, in which Wackenroder presents his ideas as though they were written by a lay-brother, who in turn re-produces various letters of mediaeval painters and finally traces the career of the musician Joseph Berglinger. This sophisticated multiple framework has been attributed to Wackenroder's reserve, – the opposite of Byron's self-display in *Childe Harold's Pilgrimage*. In Wackenroder's case the desire for anonymity may well have played some part, but the recurrent preference for the framework technique surely reflects the deliberate distancing of the physical here and now from the new realm created by the imagination: the world within – or rather beyond – the real world.

In no poet is this dichotomy as fundamental as in Novalis and none could equal his visionary evocation of new horizons. He was aware in his own life of the tension between his sense of reality, his career as a mining engineer, and his vocation as the poet of inwardness, the call to the invisible world as he put it. The transfiguring force of his imagination was brought into play in his early encounter with Sophie von Kühn; rationally he could recognize the limitations of this thirteen-year-old, even complaining that poetry interested her not a whit and that she was a cold-hearted creature, yet he did – admittedly after her death – idealize her to an unprecedented degree, not only as the sun of his life, but as a religious figure associated with Christ, the focus and inspiration of his infinite longings, the gateway to the transcendental Utopia. Banal though this example may be, it does illustrate very well Novalis' double vision, his ability to see, like Blake, *through* the real to the ideal image conjured up by the imagination. The possibility of such a dual view of the world is implicit in all his writing, although his true allegiance is to the inner vision, which comes into its own in every one of his works when the world of appearances fades as the world of imagination is realized. So the *Hymnen an die Nacht* begin characteristically with a brief tribute to light, the element of conscious, wakeful living; but almost immediately, in the second paragraph of the first hymn already, the poet turns away to the other world. Henceforth the physical phenomena of daylight are dim and dull compared to the ecstatic visions rising from the dark regions of the subconscious to which the poet yields in an intoxicated state of enthusiasm. In a radical reversal of values, it is night, darkness and death that vouchsafe Novalis an esoteric illumination as his spirit, released from the bonds of the earth, finds a paradise of dreams and visions. This progression from the outer to the inner realm is clearly evident in the style and imagery too: after the orderly, rational tribute to light with its plastic, concrete images, the poem drifts increasingly into an emotional incoherence as the poet is gripped by the chaos of darkness. The more the orderly statement of thought recedes, the more blurred the contours become and the syntax tends to dissolve as if in reflection of the vegetative softness that is being depicted. The imagery is dominated by words of fluidity ('quillt', 'träuft', 'Flut', 'floß', 'saugen', 'wogt', 'wie ein unendlich Meer', 'durchströmt') which suggest the departure from the *terra firma* of daylight into some mysterious inner region. This use of imagery is typical of Novalis' method of indirect communication, making the abstract palpable, expressing the inexpressible in the language of metaphor that was the appropriate medium for the utterance of his transcendental perceptions. His great *Märchenroman Heinrich von Ofterdingen* is entirely symbolical, departing from the norm of the novel less in its content than in its manner of narration, which is essentially poetic in that the fabric of the story is woven of an interrelated web of images. Its central symbol, the blue flower, which was to become the devise of the German Romantic movement, has several layers of significance, denoting both the objects of Heinrich's quest, Mathilde and poetry, as well as the yearning inherent in the quest itself. Heinrich's pilgrimage in search of the blue flower follows a course similar to the movement of the *Hymnen an die Nacht* : from the sober, rationalistic milieu of his home, where dreams are dismissed as mere fancies, to the enchanted land of poetry, ruled by Klingsohr, Mathilde's father. In contrast to Goethe's Wilhelm Meister, who learns to accept self-limitation within the confines of society, and also to Tieck's Franz Sternbald, whose journey degenerates into a series of Bohemian adventures, Heinrich, the born artist, follows a path that leads inwards. Starting in the real world, he gradually penetrates the realm of the imagination through his own dreams, the tales of the merchants, the encounters with the mysteries of the Orient and of nature in the figures of Zulima and the miner (who recall Mignon and the harpist in *Wilhelm Meister*). As his dormant intuitive powers are aroused, he repeatedly recognizes as strangely familiar things not rationally known to him, but rising to the surface from the inner world of which he had scarcely been aware. This phenomenon of *déjà vu* provides a clue to the trend of Heinrich's development : like the hero of *Hyazinth und Rosenblütchen*, Heinrich learns to lift the veil of appearances, to see not *with*, but *through* the corporeal eye so that he is able to perceive not the physical reality around him, but its imaginative transfiguration. The pattern of both Heinrich's and Hyazinth's progress is that of a spiral, leading upwards through the magic transforming loop of the imagination to the new, loftier world, the fulfilment of the inner vision. So in *Heinrich von Ofterdingen*, after the completion of Heinrich's journey on earth, sub-titled *Die Erwartung*,* the second part, *Die Erfüllung*† opens with a poem heralding the new world :

> Es bricht die neue Welt herein
> Und verdunkelt den hellsten Sonnenschein,

* *Promise* † *Fulfilment.*

Man sieht nun aus bemoosten Trümmern
Eine wunderseltsame Zukunft schimmern,
Und was vordem alltäglich war,
Scheint jetzo fremd und wunderbar,
Der Liebe Reich ist aufgetan,
Die Fabel fängt zu spinnen an.
Das Urspiel jeder Natur beginnt,
Auf kräftige Worte jedes sinnt,
Und so das große Weltgemüt
Überall sich regt und unendlich blüht.
Alles muß in einander greifen,
Eins durch das andre gedeihn und reifen;
Jedes in allen dar sich stellt,
Indem es sich mit ihnen vermischet
Und gierig in ihre Tiefen fällt,
Sein eigentümliches Wesen erfrischet
Und tausend neue Gedanken erhält.
Die Welt wird Traum, der Traum wird Welt
Und was man glaubt, es sei geschehn,
Kann man von weitem erst kommen sehn.
Frei soll die Phantasie erst schalten,
Nach ihrem Gefallen die Fäden verweben,
Hier manches verschleiern, dort manches entfalten,
Und endlich in magischen Dunst verschweben.[150]

Nowhere in European Romantic literature is there a more
succinct and eloquent panegyric of the esemplastic, mediating
and modifying powers of the creative imagination than in these
lines that sketch the programme of the second part of the novel.
Like Novalis himself in the *Hymnen an die Nacht*, Heinrich too,
after the death of his beloved, enters into some yonder world,
where time and space are suspended as he again passes through
the earthly experiences of the first part, this time all transfigured by the poetic imagination. In this *Märchenroman* that
transformation of the world which is the core of any *Märchen*
is actually seen to take place, and *Heinrich von Ofterdingen*
therefore represents the quintessence of the German Romantic
belief in the power of the imagination to shape its own world.

No other poet of either the *Früh-* or the *Hochromantik* could
be as uncompromisingly transcendental as Novalis. By com-

parison Tieck seems shallow, although he too in his *Märchen*
portrayed a world of the imagination, albeit totally different to
that of Novalis. The key to Tieck's works (and to his personality) lies in that phenomenal gift of fantasy that F.
Schlegel already recognized as the source of his writing. According to
contemporary testimony, Tieck frequently had hallucinatory
visions and he was certainly the exponent of a peculiar parlour-
game, the immediate invention and recital of plays on the most
far-fetched subjects (e.g. make up a play with an orang-outang
for its hero!). No wonder that such a man in his appraisal of
Shakespeare extolled above all other endowments of the poet the
free play of his imagination. This factor is very potently at work
in his own tales, which are the outcome of an imagination running riot, almost after the manner of the *Sturm und Drang*,
though more sombre in hue. With his morbid interest in the horrible and his awareness of the sinister forces lurking in nature as
a threat to man, Tieck shows a world into which the supernatural
can and does irrupt without warning – as in Kafka's works. The
domain into which Christian is drawn in *Der Runenberg*, or that
in which first Bertha and then her husband are entrapped in *Der
blonde Eckbert* may be interpreted as projections of Tieck's own
fears or as products of the characters' madness (and it is
characteristic of Tieck's narrative method that the endings of
his stories are left tantalisingly open). What is certain is that
Tieck deliberately questioned and ultimately removed the firm
basis of reality to sidle into a strange world of the imagination as
mystifying to the protagonists as to the reader. Tieck may be
branded as a popularizer, even a vulgarizer, the fountain-head
of the horror-tale; nevertheless he did fashion out of his inner
vision a highly imaginative world incarnate in such lasting
symbols as the gold of Christian's lust and the bird that represents *Waldeinsamkeit*, the enchanted land in *Der blonde Eckbert*.

This capacity to launch symbolic images was less marked
among the *Hochromantiker*, and it is interesting that this decline
in inventiveness seems to link up with a waning emphasis on
the creative powers of the imagination. By and large, the writers

of the *Hochromantik*, no doubt for lack of the primordial inner vision of a Novalis or a Tieck, preferred to build their imaginary worlds out of traditional mythological motifs such as the mermaid turned woman of Fouqué's *Undine* and the sale of one's shadow and the seven-league boots in Chamisso's *Peter Schlemihl*. Stripped of its metaphysical idealism, world-making became for these later Romantics more of a pantomine than an expression of a *Weltanschauung*. This playfulness is most evident in Brentano, a man possessed by a fantasy so capricious as to tempt him into a veritable maze of involved intrigue; even his best shortish tale, *Die Geschichte vom braven Kasperl und dem schönen Annerl* is a complex arabesque, let alone his rambling pseudo-novel *Godwi*. Yet although writers such as Fouqué, Chamisso and Brentano had not the modifying imagination to shape their own worlds, the existence of a realm other than that of physical appearances is obviously the accepted foundation of their works. Only E. T. A. Hoffmann stands out as an exception and his contribution to Romantic world-making is eccentrically original. Whereas the *Frühromantiker* saw through reality to the transcendental, the hallmark of Hoffmann's vision is that he sees and portrays *both* simultaneously. Instead of dismissing the evidence of his corporeal eye, Hoffmann recorded it alongside the other view so that his tales constantly oscillate between the real and the *Märchen* worlds. This dualism is already hinted at in the sub-title of *Der goldene Topf* : *Ein Märchen aus der neuen Zeit*,* firmly rooted, as the opening sentence establishes, in the Dresden of the day. It is in this commonplace setting of specific streets, shops and parks that the wondrous occurs as Anselmus sees the door-knocker changing into a menacing, grimacing witch and hears the rustling of the leaves turning into the seductive whisper of enchanting snakes. The yonder world is not distinct from this one, as for Novalis, but immanent in it, though the anchor of reality is never cast. For Hoffmann, again unlike his early Romantic predecessors, recognized the claims of the real world so that he made no attempt at a consistent,

* *A modern tale of the supernatural*

permanent transformation, as in *Heinrich von Ofterdingen*. Standing in fact between a declining Romanticism and a nascent Realism, he depicted the incursion of the irrational into the commonplace in a characteristically ironic, grotesque manner. The imagination is only one possible, no longer the sole valid, means of perception, and so its world of symbolical images must take its place beside the world of concrete objects.

* * *

It seems superfluous to point out now in so many words the extraordinary diversity of the workings of the imagination in the writings of the European Romantics. These differences alone, fundamental as they are, should convert those who still insist on the likeness of Romanticism throughout Europe. To take up Barzun's metaphor once more : this is a family whose physiognomy is as remarkable for the differences as for the similarities between its members.

In the case of imagination, these differences are apparent in both the theory and the practice, which are, of course, interconnected. Where the powers of the imagination are most highly extolled in the critical ideas, there the imagination is given the freest rein. In this respect there is none of that discrepancy between programme and performance that sometimes complicates the study of Romanticism. So conversely, where the role of the imagination is minimized in the literary theories, there it plays only a minor part. The clearest instance of this occurs in France : as I have tried to explain in the first part of this section, imagination was viewed there with considerable distrust as a potential threat to the truthfulness, the naturalness for which the French Romantics strove in reaction against the Neo-classical canon of fidelity to rules and to good taste. These ideals inevitably turned French Romanticism into an outward looking movement, just as the revolt against Neo-classicism resulted in a primary concern with external problems of form. Hence there was little scope or sympathy for the introverted imagination, the esemplastic, mediating and modify-

ing force envisaged in England and Germany. French sus-
picions concerning imagination were in fact confirmed when it
became associated with the disreputable brand of Romanticism,
generally known as *frénétique,** which revelled in wild outbursts
of Gothic fantasy. The constructive powers of the creative
imagination were appreciated in France many years later when
they found brilliant expression in the Symbolist poetry that
is one of the glories of French literature. Perhaps in fact
French Symbolist poetry is the more impressive because its
practices had not been anticipated in the Romantic lyric in the
same way as in Germany and England, where the poetry of the
turn of the nineteenth century is, as its name suggests, a Neo-
romantic revival over-shadowed by the wealth of its Romantic
ancestry. In this sense, the particular character of French
Romanticism, determined as it was by opposition to an overwhelming Neo-classical tradition, leads not only to a cleft
between the Romanticism of France and that of England and
Germany, but also to a deeper divergence of development lasting
right into this century.

Between the English and the Germans the relationship is
very much closer in the conception and workings of the imagination, as in most respects. On the other hand, the differences of
emphasis and degree are still sufficient to give the Romantic
movement a quite distinct aspect in the two lands. Basically
both the English and the Germans believed in the esemplastic,
mediating and modifying powers of the creative imagination.
In England, however, these powers were interpreted less dog-
matically and used with greater moderation than in Germany.
There was among the English poets a characteristic freedom in
their attitude towards imagination, a lack of uniformity that
stems perhaps from their native individualism and that permits
a wide range of approach: from the visionary mythologies of
Blake to the mingling of representation with symbolic interpretation typical of Wordsworth. But there can be no doubt of the
image's central function in English Romantic poetry, in contrast

* frenzied

to its peripheral, purely decorative position during the Augustan Age. In Germany this central function of the image was systematized in a manner alien to England. As the expression of the inexpressible, the symbolic image was a crucial point of *Frühromantik* theory, which conceived the artist's task as one unending attempt to find hieroglyphic equivalents for his transcendental visions. Taking this process a step further, the German Romantics believed that they could not only mediate their perceptions to others, but actually transform reality by poeticizing it into a world of the imagination. To see and use imagination in this way reveals an intensity, a measure of introversion and, frankly, of eccentricity that again marks the German Romantic movement off from its English counterpart.

Feeling

The Relative Importance of Feeling

————— ❀⊛❀ —————

IF one characteristic more than any other is popularly associated with Romanticism it is the unfettered expression of feeling. Nowadays the adjective 'romantic' – as in the phrases 'a romantic song' or 'a romantic story' – is commonly used to mean simply 'sentimental', while 'sentimental' in turn has fallen into disrepute as denoting mawkish, excessive feeling. Nor is this merely a careless usage of terms. Even so discerning a critic as Neville Cardus, writing recently of Busoni, called him a Neo-classic in his intellectual approach to music in reaction against the romantic use of music as a medium of individual emotional realization or projection. This widespread tendency to equate 'romantic' and 'emotional' in a somewhat peremptory fashion is, however, fraught with danger. Not so much because it is inherently false – the expression of feeling is, after all, one of the salient features of Romanticism. But it is only one among several, not necessarily the foremost, nor the very hall-mark of Romanticism, as is often assumed. Indeed, far from being primary, the expression of feeling is much rather the outcome of the individualism and supremacy of imagination that are the real foundation of the Romantic attitude. Once individualism had been firmly established, the distinctive feelings of the exceptional being assumed a totally new importance, and in the free play of the imagination they soon found a convenient outlet. The emphasis on the so-called 'personal element' is in fact a direct consequence of the shift in the whole conception of art that is the essence of the Romantic revolution. Whereas previously the artist's function had been to adapt and rearrange inherited ingredients, henceforth he was to aim at creation, for which he naturally drew on his own experiences and emotions.

It is only when seen in this context that the Romantic interest in feeling is brought into true perspective.

To approach the subject of Romantic feeling from this angle also helps to elucidate its relationship to the sentimentalism of the preceding age and to clarify the nature of that 'modification générale de la sensibilité ou de son expression artistique' [1] wrought by the Romantic movement throughout Europe. This mutation was gradually taking place in the course of the eighteenth century as the calculating reason of rationalism came to be replaced by the reasons of the heart favoured by the 'Age of Sentiment' that dawned towards the middle of the century. It was then that sensibility came into vogue, an attitude compounded of an innate goodness of heart, a melting softness ever ready to be moved, as well as an instinctive moral tact and leaning to philanthrophy. Perhaps the best definition of this otherwise vague term is offered by Mary Wollstonecraft who regarded sensibility as 'the result of acute senses, finely fashioned nerves, which vibrate at the slightest touch, and convey such clear intelligence to the brain, that it does not require to be arranged by the judgement'. [2] Sensibility thus represents the beginning of a reaction against the intellectualism, the mechanical view of the world dominant in the late seventeenth and early eighteenth centuries. Instead of being subject to the control of reason and will, man was at last to be allowed to act according to instinct, the promptings of his sensibility. Hume in his *Treatise of Human Nature* of 1739 advanced the opinion that reason is and ought to be the slave of the passions, as it was to be for the Man (and Woman) of Feeling, whose prototype was soon to appear.

This release from the straitjacket of rationalism and the concomitant emergence of feeling was common to many European lands. In England the Augustan Age brought protests against too strict a formalism, against turning poetry into a mere mechanic craft. Pope in his *Essay on Criticism* (1711) recognized that the famous rules were 'but nature methodiz'd', while Dryden plainly advocated even their infringement rather than the sacrifices of any great beauty. In place of the intransigent authoritarianism of rationalism, reasonableness was extolled in this period of compromise that succeeded in allying brilliant elegance with a certain correctness. The range and variety of Augustan literature permitted a considerable freedom, certainly sufficient to admit the nascent sentimentalism of the mid-eighteenth century. As early as the first decade of the century the comedies of Cibber and Steele with their tender scenes, declamatory speeches and torrents of tears enjoyed great popularity. With Richardson the 'Age of Sentiment' came into its own: his *Pamela* (1740) and *Clarissa Harlowe* (1747) are overflowing with an emotional morality, designed, to quote the preface to *Clarissa Harlowe*, not 'only to divert and amuse' but rather 'as a vehicle to the instruction'. Thenceforth the sentimental novel was in full spate: Goldsmith's *Vicar of Wakefield* (1766) was followed by Sterne's *Sentimental Journey* (1768), which is reputed to have given the word its European currency. By the early 1770s Richardson and Sterne were diluted and imitated in such middlebrow novels as Henry Brooke's *Juliet Grenville; or, the History of the Human Heart* (1774) and Henry Mackenzie's *Man of Feeling* (1771) in which the emotional susceptibility of a tender heart is valued above the sound judgement of a cool head – surely a clear indication of the change of attitude accomplished by the sentimental novel in the Preromantic period. The Gothic novel that flowered towards the end of the century with the stories of 'Monk' Lewis and Mrs Radcliffe also stemmed from this same current of sensibility, although the sensation aroused by these tales is a shudder of fear. With the sentimental novel, which spread rapidly throughout Europe, the English made an important contribution to Pre-romanticism.

The French on the other hand, under the sway of their seventeenth century Neo-classical tradition, seem tardy and timid in liberating feeling, specially when compared to the English. Rationalism was much more deeply ingrained in French thought since Descartes than it ever had been in the

English stream of pragmatic empiricism. Hence belief in the absolute validity of the rules and in eternal standards of good taste tended to survive surprisingly long in France, indeed right to the end of the eighteenth century. As late as 1799 La Harpe in his *Cours de littérature ancienne et moderne* presented a codified summary of the old outlook. And Voltaire confessed: 'Je n'estime la poésie qu'autant qu'elle est l'ornement de la raison',[3] though he did grudgingly make a slight concession in his *Dictionnaire philosophique* towards 'l'enthousiasme raisonnable'[4] – if that is not a *contradictio in adjecto*. Nevertheless, in spite of these strong reactionary currents, sentimentalism did infiltrate into France, albeit never with the same sweeping force as in England; moreover, during this period of transition when the former ideals were still being upheld halfheartedly, many an advance was followed by a prudent retreat. The most striking instance of such a retrogression is the development of Diderot, whose early theories were almost blatantly emotionalist. Inspired in part by admiration for Shakespeare and Richardson, Diderot for a while advocated a kind of sensationalism in drama, including the use of realistic devices in order to intensify the emotional effect. Later in his life, however, these progressive ideas were profoundly modified by his return to the basic Neo-classical tenets. But in the long run no amount of innate conservatism could block the progress of sentimentalism: in philosophy Condillac's *Traité des Sensations* (1754) marked the advent of sensualism, while on the stage feeling came to the fore in Mercier's moralistic dramas and in La Chaussée's *comédies larmoyantes*, tear-jerking tragi-comedies in which emotion-laden situations are exploited with a good deal of deliberate pathos and in a style heavy with *tendresse, sentiments si doux, douleur amère, ingratitude, désespéré, sensible, adorer,* etc. Thus, notwithstanding the persistence of the long-standing Neo-classical tradition, the way had been prepared for Rousseau's *La Nouvelle Héloïse*, whose appearance in 1761 marked a decisive break-through of the voice of feeling in France.

Paradoxically, Rousseau's voice had less immediate resonance in France than in Germany, where neither the reasonableness of the English nor the rationalism of the French was indigenous. No wonder that Gottsched's attempt to introduce a petty, pedantic Neo-classicism was such a resounding failure, except in that it provoked the first stirrings of a more fruitful aesthetics in the opposition of Bodmer and Breitinger. Gottsched's moralistic dogmatism in fact ran quite contrary to the native tradition, which can best be described as one of free irrationalism. So the violent emotionalism of the young *Stürmer und Dränger* had as its immediate source revolt against the restrictiveness of rules and literary conventions; at the same time, on a deeper level, it represents a resurgence of a characteristically German attitude that had for long lain dormant and had been partially repressed by modish foreign importations. It is also significant that the mid-eighteenth century witnessed the revival of Pietism, a brand of religious belief descended in part from Jacob Böhme's mysticism and nurtured first by Spener and Francke in the last quarter of the seventeenth century, and later by Klopstock, Jung-Stilling and K. P. Moritz. Pietism became an influential force throughout Germany after the foundation of the Herrenhut group by Graf von Zinzendorf: the sibylline Hamann was attracted by its mysticism, the family of Novalis was profoundly steeped in the Herrenhut cult and Goethe too, after his illness in Leipzig, while convalescing at home, came into contact with Pietism through his encounter with his mother's friend, Fräulein von Klettenberg, whose letters and conversations were to form the basis of the 'Bekenntnisse einer schönen Seele'* in book vi of *Wilhelm Meisters Lehrjahre*. The Pietists showed an intense fervour in their quest for God and for eternal values, which they sought not in the orthodox beliefs of organized religion but in the personal experience of the individual heart. There was a parallel movement in England in the religious revival known as Methodism which was akin to Pietism in its exaltation of religious sentiment and in the fervent devotion of its hymns, many of which Wesley had

* 'Confessions of a tender soul'

translated from German. But Methodism spread only slowly
and was in the late eighteenth century a less potent force in
England than Pietism in Germany. Pietism fostered both an
introverted individualism through the importance it attached
to the analysis of the soul and, above all, an immense growth
of emotionalism in that everything was to be apprehended
through intimate revelation, through the personal feelings of
the sensitive heart. 'Ganz Empfindung' [5] is Goethe's phrase to
describe his 'schöne Seele' * at the very outset. This tender,
somewhat sentimental emotionalism of the Pietists was then
fused with the dynamic, ecstatic outbursts of the *Sturm und
Drang* in Goethe's *Werther*, which was as much of a landmark in
the evolution of sentimentalism in Europe as Rousseau's
Nouvelle Héloïse and the novels of Richardson.

It is therefore evident that the Romantics did not initiate
the prominence given to feeling for which they are both
credited and blamed. In England and Germany and also –
though to a rather lesser extent – in France, there was a stream
of sentiment in the eighteenth century so that emotionalism of a
kind was in full bloom before the emergence of any specific
Romantic movement. The enthusiastic reception accorded
throughout Europe to the supposed works of Ossian – poems
'calculated to please persons of exquisite feelings of heart', as
Macpherson stated in his preface to the new edition of 1773 – is
evidence of the widespread taste for this effusive style of writing.
This eighteenth-century emotionalism can most appropriately
be characterized by the word sentimentalism, used not in any
pejorative sense, but in as much as it implies a certain con-
ventionality of both feeling and expression. It is not only the
comédies larmoyantes of La Chaussée and the third-rate German
anacreontic poetry of the time that abound in the standard
figures of rhetoric, reflections of a stock-in-trade sensibility.
Even Richardson's *Clarissa Harlowe* is full of this type of
phraseology: the heroine's heart 'flutters', 'throbs', is 'in
visible palpitations', 'cut by daggers' and 'set a-bleeding';

* 'tender soul'

there is much 'beseeching', 'entreating' and on every other page
'weeping' as tears 'trickle down her bosom', 'bedew her neck',
'bathe her worthy bosom', flowing from her 'deluged eye.'
But this is, at least to the reader of today, a stilted sentimentality, overlaid with moralism and compensating in extravagance
of expression for what it lacks in immediacy and genuineness.

Here the vital distinction arises between the emotionalism
of the mid-eighteenth century and that of the Romantics:
whereas the former was broadly generalized into a set pattern of
responses, the latter was – or affects to be – essentially *personal*
feeling surging directly from experience into an autobiographical
confession. The conventional lyre of Parnassus was replaced
by the strings of the human heart, as Lamartine put it in the
first preface to his *Méditations. La Nouvelle Héloïse* stands
poised midway between the two; in *Werther*, however, the
transmutation has been completed. Goethe himself was fully
conscious of the source of his writings: in *Dichtung und
Wahrheit* he explains that, since the affairs of the heart ('die
Angelegenheiten des Herzens') had always been of prime
importance to him, his poems were so much a precipitate of his
own feelings as to form 'Bruchstücke einer großen Konfession'.[6]
This famous phrase could in fact be applied to a fair amount of
Romantic writing, but not to the products of the 'Age of
Sentiment', which expresses less *spontaneous* than *calculated*
feeling, for the emancipation from rationalism was not yet so
total as to obliterate the mind altogether. The really momentous
break came not with the negative rejection of rationalism, but
with the positive new beginning under the aegis of individualism
and imagination. The expression of feeling could only become
personal, as it did in *Werther*, after the imaginative perceptions
of the individual had been accepted as the basis of artistic
creativity. In that context feeling then appeared in quite
another guise and role than in the 'Age of Sentiment'.

Instead of being a mere repository of the tender sentiments
aroused by sensibility, the human heart represented to the
Romantics the very key to the universe: 'Das Herz ist der

Schlüssel der Welt und des Lebens',[7] according to Novalis. Werther had already recognized this although, characteristically, he put it into more specifically personal terms when he wrote of 'dies Herz, das doch mein einziger Stolz ist, das ganz allein die Quelle von allem ist, aller Kraft, aller Seligkeit und alles Elends'.[8] Rousseau too was convinced of the primacy of feeling: 'Je sentis avant de penser: c'est le sort commun de l'humanité' [9] he commented at the beginning of his *Confessions*, and idealist that he was, he reached the conclusion that 'le coeur fait le vrai bonheur'.[10] On the whole, however, the Romantics envisaged the heart not only, or even primarily, as the fountainhead of happiness and sorrow, but particularly as an organ of knowledge. As a corollary to the rejection of rationalism, the mind was demoted from its controlling position and replaced by the heart as the means of perception: 'The feelings will set up their standard against the understanding, whenever the understanding has renounced its allegiance to the reason',[11] to use Coleridge's words. 'Only what we feel, we know' could well have been the motto of the Romantics; the heart must be believed before the reason because here lies that essential part of man wherein he is linked to the universal spirit. So Coleridge repeatedly asserted that feeling and the response of the heart were a better test of truth than logic; he warned Southey that 'a metaphysical solution, that does not instantly tell you something in the heart is grievously to be suspected'.[12] And because he believed that poetry should be a 'synthesis of thought and feeling',[13] he lamented: 'I *think* too much for a *poet*.' [14] Yet as a critic Coleridge's distinctive quality is epitomized by the phrase: 'I no sooner felt than I sought to understand';[15] first he felt keenly and then he tried to understand and analyse what he had felt. The same subservience of the intellect to the emotional capacity ('ce qu'on a analysé' as against 'ce qu'on éprouve') was one of the main points of Guiraud's exposition of the principles of French Romanticism under the heading *Nos Doctrines* in *La Muse Française* of January 1824. And this was also the approach that Deschamps recommended to his countrymen, whom he criticized in the preface to his *Études françaises et étrangères* for comprehending more and better than they could feel, forgetting, as they tended to, that poetry had to reach the heart. This the Germans were not likely to overlook after the impact of the *Sturm und Drang*, and if perchance they did, Wackenroder and Tieck, in the *Herzensergießungen eines kunstliebenden Klosterbruders* and in the *Phantasien über die Kuns* enthusiastically proclaimed the concept of art as an expression of feeling, to be appreciated by the heart, not the head, Similarly, for Schleiermacher the act of artistic creation was a kind of self-manifestation, tantamount to an externalizing of feeling. But to the German Romantics feeling was the gateway to much besides art. In *Die Lehrlinge zu Saïs*, Novalis showed that nature too could only be grasped by a loving heart, not by the ratio-cination of science or philosophy, for even the scientist had to be guided in his experiments by a mysterious instinct, that springs from feeling. And Novalis added the marginal comment 'Nicht das Herz?' * to an aphorism of F. Schlegel, who main-tained that the imagination was man's organ for the perception of the divine. In emphasizing the role of feeling in religion, in accordance with his Pietist background and upbringing, Novalis concurred with Schleiermacher who defined the essence of religion as 'weder Denken noch Handeln, sondern An-schauung und Gefühl'.[16] Throughout the *Reden über die Religion* Schleiermacher constantly insisted on the emotional nature of religious faith, and as if to underline his own belief he was quite carried away into a declamatory, not to say sentimental manner.

The part that feeling played for the Romantics is therefore both different in quality and far wider in scope than would have been possible for the conventional sensibility of the eighteenth century. The stock emotionalism of the 'Age of Sentiment' was replaced by a personal intensity in perception and expression. The difference is well brought out in Hugo's remark: 'Ce n'est point réellement aux sources d'Hippocrène, à la fontaine de Castalie, ni même au ruisseau du Permesse, que le poète

* 'Not the heart?'

puise son génie; mais tout simplement dans son âme et dans son coeur.' [17] The subjective feelings of the imaginative individual formed the material of poetry, the basis of art, in Hugo's phrase from the preface to *Les Feuilles d'Automne*. So feeling was invested with a powerful new role in the Romantic ideology and even with a new mystical significance. Just as reason had been the universal yardstick of the seventeenth century, now it was feeling that was supposed to provide access to the whole universe, like some magical 'Open Sesame'. This essentially emotional approach is at once a source of strength and of weakness in Romanticism. The latter becomes most apparent in Romantic thought, which is by and large prone to vagueness and diffuseness, not to say confusion for all its flashes of vivid insight; that these peculiarities stem from the dominance of feeling over reason seems beyond doubt. On the other hand, the stress on feeling as the core of art led the Romantics to a greater intensity and to a truer understanding of aesthetic appreciation. In place of the moralistic purpose previously attributed to art, its emotional effect was now brought to the fore. Novalis indeed defined poetry as 'eine Gemütserregungs-kunst',[18] and Coleridge accepted the same criterion when he contrasted poetry and science :

'The common essence of all' (the arts) 'consists in the excitement of emotion for the immediate purpose of pleasure through the medium of beauty; herein contradistinguishing poetry from science, the immediate object and primary purpose of which is truth and possible utility'.[19]

This emotion is excited in the reader because the poet himself is endowed with a greater capacity and depth of feeling beyond the limits of ordinary men; his is 'a life of sensations rather than thoughts',[20] sensations subsequently expressed in his writings, which can thus make others 'feel vividly, and with a vital consciousness emotions which ordinary life rarely or never supplies occasions for exciting, and which had previously lain unawakened.' [21] Always the core of this new type of poetry 'ist eben die Begeisterung, oder das höhere und schönere Gefühl' [22] uppermost in both poet and audience.

This emphasis on feeling as the mainspring of Romantic art led to a concentration on content rather than form. The Romantic, individualistic, introverted and imaginative by temperament, tended to prize emotional experience for its own sake and to devote himself to the exploration and extension of such experience. This was certainly Coleridge's pre-occupation, and it may have encouraged his opium-taking in the same way as writers of to-day are tempted to experiment with hallucinatory drugs. This does not, of course, mean that the Romantics proposed and made no innovations in form : the *Frühromantiker* were full of plans for the evolution of the *Roman* and the *Mischgedicht*, while some of the French Romantics seemed for a time virtually obsessed with technical problems. Nevertheless, on the whole, the expression of emotional, imaginative experience was more important to the Romantic than the actual form in which it was cast. For this reason Romantic art is frequently contrasted with Classical art, which aspires to the balanced perfection of a harmonious beauty. Such a sweeping, schematic antithesis is fraught with the pitfalls of any dogmatic oversimplification. On the other hand, it cannot be denied that Romantic art does appear to disregard form. Hence it succeeds best in the shorter, freer form of the lyric, carried along by a single imaginative, emotional impetus. Even longer poems, as in Keats' case, tended to come to grief, while in the novel the concentration on the sentimental content was undoubtedly at the expense of formal considerations. In his *Observations* on *Obermann* for instance, Sénacour freely admitted :

> Ces lettres ne sont pas un roman. Il n'y a point de mouvement dramatique, d'événements préparés et conduits, point de dénouement; rien de ce qu'on appelle l'intérêt d'un ouvrage.
> On y trouvera des descriptions; de celles qui servent à mieux faire entendre les choses naturelles, et à donner des lumières, peut-être trop negligées, sur les rapports de l'homme avec ce qu'il appelle l'inanimé.[23]

Moreover, even when the Romantics did profess an interest in form, they were still carried away by an imaginative emotionalism, so that some of the technical experiments led, paradoxically, not to the hoped-for expansion of the conventional moulds but rather towards their dissolution. This happened most strikingly in the case of the German *Roman*, which was, according to the theories of the *Frühromantiker*, to become the central vehicle for the art of the future. Even allowing for the highly idiosyncratic interpretation of the term novel to include the plays of Shakespeare, the whole project was hardly feasible from the outset and the results were little short of disastrous. F. Schlegel's *Lucinde*, intended as an example of the new type of writing, was branded an anti-novel ('ein Unroman') by the critically discerning A. W. Schlegel because the usual backbone of a novel, plot and characterization, were abandoned in favour of a kernel of feeling, which was to hold the disparate sections together. Other so-called novels were but slightly less bizarre : the *Herzensergießungen eines kunstliebenden Klosterbruders* consists of a loosely grouped collection of eighteen fragments, unified by their common focus on art; *Franz Sternbalds Wanderungen* by Tieck meanders away into a series of digressions, while Brentano's *Godwi* has rightly been called a novel run wild; even Novalis' *Heinrich von Ofterdingen* remained a fragment, and it too reveals the tendency to break up the accepted narrative form.

Nowhere is this danger of the dissolution of form through the intervention of feeling and imagination more apparent than in the atrophy of drama. It is naïve to wonder, as one critic has done recently, why 'in view of the opportunities . . . none of the Romantics was able to achieve a successful acting play'.[24] The theatrical opportunities may well have been manifold, but the first prerequisite of 'a successful acting play' is a well-defined, finite shape, that is to say the very opposite of the expansive, emotional, imaginative expression preferred by the Romantics. In the whole Romantic movement, in its emphasis on individual experience, in its imaginative explorations and in its subjectivity there lay a principle inimical to dramatic creation. 'The age we live in', wrote Hazlitt in the *London Magazine* of April 1820, 'is critical, didactic, paradoxical, romantic, but it is not dramatic.' For of all the literary genres drama is the most objective, the representational form *par excellence*, and as such the least appealing or fitting to the true Romantic's imaginative, emotional approach. This basic incompatibility between the nature of drama and the inclinations of the Romantic accounts for the Romantics' slight interest in this extrovert form. 'Dem dramatischen Dichter ist es nicht vergönnt begeistert zu träumen, er muß den geradesten Weg zu seinem Ziele gehen',[25] wrote A. W. Schlegel; this was not the manner of the Romantic, who substituted picturesque local colour for the austere plasticity of ancient tragedy, and replaced tragic guilt by passion. So when the Romantics did venture into the dramatic field, they produced either 'plays which are not literature' or 'literary exercises which are not in the fullest sense plays'.[26] Dramatized mythological poems such as Byron's *Cain* and Shelley's *Prometheus Unbound* and *Hellas*, both of which bear the significant sub-title 'A Lyrical Drama', would fall into the latter category, together with the lyrical outpourings of a work like *Manfred* that presents a series of situations without any dramatic conflict. All these, as well as Coleridge's *Remorse*, are dramas of stagnation, in which the action is nothing and the poetry everything. This indeed was the justified complaint of audiences, whose impatience and boredom found vent in George Darley's *Letter to the Dramatists of the Day* (1821). No wonder that this time witnessed an immense increase in the number of printed plays: van Tieghem estimates that of the plays printed in the first three decades of the nineteenth century barely a quarter were ever performed.[27] This fact is hardly surprising considering the difficulties that would face the producer of some of these plays that were either, like those of Byron, static effusions of feeling, or else complex arabesques of an imagination running riot, such as Tieck's *Der gestiefelte Kater* or *Die verkehrte Welt*. In both these satires the dramatic illusion is so

P

persistently broken by interruptions from an audience and all dramatic conventions are so systematically sabotaged as to result in utter chaos, travesties of drama in much the same way as *Lucinde* is an involuntary burlesque of the novel. In all these cases the Romantic showed himself unwilling to fulfil the aesthetic demands of the dramatic genre, which requires a degree of intellectual control. The Romantic preferred to yield to his heart and his instinct, to let his feelings flow forth and his caprice range unchecked : this is not the stuff of drama.

Only when their distinctive characteristics were attenuated, could the Romantics produce effective plays. Thus the German *Schicksalstragödie,** perfected by Zacharias Werner in his melodramatic *Der 24. Februar*, exploited the current fascination with the uncanny and irrational in a lurid, superficial manner, not unlike the Gothic novel. Similarly Shelley, in spite of his dislike of drama and his assertion that he was 'too metaphysical and abstract, too fond of the theoretical and the ideal, to succeed as a tragedian',[28] wrote a moving play, *The Cenci*, well constructed and tightly packed with action that springs from clashes of character. Yet *The Cenci*, significantly, was an exception among Shelley's works, 'written without any of the peculiar feelings and opinions which characterize my other compositions; I have attended simply to the impartial development of such characters as it is probable the persons represented really were.'[29] Furthermore, Shelley took care to point out that 'I have avoided with great care in writing this play the introduction of what is commonly called mere poetry'.[30] It is certainly no coincidence that the least personal, the least poetic of Shelley's works, that most divorced from subjective emotions should be successful as a drama. And the French produced more dramas during the early nineteenth century than either the English or the Germans partly because their brand of Romanticism was in fact so unlike the imaginative idealism of their Anglo-Saxon and Teutonic contemporaries. Even so Francophile a critic as von Tieghem has conceded that French Romantic drama was devoid of 'les

* 'tragedy of fate'

points les plus avancées du romantisme imaginatif et lyrique'.[31]
Since the French Romantic movement was to a considerable
extent inspired by opposition to an out-worn Neo-classicism,
its drama naturally evolved in rebellion to the rigid rules of the
seventeenth century. It was, therefore, in many respects similar
to the German *Sturm und Drang* type of drama, in the Shakespearean tradition rather than specifically Romantic, concerned
above all with the conquest of freedom. A comparison of such
plays as Hugo's *Hernani* and *Ruy Blas* or Musset's *Lorenzaccio*
with, say, Byron's or Shelley's dramatic poems or with Tieck's
caprices only serves to show how far removed certain products
of the French Romantic school are from the mainstream of
European Romanticism. The vehemence, the worship of the
great, forceful hero even if a criminal, the historical setting, the
declamatory style of the French dramas all proclaim their kinship with the early plays of Goethe and Schiller and with
Shakespeare. *Manfred, Cain* and *Prometheus Unbound*, on the
other hand, are remarkable for fine lyrical passages of real
feeling, while Tieck's plays and even the melodramas of
Zacharias Werner abound in imagination. They are, however,
less effective theatrically as dramas than the French plays because the Romantic principles of feeling and imagination on
which they are based, are inimical to the finite, objective
character of the genre.

In the prominence given to drama the French Romantics once
again differed from their counterparts in England and Germany.
Romantic drama aroused little interest in England and Germany
and attracted excessive attention in France, where it was
Romantic chiefly in name. Perhaps, though, the passion with
which the French Romantics debated problems of dramatic
technique could be cited as another instance of that dominance
of feeling over reason characteristic of the Romantic approach
to life and art.

The Expression of Feeling

<hr/>

THAT the personal feelings of the imaginative individual form the basis of art was unanimously accepted by the Romantics. There is indeed hardly any other tenet in the Romantic credo on which so remarkable a degree of agreement is found throughout Europe. But in the ways in which that fundamental feeling is actually expressed in the writings of various poets there are immediate and profound differences, depending both on the poet's own personality and on the literary tradition in which he is embedded. It is illuminating to borrow – and extend – Hugo's vivid image from the preface to *Les Feuilles d'Automne*, where he compared the human heart to the earth:

> Le coeur humain est comme la terre, on peut semer, on peut planter, on peut bâtir tout ce qu'on veut à sa surface; il n'en continuera pas moins à produire ses verdures, ses fleurs, ses fruits naturels; mais jamais pioches ni sondes ne le troubleront à de certaines profondeurs; mais de même qu'elle sera toujours la terre, il sera toujours le coeur humain; la base de l'art, comme elle de la nature.[32]

Just as the earth is the ground common to all nature, though it produces shrubs, flowers and trees of various species according to the characteristics of the soil and the climate of the region, so the feelings of the human heart are the basis of Romantic art, but like the vegetation of the earth, they may become manifest in differing styles and with varying intensity. Thus there emerges once again in the expression of feeling, as in the effects of individualism and the workings of the imagination, a pattern of national as well as individual divergences within a basic structure of similarity.

The fruitful soil for Romantic poetry then is the belief that it springs from 'the spontaneous overflow of powerful feelings'.[33] That phrase of Wordsworth's is probably the most familiar piece of Romantic theory in the English language, and as such has made no small contribution to the widespread equation of Romanticism with the outpouring of feeling. However hackneyed it may seem to us, it nevertheless neatly sets forth a conception of poetry held by most of the European Romantics, albeit with certain variants of emphasis and interpretation. In as far as it was a common denominator, it provides a convenient starting-point for an examination of Romantic poetry, particularly with a view to discerning those variants. For the sake of clarity, the two main notions in Wordsworth's phrase, that of an 'overflow' and that of spontaneity will be discussed separately.

A. *'Overflow'*

Although it was Wordsworth who formulated the idea of good poetry as an 'overflow of powerful feelings', he himself was far from an unqualified acceptance of this concept. He certainly upheld the primacy of feeling, the view that the mainspring of poetry is emotion, yet it is significantly 'emotion recollected in tranquillity',[34] to quote another well-worn dictum. This implies none of that wild passion conjured up by the term 'overflow', but rather a reflecting detachment on the part of the poet who expresses his feelings to some purpose. To Wordsworth poetry was in fact a more serious business than the self-indulgent outpouring of personal emotions:

> Poetry is the most philosophic of all writing: its object is truth, not individual and local, but general and operative; not standing upon external testimony, but carried alive into the heart by passion; truth which is its own testimony, . . . Poetry is the image of man and nature.[35]

Feeling was thus for Wordsworth a means whereby to convey to men's hearts that ultimate truth which is the real quest of his poetry. Accordingly each of his poems, he maintained, has a purpose, a *worthy* purpose : 'to follow the fluxes and refluxes of the mind when agitated by the great and simple affections of our nature.' [36] All this is very different from what might be expected from a poet who sees the origins of poetry in 'the spontaneous overflow of powerful feelings'. The essential point to grasp is that the expression of feeling was never an end in itself to Wordsworth, but rather a means subordinate to a higher purpose. For this reason there is no contradiction between Wordsworth's advocacy of feeling and his avowed moral intent. In a lengthy footnote in the second *Preface to the 'Lyrical Ballads'* [37] Wordsworth outlined the underlying object, the moral sentiment inherent in several of his poems including *The Idiot Boy, Simon Lee, The Brothers, We are Seven,* etc. This awareness of a deeper purpose in poetry beyond the personal expression of feeling is borne out by Wordsworth's picture of the poet not as a prophet in an ivory tower but as 'a man speaking to men', admittedly 'a man . . . , endowed with more lively sensibility, more enthusiasm and tenderness, who has a greater knowledge of human nature, and a more comprehensive soul than are supposed to be common among mankind'.[38] Nonetheless, for all his gifts, this is an artist who travels at men's sides as well as occasionally before them, to use Wordsworth's own words from a letter to John Wilson, in which the moral aim of poetry is made quite explicit : 'A great poet ought to rectify men's feelings, to render their feelings more sane, pure, and permanent.' [39] Poetry then was to Wordsworth much more than an 'overflow of powerful feelings', a straightforward 'Herzensergießung'* in Wackenroder's telling term; it has a definite social and moral function that is performed through the intermediacy of the poem's emotional drive. In the combination of these two usually disparate elements lies the special quality of Wordsworth's poetry. The novel – indeed, at the time even revolutionary – title of his collection, *Lyrical Ballads,* hinted at a fusion of two strains, the emotional and the narrative, whereby the lyrical ballad became the vehicle of

---

* 'outpouring of feeling from the heart'

personal feeling objectified. Starting from his own emotional reaction to an incident or a scene, Wordsworth recounted it in the substance of the poem in order to lead back at the end to the original emotional impetus. This is his method in the two poems *I wandered lonely as a cloud* and *Resolution and Independence*, whose genesis can be traced back directly to the happenings recorded in his sister's journal. Both are carried along by the 'powerful feelings' that inspire the descriptions and the meaning contained in them; both in fact bear out Wordsworth's contention 'that the feeling therein developed gives importance to the action and situation, and not the action and situation to the feeling'.[40] In his finest poems Wordsworth achieved a rare harmony of the lyrical and the epic, feeling and narrative. There may well be two voices in his poetry: the one that has been called Augustan that is heard in the accuracy of observation, the colloquial realism, the sober factuality that keeps the eye riveted on the object, and the other, Romantic in its depth of feeling, its refreshing idealism and its imaginative modification of phenomenal reality.[41] In unison these two voices are the source of Wordsworth's strength as a poet, each checking the potential excesses of the other. Therefore the 'powerful feelings' reside in his poems, rather than actually 'overflow' from them, for the subjective call of emotion is counterbalanced by the objective voice of social communication. Wordsworth sought

<blockquote>
to control
Rebellious passion: for the Gods approve
The depth, and not the tumult, of the soul.[42]
</blockquote>

Opposed to violence of feeling, he chose rather to portray the quieter heroism of endurance in *Michael*, *Simon Lee*, *Resolution and Independence*, *Ruth*, to name only a few. Throughout Wordsworth's poetry, the feelings, powerful though they be, remain under the poet's control to be used to good purpose.

Although Wordsworth's manner is far too individual to be regarded as typical, in a sense he is nevertheless characteristic of the way in which the English Romantics approached the

expression of feeling. For there is by and large little vehement
'overflow' of feeling in English Romantic poetry and even less
of those intimate confidences in which the French writing of the
period abounds. Perhaps the English esteem of moderation and
good sense, the tradition of reserve, had a tempering effect.
Keats certainly exalted feeling, even criticizing Milton on the
grounds that 'he did not think into the human heart as Wordsworth has done'.[43] But to Keats feeling meant not so much
personal sentiment as the emotional experience of beauty. His
own poems bear witness to the truth of his statement: 'I never
wrote one single line of poetry with the least shadow of public
thought.'[44] Keats was profoundly convinced that 'with a great
poet the sense of Beauty overcomes every other consideration',[45]
and in a letter of 22 December 1817 he wrote to his brothers
that 'the excellence of every Art is its intensity'.[46] It is this
glorification of beauty as an absolute standard that has earned
Keats the reputation of an intellectual, a pure, an aesthetic poet.
Yet he was passionate in expressing the beliefs of his heart,
which form the matter of his poetry and which he prized above
personal feelings. Thus Keats, like Wordsworth, represents a
modified 'overflow of powerful feelings', and the same may be
said, perhaps surprisingly, of Byron, who is generally considered
the most blatantly exhibitionist of the English Romantic poets.
In contrast to his iconoclastic views on the role of the imagination, he did conform to the Romantic estimate of feeling:
'poetry is the expression of excited passion.'[47] But in Byron's
poetry two voices are as clearly audible as in that of Wordsworth; besides the voice of 'excited passion' telling of itself,
there is the increasingly loud mocking note of self-irony. The
balance between these two oscillates: in the mawkish intemper-
ances of *Childe Harold's Pilgrimage* the former is dominant; in
the satirical realism of *Don Juan*, however, Byron's ironic wit
turns one of the world's traditional sentimental stories into a
gay tale of comical disillusionment. This raillery, which is one
of the chief features of Byron's writings, countered any tendency
to any undue indulgence in feeling.

Among the English Romantic poets, it is not Byron but Shelley whose poetry is the most unalloyed 'overflow of powerful feelings'. This may well account, in part at least, for the disfavour into which Shelley has recently fallen. The following passage sums up the contemporary case against Shelley : 'He is sentimental : that is, he calls for a greater display of emotion than the modern reader feels to be warranted by the occasion. He employs pronounced, intoxicating, hypnotic rhythms that seem to be trying to sweep the reader into hasty emotional commitments.' [48] It is true that the strongest impression made by Shelley's poetry is an emotional quality, which defines itself more precisely than the rather vaguely outlined situations and ideas that aroused it. This, however, is an outcome of Shelley's theory of aesthetic creation : the moment of inspiration appeared to him the highest climax, the fleeting vision of transcendent reality; beside this, the mind in composition was a mere 'fading coal', as he put it in *The Defence of Poetry*. Accordingly Shelley was, perhaps subconsciously, somewhat unwilling to use his rational mind to shape the magnificent inspiration. In consequence some of his poems seem to spring like the song from the skylark :

> Pourest thy full heart
> In profuse strains of unpremeditated art.

This 'unpremeditated' outpouring of the 'full heart' suggests the use of language for as direct as possible an expression of emotional states, dependent as little as possible on intellectual analysis and ordering, thereby fulfilling Shelley's ideal as a poet. The focus is always on the original emotional inspiration, which is conveyed in a succession of rapturous cries, in that superabundance of images, for which Shelley is as frequently criticized as for his alleged sentimentality. The two are facets of the same unchallenged supremacy of 'powerful feelings' which flow out in a profusion of images :

> I fall upon the thorns of life! I bleed!

> A heavy weight of hours has chained and bowed
> One too like thee : tameless, and swift, and proud.

Shelley exclaimed in the *Ode to the West Wind*. In such laments
as this or the closing stanza of *The Indian Serenade* :

> Oh lift me from the grass!
> I die! I faint! I fail!
> Let thy love in kisses rain
> On my lips and eyelids pale.
> My cheek is cold and white, alas!
> My heart beats loud and fast; —
> Oh! press it to thine own again,
> Where it will break at last

there is a streak of self-dramatization, of self-pity alien to the
English liking for stoicism. In this, as in his attitude to nature,
Shelley was indeed closer to his French contemporaries than to
his own compatriots. Like Lamartine and Musset, Shelley
believed that 'our sweetest songs are those that tell of saddest
thought.' [49] Yet overflowing with emotion though Shelley may
seem when measured against Wordsworth and Keats, he appears
on the contrary quite restrained beside, say, Lamartine with his
constant jeremiads :

> Ma harpe fut souvent de larmes arrosée;
> Mais les pleurs sont pour nous la céleste rosée;
> Sous un ciel toujours pur le coeur ne mûrit pas. [50]

The ornamentation of Lamartine's loaded imagery suggests
something of the pleasure derived from the tears liberally
scattered throughout his poetry. How the baroque conceits of
Lamartine's expression contrast with the simple starkness of
Shelley's line, quoted above, which states a similar idea! Only
through a comparative study can a correct assessment be made
of the degree of Shelley's sentimentality.

The restraint of the English poets does not become fully
apparent until it is measured against the exuberance of the
French, who wanted to 'burn the paper' instead of 'recollecting
emotion in tranquillity'. The 'overflow of powerful feelings' was

undoubtedly strongest in France, where it took the form of personal poetry. The poems of Lamartine, Musset and Hugo hold up a mirror to the poet's intimate life by presenting a kind of journal of impressions, ideas and primarily, of course, of feelings. Like the fight for individual freedom and the quest for naturalness, this deliberate emphasis on the personal element and the consequent spate of confessional poetry formed part of the reaction against a Neo-classicism that held the ego to be hateful. In this historical setting Mme de Staël's *De la Littérature* and *De l'Allemagne* appeared like manifestoes in favour of Romantic subjectivism. With her admiration for sensibility of every kind, she interpreted Shakespeare as the master of pathos and Goethe as the head of the melancholy school. She made the presence of sensibility one of the criteria for distinguishing between ancient and modern literature : 'la poésie des anciens est plus pure comme art, celle des modernes fait verser plus de larmes,' [51] and realizing as she did that French literature was in need of a new direction, she pointed to the development of subjectivism as a possible path. Thenceforth the emphasis was incessantly on the role of feeling, the heart in artistic creation : 'le coeur seul est poète,' [52] wrote Chénier, while Soumet, in a review of Hugo's *Nouvelles Odes* in *La Muse Française*, demanded that writers should possess first and foremost what he called 'le génie des émotions'.[53] The Romantic poets themselves were almost unanimous on this point. For Musset the issue was clear : 'L'art, c'est le sentiment,' [54] he laid down. Hugo's views were very similar : 'Qu'est-ce en effet qu'un poète ? Un homme qui sent fortement, exprimant ses sensations dans une langue plus expressive. La poésie, ce n'est presque que sentiment.' [55] The sole exception to this glorification of feeling was Vigny, whose admiration for stoicism in the face of suffering led him to a scale of values other than that of his contemporaries :

> Il y a plus de force, de dignité et de grandeur dans les poètes *objectifs* épiques et dramatiques tels qu'Homère, Shakespeare,

Dante, Molière, Corneille, que dans les poètes *subjectifs* ou
élégiaques se peignant eux-mêmes et déplorant leurs peines
secrètes, comme Pétrarque.[56]

It was in keeping with this judgement that Vigny estimated the
heart, if not exactly inferior, at least subject to the intellect:
'Le coeur existe bien, moralement parlant. On sent ses mouve-
ments de joie et de douleur; mais c'est une chambre obscure
dont la lumière est la tête.' [57] In this respect, as in his attitude
to imagination, Vigny stood somewhat apart from the French
Romantic poets, whose statements are startlingly like the
theories of the young *Stürmer und Dränger* in the Germany of
the early 1770s; in fact the situation of the French Romantics
in the first three decades of the nineteenth century bears a
striking resemblance to that of the earlier German group in
that both were in revolt against a tradition that had become
exhausted and sterile and so both were fighting to make a new
start. Lamartine was conscious of this renaissance when he
described the Romantic movement as a 'résurrection du sentiment moral et poétique' [58] in *Des Destinées de la Poésie*, a survey
of the history of poetry in which he attacked the rationalistic
past in contrast to the spiritual, poetic present and future. For
Lamartine, moreover, and indeed for all the French Romantics,
it was sensibility, rather than imagination, which was the poet's
cardinal quality. French Romantic theory thus differs from
English and German in laying as great a stress on feeling as the
Sturm und Drang had done. This is to the detriment of imagination, that played so decisive a part in English and German
Romanticism, but did not really come to the fore in France until
the Symbolist period later in the nineteenth century. What first
appears as a mere question of varied emphasis eventually turns
out to be a basic divergence of character.

Where imagination reigned supreme, as in England and
Germany, it was the poet's visions of a transcendent reality that
stood in the foreground. Whereas in France, where feeling far
outdid imagination in importance, poetry was envisaged as the

direct product of emotion. Hence personal poetry achieved a prominence in France unparalleled elsewhere. The French Romantics were convinced that 'les grands écrivains ont mis leur histoire dans leurs ouvrages. On ne peint bien que son propre coeur, en l'attribuant à un autre'.[59] Chateaubriand took this doctrine of utter, inevitable subjectivism so far as to interpret Milton's portrayal of Adam and Eve as a reflection of the English poet's own relationship to his wife! Notwithstanding this exaggeration, Chateaubriand's view found ample resonance among the Romantics. Stendhal, with his insistence on sincerity, held that 'on ne peut peindre ce qu'on n'a pas senti'.[60] Hugo was even more specifically autobiographical for he believed that the figure of the author stands out clearly from every work. In the 1822 preface to the *Odes et Ballades* he called poetry 'tout ce qu'il y a d'intime dans tout' [61] – hardly the most illuminating of definitions, but one that again underlines the inward, personal nature of poetry in Hugo's eyes. This is borne out once more in the preface to *Les Rayons et les Ombres*, where Hugo extolled 'cette profonde peinture du moi' [62] as the summit of the poet's achievements : surely a clear brief for the extreme subjectivism of the French Romantic lyric. Lamartine was no less explicit in his confession : 'je m'exprimais moi-même pour moi-même.' This he elaborated in his argument that poetry was for him a kind of personal catharsis : 'Ce n'était pas un art, c'était un soulagement de mon propre coeur, qui se berçait de ses propres sanglots . . . Ces vers étaient un gémissement ou un cri de l'âme.' [63] Lamartine himself gave the most pertinent characterization of the resultant poems when he referred to them as 'des retours sur moi-même, des plaintes ou des délires personnels'.[64] This description would be equally apposite to much of Musset's poetry, the most totally self-centred poetry of the whole Romantic movement. The form in itself is already significant for it is no coincidence that Musset frequently chose to express himself in dialogue, a dialogue that is really a monologue in that the exchanges are between the poet and his muse, that is two aspects of himself, or between the poet and his

vision of his double, 'qui me ressemblait comme un frère.' [65]
Lamartine too wrote a dialogue between his soul and himself
('dialogue entre mon âme et moi') in *La Vigne et la Maison*,
but in Musset's case, all his poetry in effect consists of exchanges
between the various aspects of his ego. He holds a mirror up to
himself, as he listens to the voice of his heart :

> La bouche garde le silence
> Pour écouter parler le coeur.[66]

Again and again Musset returned to this favourite theme, the
primacy of the heart, of feeling in poetry :

> De ton coeur ou de toi lequel est le poète ?
> C'est ton coeur. . . .[67]

> Ah frappe-toi le coeur, c'est là qu'est le génie.[68]

> Sachez-le. – c'est le coeur qui parle et qui soupire
> Lorsque la main écrit. – c'est le coeur qui se fond ;
> C'est le coeur qui s'étend, se découvre et respire
> Comme un gai pèlerin sur le sommet d'un mont.[69]

And this heart, which pours its feelings out into the poems is
'mon faible coeur',[70] always an afflicted heart. For Musset
believed that sorrow was almost a necessary prerequisite of
poetry; in the famous lines that introduce the comparison of the
poet to a pelican in *La Nuit de Mai* he wrote :

> Rien ne nous rend si grands qu'une grande douleur,
> Mais, pour en être atteint, ne crois pas, ô poète,
> Que ta voix ici-bas doive rester muette.
> Les plus désespérés sont les chants les plus beaux,
> Et j'en sais d'immortels qui sont de purs sanglots.[71]

The parallel, in content between these lines and Shelley's

> Our sweetest songs are those that tell of saddest thought.

is quite obvious. Yet the context, the tone and the whole underlying attitude are so different as to give some measure of the
range of feeling within the Romantic movement. Shelley accepts
pain and sorrow as a part of life, as a foil to its joy :

We look before and after,
And pine for what is not;
Our sincerest laughter
With some pain is fraught;
Our sweetest songs are those that tell of saddest thought.

Yet if we could scorn
Hate, and pride, and fear;
If we were things born
Not to shed a tear,
I know not how thy joy we ever should come near.[72]

There is a calm, a balance in these stanzas that is reflected in their very form. Musset, on the other hand, constantly raised the pitch to the melodramatic by his deliberate exaltation and exploitation of suffering, and this tendency is plainly apparent in the imagery (e.g. 'de purs sanglots', the pelican) and in the oratorical style of his *Nuits*. In Musset's poetry the 'overflow of powerful feelings' characteristic of the French Romantic lyric became a veritable deluge.

Vigny alone forms an exception in his detachment from personal sentimentality just as his evaluation of imagination diverged from that of his compatriots. Vigny indeed rejected the fashionable exhibitionism of the tearful Romantic poets with as much vehemence as Leconte de Lisle, who accused them of selling their sorrows. Curiously, Vigny even used the same image in *Chatterton*: 'Ouvrir son coeur pour le mettre en étalage sur un comptoir! S'il a des blessures, tant mieux! il a plus de prix; tant soit peu mutilé, on l'achète plus cher!' [73] Although Vigny often showed compassion for human suffering, he never glorified it and his greatest admiration was for the nobility of stoical endurance, for his faith lay in the human spirit ('l'esprit pur') as the ultimate vehicle of progress. This moralistic strain suggests a certain resemblance to Wordsworth alongside their similar use of imagery. It is perhaps worth noting that Vigny had a strong interest in English poetry since his youth and eventually married an English woman. Thus, with emotions no less deep or intense than his contemporaries,

Vigny shunned too facile and effusive a manner of expression;
the word 'I', he wrote in an entry in the *Journal d'un Poète* on
31 January 1835, seemed to him the hardest word to pronounce
in a becoming manner. Instead he translated his personal
feelings into generalizations, conveyed not so much directly as
in parables and images. Again the role of feeling is in inverse
ratio to that of the imagination. Moreover, Vigny's restraint in
the expression of feeling was accompanied by a preoccupation
with form, part of the same attempt to impose order on verbal
as well as emotional chaos. In this respect Vigny was ahead of
the French Romantic poets. Gradually Hugo, Lamartine and
even Musset came to realize the limitations of a lyricism that
recorded only the 'overflow of powerful feelings' and attached
increasing importance to the social function of poetry. Nevertheless, it is the French Romantics who are chiefly responsible for
the widely diffused image of Romantic poetry as a sentimental
effusion of subjective feelings.

There was far less of this among the German Romantics
than among the French; in fact there was surprisingly little
'overflow of powerful feelings'. This moderation in the expression of emotion is all the more unexpected from a group that
espoused the Fichtean philosophy of subjectivism, fostered the
primacy of the individual, coined the term *Herzensergießung*
and altogether tended to extremism in both doctrine and practice. There would seem, however, to be several reasons for the
lack of 'overflow' in German Romanticism. The first could be
called historical: the great break-through of subjective feeling
had already been accomplished by the *Sturm und Drang*. What
the French Romantics were fighting for in the 1820s – liberation
from the yoke of literary rules, freedom of individual expression,
the release of emotion and imagination – all this had been
achieved in the 1770s in Germany in the tremendous explosion
of dynamic impetus known as the *Sturm und Drang*. It was then
that the rather conventional feelings and worn figures of speech
characteristic of the sentimentalism of Klopstock's predecessors
were ousted by the vigorous natural impulses of the young

Goethe and Schiller and their fellow 'Stormers'. It was then also that *Werther* was born. So that the conception of poetry as an outpouring of emotion was fully accepted in Germany many years before the Romantic school as such emerged. In consequence, the *Frühromantiker* saw little need to assert this notion since it was already taken for granted, just as the English paid scant heed to the individualism that was inherent in their tradition.

With the primacy of feeling safely posited, the German Romantics concentrated on the elaboration of a radical new theory of imagination. Although this shift of emphasis was in itself an outcome of the full acceptance of feeling as the basis of poetry, it was in turn instrumental in a certain recession of feeling from the supreme position it had held in the *Sturm und Drang*. This is a matter of balance common to the whole of the Romantic movement: it is like a seesaw, with feeling at one end and imagination at the other; in proportion as the one rises, the other goes down, and vice versa. Among the French Romantics, where imagination was viewed with some distrust, feeling shot up in importance, except for Vigny, who kept a more level keel. The English on the whole maintained a fairly even balance, perhaps slightly weighted towards imagination, and very much so in the case of Blake. In this seesaw the Germans came down decidedly on the side of imagination. The personal emotional experience fundamental to Romantic art, was sublimated and expanded to have a wider meaning – in other words, transformed by means of the imagination in the same way as the *Frühromantiker* sought to transform the whole world. For example, Wackenroder's impressions of the baroque towns of Southern Germany turned into a paean of the art of the Middle Ages in the *Herzensergießungen eines kunstliebenden Klosterbruders*. Similarly Novalis' esoteric visions at Sophie's grave were, in the course of the *Hymnen an die Nacht*, invested with a universal significance valid for all mankind through the association with Christianity. Hoffmann's double life as artist and lawyer found its precipitate in the dualism of

Q

his tales. In each case the purely personal feeling was transmuted
into an imaginative perception: the 'overflow' was directed
along special channels. In the same way the *Hochromantiker*
expressed feeling in their lyrics not directly and subjectively
in the manner of the French Romantic poets, but rather music-
ally and in images. Their poems are softer, more fluid, more
emotional than the lyrical ballads or odes of the English
Romantics, which communicate a distinct content, whereas the
German lyrics are above all carriers of mood, the famous
Stimmung. Brentano, Eichendorff, Uhland and Mörike all
created atmosphere by means of rhythm, sound pattern and a
series of suggestive images. A poem such as Brentano's
Abendständchen depends for its mysteriously hypnotic effect on
the use of repetition, long dark vowels, synesthesia and vague,
swimming pictures that seem to dissolve into the very mood
they conjure up. The whole poem is charged with emotion, yet
none is stated point-blank. The same oblique method is characteristic of Uhland's *Frühlingsglaube* in which the phenomena of
nature are personified in order to bring out that coming to life
in spring that is the poem's theme. The joy of spring is conveyed
by the repeated chorus, the vocatives, the exclamations, the
spotlight on words such as *schaffen* and *blühen** that tell of the
renewal of life: the feeling behind *Frühlingsglaube* is instilled
into pregnant images and sounds. This is equally true of
Eichendorff's *Mondnacht*; the opening picture of the moonlit
night –

> Es war, als hätt' der Himmel
> Die Erde still geküßt,
> Daß sie im Blütenschimmer
> Von ihm nur träumen müßt.[74]

– is at once both realistic and highly imaginative. The poet
appears only to be describing the texture of the moonlit night:
the rustle of the forest, the gentle swaying of the corn, the
silence; but at the same time he is evoking all the enchantment

---

* create and blossom

of such a night, the curious sense of peace that lulls mind and soul. Once again an emotional state has found expression through an imaginative perception. Thus the ascendancy of the imagination in German Romanticism acted as a check on the direct 'overflow of powerful feelings'.

Another controlling factor can be discerned in the strange concept of irony as elaborated by F. Schlegel. This was no ordinary irony, no mere sarcastic mockery, but, as F. Schlegel put it, a higher irony, a constant agility of the mind that never loses sight of the whole game of life. Unfortunately F. Schlegel's aphorisms, hardly models of clarity at any time, seem particularly opaque on the subject of irony. The best short explanation, to my mind, is that of R. Huch, who described Romantic irony as 'ein geistiges Fliegenkönnen'.[75] This clever phrase implies the self-detachment that is the essence of any irony, low or high. This was, moreover, hinted in A. W. Schlegel's comment on irony as 'ein in die Darstellung selbst hineingelegtes mehr oder weniger leise angedeutetes Eingeständnis ihrer übertreibenden Einseitigkeit in dem Anteil der Fantasie und Empfindung'.[76] With his customary perspicacity A. W. Schlegel realized that irony could be a corrective to those excesses to which German Romanticism was prone. In its self-conscious awareness of itself, of its own feelings and attitude, irony already goes some way to the redress of immoderation. This ability demanded of the artist to raise himself above himself, in F. Schlegel's jargon, is part of the sophistication of German Romanticism, as well as a confession of its own artificial refinement. This is surely implicit in Novalis' startling admission in the first *Blütenstaub* fragment: 'Wir suchen überall das Unbedingte, und finden immer nur Dinge'[77] – ironical also in its clever play on the words 'unbedingt' and 'Ding'. However bizarre the workings of this irony may have been in many instances, there can be no doubt as to one of its side-effects: it was by its very nature bound to curb any extravagant 'overflow' of feeling.

Had the French Romantics possessed the kind of self-detachment that is a prerequisite of irony, they could not have

indulged in so heedless an effusion of personal emotions. Nor
was there any equivalent to this type of irony among the English
Romantics except perhaps in the satirical humour of Byron.
But in England the innate aversion to display and the moral
earnestness sufficed to counteract any 'overflow of powerful
feelings' as effectively as the ascendancy of imagination and the
concept of irony in Germany. The popular idea of Romantic
poetry as an effusion of sentiment is fulfilled only in France.

B. *'Spontaneous'*

The adjective chosen by Wordsworth to describe the 'overflow of powerful feelings' refers to a quality that is, like the
outpouring of sentiment itself, generally attributed to Romantic
art. In fact emphasis on spontaneity, in one sense or another,
was an essential part of the total reorientation underlying the
rise of Romanticism throughout Europe, no doubt in reaction
to the previous cult of so-called correctness. But the interpretation given to 'spontaneous' varied considerably from
writer to writer, from group to group and from country to
country, depending as much on individual preferences as on the
historical context. So once again the fundamental similarity that
first meets the eye is profoundly modified on closer inspection.

For Wordsworth himself 'spontaneous' was synonymous with
'natural', as Coleridge realized when he defined Wordsworth's
programme for the *Lyrical Ballads* in chapter XIV of *Biographia
Literaria* as 'faithful adherence to the truth of nature'. In
contrast to the elegance and wit cultivated by the Augustans,
Wordsworth sought above all that which he called 'spontaneous'. So novel was this type of poetry that he had to add to the
second edition of the *Lyrical Ballads* the preface in which he set
out his aims and methods : 'The principal object, then, proposed
in these poems was to choose incidents and situations from
common life, and to relate or describe them, throughout, as
far as was possible, in a selection of language really used by

men.' [78] Spontaneity, in the sense of naturalness, thus had two facets for Wordsworth: subject matter and language. In the original *Advertisement* to the *Lyrical Ballads* of 1798 Wordsworth already advocated 'a natural delineation of human passions, human characters and human incidents',[79] as the stuff of poetry. This view forms the basis for Wordsworth's preference for domestic themes and rustic settings, to which his contemporaries, however, took such exception that he offered a lengthy apologia in the *Preface* of 1800:

> Humble and rustic life was generally chosen, because, in that condition, the essential passions of the heart find a better soil in which they can attain their maturity, are less under restraint, and speak a plainer and more emphatic language; because in that condition of life our elementary feelings co-exist in a state of greater simplicity, and consequently, may be more accurately contemplated, and more forcibly communicated; because the manners of rural life germinate from those elementary feelings, and, from the necessary character of rural occupations, are more easily comprehended, and are more durable; and, lastly, because in that condition the passions of men are incorporated with the beautiful and permanent forms of nature.[80]

This appraisal of simple life and people was, of course, not new at the time; the growing interest in folk-song had drawn attention to the utterances of ordinary people, such as Herder had recommended:

> 'Wer noch bei uns Spuren von dieser Festigkeit finden will, der suche sie ja nicht bei solchen' (i.e. gelehrten Leuten): 'unverdorbne Kinder, Frauenzimmer, Leute von gutem Naturverstande, mehr durch Thätigkeit als Spekulation gebildet, die sind, wenn das was ich anführte, Beredsamkeit ist, alsdenn die einzigen und die besten Redner unsrer Zeit'.[81]

But in Herder's case this plea stemmed from a Rousseauistic worship of the primitive, as exemplified by Ossian; its latent motive was a rejection of present reality in favour of the distant: in other words, it was a Romantic procedure. Whereas Wordsworth created his poetry out of the natural human life close at hand: the 'incidents and situations from common life' are so portrayed as 'to throw over them a certain colouring of imagination, whereby ordinary things should be presented to the mind in an unusual aspect'.[82] What Wordsworth was really attempting was better formulated by his collaborator on the *Lyrical Ballads*, Coleridge, in his comment in chapter XIV of *Biographia Literaria*:

> Mr Wordsworth . . . was to propose to himself as his object to give the charm of novelty to things of everyday, and to excite a feeling analogous to the supernatural, by awakening the mind's attention from the lethargy of custom, and by directing it to the loveliness and the wonders of the world before us; an inexhaustible treasure, but for which, in consequence of the film of familiarity and selfish solicitude, we have eyes, yet see not, ears that hear not, and hearts that neither feel nor understand.

How perceptive and articulate a critic Coleridge was. It was indeed in lending 'the charm of novelty to everyday things' that the innovation of the *Lyrical Ballads* lay. In an age when men were wont to search for the simple and spontaneous among primitive peoples in distant lands (e.g. Rousseau, Chateaubriand, Bernardin de Saint-Pierre, Herder, Coleridge's and Southey's Pantisocratic project), Wordsworth discovered it in the daily round of unaffected country-folk. Again and again in poems too numerous to mention he drew a picture of the domestic affections (his own phrase in a letter to Charles James Fox about *Michael*) and sorrows of the rustics he knew; often too he made children or idiots the subjects of his poems because their feelings and utterances flow out all the more spontaneously. Nowhere is Wordsworth's kinship with the German Poetic Realists of the mid-nineteenth century more apparent than in this concentration on the ordinary affairs of the world around us. Like the Poetic Realists, he appreciated the small, unpretentious things in the world around us, the quiet heroism of the enduring heart. Wordsworth nearly always took a real happening or figure as his starting-point; his own notes and references to his sister's *Journal* show how many poems grew out of minute observation of a natural object, which retains its features though charged with significance. He had the power, like the Poetic Realists, to make common things, in their utmost detail, expressive. Moreover, he insisted on using 'the language of conversation in the middle and lower classes',[83] for the poet, he argued, 'must express himself as other men express themselves' [84] instead of in some peculiar poetic direction. By opting for the language of ordinary men, Wordsworth was pursuing his own quest for the spontaneous in the sense of the natural. Hence much of his best poetry has a directness, a simplicity, a firmness, a realism that is in startling contrast to the fanciful effusiveness usually associated with the Romantic expression of feeling.

Wordsworth was in fact too realistic for many of his contemporaries who criticized and scoffed without mercy. The most vehement attacks came from the critic Jeffrey and from Blake: 'I see in Wordsworth the Natural Man rising up against the Spiritual Man Continually, and then he is No Poet but a Heathen Philosopher at Enmity against all true Poetry or Inspiration.' [85] Extreme though this condemnation is, it was only to be expected from a poet who recognized the validity of nothing other than the inner, imaginative vision. What is more, Blake was to some extent right in so far as the ideal of spontaneity as naturalness, which was Wordsworth's interpretation, is alien to the essence of Romanticism with its overriding emphasis on imaginative transfiguration. There were other, though less weighty criticisms: Shelley's accusation of dullness in the satirical *Peter Bell, the Third* and Tennyson's witticism that Wordsworth's poetry is in parts 'thick-ankled'.[86] The most judicious assessment was that of Coleridge, who found fault with the 'INCONSTANCY' [87] of Wordsworth's style, which led to 'anti-climax and hyper-climax', and who sensed in Wordsworth's poetry 'a something corporeal, a matter-of-factness, a clinging to the palpable, or often to the petty'.[88]

Notwithstanding these often well founded objections, Wordsworth's championship of the spontaneous, the natural in language and theme is indicative of an important streak in English Romanticism, one that distinguishes it quite fundamentally from its German and French counterparts, namely its realism. In almost all of its theories and works, with remarkably few exceptions, the English Romantic movement is characterized by a certain moderation, in contrast to the excesses of the French and the Germans, as though the English tradition of good sense, level-headedness, and pragmatism were conspiring to maintain an even balance, so that English Romantic writing never lost the redressing element of realism. Wordsworth was by no means alone in his plea for more natural language; in the preface to *The Cenci* Shelley recommended 'the real language of men in general' for 'I entirely agree with those modern critics who assert that in order to move men to true sympathy we must use the familiar language of men'.[89] Likewise Coleridge believed that 'works of imagination should be written in very plain language; the more purely imaginative they are the more necessary it is to be plain'[90] — a comment particularly interesting in view of his own procedure in such poems as *The Ancient Mariner*, *Christabel* and *Kubla Khan*, in which he translated the weird world of his visions into relatively concrete pictures :

> In Xanadu did Kubla Khan
> A stately pleasure-dome decree :
> Where Alph, the sacred river, ran
> Through caverns measureless to man
> Down to a sunless sea.
> So twice five miles of fertile ground
> With walls and towers were girdled round :
> And there were gardens bright with sinuous rills,
> Where blossomed many an incense-bearing tree;
> And here were forests ancient as the hills,
> Enfolding sunny spots of greenery.

The language of *Kubla Khan* can hardly be called 'plain', yet the whole description as such does convey a certain outlandish reality. Its almost tangible quality becomes more evident when it is placed beside Novalis' evocation of his dream-world in the second part of *Heinrich von Ofterdingen* :

Sie waren jetzt auf einen geräumigen Platz im Holze gekommen, auf welchem einige verfallne Türme hinter tiefen Gräben standen. Junges Gebüsch schlang sich um die alten Mauern, wie ein jugendlicher Kranz um das Silberhaupt eines Greises. Man sah in die Unermeßlichkeit der Zeiten und erblickte die weitesten Geschichten in kleine glänzende Minuten zusammengezogen, wenn man die grauen Steine, die blitzänlichen Risse und die hohen schaurigen Gestalten betrachtete. So zeigt uns der Himmel unendliche Räume in dunkles Blau gekleidet und wie milchfarbne Schimmer, so unschuldig wie die Wangen eines Kindes, die fernsten Heere seiner schweren ungeheuren Welten.[91]

Whereas Coleridge's words conjure up before the reader's eyes a mysterious, private pleasure-garden, Novalis' setting, after a fairly precise start, evaporates alarmingly into a mystical perception of transcendental truths (as indeed does the whole novel). Coleridge's 'imaginative realism' – to borrow Bowra's apt phrase [92] – is even better illustrated by *The Ancient Mariner* in which the unnatural events seem to develop from natural elements so that the whole narrative is veiled in a mysteriousness into which the reader is drawn as compulsively as the wedding-guest. The tale's hypnotic effect derives from the directness of the story-telling, from the simplicity of the diction with its discriminating use of repetition, imagery and musical cadence, and not least from the realism of the description full of gruesome details from the known world that lend conviction to the supernatural. With what ease and apparent spontaneity Coleridge creates the mariner's world :

> And now there came both mist and snow,
> And it grew wondrous cold :
> And ice, mast-high, came floating by,
> As green as emerald.

> And through the drifts, the snowy clifts
> Did send a dismal sheen :
> Nor shapes of men nor beasts we ken –
> The ice was all between.

> The ice was here, the ice was there,
> The ice was all around :

> It cracked and growled, and roared and howled,
> Like noises in a swound!

Who could refrain from shuddering at this vivid evocation of a world that is, like Kafka's, both real and unreal. Coleridge's poems may have been inspired by the visions of his imagination, but their success is due in no small measure to the realism of presentation which gives them their special cogency.

Keats too, for all his reputed aestheticism and his conscious development of his poetic powers, insisted on the need for a spontaneous, natural flow of poetry. In a letter to John Taylor of 27 February 1818 he demanded that imagery 'should like the sun come natural natural', and he repeated the same key word when he went on to posit as an axiom 'that if poetry comes not as naturally as the leaves to a tree it had better not come at all'.[93] Keats' imagery in his finest poetry is indeed so totally integrated into the very fabric of the poem (e.g. *Ode to Autumn*, *Ode to a Nightingale*) as to seem entirely 'natural natural'. Moreover, his poetry does appear to come 'as naturally as the leaves to a tree' in that the imaginative transfiguration evolves out of a precise observation of reality, such as is not usually credited to Keats. The atmosphere grows out of a kaleidoscope of realistic details; for instance the coldness of *The Eve of St Agnes* comes home in the opening verse in a series of distinct pictures:

> St Agnes' Eve – Ah, bitter chill it was!
> The owl, for all his feathers, was a-cold;
> The hare limp'd trembling through the frozen grass,
> And silent was the flock in woolly fold:
> Numb were the Beadsman's fingers, while he told
> His rosary, and while his frosted breath,
> Like pious incense from a censer old,
> Seem'd taking flight for heaven. . . .

Even a poem so completely imaginative in its perception as the *Ode to Autumn* has a realism that is all too often overlooked:

> And full-grown lambs loud bleat from hilly bourn;
> Hedge-crickets sing; and now with treble soft

The red-breast whistles from a garden-croft;
And gathering swallows twitter in the skies.

Thus in England spontaneity was interpreted as naturalness and this in turn fostered a strain of realism evident in both observation and expression. It is perhaps worth recalling in this context that in the 1959 exhibition of European Romantic art the English pictures stood out in that they were chiefly landscapes (Constable, Turner, Crome, Ward), inspired by real scenes, as against the symbolical images that dominated the paintings of Delacroix, Friedrich, Runge, Schwind, Overbeck. Such clear-cut distinctions are, of course, invidious, as is revealed by a glance at the drawings or writings of Blake, who was totally possessed by his imaginative visions. But this glaring exception, proof again of English individualism, does not invalidate the contention that on the whole the English remained in closer contact with reality than either the Germans or the French. The real was never severed from the ideal, as with the *Frühromantiker*; on the contrary, Coleridge repudiated Schelling's opposition of real and ideal as false. The real was completely integrated with the imaginative in the poetry of Wordsworth, Coleridge and Keats. With Byron or a sceptic such as Peacock, the two elements jostled each other quite happily. Byron's ambiguous attitude towards the Romantic hero and his technique of deliberate anti-climax in the repeated drop from the sublimity of the ideal to the banality of the real brand him as much a Realist as a Romantic. And this is equally true of Peacock with his good sense, his practical pragmatism, his awareness of the absurd on the one hand, and on the other, his idealism, his delight in the past as a time of organic unity, and his occasional unabashed sentimentality. So Romanticism was never divorced from Realism in England as on the Continent. The whole development of English literature was evolutionary in character and therefore not given to such violent swings. It is perhaps worth adding that the Industrial Revolution was less of a revolution in England than in either France or Germany because it started early and advanced gradually with little of the sudden shock it produced on the Continent. Similarly, in literature there were no sharp divisions; indeed, on the very fringes of the Romantic movement in England a vigorous realism flourished in Scott's descriptions of low life, in Burns' robust portrayal of Scotland, in Crabbe's faithful picture of rural England and in the psychological insights of Jane Austen's social novels. The presence of this current of Realism both within and alongside English Romanticism in itself prevented that extremism to which Romanticism was by nature inclined and to which it tended to succumb in France and Germany.

The equipoise of the English is once again thrown into relief by comparison with the French, for whom spontaneity had such different implications. In the battles of the French Romantic revolution the demand for spontaneity was one of the chief clarion-calls. Spontaneity was to lyric poetry what emancipation from the three unities was to drama : the symbolical quintessence of the freedom for which the French Romantics were fighting. Whereas Boileau had advised :

> Aimez donc la raison; que toujours vos écrits
> Empruntent d'elle seule et leur lustre et leur prix.[94]

the Romantics made the drastic reversal embodied in Musset's words : 'Mon premier point sera qu'il faut déraisonner.' [95] The same rejection of the old standards is implied in Hugo's observation, in the preface to the *Orientales*, that the French had always modelled themselves on Boileau, while other nations looked to Homer, Dante, Shakespeare, who had come to be regarded as the prototypes of Romanticism. In place of the conventionally correct, but restrained writing of the past, the Romantics therefore sought above all spontaneity, which to them meant the direct outpouring of feeling without the control of any aesthetic discipline that might savour of the former restrictions. In fact this creed of spontaneity was very similar to that of the German *Stürmer und Dränger*, who had likewise thrown all the sterile rules overboard. As in the Germany of the early 1770s, in France some fifty years later the floodgates of emotion were thrown open in a tremendous upsurge of enthusiasm. Poetry was to be a 'spontaneous overflow of powerful feelings', rushing unchecked straight from the heart. Whole works were to be 'plutôt improvisés que composés' [96] according to Mme de Staël, one of the leading apostles of this inspirational conception of writing. In the very first chapter of *De la Littérature* already she had expressed the view that modern poetry, consisting as it did predominantly of eloquent passion, was the child of enthusiasm set on fire. This notion that every book should 'jaillir d'un seul jet' [97] and be published without revision persisted with a peculiar tenacity throughout the statements of the French Romantics. Lamartine, for instance, boasted in the *Avertissement* to his *Harmonies* :

> Voici quatre livres de poésies écrites comme elles ont été senties, sans liaison, sans suite, sans transition apparente : la nature en a, mais n'en montre pas; poésies réelles et non feintes, qui sentent moins le poète que l'homme même, révélation intime et involontaire de ses impressions de chaque jour, pages de sa vie intérieure inspirées tantôt par la tristesse, tantôt par la joie. . . .[98]

This is evidently a very different kind of spontaneity to that practised by the English poets. Although the French Romantics also aimed at truth and naturalness, they referred these ideals more particularly to drama, where they strove for realism in opposition to the artificiality of the rule-ridden plays of their predecessors. But in the field of lyric poetry, truth and naturalness were not conceived as in England to denote 'faithful adherence to the truth of nature' in both matter and manner, but rather as the truth of the heart's emotions, to be expressed exactly as they were felt ('écrites comme elles ont été senties'). Thus the English interpretation of spontaneity led to a more realistic type of poetry, whereas the French exaltation of spontaneity as equivalent to purely inspirational writing tended to reinforce the emotional currents of their brand of Romanticism with its strong emphasis on personal feeling. 'Être touché' was 'le véritable art' [99] when poetry became exclusively a product of the 'spontaneous overflow of powerful feelings'.

This overriding concern in French Romantic poetry with content and spirit had as its corollary a certain disregard for form. It is a curious contradiction within the French Romantic movement that so much thought, space and energy were devoted to the controversies surrounding dramatic form, while at the same time little heed was paid to questions of poetic form. When Hugo discussed verse form in the preface to *Cromwell*, he was referring to dramatic, not lyrical verse. Poetic theory was hardly more than a passionate plea for the free flow of emotion, and this conception of poetry as pure feeling with its worship of spontaneity led to a neglect, often even a scorn of conscious form in the belief that the first flush of inspiration was bound to produce the best results. The certainty that 'le coeur seul est poète' had as its complement – in fact literally, in the other half of Chénier's Alexandrine – the conviction that 'l'art ne fait que des vers'.[100] The turmoil in the poet's heart was to be reflected in – not corrected by – the language and form of the spontaneous poem. It is hardly surprising that this resulted in poetry that was not only effusive to the point of excess, but also rather loose in form, lacking the density and concision characteristic of the finest lyrics. There is too much abundance on the surface and too little of that hidden wealth that makes each reading of any really great poem an exciting voyage of discovery. For this reason many of Lamartine's and some of Musset's poems seem to go on far too long; the words continue so surge out as if uncontrolled, after the substance of the poem has made its impact. As Gilman has pointed out, 'French Romantic poetry is rich in great passages rather than in great poems. Rarely does a poem of any length maintain a high level throughout'.[101] *Le Lac*, for instance, after the grandiose and poignant image of the opening, relapses into the rather ponderous, repetitive rhetoric of its second half. Similarly, Hugo's *A Villequier* loses its initial impetus as it lapses disappointingly into platitudinous exclamations. Both these poems confirm

Gilman's belief that it is the intrusion of false rhetoric that accounts for the striking unevenness of many French Romantic poems. Lacking the check inherent in a finite form, such as the sonnet, the poet could all too easily surrender to the flow of emotion – hollow as well as genuine. Thus the element of theatricality, which is undeniably present in French Romantic poetry, is in some subterranean way connected with the neglect of form that is a consequence of the cult of spontaneity.

The exaltation of feeling above all else led not only to diffuseness of form, for fear that orderliness might blunt the direct expression of emotion, but also to an undue display of passion in grandiloquent rhetoric, as though the poet were speaking from the rostrum rather than pouring out his heart for his own relief. This declamatory quality of the French Romantic lyric has frequently been noted. It is most evident in Hugo's early work with its whole paraphernalia of exclamations, repetitions, contrasts and sonorous endings :

> Heureux qui de l'oubli ne fuit point les ténèbres!
> Heureux qui ne sait pas combien d'échos funèbres
>   Le bruit d'un nom fait retentir!
>   Et si la gloire est inquiète,
>   Et si la palme du poète
>   Est une palme de martyr!
>
> Sans craindre le chasseur, l'orage ou le vertige,
> Heureux l'oiseau qui plane et l'oiseau qui voltige!
>   Heureux qui ne veut rien tenter!
>   Heureux qui suit ce qu'il doit suivre!
>   Heureux qui ne vit que pour vivre,
>   Qui ne chante que pour chanter! [102]

The same oratorical devices (enumerations, exclamations, contrasts) are just as common throughout Lamartine's verse :

> O lac! rochers muets! grottes! forêt obscure!
> Vous que le temps épargne ou qu'il peut rajeunir;
> Gardez de cette nuit, gardez, belle nature,
>   Au moins le souvenir.[103]

Similar examples abound on every page, and as in the case of

Musset, these rhetorical outbursts are generally associated with a blatant self-melodramatization :

> O Muse! que m'importe ou la mort ou la vie ?
> J'aime, et je veux pâlir; j'aime, et je veux souffrir;
> J'aime, et pour un baiser je donne mon génie;
> J'aime, et je veux sentir sur ma joue amaigrie
> Ruisseler une source impossible à tarir.[104]

The mawkish emotionalism of the situation has spilled over into the technique and language. The spontaneity that bred naturalness and thence realism in England brought forth rhetoric in France.

This strain of oratorical rhetoric in French Romantic poetry has been interpreted as a vestige of the old Neo-classical habits against which the Romantics were up in arms. Hugo may have shouted : 'Aux armes, prose et vers! formez vos bataillons!' and vaunted that :

> sur les bataillons d'alexandrins carrés,
> Je fis souffler un vent révolutionnaire.
> Je mis un bonnet rouge au vieux dictionnaire.[105]

But whether the technical liberalization introduced by the Romantic poets really implied a radical break with the past is open to question. Many critics have discussed this point at length : Hazard, for example, has argued that French Romantic poetry always retained 'ses qualités traditionelles : goût obstiné de la composition et de l'ordre, clarté, netteté; modération au moins relative : prompte reprise après les abandons; raison toujours vigilante'.[106] His conclusion – that 'l'esprit classique n'a pas tellement perdu ses droits, même sur notre romantisme, qu'il ne s'oppose aux excès et aux fureurs incohérentes du sentiment' [107] – coincides with that of Moreau who, in his tendentious book *Le Classicisme des Romantiques*, espied Classicism in every use of a word such as *char*,* indeed, even in any interest in human nature, without, however, really

* chariot

defining either Classicism or Romanticism beyond distinguishing between the unity of the former and the diversity of the latter. Nevertheless there is some truth in Moreau's contention of a certain 'sagesse cachée' [108] not only in so reasoned and reasonable a work as Stendhal's *Racine et Shakespeare*, but also in the apparently iconoclastic preface to *Cromwell* in its great reliance on such terms as *cependant* and *en effet*,* and particularly in Hugo's tendency to see and explain everything in terms of antithesis. This marked preference for antithesis in French Romantic poetry can be seen as merely another form of the Classical love of symmetry, just as its emotional grandiloquence comes strangely to resemble the rhetorical oratory of Neo-classicism. Whether, in the last resort, these technical factors add up to a tyranny of Classicism over French Romanticism remains a very debatable point, and there is no need to go as far as Strich, who saw France as the land of Classicism, the un-Romantic nation *par excellence*.[109] On the other hand, there can be no doubt that the declamatory tone and the flowery style of an overflowing emotionalism stifle all pretensions of spontaneity. The means used to achieve spontaneity in France are, paradoxically, self-defeating so that the French Romantic lyric still appears self-conscious beside the naturalness of the English.

The difference is well illustrated by a juxtaposition of two poems, one French, one English, both on the same theme and both, by a curious coincidence, written in the year 1819 : Lamartine's *L'Automne* and Keats' *Ode to Autumn*.† For Lamartine autumn is above all a time of death and mourning : in the very first stanza the dominant idea of ending and fading is brought out in such phrases as 'bois couronnés d'un reste de verdure', 'feuillages jaunissants', 'le deuil de la nature', and later there are explicit references to 'ces jours d'automne où la nature expire', to the charms of this season :

> C'est l'adieu d'un ami, c'est le dernier sourire
> Des lèvres que la mort va fermer pour jamais.

* however and indeed
† For texts of poems and translation see Appendix B.

R

This moribund aspect of nature pleases the poet because it mirrors his own melancholy – 'convient à la douleur'; just as the joys of summer are over with the advent of autumn that leads to the desolation of winter, so the poet too feels his life drawing to a close. Throughout the poem this parallel is implied between the season and the poet's life, culminating in the final stanza with 'la fleur tombe' and its corresponding echo, 'moi, je meurs'. But although the poem bears the title *L'Automne*, surprisingly little is really said about it; only the first and the third stanzas are given to an interpretation of autumn and even this dwells far more on mood than on descriptive detail. The rest of the poem, certainly from the fourth stanza onwards, where the comparison between the autumn without and the autumn within is made in the lines beginning:

> Ainsi, prêt à quitter l'horizon de la vie,
> Pleurant de mes longs jours l'espoir évanoui,
> Je me retourne encore . . .

– from this point on *L'Automne* is solely concerned with the poet's own emotions, as the preponderance of 'je' indicates. Lamartine is beset with an undefined grief, a kind of *mal du siècle* perhaps ('je suis d'un pas rêveur le sentier solitaire') that drives him to despair of future happiness. It is this that really forms the main theme of the poem, for which the autumnal season merely provides a starting-point. In the central section (stanzas iv–viii), without a mention of autumn except the closing comparison of himself to the dropping flower-petals, Lamartine paints a vivid picture of his lachrymose state of mind, mobilizing sundry rhetorical devices at his disposal (enumerations, exclamations, antithesis) to achieve the desired effect:

> Terre, soleil, vallons, belle et douce nature,
> Je vous dois une larme sux bords de mon tombeau!
> L'air est si parfumé! la lumière est si pure!
> Aux regards d'un mourant le soleil est si beau!

'Aux regards d'un mourant' is perhaps the operative phrase:

Lamartine gives a melodramatic impression of autumn as it appears to a man who imagines himself to be dying.

Keats, ironically, really was already dying when he wrote his *Ode to Autumn*, yet he sees it 'with rosy hue' as a time not of death but of harvest. From the outset he emphasizes the richness of autumn's gifts ('mellow fruitfulness', 'fill all fruit with ripeness to the core', 'swell the gourd', 'plump the hazel shells with a sweet kernel', 'set budding more, / And still more, later flowers') and his is 'the maturing sun' in contrast to Lamartine's 'soleil pâlissant'. The abundance and gentleness that are the main features of autumn in Keats' eyes are reflected in the stately lines, the long vowels, the whole slow, dignified movement of these ample verses that seem as laden with riches as the season itself. With barely a backward glance at 'the songs of Spring' Keats gladly accepts autumn for 'thou hast thy music too'. This is the only fleeting note of reflection in an ode that is entirely about autumn. Keats responds to autumn with his sense of sight, of taste, of touch and of hearing; he brings it to life in his remarkable pictorial imagery, personifying it first as the 'close bosom-friend of the maturing sun', then 'sitting careless on a granary floor' or 'on a half-reap'd furrow sound asleep', or 'like a gleaner', or watching 'by a cyder-press, with patient look', all images drawn from the harvesting that symbolizes autumn's wealth. In this sustained evocation of the figures and moods of autumn there is never any intrusion of the poet's own feelings, such as virtually obliterates autumn in Lamartine's poem. Keats seems to disappear into the very fruits of autumn, emerging only in the last stanza to observe and describe after the briefest of questionings :

> Where are the songs of Spring? Ay, where are they?
> Think not of them, thou hast thy music too, –
> While barred clouds bloom the soft-dying day,
> And touch the stubble-plains with rosy hue;
> Then in a wailful choir the small gnats mourn
> Among the river sallows, borne aloft
> Or sinking as the light wind lives or dies;

Such a description would be inconceivable to Lamartine who is totally absorbed in his own emotions. His poem springs from a cultivation of personal feeling while Keats' *Ode to Autumn* grows out of a delight in the sensuous beauty of the world around him, a delight most acutely experienced by a man aware of the likelihood of early death. Keats' poem gives an imaginative illumination of what he has seen and felt in autumn; his perception is so intense and his expression is at once so vivid and so apt as to transfigure this season for the reader, to whom autumn must surely always be 'the season of mists and mellow fruitfulness'. The chief impression derived from Lamartine's poem, on the other hand, is of the poet's own feelings, the grief of a man who had indeed been struck by a deep sorrow, but who seems, almost voluptuously, to enjoy it as he displays it in a torrent of picturesque oratory. In spite of the danger of generalizing from a comparison of single works, it is tempting to see in the contrast between these two poems an image of the difference between the English and the French Romantic lyric.

To complete the spectrum, a glance at one of Eichendorff's autumn poems, *Herbstweh,** reveals the qualities of the German lyric as practised by the poets of the *Hochromantik*. Much briefer than either of the other two poems, *Herbstweh* makes the impression of a folk-song. Its thought is as uncomplicated as its language, composed as it is mostly of short words and direct statements ('ich bin so müd' ', 'bald kommt der Winter'). It has the abruptness of the folk-song, launching straight into the subject without preliminary description, and conveying unequivocally the weariness that is common to the season and to the old man, the decline of both the year towards the snow of winter and of the human life towards the grave. Yet for all its apparent simplicity and directness, it is not so much a poem of statement as of a state in that its primary intent is the evocation of an atmosphere. This is evident from the opening line, devoid of a verb, a phrase that seeks to set a mood rather than to impart a fact. And all the words are chosen to reinforce the dominant

---

* For text and translation see Appendix B.

atmosphere of a gentle melancholy without drama, after the heat of summer and life's passions are spent: 'müd' ', 'welk', 'verblüht', as well as the repeated 'fallen'. This is a fine example of what is known as a *Stimmungsgedicht*, a poem that evokes a mood, such as the poets of the *Hochromantik* cultivated.

Herbstweh has, too, a certain spontaneity, but very different in kind to that of the English and French Romantic poems – a spontaneity that is comprehensible only in the context of the peculiar predicament of the *Hochromantiker* which requires some elucidation. First it is vital to make a clear distinction between the *Frühromantik* and the *Hochromantik* : the former frankly cared little for spontaneity, a quality that had featured prominently in the programme of their predecessors, the *Stürmer und Dränger*. Consequently the *Frühromantiker* sought not so much to express their feelings freely, since this had after all been done already, as rather to mediate their imaginative perception of the transcendental. So theirs was a highly sophisticated, indeed one might quite fairly say, an over-sophisticated art, fervent in character, exclusive in appeal, with strong religious, mystical overtones. By contrast, the *Hochromantik*, in retreat from the complexities of *Frühromantik* transcendentalism, returned more towards the ideals of the *Sturm und Drang*. For instance, the *Sturm und Drang* interest in the past, specially in the Middle Ages, which the *Frühromantiker* had interpreted as a vaguely Christian Utopia, became with the *Hochromantiker* a part of their growing national consciousness. Pride in the German heritage took a practical form in the study of the origins of the German language as well as of German literature. Hence the primitive utterances of the folk-song or tale fascinated the *Hochromantiker* at least as much as they had Herder, with the difference that the latter collected the songs of all peoples, as the title of his anthology, *Stimmen der Völker* indicates, whereas Brentano's and Arnim's *Des Knaben Wunderhorn* concentrated solely on German songs, like Görres' *Die teutschen Volksbücher*, tales that had been passed on orally from generation to generation in German families.

It was through this revival of interest in folk-song that the *Hochromantiker* learned to prize spontaneity, in place of the excessive self-consciousness implied by the *Frühromantik* concept of irony. The traditional *Volkslied*, reputed to be spontaneous song, was now extolled as a model of naturalness and simplicity and contrasted with the modern artist's *Kunstlied* which, however well wrought – or *because* it was well wrought – could not equal the direct impact of the natural utterance. This glorification of all so-called *Naturpoesie* at the expense of *Kunstpoesie** is the recurrent theme of Tieck's *Die altdeutschen Minnelieder*, Arnim's *Von Volksliedern* Görres' introduction to *Die teutschen Volksbücher* and J. Grimm's correspondence with Arnim in 1811. The distinction between 'natural' and 'created' poetry is somewhat reminiscent of Schillers' division into 'naïve' and 'sentimental', although the Romantics were much more drastic in that all modern writing was branded as the product of reflection, and therefore dismissed as inferior to the instinctive, spontaneous poetry of the ancient bards. The dangers of such an indiscriminate generalization are fully illustrated by the ridiculous Ossian episode when the whole of Europe was hoaxed into a craze for this spurious primitive poetry. Obviously this sudden cult of naturalness after a phase of metaphysical sophistication was not without artificiality, as is betrayed by the tortuous style of several of these pleas for spontaneity :

> Die Gelehrten indessen versaßen sich über einer eigenen vornehmen Sprache, die auf lange Zeit alles Hohe und Herrliche vom Volke trennte, die sie endlich doch entweder wieder vernichten oder allgemein machen müssen, wenn sie einsehen, daß ihr Treiben aller echten Bildung entgegen, die Sprache als etwas Bestehendes für sich auszubilden, da sie doch notwendig ewig flüssig sein muss, dem Gedanken sich zu fügen, der sich in ihr offenbart und ausgießt; denn so und nur so allein wird ihr täglich angeboren, ganz ohne künstliche Beihülfe. Nur wegen dieser Sprachtrennung in dieser Nichtachtung des besseren poetischen Teiles vom Volke mangelt dem neueren Deutschland

---

* The contrast is between *Naturpoesie*, 'natural' poetry, i.e. folk-song, traditional tales and *Kunstpoesie*, 'artistic', created poetry.

großenteils Volkspoesie, nur wo es ungelehrter wird, wenigstens überwiegender in besondrer Bildung der allgemeinen durch Bücher, da entsteht manches Volkslied, das ungedruckt und ungeschrieben, zu uns durch die Lüfte dringt, wie eine weiße Krähe.[110]

What a fine case of the pot calling the kettle black!

Fortunately the practitioners of spontaneity were less constrained than the theoreticians. Indeed, the lyricists of the *Hochromantik* were remarkably successful in capturing the tone and atmosphere of the folk-songs which they took as their models, as *Herbstweh* shows. They aimed not so much to imitate as to re-create the naturalness of the folk-song in their own poems. It is a measure of their achievement that many Germans are unable to discriminate the genuine from the made folk-song, so fully have many of the poems of Mörike, Eichendorff, Uhland and Heine – some further enhanced by the musical settings of Schubert, Schumann and Mendelssohn – become a part of the national heritage. These lyrics owe their immediate appeal and their immense popularity to a whole combination of factors: in this deliberate attempt at a renewal of the folk-song certain favourite figures and themes, already associated with folk-poetry, were chosen: the shepherd, the fisherman, the miller, the gypsy, the maiden at her spinning-wheel, the mother at her child's cradle, the forsaken lover, the traveller etc. Even more important was the use of particular forms (for instance, the ballad) and above all of a style and manner of expression as direct and unadorned as that of the true folk-song. This is an art of apparent artlessness as either a tale is told or a mood evoked with an ease and simplicity that almost defy intellectual examination. With a poet of such conscious skill as Heine the source of his effectiveness can still be discerned in the clever technique of repetitions, of long and short words, of alliteration and assonance, but when the lyric of the *Hochromantik* comes closest to the folk-song, its spontaneity is beyond analysis. Faced with Uhland's *Der gute Kamerad* even so intelligent a critic as Korff [111] all but admitted defeat.

These lyrics of the *Hochromantik* seem to invite comparison
with the poems of Wordsworth since both aspire to naturalness
as their ideal. Like Wordsworth, who wrote about a reaper, a
leech-gatherer, an old Cumberland beggar and so forth, the
Hochromantiker often took ordinary people as their subjects:
the shepherd, the soldier, the maiden at work in the kitchen.
These characters, however, are generalized prototypes, usually
without name, whereas Wordsworth's figures are more specific,
inspired in many cases by people he had actually met. Whether
they were prompted by a particular incident or not, Wordsworth's poems tend to start from a visual impetus:

> Behold her, single in the field,
> Yon solitary Highland lass!
> Reaping and singing by herself,
> Stop here, or gently pass!
> Alone she cuts and binds the grain,
> And sings a melancholy strain;

These are the opening lines of *The Solitary Reaper*; the same
habit of beginning with a picture is found in *The Old Cumberland
Beggar* and in many other poems:

> I saw an aged Beggar in my walk;
> And he was seated, by the highway side,
> On a low structure of rude masonry
> Built at the foot of a huge hill, that they
> Who lead their horses down the steep rough road
> May thence remount at ease. The aged Man
> Had placed his staff across the broad smooth stone
> That overlays the pile; and, from a bag
> All white with flour, the dole of village dames,
> He drew his scraps and fragments, one by one;
> And scanned them with a fixed and serious look
> Of idle computation. In the sun,
> Upon the second step of that small pile,
> Surrounded by those wild unpeopled hills,
> He sat, and ate his food in solitude:
> And ever, scattered from his palsied hand,
> That, still attempting to prevent the waste,
> Was baffled still, the crumbs in little showers

Fell on the ground; and the small mountain birds,
Not venturing yet to peck their destined meal,
Approached within the length of half his staff.

The first impression is therefore predominantly visual, with close concentration on a real object which Wordsworth has observed and described with a meticulous attention to detail. Only later in the course of the poem does the visual fuse with the visionary when the object's significance becomes apparent. In the lyric of the *Hochromantik*, on the other hand, the visual element is of far less importance; instead of having an autonomous existence, as in Wordsworth's poems, it is always associated with, indeed subject to the emotional context. At the beginning of Eichendorff's *Das verlassene Mägdlein* –

> Früh, wenn die Hähne krähn,
> Eh' die Sternlein verschwinden,
> Muß ich am Herde stehn.
> Muß ich Feuer zünden.
>
> Schön ist der Flammen Schein,
> Es springen die Funken;
> Ich schaue so drein,
> In Leid versunken.[112]

– the descriptive touches act as a framework to the human figure : in the first stanza the bleakness of early morning colours the dreariness of the girl's menial tasks, while in the second the warmth, beauty and movement of the flame contrast with the stasis induced in her by her sorrow. Moreover the descriptive elements, like the characters themselves, remain generalized (the cocks, the stars, the flames) as against Wordsworth's eye for very precise detail. In the lyric of the *Hochromantik* description serves almost exclusively to set the atmosphere. Thus Eichendorff's *Das zerbrochene Ringlein* starts with this apparently simple, yet strangely hypnotic phrase :

> In einem kühlen Grunde
> Da geht ein Mühlenrad [113]

With its long dark vowels and mysteriously slow movement it is a superb introduction to the poem's haunting sadness.

Das zerbrochene Ringlein shows yet another characteristic of the *Hochromantik* lyric : the tendency to monologue, explicitly, as in *Das verlassene Mägdlein,* Eichendorff's *Der Einsiedler,* Uhland's *Der gute Kamerad,* or implicitly when the poet muses to himself. Wordsworth too allowed his characters to speak, but more often than not his poems took the form of a conversation : *The Fountain, We are Seven, The Two April Mornings, Expostulation and Reply.* The exchange between two people suggests an orientation outwards, towards others, whereas the German technique of monologue looks essentially inwards into the one person whose feelings are expressed. Mörike and Eichendorff identified themselves with their subject, illuminating it from inside, so to speak, while Wordsworth contemplated his object from outside, standing aside to comment at a distance from a social rather than a psychological point of view. *The Solitary Reaper* presents the picture of the girl at work in the fields and the sound of her song; *Das verlassene Mägdlein* leaves us less with a picture than with an impression of the girl's state of mind. Yet for all its emotional depth, its vocabulary looks in fact simpler and more spontaneous than that of *The Solitary Reaper*; in its apparent artlessness, however, a good deal of artfulness lies hidden. Both achieve a kind of naturalness; Wordsworth's is the more straightforward naturalness, stemming from his observation of reality; that of the *Hochromantiker* is of a more stylized character, determined by the introverted, imaginative approach typical of German Romanticism. Hence the *Hochromantiker* were as deeply committed to the evocation of mood and atmosphere as Wordsworth was to the objects and figures of the outer world. To him spontaneity in poetry meant the description, in plain language, of ordinary sights and happenings. To the *Hochromantiker* it signified a highly articulate re-creation of naïvety. And to the French it spelt the outpouring of personal emotion with as much eloquence as could be mustered. The interpretations of the one, seemingly simple term could hardly be more diverse in theory and in practice.

*   *   *

There is thus in the role and expression of feeling in European Romanticism the same interplay of similarities and differences between the various lands as in the case of individualism and imagination. Once again a certain common foundation exists in the universal agreement on the importance of feeling as such, although from the very outset divergences of emphasis become apparent. In France, there is a much more vociferous advocacy of the central place of feeling in poetry than in either England or Germany. In the actual expression of feeling it is the differences that predominate in a whole gamut of possible attitudes ranging from the restrained earnestness and realistic tendencies of the English to the rhetorical exuberance of the French, while the complex German notion of irony and the equally self-conscious cult of spontaneity represent more sophisticated attitudes towards the expression of feeling. These variations derive largely from the diversity of the historical background in the various lands. In France the outburst of emotion was at its most violent and took the form of a glorification of personal feeling poured forth in highly emotional terms because these very features had been so rigorously repressed by the rules, the good taste, the propriety (*bienséance*), that mattered so much to Neo-classicism. Hence one salient aspect of the French Romantic movement in its revolt against tradition was the adoption of a view of poetry centred on the expression of emotion. In England and Germany, on the other hand, this break-through had already been accomplished. In England the emancipation from rationalism came fairly gradually and was therefore far less explosive than in France. Nor had there ever been such suppression as across the Channel, so that the course of English literature is more of an easy-going evolution. The development of German literature was of a less even tenor, but its revolution came earlier than that of the French with the *Sturm und Drang*

of the 1770s that established once and for all the primacy of
feeling. The *Frühromantiker* accordingly took this for granted
and laid the main emphasis on the imagination. Even the subsequent *Hochromantik* retreat from transcendentalism in favour
of a greater naturalness still did not imply a simple expression
of feeling. The divergences between the three Romantic movements appear indeed to be greater in this field than elsewhere,
paradoxical though this conclusion may seem in the light of the
popular association of Romanticism in any shape or form with the
outpouring of feeling. On closer scrutiny, however, the imagination is seen to play a far more vital part in the genuine Romantic
work than feeling. And because the balance between these two
elements – imagination and feeling – oscillates so considerably
from country to country, the face of Romanticism has, within
its family resemblance, such markedly different features.

  Just how different these can be is vividly illustrated by three
poems* all concerned with the same theme, the poet's sense of
desolation at the loss of a dear friend. True, in Wordsworth's
case the loss was metaphorical for in *A Complaint* he was
writing of Coleridge's growing estrangement, whereas both
Lamartine in *L'Isolement* and Novalis in the *Hymnen an die
Nacht* were lamenting the physical death of the beloved, but the
situations are sufficiently similar to warrant comparison. Given
this thematic affinity, the three poems could hardly be more
diverse. Wordsworth's is by far the most restrained in the
expression of emotion, and incidentally also the shortest. Starting with the direct statement

There is a change – and I am poor;

that makes a forceful impact by its very bareness, the poem leads
back in the closing lines to a reiteration of this central idea,
even with the same key words, 'change' and 'poor' :

– Such change, and at the very door
Of my fond heart, hath made me poor.

* For texts of poems and translations see Appendix C.

This modified repetition gives the poem a rounded, compact form, while the phrase now added in parenthesis ('and at the very door/Of my fond heart') hints, still with some reticence, at the depth of Wordsworth's grief. Between these direct statements at the beginning and the end, the main part of the poem is encompassed in a long dual image, that of the fountain and the well. Previously his friend's love was like a fountain

> Whose only business was to flow;
> And flow it did;

By this repetition of the word 'flow' and by the use in the second stanza of the adjectives 'murmuring, sparkling, living', Wordsworth stresses the liveliness, the constant, generous renewal of the gifts so freely bestowed by 'that consecrated fount' of love. This appraisal of the fountain, denoting the past state, makes all the more crass the contrast with the present that is likened to 'a comfortless and hidden well'. The image remains within the same province, that of water, but the static, somehow closed-in existence of the well is the opposite of the fountain's open-hearted flow :

> A well of love – it may be deep –
> I trust it is, – and never dry;
> What matter ? if the waters sleep
> In silence and obscurity.

The disjointed phrases, separated by dashes, seem to come in fits and starts like water extracted with difficulty out of an awkward well, whereas the first half of the poem flowed as smoothly as the fountain. The rhetorical questions of the latter half also suggest the 'silence' of the well's 'sleeping', unresponsive waters as against the 'murmuring' of the fountain. By clothing his emotion in imagery Wordsworth has avoided any excessive overflow of personal feeling. Indeed, the imagery fulfils several functions simultaneously : it achieves an imaginative transfiguration of the subject matter; it diverts the attention – momentarily – from the emotional content through its realistic evocation of fountain and well; and finally, most important of all, the contrast between fountain and well brings home the nature of the change that has made the poet poor infinitely better than any succession of laments. The poem is thus artistically complete and, for all its innate restraint, emotionally satisfying.

Wordsworth's poem is entitled *A Complaint* but it contains so much less complaining than Lamartine's *L'Isolement* or, for that matter, Novalis' *Hymnen an die Nacht*. Yet Lamartine does not begin with his complaint as Wordsworth did; the first four stanzas, almost a third of the poem, are devoted to the setting. The aim is not so much precise description of a place as evocation of an atmosphere: the details of the landscape remain generalized and hazy, disappearing like the meandering stream 'en un lointain obscur'. Already the real world fades before the more imperative demands of the poet's inner realm of feeling. The opening lines:

> Souvent sur la montagne, à l'ombre du vieux chêne
> Au coucher du soleil, triste   ent je m'assieds;

set the mood as the poet's sadness is in consonance with the gloom of twilight, the shadowiness of the whole panorama before him, the sombre colouring of the woods and the solemn sound of the church-bells. This first part of *L'Isolement* is clearly in the melancholy graveyard tradition of the mid- and late eighteenth century, strongly reminiscent of Gray's *Elegy written in a country churchyard* where

> The curfew tolls the knell of parting day . . .

Moreover, Lamartine's occasional lapses into conventional poetic phraseology ('le char vapoureux de la reine des ombres' or, later, 'sur le char de L'Aurore') seem to indicate at least some degree of indebtedness to his predecessors. But this description is a mere preliminary, for the poet soon turns his gaze away, his 'âme indifférente' finding no joy in the 'doux tableaux' of this world. And so the middle section brings the substance of his lament, neatly embodied in the seventh stanza, exactly at the centre of the poem:

Que me font ces vallons, ces palais, ces chaumières ?
Vains objets dont pour moi le charme est envolé ;
Fleuves, rochers, forêts, solitudes si chères,
Un seul être vous manque, et tout est dépeuplé !

Here, as indeed throughout *L'Isolement*, Lamartine uses many
of the familiar stylistic devices of oratory (enumerations,
exclamation, rhetorical question, antithesis) for an emphatic
effect. What a contrast between Wordsworth's discreet, yet
forceful imagery and Lamartine's emotional display. The difference in poetic technique is inseparable from an underlying
divergence of attitude : the dignified restraint of Wordsworth's

There is a change – and I am poor

as against the self-pity implied by Lamartine's

Et je dis: "Nulle part le bonheur ne m'attend".

The extravagance of Lamartine's sorrow heightens in the third
part of the poem when he expresses his hope for reunion with the
beloved in some future yonder realm. But in spite of the poet's
ardour, a certain doubt hangs over these lines, a doubt that is
indicated by the 'peut-être' that introduces his speculations
as well as by the recurrence of the conditional tense and the un-
answered questions. Thus, even though Lamartine declares :

Il n'est rien de commun entre la terre et moi,

he promptly in fact returns to this earth, quite literally in the
final stanza :

Quand la feuille des bois tombe dans la prairie,
Le vent du soir s'élève et l'arrache aux vallons :
Et moi, je suis semblable à la feuille flétrie :
Emportez-moi comme elle, orageux aquilons !

It is a fine flourish on which to end a poem, and characteristic
of *L'Isolement* in its calculated exploitation of a felicitous
image. Emotionalism and rhetoric go hand in hand with
Lamartine.

Novalis' *Hymnen an die Nacht* are totally different to both

Wordsworth's *A Complaint* and Lamartine's *L'Isolement*, although the initial impetus is the same sense of loss as in the
English and French poems. There is a superficial parallel to
Lamartine's lyric when Novalis starts with a tribute to light
that is, like Lamartine's atmospheric evocation of the scene,
preparatory to the central theme. Still the resemblance to
Lamartine continues as Novalis turns away from the physical
phenomena of the day-light world :

> Abwärts wend ich mich zu der heiligen, unaussprechlichen,
> geheimnisvollen Nacht.

This implies a much more radical rejection of the whole realm of
light and life than that of Lamartine who, for all his indifference
and detachment, does remain rooted within reality : 'je contemple la terre' – albeit 'ainsi qu'une âme errante'. Hence
Lamartine's excursion 'au delà des bornes' of this universe
is purely speculative, couched in the conditional tense and
prefaced by 'peut-être', and although he asks himself :

> Sur la terre d'exil pourquoi resté-je encore ?

he nonetheless links himself more closely to the earth in the
final comparison of himself to a withered leaf. Lamartine looks
outwards, as in *Le Lac* and *L'Automne*, projecting his feelings
on to the world of nature around him. Whereas the path of
Novalis leads inwards ('Nach Innen geht der geheimnisvolle
Weg') so that for him 'Fernab liegt die Welt, in eine tiefe
Grube versenkt'. Guided by a complete faith in his innermost
instincts, he takes an irrational leap into the dark, where he is
welcomed by mystical visions of his mother and his beloved.
Novalis conveys these experiences in the present tense, in an
ecstatic style, disjointed through excitement. This suggests
the immediacy and impact of his visions, and contrasts both
with the sobriety of his own initial tribute to light, and even
more pointedly with Lamartine's suppositional approach :

> Là, je m'enivrerais à la source où j'aspire ;
> Là, je retrouverais et l'espoir et l'amour.

What is hypothetical to Lamartine becomes real to Novalis : 'Sie sendet mir dich – zarte Geliebte, liebliche Sonne der Nacht, – nun wach ich – denn ich bin dein und mein, – du hast die Nacht mir zum Leben verkündet.' In the total reversal of normal values that follows this esoteric moment of illumination Novalis voluptuously accepts night and death as the meaningful parts of human existence, for which he longs while enduring the periods of daylight. Lamartine's speculation about a world beyond is no more than a passing day-dream, while Novalis is firmly convinced of the absolute reality of the inner realm which he has created. As in *Heinrich von Ofterdingen*, the ordinary world is discarded to make way for this higher sphere fashioned by the inner eye. So Novalis' grief at the death of Sophie is transfigured by means of the poet's imagination into a joyous new beginning. Far from remaining enclosed in his sorrow after the manner of Lamartine and Wordsworth, whose image of the well suggests confinement, Novalis embarks on a great expansive re-discovery of life in the light of his revelation when he goes on, in the last two hymns, to re-interpret the history of mankind and the Christian religion in terms of the antithesis between night and day, death and life. Thus the main theme of the *Hymnen an die Nacht*, the salvation of the individual and of mankind through the illumination of death and darkness, is reiterated on a less personal level. In keeping with the German Romantic demand for an all-embracing poetry, Novalis has broadened his own experience into universal significance, associating Sophie, the source of his true vision, with Christ, the saviour of mankind. This tendency to universalize is a distinctive German characteristic, quite alien to either the English or the French Romantics.

The difference is reflected also in the form of the three poems : Wordsworth's is taut and concise, achieving a remarkable concentration through the density of its imagery. Beside Wordsworth's *A Complaint*, Lamartine's *L'Isolement* appears somewhat diffuse with its oratorical devices, and decidedly conventional in its use of a regular four-line stanza with a

s

repeated ABAB rhyme-scheme. But both remain within the compass of the lyric genre, whereas the *Hymnen an die Nacht* expand beyond these limits as the dynamic flow of revelation surges out in powerfully dithyrambic rhythms that alternate freely between prose and verse. The more Novalis' vision grips him, the more does outer reality dissolve and with it also the form, grammatical and structural. The syntax breaks down into a series of ecstatic cries, separated by dashes, the contours become blurred through the avoidance of visual details and the consistent preference for terms of fluidity ('quillt', 'träuft', 'Flut', 'saugend', 'schwimmt', 'Woge', 'hinabgespült', 'rinnt aufgelöst') that suggest the gradual drift into the semi-conscious state of dream and imagination.

Novalis' *Hymnen an die Nacht* are thus less a direct expression of feeling than a record of an esoteric experience. Novalis reacts to the sorrow of Sophie's death as much with his imagination as with his heart – if not more so – so that the personal grief is transfigured into a mystical revelation, valid for all mankind. The *Hymnen an die Nacht* are typical of German Romanticism in this supremacy of the transforming imagination as well as in the expansive movement, the fluidity of form and language and the whole fervid tone. These qualities distinguish Novalis' rhapsody sharply from Wordsworth's *A Complaint* which has many features characteristic of English Romanticism : the balance of feeling and imagination, a certain freshness and directness, a close relationship to the real, particularly to nature, and an economy of form equalled only by the restraint of its emotion. No wonder that Hazlitt, accustomed to such poems as those of Wordsworth and Keats, criticized French poetry as 'frothy verbiage or a mucilage of sentiment without natural bones or substance' in contrast to 'ours' which 'constantly clings to the concrete, and has a purchase upon matter'. With a sure aim, Hazlitt went on to diagnose the reason for what he called the lack of 'combination of internal feeling with external imagery' in French poetry. 'Outward objects', he maintained, 'interfere with and extinguish the flame of their imagination :

with us they are the fuel that kindles it into a brighter blaze'.[114] Where Wordsworth draws strength from nature imagery (fountain and well), Lamartine can only assimilate the outer world to his own mood. His poem is a display of emotion and technical skill; personal feelings are poured out in a fashion that seems to justify Vigny's harsh judgement: 'Lamartine est un poète d'enivrement sans bornes, sans forme'.[115] This is the weakness of French Romantic poetry, and it springs from a strange backwardness of the imaginative powers, an underestimation of their role in artistic creativity, in curious contrast to the fundamental defect of most German Romantic works, which stems from an overestimation, an excessive exuberance of the imagination. The differences between these three poems are, therefore, not only a matter of personal idiosyncracies; they also reflect and illustrate the deep divergences between the three Romantic movements.

Conclusion: Perspective

FROM a confrontation of three poems as heterogeneous as
A Complaint, *L'Isolement* and the *Hymnen an die Nacht* it is the
differences between the faces of Romanticism in England,
France and Germany that become apparent rather than the
similarities. Nor is this by any means an isolated example
chosen specially for the sake of making a point. Again and
again, in each genre, the same divergences are perceptible: in
the differences between the three historical novels, *Waverley*,
Notre-Dame de Paris and *Heinrich von Ofterdingen*, or between
the three dramas *Manfred*, *Hernani* and *Die verkehrte Welt*. So
much so that it would indeed seem easier to be convinced of
the diversity of the Romantic movement than of its fundamental
unity in view of its manifold manifestations. This may explain
why critics have generally tended to argue in favour of the
likenesses in an attempt to introduce some semblance of
order and cohesion into the maze that is Romanticism. But the
undue insistence on resemblances, to which this kind of approach
has only too often led, produces a final picture of a remarkable
uniformity – a picture that is patently a distortion. On the other
hand, to dwell on the differences, as I have done, in, for instance,
the treatment of the Romantic hero, the attitude to nature, the
uses of imagery, the expression of feeling, as well as in the
theoretical tenets – this too is fraught with danger in that it
may leave the impression simply of a totally bewildering
variety. Both defeat the underlying purpose of any comparative
study, which aims surely to achieve a more balanced view, a
truer perspective than is possible from the isolated analysis of a
single national literature, however rich in itself.

In one respect the present comparison has perhaps brought

Romanticism into sharper focus in so far as the specific national character of each Romanticism has emerged more clearly from this juxtaposition of ideas and works. Thus the extremism, the bias towards metaphysical speculation, the idealism that is the mainspring of German Romanticism sets off the moderation, the streak of realism, the good sense that mark its English counterpart. While English Romanticism, seen only in the context of the development of English literature, may appear far-fetched in its flights of fancy, its real nature – if the pun is permissible – is only appreciated in relation to its infinitely more fanciful Continental equivalents. In this case the comparison makes a vital corrective. Similarly, the vehemence, the emotionalism, the pleas for freedom of expression that are at the core of French Romanticism become less perplexing when considered in the right framework. The parallel that has so often suggested itself in the course of this study between French Romanticism and the German *Sturm und Drang* is an illuminating one : because of its literary and historical background the French Romanticism of the early nineteenth century was more akin to the German revolt of the 1770s than to the imaginative experimentation typical of English and German Romanticism. This was to come in France later in the nineteenth century with the Symbolist poets, whose works represent the French version of what is known as Romanticism in England and Germany. From these national distinctions come the differences in the faces of Romanticism.

And yet, even while trying to pinpoint the forms and sources of divergence, one cannot but be struck by that family likeness that is as tantalising as it is undeniable. Is it at all possible to come to terms with this paradox, to interpret this strange similarity-*cum*-diversity in a satisfying manner – and without adding yet another to the welter of theories already beleaguering Romanticism? This is the crucial question in any attempt to grasp the phenomenon of Romanticism, and it is one that can, by its very nature, be answered only in a tentative fashion.

* * *

In the context of the development of Western literature, Romanticism appears as a tremendous creative renewal, of a force equalled perhaps only by the Renaissance. The very words used to describe Romanticism point to the renewal that it implied, phrases such as 'the awakening of the imagination', 'the renascence of feeling', 'the religious revival', 'the active reawakening of a creative impulse', which abound in critical discussions of the Romantic movement. This renewal was, in part at least, forced on the Romantics by their singular historical position. Whereas the Renaissance derived its chief inspiration from a re-vivification of Classical ideals, Romanticism had no equally convenient models at hand. The consistent and manageable structure, which the Renaissance had built out of the stones of Classical Antiquity, had fallen increasingly into disarray. In this state of stalemate the Romantics too looked back to the past: Sainte-Beuve pointed to the sixteenth century in his *Tableau historique et critique de la poésie française au XVIième siècle*; the English turned to Shakespeare and the Pre-Restoration poets, while the Germans heeded the voice of Jacob Böhme and of their traditional folk-songs and folk-tales. The very catholicity of the Romantics' reading – the Bible, Dante, Shakespeare and Calderón – reveals their lack of backing from any consistent system such as buttressed the Renaissance. Herein, however, lies the peculiar strength of the Romantic renewal: it was not just a revival of older ideals that had been forgotten for a while, it was a real new beginning. Rising in contrast to the ruins of Neo-classicism, its aesthetics were nothing short of revolutionary: its emphasis on the individual and its insight into the powers of the imagination were turning-points in the evolution of European thought as well as the cornerstones of the creative renewal.

And so the history of the Romantic movement is one long story of innovation from the early stirrings of Pre-romanticism onwards: the new sensibility, the new lyrical prose style, the new outpouring of feeling, the new experiments with the form of the novel, the new freedom of the drama, the new uses of imagery, the new attitude to nature, and so forth. Each and every Romantic poet and thinker, however idiosyncratic in manner or ideas, partook in some way or other in this creative renewal. Their works may not always have been new in the absolute sense, but they were new within the context of their country and setting. Thus the lyrics of Lamartine's *Méditations Poétiques* were as much of an innovation in the France of 1820 as Blake's *Songs of Innocence* were in the England of 1787, however much they may actually differ in style and content. The same is true of the impact of Wordsworth's *Lyrical Ballads* in England in 1798 and of Novalis' almost contemporaneous, but totally dissimilar *Hymnen an die Nacht*. The examples could be multiplied endlessly: to take the three dramas cited earlier, *Manfred*, *Hernani* and *Die verkehrte Welt*: each of these also represented an entirely new departure on its appearance. Or again, Musset's *Nuits* were as novel as Keats' *Odes*, and Wackenroder's *Herzensergießungen eines kunstliebenden Klosterbruders* were as daring an experiment as Coleridge's *Ancient Mariner*. Every one of these works is quite distinct in both content and form from its eighteenth-century predecessors. The poetry of Blake, Wordsworth, Coleridge, Shelley, Keats, and even Byron – for all his affinities to the earlier satirical tradition – is palpably different to that of Pope and Dryden, just as the writings of Hugo, Lamartine, Musset and Vigny are other in character to those of Delille and La Chaussée; and the works of Novalis, Tieck, Hoffmann and Brentano stand apart from those of Haller and Klopstock. However diverse the products of Romanticism are, they share this common denominator of a creative renewal in the sense that the innovations in technique and ideology introduced by the Romantics were no mere quest for the newfangled, but the expression of a deep-rooted need: the need for an artistic regeneration. It is this, rather than any tangible feature, that holds the Romantic family together and that distinguishes the poets of the late eighteenth and early nineteenth centuries from those of other periods who may well have some of the qualities associated with Romanticism. Who would deny, for instance, that Homer or Racine, Shakespeare or Dante possessed creative imagination? – and it is no coincidence that the latter were claimed by the Romantics as their ancestors. But to pick out single traits in this fashion is a dangerous method, as Etiemble so convincingly showed when he illustrated European Pre-romanticism by reference to Chinese poets of the pre-Christian era. This is in fact the approach of Little Jack Horner, pulling out the plums without noticing the fruit-cake from which they came. In the case of Romanticism, individualism, imagination, the expression of feeling are the 'plums', synthesized in the idea of a creative renewal.

That this renewal in itself took various forms was to be expected, for its direction and force were determined by local circumstances. In the same way as 'the effects of Cartesian rationalism, Lockean empiricism, and Leibnizian idealism are imprinted on the criticism of the three leading nations',[1] so the background, both past and present, affected each country's Romanticism, thus accounting, at least in some degree, for the differences between the movements to which the same name is given. Broadly speaking, the Romantic renewal had two aspects : either it was orientated backwards, dominated by the Neo-classical past and at pains to be rid of it; or it was forward-looking, concerned with the establishment of an aesthetics and a poetry in consonance with modern views. The character of each Romantic movement was shaped by the supremacy of the one or the other, and this in turn depended on the native literary tradition.

The Romanticism that most consistently fixed its gaze backwards is that of France, where the past was ever in men's consciousness. The French felt – indeed many still feel – that the true glory of their literature lay in the seventeenth century; hence that 'complesso d'eredità'[2] in their relationship to the past, of which they have tended to remain prisoners and often victims. By the beginning of the nineteenth century, the Neo-classical tradition had become stale and spent; yet it still persisted without having forfeited much of its old authority.

The rules of the three unities were the straightjacket of drama, just as the rigid Alexandrine crippled lyric poetry. No wonder that French Romanticism was so deliberately anti-Classical, so determined to cast off the yoke at long last. For this reason the aesthetic discussions in the journals of the 1820s constantly weigh up the new against the established practices. There is no parallel to this approach either in England or in Germany, where the past threw no such overwhelming shadow as in France. Nor did other lands witness the acrimonious arguments that accompanied the emergence of French Romanticism, the whole series of charges culminating in the pitched battle of *Hernani*. The violence of the opposition in itself indicates the strength and persistence of Neo-classicism. So French Romanticism needed its aggressive, propagandist momentum to assert itself. In its rebellious character and liberating aims it was very like the German *Sturm und Drang*, and the kinship is borne out by their common emphasis on concepts such as genius, nature and feeling, as well as by the phrases used to describe French Romanticism, which would be equally appropriate to the *Sturm und Drang*: 'bruyant', 'théâtral', 'sa recherche du cas exceptionel, du contraste criant', 'son mépris de la tradition et des conventions'.[3] It should not be forgotten either that the Germans whom Mme de Staël had introduced to the French were just the *Stürmer und Dränger*, while from a recent study[4] it would seem that Hugo's acquaintance with German literature was confined entirely to the poets of the *Sturm und Drang*. Even this century the French conception of Romanticism is still such as to advocate that 'il faudrait tout au moins appeler romantique le mouvement du groupe poétique de Göttingen et surtout celui de la période d'*assaut et élan* (*Sturm und Drang*) entre 1770 et 1780.'[5] Like the *Sturm und Drang*, French Romanticism sought to begin its renewal by a vehement rejection of what had gone before. It was in contravention of the Neo-classicism of the seventeenth century that its salient features evolved: the freedom of dramatic technique, the focus on the ego, the unrestrained outpouring of emotion, the emphasis on truth to nature. But whatever the objections to the tenets and practices of French Romanticism, whatever its limitations and failings, it did have a liberalizing effect by its outspoken renunciation of worn and weary ideas. In the works of Lamartine, Hugo, Vigny and Musset there was clearly a new spark of life.

By contrast, the whole tendency of the Romantic movements in England and Germany was decidedly forward-looking. While French critical theories were directed against the past, the English and Germans were more concerned with the future. Neither country was as heavily burdened with authoritative precedents as France : in Germany Neo-classicism was a foreign importation, which never really took root on Teutonic soil even before it was questioned by the Enlightenment and dismissed by the *Sturm und Drang*; and in England its rigid dogmatism was so considerably tempered by empirical good sense as to lose its air of intransigence. This difference in the antecedents to Romanticism in the three literatures may explain why the creative renewal too was divergent in direction : where the past still loomed large, as in France, to combat it was the first imperative; on the other hand, where old scores had been settled, as in Germany, or hardly seemed to need settling, as in England, the Romantics were free to advance as they chose. Thus the French Romantics, in their struggle with the past, demanded and practised freedom to write as they pleased, whereas for the English and the Germans it was the imagination that was paramount in their exploration of future possibilities.

The contrast is greatest between France and England, between the revolutionary and the evolutionary emergence of Romanticism. As against the paroxysms that shook France, across the Channel the reorientation came in a gradual shift of outlook as new notions infiltrated almost imperceptibly in the course of the eighteenth century. It is surely no coincidence that England contributed the most and France the least to Preromanticism. Because of the English gift for compromise the new ideas were somehow assimilated to the old without any sudden break in continuity such as occurred in France. This sense of belonging to the native tradition distinguishes Romanticism in England from the Romanticism of France which ran counter to all that had gone before. Moreover, the Romantic movement never sought to assume an incontestable sway in England; even in its heyday many eighteenth-century elements persisted alongside it in the poetry of Byron and Clare, as well as in the current of realism in Peacock, Jane Austen, Scott, not to mention Wordsworth himself. English Romanticism could in fact afford to be tolerant and broad in scope because it did not, as in France and Germany, have to be militant. It was unorganized, without leaders or journals or definite programmes, a loose, informal movement, 'a warm intuitive muddle',[6] with a large body of highly suggestive critical remarks rather than any clearly formulated, systematic theory. For this reason it would hardly be possible to collect the corpus of thought of the English Romantics in the way that Kluckhohn has done for the Germans in *Das Ideengut der deutschen Romantik.* Nor is it feasible to classify the English Romantics in any helpful way. It is in fact difficult to generalize at all about the Romantic movement in England because it was so varied, so uncodified, so independent. This is reflected in the quality of its creative renewal which, with true English adaptability, grew as if naturally and organically without any of the sudden jolts that troubled the French. In place of the planned, concerted beginnings launched by the various groups in France, England saw a whole series of new departures in Blake's symbolism, Wordsworth's poetic realism, Coleridge's surrealism, Shelley's aesthetic sensualism, Keats' subtle blend of realistic observation and imaginative transfiguration, Byron's oscillation between satirical hardness and emotional softness. The range and variety of this creative renewal is simply staggering.

It was almost as brilliant in Germany where it was, however, driven to a strange course by the urge somehow or other to outdo the greatness of Goethe and Schiller. It is often forgotten that the Romantic movement forms an integral part of the glorious age of German literature, the so-called *Goethezeit* spanning the whole length of Goethe's creative life from about 1770 to his death in 1832. By the closing years of the eighteenth century when the first Romantic circle took shape, German literature was already experiencing a decisive regeneration in the hands of Goethe and Schiller. The Romantics were fully aware of this; hence their deeply ambivalent attitude to Goethe. His early ideals, dating from his *Sturm und Drang* period, were sufficiently like their own to evoke their enthusiastic approval, but his subsequent development towards a more mature outlook, as exemplified in *Wilhelm Meister*, met with a disapproval amounting to hostility. The *Frühromantiker* therefore determined not only to correct Goethe (*Heinrich von Ofterdingen* was intended as an anti-*Wilhelm Meister*), but also to outstrip him. So they were impelled to that extremism that characterizes so much of their writing, and for this reason too they repeatedly emphasized that theirs was the poetry not so much of the present as of the future, an infinite, progressive poetry, still in the process of evolution, as F. Schlegel put it in the 116th *Athenäum* Fragment. This was a subtle way of dealing with the past: recognizing its achievements as great but somehow limited, and going on from there to herald a higher poetry that was to embrace the poetry of science, of religion, of every human activity indeed, as well as the so-called poetry of poetry. There was undoubtedly an element of the bizarre and the megalomaniac in this programme which contrasts strangely with the moderation and good sense of the English Romantics, who showed little desire to go beyond the boundaries of the various arts and equally little liking for startling techniques such as oxymoron, paradox, contradiction of every kind, so dear to both the Germans and the French in their common aim of making an impression. Yet nowhere in Europe was there a more lively awareness of the need for a creative renewal than among these German Romantics because of the very extremity of their position. They set out with the avowed aim of poeticizing the whole universe, thereby taking the ideal of creative renewal to its logical, if somewhat absurd extreme, just as Fichte carried protectionism to its absolute extreme in *Der geschlossene Handelsstaat*. The organ of this renewal, of this poeticization was the artist's creative imagination, the source of new perceptions, new forms, new styles, entire new worlds. It was this conception of the function of the artist's imagination that gave German Romanticism its distinctive mystical, pseudo-religious tinge. Starting as an attempt to equal or surpass the splendour of Goethe and Schiller, the German Romantics' creative renewal was soon elevated to the metaphysical. As an artistic renewal, however, it became effective only when the speculative was activated into the creative : thus while the *Frühromantiker* made a major contribution to aesthetics, it was the *Hochromantiker* who produced most of the poetic works on which the fame of German Romanticism rests.

In these ways the creative renewal too is adapted to the particular circumstances, to the indigenous tradition of each land and each literature. But whatever its special direction, it is inherent in every one of the Romantic movements as a prime activating force, and as such it forms the flexible bond that holds together this very diverse family.

*   *   *

Ultimately it is as a creative renewal that Romanticism is of significance in the history of European literature. Romanticism not only carried out the 'task of reconstruction' after 'the critical philosophers of the eighteenth century had destroyed their own dwelling-place'.[7] The reorientation from a predominantly imitative Neo-classicism to a self-confident assertion of the powers of the individual imagination was a decisive watershed in the history of mankind, comparable in effect – to continue the geographic metaphor – to the climatic barrier of the Alps in Europe. Just as the weather North of the Alps differs perceptibly from that South of the great divide, so Romantic and post-Romantic art is recognizably other than that which preceded it, however many precursors may be found. The change is not a question of range or of technical freedom,

although both of these increased immensely in consequence of
the Romantic revolution in aesthetics. But the really crucial
innovation was less tangible : during the Romantic period for
the first time the creative imagination was widely accepted as
the mainspring of the arts. The objective yardsticks largely
prevalent until then were replaced by subjective criteria that
paved the way for a new art, less harmonious than that of the
past, but infinitely richer in all manner of experimentation.
This watershed in artistic perception and expression coincided
with the cataclysm of the French Revolution that gave a deep
jolt to the social organization of Europe; these were, moreover,
the years in which the vast economic reshapings of the
Industrial Revolution began. There is good ground for the
argument that the roots of the modern age, socially, economically and artistically are embedded in the Romantic period.

The after-effects of Romanticism as a creative renewal are
still potent even to-day for the Romantics opened up so many
new possibilities that they themselves could often only grope
their way, and it was left to their successors in the nineteenth
and twentieth centuries to reap the full harvest. There is much
truth in Baudelaire's claim : 'qui dit romantisme, dit art
moderne'.[8] Certainly the Symbolist movements that flourished
throughout Europe in the latter years of the nineteenth century
are not without cause sometimes called Neo-romanticism, for
their view of poetry and their practices are profoundly indebted
to their predecessors. For the Symbolists as for the Romantics,
the world of art was the only true world, which the visionary
artist-adventurer explored with the intuitive powers of his
imagination that enabled him to perceive the hidden relationships between the visible and the invisible. These correspondences were embodied in the magical symbols, whose
function was the same as that of the Romantic image : to express
the inexpressible, to mediate the artist's private perception of
the transcendental. The affinity between the French Symbolists
and the German Romantics is too obvious to require much
elaboration. The conception of the imagination is closely

parallel : 'mystérieuse faculté que cette reine des facultés',[9] wrote Baudelaire; 'elle est la synthèse';[10] 'elle crée un monde nouveau';[11] 'elle est positivement apparentée avec l'infini'.[12] Like Novalis, Tieck and Hoffmann, Nerval, Mallarmé and Rimbaud created their own worlds; Nerval indeed began his *Aurélia* with the categoric statement : 'Le Rêve est une seconde vie',[13] and went on to describe his own second life, 'l'épanchement du songe dans la vie réelle',[14] imaginative dreams that alienated him more and more from reality as he plunged into the visions of the night. Moreover, the Symbolists' cult of synesthesia, as well as their belief in the interdependence of all the arts, are an extension of the Romantic demand for the mingling of genres. There is considerable justification for regarding these poets as the true French Romantics, as some critics have indeed done.

In Symbolism and also in the tendency known as 'Art for art's sake' the heritage of Romanticism is clearly apparent; in a number of other movements and writers its force is less plain but no less powerful. Impressionism in art is inconceivable except in the wake of Romanticism, and this also holds true of Surrealism with its concentration on the unexplored possibilities of the unconscious, its aim of releasing the underground world of dreams, fantasies, hallucinations. And Existentialism too in its subjective reappraisal of life is surely descended from Romanticism; the sensations experienced by Antoine Roquentin, the hero of Sartre's *La Nausée*, are strangely like a twentieth century version of the Romantic *mal du siècle*, stemming from the over-active imaginings of an isolated, hypersensitive individual. In fact, all twentieth-century experimental fiction rests on a foundation of Romanticism in its move from the real to the imaginative world of dreams, myths and mysteries, its search for new symbols and new forms, its exploration of time and space, its rejection of plot in favour of an organic structure dependent on an associative sequence of recurrent images. The whole technique of interior monologue, stream of consciousness, by which is meant that the tale is told from within the mind of a fictitious character or characters, derives from the Romantic preference for seeing not the surface appearance but the inner reality beneath it. In this sense James Joyce's *Finnegans Wake* represents perhaps the extreme, the *reductio ad absurdum* of Romanticism. Undoubtedly all the anarchic individualism, the ebullient imaginativeness and the emotional vehemence of twentieth-century art are already implicit in Romanticism.

Whether this aftermath of the Romantic revolution in aesthetics has effected a disruption or a regeneration of the European cultural tradition has for many years been a subject of debate. On the one hand, critics such as Pierre Lasserre in *Le Romantisme français* (Paris 1907) and Irving Babbitt in *Rousseau and Romanticism* (Cambridge, Mass., 1919) have seen Romanticism as a sickness, the source of vicious confusion, a substitute for genuine spiritual effort that has led inevitably to the moral bankruptcy of modern man. In the arts the detractors of Romanticism have held it responsible for chaos and disorder of every kind masquerading as self-expression, a reflection of the artist's feelings with a total contempt for form. Action painting, novels to be read in any chance sequence, indeterminate music that leaves the order of sections and even the choice of notes to the performer: all these have been condemned as sheer sensationalism. At the opposite pole are those who evaluate Romanticism in a positive fashion as the harbinger of a new flexibility of artistic form, a new freedom in experimentation as well as of organic thinking, of seeing and experiencing from the inside, so to speak. Foremost among these is Morse Peckham, who has interpreted the whole nineteenth century as a period of reconstruction, innovation and reorientation (*Beyond the Tragic Vision* (New York 1962)) that broke in with the collapse of the Enlightenment. Once again, what is so striking is the amazing range of after-effects and the queer assortment of progeny – Proust and Kafka, Picasso and Chagall, Mahler and Messiaen, Brecht and Beckett – rightly or wrongly attributed to Romanticism by both its critics and its defenders. Those culture-conscious citizens of La Ferté-sous-

T

Jouarre, M. Dupuis and M. Cotonet, would be even more
bewildered by the whole problem of Romanticism in the 1960s
than they were in the 1830s.

★   ★   ★

What then emerges from this attempt to see the Romantic
movements in England, France and Germany comparatively,
each in the light of the others and also in the historical perspective of their respective origins? No simple formula, unfortunately, to settle once and for all the perplexities of M. Dupuis and
M. Cotonet; only the conviction of the fundamental multi-
formity of Romanticism. If not the proverbial 'all things to all
men', it certainly signifies many things to many men. Herein
surely lies the main reason why the term has so far defied
definition and continues to puzzle and annoy. Any attempt to
capture its meaning in a single slick phrase is a denial of its
quintessential character and therefore doomed to failure.

And this holds equally, if not more so, of the endeavour to
determine the interrelationship of the European Romantic
movements. The comparative study of literature does not
produce neat, slogan-like classifications – unless the critic sets
out with a preconceived scheme into which the material is
fitted as best can be. If, however, the facts are not ruthlessly
dragooned into a rigid pattern, the results are bound to be less
impressive. But for the penalty of a certain inconclusiveness the
reward is truthfulness. So, renouncing hope of an easy solution,
one must in the last resort accept a compromise, recognizing the
family likeness in the manifestations of European Romanticism
but also the great variations of feature and the many permutations. At best the highly intricate web of similarities and
differences that forms the fabric of European Romanticism
could be characterized in the phrase that Coleridge used to
describe beauty: 'Multeïty in Unity'.[15] Perhaps we should do
Romanticism more justice if we ceased the search for that
elusive unity and began rather to appreciate its multeïty.

Appendix A
Chronological Chart

	ENGLAND	GERMANY	FRANCE
1726 –30	Thomson: *Seasons*		
1740		Bodmer: *Kritische Abhandlung von dem Wunderbaren in der Poesie*	
1742	Young: *Night Thoughts*		
1745	Akenside: *Pleasures of Imagination*		
1747	Richardson: *Clarissa Harlowe*		
1750	Gray: *Elegy in a Country Churchyard*		
1754			Condillac: *Traité des Sensations*
1755			
1758			Diderot: *Discours sur la Poésie Dramatique*
1759	Young: *Conjectures on Original Composition*	Lessing: *Literaturbriefe*	
1760	MacPherson: *Fragments* ⟶ Translation		
1761			Rousseau: *La Nouvelle Héloïse*
1762	MacPherson: *Fingal,* translation from Ossian		
1764	⟶ Translation		
1765	Percy: *Reliques*		
1766		Herder: *Fragmente über die neuere deutsche Literatur*	
1767		Lessing: *Hamburgische Dramaturgie*	
1769		Herder: *Journal meiner Reise*	
1770			
1773		*Von deutscher Art und Kunst*	
1774		Goethe: *Götz von Berlichingen* Goethe: *Werther*	

	ENGLAND	GERMANY	FRANCE
1775		First translation of Shakespeare	
1776		Klinger : *Sturm und Drang*	
1778		Herder : *Stimmen der Völker*	Rousseau : *Rêveries du Promeneur Solitaire*
1781		Schiller : *Die Räuber* Kant : *Kritik der reinen Vernunft*	Rousseau : *Confessions*
1787	Blake : *Songs of Innocence*		B. de St-Pierre : *Paul et Virginie*
1788		Kant : *Kritik der praktischen Vernunft*	
1790		Kant : *Kritik der Urteilskraft*	
1791			B. de St-Pierre : *La Chaumière Indienne*
1792			Rouget de Lisle : *La Marseillaise*
1794	Blake : *Songs of Experience*	Fichte : *Wissenschaftslehre* Schiller : *Uber naïve und sentimentalische Dichtung*	
1796	Coleridge : *The Aeolian Harp*		
1797		A. W. Schlegel : Translation of Shakespeare Schelling : *Ideen zu einer Philosophie der Natur* Tieck : *Volksmärchen* Wackenroder : *Herzensergießungen eines kunstliebenden Klosterbruders*	
1798	Wordsworth : *Lyrical Ballads* Coleridge : *The Ancient Mariner Frost at Midnight Fears in Solitude The Nightingale*	*Athenäum*	
1799		Schleiermacher : *Reden über die Religion* F. Schlegel : *Lucinde*	La Harpe : *Cours de littérature ancienne et moderne*
1800	Wordsworth : *Michael Ruth*	Novalis : *Hymnen an die Nacht*	Mme de Staël : *De la Littérature*
1801			Chateaubriand : *Atala*
1802	Coleridge : *Dejection*	Novalis : *Heinrich von Ofterdingen*	Chateaubriand : *Génie du Christianisme*
1804			
1805	Wordsworth : *Prelude*	Arnim u. Brentano : *Des Knaben Wunderhorn* (—1808)	Chateaubriand : *René*

	ENGLAND	GERMANY	FRANCE
1806		Fichte : *Reden an die deutsche Nation*	
1807		Görres : *Die teutschen Volksbücher*	Lemercier : *Christophe Colomb*
1809		A. W. Schlegel : *Vorlesungen über dramatische Kunst und Literatur*	
1810			
1812	Byron : *Childe Harold*	Grimm : *Märchen*	
1813	Shelley : *Queen Mab*	Arndt : *Lieder für Teutsche*	Mme de Staël : *De l'Allemagne* → Translation
1814	Wordsworth : *The Excursion* Byron : *The Corsair* *Lara* *Bride of Abydos* Scott : *Waverley*	Rückert : *Geharnischte Sonette* Körner : *Leyer und Schwert* Chamisso : *Peter Schlemihl*	
1815	Wordsworth : *Poems* Translation	Hoffmann : *Elixiere des Teufels* Uhland : *Gedichte* Tieck : *Phantasus*	
1816	Byron: *Siege of Corinth* *Prisoner of Chillon* Coleridge : *Kubla Khan* *Christabel* Shelley : *Alastor*		
1817	Byron : *Manfred* Keats : *Poems* Coleridge : *Sibylline leaves* *Biographia Literaria*	Hoffmann : *Nachtstücke*	
1818	Keats : *Endymion* Hazlitt : *Lectures on the English Poets* Peacock : *Nightmare Abbey*		
1819	Byron : *Don Juan* (—1824) *Mazeppa* Keats : *Eve of St. Agnes* Shelley : *The Cenci*	Hoffmann : *Die Serapionsbrüder* Schopenhauer : *Die Welt als Wille und Vorstellung*	
1820	Keats : *Hyperion* *Lamia* Shelley : *Prometheus Unbound*		Lamartine : *Méditations Poétiques* *Conservateur Littéraire* Lebrun : *Maria Stuart*
1821	Byron : *Cain* *Sardanapalus* Shelley : *Adonais* *Epipsychidion* *Defence of Poetry*	Hoffmann : *Kater Murr*	*Société des Bonnes-Lettres*

	ENGLAND	GERMANY	FRANCE
1821	De Quincey: *Confessions of an English Opium Eater*		
1822	Shelley: *Hellas* Byron: *Vision of Judgement*	Hoffmann: *Meister Floh* Heine: *Gedichte*	Vigny: *Poèmes* Hugo: *Odes*
1823	Carlyle: *Life of Schiller*		Lamartine: *Nouvelles Méditations Poétiques* Stendhal: *Racine et Shakespeare* Hugo: *Han d'Islande* *Muse Française*
1824	Byron: *The Island* Shelley: *Posthumous Poems* *Triumph of Life*	Mörike: *Gedichte*	Mercure du XIX siècle Vigny: *Éloa* Hugo: *Odes Nouvelles* *Le Globe*
1825	Hazlitt: *Spirit of the Age* Coleridge: *Aids to Reflection*	Tieck and Schlegel: Shakespeare Translations (–1833)	
1826		Eichendorff: *Taugenichts* Heine: *Harzreise* Kerner: *Gedichte* Hölderlin: *Gedichte* Tieck: *Aufruhr in den Cevennen*	Hugo: *Odes et Ballades* Vigny: *Poèmes* *Cinq Mars*
1827		Heine: *Buch der Lieder* *Reisebilder*	Hugo: *Cromwell*
1828	Carlyle: *Goethe*		Sainte-Beuve: *Tableau historique*
1829	Carlyle: *Novalis*		Vigny: *Othello* *Poèmes* Deschamps: *Préface des Études françaises et étrangères* Hugo: *Les Orientales*
1830			Hugo: *Hernani* Lamartine: *Harmonies Poétiques* Gautier: *Poésies* Musset: *Contes d'Espagne et d'Italie*
1831	Peacock: *Crotchet Castle*		Hugo: *Notre-Dame de Paris* *Feuilles d'Automne*
1832		Lenau: *Gedichte*	Hugo: *Le Roi s'amuse* Vigny: *Stello*
1833	Carlyle: *Sartor Resartus*		Musset: *Les Caprices de Marianne* *Rolla*
1834			Musset: *On ne badine pas avec l'amour* *Lorenzaccio* *Fantasia*

ENGLAND	GERMANY	FRANCE
1835		Vigny: *Chatterton* *Servitude et Grandeur Militaires* Hugo: *Chants du Crépuscule* Musset: *La Nuit de Mai* *La Nuit de Décembre*
1836	Immermann: *Die Epigonen*	Musset: *La Nuit d'Août* *Il ne faut jurer de rien* *Confession d'un enfant du siècle* *Lettres de Dupuis et Cotonet* Lamartine: *Jocelyn*
1837	Eichendorff: *Gedichte*	Musset: *La Nuit d'Octobre* Hugo: *Les Voix Intérieures*
1838	Mörike: *Gedichte* Lenau: *Gedichte*	Hugo: *Ruy Blas* Lamartine: *La Chute d'un Ange* Musset: *L'Espoir en Dieu*
1839		Lamartine: *Recueillements Poétiques*

Appendix B

Keats : *Ode to Autumn*
Lamartine : *L'Automne*
Eichendorff : *Herbstweh*

I

Season of mists and mellow fruitfulness,
  Close bosom-friend of the maturing sun;
Conspiring with him how to load and bless
  With fruit the vines that round the thatch-eves run;
To bend with apples the moss'd cottage trees,
  And fill all fruit with ripeness to the core;
    To swell the gourd, and plump the hazel shells
  With a sweet kernel; to set budding more,
And still more, later flowers for the bees,
Until they think warm days will never cease,
    For Summer has o'erbrimmed their clammy cells.

II

Who hath not seen thee oft amid thy store?
  Sometimes whoever seeks abroad may find
Thee sitting careless on a granary floor,
  Thy hair soft-lifted by the winnowing wind;
Or on a half-reap'd furrow sound asleep,
  Drowsed with the fume of poppies, while thy hook
    Spares the next swath and all its twinèd flowers:
And sometimes like a gleaner thou dost keep
  Steady thy laden head across a brook;
Or by a cyder-press, with patient look,
    Thou watchest the last oozings hours by hours.

III

Where are the songs of Spring? Ay, where are they?
  Think not of them, thou hast thy music too, –
While barrèd clouds bloom the soft-dying day,
  And touch the stubble-plains with rosy hue;
Then in a wailful choir the small gnats mourn
  Among the river sallows, borne aloft
    Or sinking as the light wind lives or dies;
And full-grown lambs loud bleat from hilly bourn;
  Hedge-crickets sing; and now with treble soft
  The red-breast whistles from a garden-croft;
    And gathering swallows twitter in the skies.

Salut, bois couronnés d'un reste de verdure !
Feuillages jaunissants sur les gazons épars ;
Salut, derniers beaux jours ! le deuil de la nature
Convient à la douleur et plaît à mes regards.

Je suis d'un pas rêveur le sentier solitaire ;
J'aime à revoir encor, pour la dernière fois,
Ce soleil pâlissant, dont la faible lumière
Perce à peine à mes pieds l'obscurité des bois.

Oui, dans ces jours d'automne où la nature expire,
A ses regards voilés je trouve plus d'attraits ;
C'est l'adieu d'un ami, c'est le dernier sourire
Des lèvres que la mort va fermer pour jamais.

Ainsi, prêt à quitter l'horizon de la vie,
Pleurant de mes longs jours l'espoir évanoui,
Je me retourne encore, et d'un regard d'envie
Je contemple ces biens dont je n'ai pas joui.

Terre, soleil, vallons, belle et douce nature,
Je vous dois une larme aux bords de mon tombeau !
L'air est si parfumé ! la lumière est si pure !
Aux regards d'un mourant le soleil est si beau !

Je voudrais maintenant vider jusqu'à la lie
Ce calice mêlé de nectar et de fiel :
Au fond de cette coupe où je buvais la vie,
Peut-être restait-il une goutte de miel !

Peut-être l'avenir me gardait-il encore
Un retour de bonheur dont l'espoir est perdu !
Peut-être, dans la foule, une âme que j'ignore
Aurait compris mon âme, et m'aurait répondu ! . . .

La fleur tombe en livrant ses parfums au zéphyre ;
À la vie, au soleil, ce sont là ses adieux :
Moi, je meurs ; et mon âme, au moment qu'elle expire,
S'exhale comme un son triste et mélodieux.

Welcome, woods capped with a vestige of green!
Leaves yellowing on the scant grass;
Welcome, last fine days! the mournful face of nature
Accords with my grief and pleasures my eye.

I follow the secluded path in pensive mood;
I like to see again, for the last time,
This waning sun, whose dim light
Hardly breaks into the darkness of the woods.

Yes, in these autumn days when nature is dying,
In its veiled features I find great allure;
It is a friend's farewell, the last smile
On lips that death will soon close for ever.

Thus, ready to leave the fields of life,
Lamenting the lost hopes of my lingering days,
I turn back once more, and with a longing gaze
I survey the delights that have not been mine.

Earth, sun, valleys, beauteous gentle nature,
I owe you a tear from the brink of my grave!
The air is so sweet! the light is so bright!
In the eyes of a dying man the sun is so beautiful!

I would now wish to drain to the dregs
This draught of nectar and of gall;
At the bottom of this cup of life
Perhaps there was still a drop of honey!

Perhaps the future still had in store
A renewal of happiness no longer awaited!
Perhaps, in the crowd, a soul unknown to me
Would have understood my soul and responded to me.

The petals drop, scattering their fragrance to the wind;
That is their farewell to life, to the sun:
And I, I am dying; and my soul, passing away,
Dissolves into a sad sweet song.

So still in den Feldern allen,
Der Garten ist lange verblüht,
Man hört nur flüsternd die Blätter fallen,
Die Erde schläfert – ich bin so müd'.

Es schüttelt die welken Blätter der Wald,
Mich friert, ich bin schon alt,
Bald kommt der Winter und fällt der Schnee,
Bedeckt den Garten und mich und alles, alles Weh.

So still in all the fields,
The garden has long since withered,
The only sound is the rustle of falling leaves,
The earth slumbers – I am so weary.

The wood casts its faded leaves,
I feel cold, I am now old,
Soon winter will come and snow will fall,
Covering the garden and me and all, all woe.

Appendix C

Wordsworth : *A Complaint*

Lamartine : *L'Isolement*

Novalis : *Erste Hymne* and *Dritte Hymne*
of *Hymnen an die Nacht*

u

There is a change – and I am poor;
Your love hath been, nor long ago,
A fountain at my fond heart's door,
Whose only business was to flow;
And flow it did; not taking heed
Of its own bounty, or my need.

What happy moments did I count!
Blest was I then all bliss above!
Now, for that consecrated fount
Of murmuring, sparkling, living love,
What have I? shall I dare to tell?
A comfortless and hidden well.

A well of love – it may be deep –
I trust it is, – and never dry:
What matter? If the waters sleep
In silence and obscurity.
Such change, and at the very door
Of my fond heart, hath made me poor.

Souvent sur la montagne, à l'ombre du vieux chêne
Au coucher du soleil, tristement je m'assieds ;
Je promène au hasard mes regards sur la plaine,
Dont le tableau changeant se déroule à mes pieds.

Ici, gronde le fleuve aux vagues écumantes ;
Il serpente, et s'enfonce en un lointain obscur ;
Là, le lac immobile étend ses eaux dormantes
Où l'étoile du soir se lève dans l'azur.

Au sommet de ces monts couronnés de bois sombres,
Le crépuscule encore jette un dernier rayon ;
Et le char vaporeux de la reine des ombres
Monte, et blanchit déjà les bords de l'horizon.

Cependant, s'élançant de la flèche gothique,
Un son religieux se répand dans les airs :
Le voyageur s'arrête, et la cloche rustique
Aux derniers bruits du jour mêle de saints concerts.

Mais à ces doux tableaux mon âme indifférente
N'éprouve devant eux ni charme ni transports ;
Je contemple la terre ainsi qu'une âme errante :
Le soleil des vivants n'échauffe plus les morts.

De colline en colline en vain portant ma vue,
Du sud à l'aquilon, de l'aurore au couchant,
Je parcours tous les points de l'immense étendue,
Et je dis : 'Nulle part le bonheur ne m'attend'.

Que me font ces vallons, ces palais, ces chaumières ?
Vains objets dont pour moi le charme est envolé ;
Fleuves, rochers, forêts, solitudes si chères,
Un seul être vous manque, et tout est dépeuplé !

Quand le tour du soleil ou commence ou s'achève,
D'un oeil indifférent je le suis dans son cours ;
En un ciel sombre ou pur qu'il se couche ou se lève,
Qu'importe le soleil ? je n'attends rien des jours.

LAMARTINE: *Solitude*

In the shade of the old oak-tree up on the hills
At sunset I often sit to rest in melancholy mood;
My gaze wanders at random over the plain,
Over its changing aspect down beneath me.

Here the river with its foaming waves rolls along;
It meanders away into the hazy distance;
There lies the tranquil lake with its sleeping waters
That reflect the evening star rising in the sky.

On the top of those peaks capped by dark woods,
Twilight still sheds a last ray of light;
And the ethereal chariot of the queen of night
Rises and casts a white shimmer over the horizon.

Meanwhile, ringing out from the Gothic spire,
A religious cadence fills the air:
The traveller halts, and the country bell
Adds its sacred harmonies to the day's dying sounds.

But my soul is indifferent to these sweet sights
And feels no delight nor rapture;
I gaze at the earth like a stray soul:
The sun of the living does not warm the dead.

Looking in vain from hill to hill,
From south to north, from east to west,
I survey the whole range of this vast expanse,
And I tell myself: 'Nowhere is there happiness for me'.

What matter these valleys, these mansions, these cottages to me?
Futile objects that hold no delight for me;
Rivers, rocks, forests, beloved nooks of solitude,
One being is absent, and all is empty!

Whether the sun begins or ends its day,
I follow its path with indifference;
Whether it sets or rises in a dull or bright sky,
What care I for the sun? I expect nothing.

Quand je pourrais le suivre en sa vaste carrière,
Mes yeux verraient partout le vide et les déserts :
Je ne désire rien de tout ce qu'il éclaire ;
Je ne demande rien à l'immense univers.

Mais peut-être au delà des bornes de sa sphère,
Lieux où le vrai soleil éclaire d'autres cieux,
Si je pouvais laisser ma dépouille à la terre,
Ce que j'ai tant rêvé paraîtrait à mes yeux ?

Là, je m'enivrerais à la source où j'aspire ;
Là, je retrouverais et l'espoir et l'amour,
Et ce bien idéal que toute âme désire,
Et qui n'a pas de nom au terrestre séjour !

Que ne puis-je, porté sur le char de l'Aurore,
Vague objet de mes voeux, m'élancer jusqu'à toi !
Sur la terre d'exil pourquoi resté-je encore ?
Il n'est rien de commun entre la terre et moi.

Quand la feuille des bois tombe dans la prairie,
Le vent du soir s'élève et l'arrache aux vallons :
Et moi, je suis semblable à la feuille flétrie :
Emportez-moi comme elle, orageux aquilons !

If I could follow the sun in its full course,
I would see everywhere emptiness and deserts :
I wish for nothing under its bright rays;
I seek nothing in the wide world.

But perhaps beyond the limits of its realm,
There where the real sun lights other skies,
If I could leave my earthly form,
The object of my dreams would appear before me?

There I would drink my fill from the spring of my desiring;
There I would again find hope and love,
And that ideal state that every soul seeks,
And that has no place nor name on earth!

Why can I not rise on the chariot of Dawn
Towards you, shadowy figure of my aspirations!
Why am I still banished to this earth?
We have nothing in common, the earth and I.

When the forest leaves fall in the meadows,
The rising wind at eventide sweeps them from the valleys :
And I, I am like a withered leaf:
Carry me too away, tempestuous blasts!

Erste Hymne

Welcher Lebendige, Sinnbegabte, liebt nicht vor allen Wundererscheinungen des verbreiteten Raums um ihn das allerfreuliche Licht – mit seinen Farben, seinen Strahlen und Wogen, seiner milden Allgegenwart, als weckender Tag. Wie des Lebens innerste Seele atmet es der rastlosen Gestirne Riesenwelt und schwimmt tanzend in seiner blauen Flut – atmet es der funkelnde, ewigruhende Stein, die sinnige, saugende Pflanze und das wilde, brennende, vielgestaltete Tier – vor allen aber der herrliche Fremdling mit den sinnvollen Augen, dem schwebenden Gange und den zartgeschlossenen, tonreichen Lippen. Wie ein König der irdischen Natur ruft es jede Kraft zu zahllosen Verwandlungen, knüpft und löst unendliche Bündnisse, hängt sein himmlisches Bild jedem irdischen Wesen um. Seine Gegenwart allein offenbart die Wunderherrlichkeit der Reiche der Welt.

Abwärts wend ich mich zu der heiligen, unaußprechlichen, geheimnisvollen Nacht. Fernab liegt die Welt – in eine tiefe Grube versenkt – wüst und einsam ist ihre Stelle. In den Saiten der Brust weht tiefe Wehmut. In Tautropfen will ich hinuntersinken und mit der Asche mich vermischen. – Fernen der Erinnerung, Wünsche der Jugend, der Kindheit Träume, des ganzen Lebens kurze Freuden und vergebliche Hoffnungen kommen in grauen Kleidern, wie Abendnebel nach der Sonne Untergang. In andern Räumen schlug die lustigen Gezelte das Licht auf. Sollte es nie zu seinen Kindern wiederkommen, die mit der Unschuld Glauben seiner harren?

Was quillt auf einmal so ahndungsvoll unterm Herzen und verschluckt der Wehmut weiche Luft? Hast auch du ein Gefallen an uns, dunkle Nacht? Was hältst du unter deinem Mantel, das mir unsichtbar kräftig an die Seele geht? Köstlicher Balsam träuft aus deiner Hand, aus dem Bündel Mohn. Die schweren Flügel des Gemüts hebst du empor. Dunkel und unaußprechlich fühlen wir uns bewegt – ein ernstes Antlitz seh ich froh erschrocken, das sanft und andachtsvoll sich zu mir neigt und unter unendlich verschlungenen Locken der Mutter liebe Jugend zeigt. Wie arm und kindisch dünkt mir das Licht nun, wie erfreulich und gesegnet des Tages Abschied! – Also nur darum, weil die Nacht dir abwendig macht die Dienenden, säetest du in des Raumes Weiten die leuchtenden Kugeln, zu verkünden deine Allmacht – deine Wiederkehr – in den Zeiten deiner Entfernung. Himmlischer als jene blitzenden Sterne dünken uns die unendlichen Augen, die die Nacht in uns geöffnet. Weiter sehn sie als

First Hymn

What living creature, endowed with all his senses, does not love
the joys of light more than all the marvellous things around him –
light with its colours, its rays and waves, its gentle presence throughout the waking day. It is like the very soul of life, the breath of the
stars' huge, moving universe floating and dancing in the blue ether –
the breath of the sparkling, static stone, of the pensively feeding
plant, of the wild animal in its many forms – but above all of the lordly
stranger with the intelligent eyes, the elastic gait and the delicately
poised, resonant lips. As king over earthly nature, it calls for countless
transformations, forms and dissolves infinite unions, imprints its
heavenly image on all things terrestrial. Only its presence reveals the
splendours of earth's realm.

I turn away towards the holy, unutterable, mysterious night.
Far off lies the world – submerged in a deep vault – desolate and
lonely its sojourn. The strings of my heart are moved by a profound
melancholy. I want to dissolve into the dew and mingle with the
ash. Remote memories, the desires of my youth, the dreams of my
childhood, the brief joys and vain hopes of my whole life appear
clad in grey, like the evening mist after sunset. Light has pitched
its gay tents elsewhere. Will it never return to its children, who
wait with the faith of the innocent?

What is it that suddenly stirs within my heart, dispelling the
soft atmosphere of melancholy? Do you too find pleasure in us, dark
night? What is it that you hold beneath your cloak that touches my
soul with hidden power? A precious balsam trickles from your hand,
from the bunch of poppies. You lift the soul's heavy wings. We feel
ourselves moved in some dark, unutterable manner – with a start of
joy I see a calm face, turned towards me in tender solicitude, and
beneath the mass of curls it is my mother in her youth. How poor and
childish light now seems, how joyful and blessed the close of day! –
For this reason then because night alienates your vassals, you sowed
the shining spheres far and wide, to proclaim your omnipotence – your
return – during your absence. The infinite eyes that night has opened
for us seem more divine than those glittering stars. They see further
than the palest of those countless hosts – without need of light they
penetrate the depths of a loving soul – filling a higher dimension
with indescribable bliss. Praise to the queen of the world, the noble
herald of holy worlds, the guardian of happy love! She sends me you,
my dearly beloved – enchanting sun of the night – now I am awake –

die blässesten jener zahllosen Heere – unbedürftig des Lichts durch-
schaun sie die Tiefen eines liebenden Gemüts – was einen höhern
Raum mit unsäglicher Wollust füllt. Preis der Weltkönigin, der
hohen Verkündigerin heiliger Welten, der Pflegerin seliger Liebe! Sie
sendet mir dich – zarte Geliebte – liebliche Sonne der Nacht, – nun
wach ich – denn ich bin dein und mein, – du hast die Nacht mir zum
Leben verkündet – mich zum Menschen gemacht – zehre mit Geister-
glut meinen Leib, daß ich luftig mit dir inniger mich mische und dann
ewig die Brautnacht währt!

Dritte Hymne

Einst, da ich bittre Tränen vergoß, da in Schmerz aufgelöst
meine Hoffnung zerrann und ich einsam stand am dürren Hügel, der in
engen, dunkeln Raum die Gestalt meines Lebens barg – einsam, wie
noch kein Einsamer war, von unsäglicher Angst getrieben, kraftlos,
nur ein Gedanken des Elends noch, – wie ich da nach Hülfe umher-
schaute, vorwärts nicht konnte und rückwärts nicht, und am fliehenden,
verlöschten Leben mit unendlicher Sehnsucht hing: da kam aus
blauen Fernen, von den Höhen meiner alten Seligkeit, ein Dämmer-
ungsschauer – und mit einem Male riß das Band der Geburt, des
Lichtes Fessel. Hin floh die irdische Herrlichkeit und meine Trauer
mit ihr – zusammen floß die Wehmut in eine neue, unergründliche
Welt, – du Nachtbegeisterung, Schlummer des Himmels, kamst
über mich – die Gegend hob sich sacht empor – über der Gegend
schwebte mein entbundner, neugeborner Geist. Zur Staubwolke
wurde der Hügel – durch die Wolke sah ich die verklärten Züge der
Geliebten. In ihren Augen ruhte die Ewigkeit – ich faßte ihre Hände,
und die Tränen wurden ein funkelndes, unzerreißliches Band. Jahr-
tausende zogen abwärts in die Ferne, wie Ungewitter. An ihrem Halse
weint ich dem neuen Leben entzückende Tränen. – Es war der erste,
einzige Traum – und erst seitdem fühl ich ewigen, unwandelbaren
Glauben an den Himmel der Nacht und sein Licht, die Geliebte.

for I am yours and mine – you have turned night into life for me –
have made me a human being – consume my body with supernatural
passion so that my ethereal self may be more intimately mingled with
you and the wedding night last for ever!

Third Hymn

Once, when I was shedding bitter tears, when my hopes evaporated
into grief, and I stood alone on a bleak hillock that held the focus of my
life in its dark confines – more alone than any lone creature had ever
been, driven by indescribable anxiety, devoid of strength, conscious
only of one great misery, – as I looked round for help, unable to
advance or withdraw, clinging with boundless longing to a departing,
lost life : – there came from the dim blue distance, from the heights of
my former happiness, a tremor of dawn – and all of a sudden the
umbilical cord tore, the fetters of light. Earthly splendour vanished
and with it my grief – my melancholy flowed over into a new unfathomable world, – you, ecstasy of night, slumber of heaven, came
upon me – the countryside rose gently – over it floated my liberated
spirit, reborn. The hillock turned into a cloud of dust – through the
cloud I saw the transfigured traits of my beloved. In her eyes was all
eternity – I took her hands and my tears became a sparkling, in-
destructible link. Thousands of years receded into the distance, like a
thunder-storm. At her bosom I wept tears of joy at this new life. – It
was the first, the only dream – and only since then have I felt an
eternal, immutable faith in the heaven of night and its light, my
beloved.

Notes and Translations

———— ❖ ————

INTRODUCTION: FOCUS

1. J. Barzun, *Classic, Romantic and Modern* (1962), p. 71.
2. P. van Tieghem, *Le Romantisme dans la littérature européenne* (1948.)
3. R. Wellek, 'The concept of Romanticism in literary history', in *Concepts of Criticism* (Yale U.P., New Haven and London, 1963), p. 160.
4. R. Etiemble, *Comparaison n'est pas raison* (1963), p. 70: 'as I had been asked to take a course at Montpellier on *pre-romanticism* in Europe at the end of the eighteenth century, I gathered from the histories of literature all the topics that had to be dealt with: nature, landscape as a reflection of a state of mind, passionate love, fate, sensibility, the fleetingness of time, ruins and so forth: I gave a course, as conventional as could be, at the end of which I added: "I wish to point out to you that all my quotations illustrating the emergence of Pre-romanticism in Europe are taken from Chinese poets between the time of K'iu Yuan, who lived before the Christian era, and the period of the Song" '.
5. A. C. Dunstan, 'German influence on Coleridge', in *Modern Language Review*, XVII and XVIII (1922 and 1923).
   L. A. Willoughby, 'Coleridge and his German contemporaries', in *English Goethe Society* (1934).
   L. A. Willoughby, 'Coleridge und Deutschland', in *Germanisch-Romanische Monatsschrift*, XXIV (1936).
6. F. Baldensperger, *Goethe en France* (1907).
7. E. Eggli, *Schiller et le romantisme français* (1927).
8. L. Reynaud, *L'Influence allemande en France au 18ième et 19ième siècle* (1922).
9. W. F. Schirmer, *Der Einfluss der deutschen Literatur auf die englische im 19. Jahrhundert* (Halle/Saale, 1947).
   F. W. Stokoe, *German influence in the English Romantic period* (Cambridge, 1926).
10. M. A. Smith, *L'Influence des Lakistes sur les Romantiques français* (1920).

J. Texte, 'Wordsworth et la poésie Lakiste en France', in *Études de littérature européenne* (1898).

11. Dunstan, in *MLR* xviii 197.
12. Barzun, *Classic, Romantic and Modern*, pp. 155–8.
13. *English Romantic Poets*, ed. M. H. Abrams (Oxford U.P., 1960), pp. 3–24.
14. *English Romantic Poets*, p. 6.
15. *English Romantic Poets*, p. 16.
16. A. W. Schlegel, *Vorlesungen über dramatische Kunst und Literatur* (Mohr & Winter, Heidelberg, 1817), p. 13: 'the particular spirit of modern art, in contrast to ancient or classical art'.
17. F. Schlegel, *Gespräch über die Poesie*, in *Kritische Schriften*, ed. W. Rasch (Hanser Verlag, Munich, 1956), p. 324: 'I beg of you, however, not to jump to the conclusion that the romantic and the modern are entirely synonymous to me.'
18. F. Schlegel, in *Kritische Schriften*, p. 324: 'the romantic is not only a type of poetry, but also an element of poetry'.
19. F. Schlegel, in *Kritische Schriften*, p. 322: 'that is romantic which depicts emotional matter in an imaginative form'.
20. F. Schlegel, in *Kritische Schriften*, p. 299.
21. F. Schlegel, in *Kritische Schriften*, p. 312: 'it is in the East that we must seek the most sublime instances of the romantic'.
22. F. Schlegel, *Geschichte der alten und neuen Literatur* (Verlag Ferdinand Schöningh, Munich, 1961), p. 285: 'the really distinctive feature of the romantic, in so far as we still distinguish between the romantic and the Christian-allegorical'.
23. F. Schlegel, *Geschichte der alten und neuen Literatur*, p. 284: 'among dramatists, Calderon is the most Christian, and for that reason also the most romantic'.
24. F. Schlegel, in *Kritische Schriften*, p. 37: 'caprice'.
25. Stendhal, *Racine et Shakespeare* (Le Divan, Paris, 1928), p. 106: 'All the great writers were romantic in their day'.
26. Stendhal, *Racine et Shakespeare*, p. 114: 'the Roman artists were romantic; they represented what, in their day, was true and consequently moving to their compatriots'.
27. Stendhal, *Racine et Shakespeare*, p. 43: 'Romanticism is the art of offering people the literary works which are likely to give them the greatest possible pleasure, having due regard to contemporary habits and beliefs. Classicism, on the other hand, offers them the literature which gave the greatest possible pleasure to their great-grandparents.'
28. *Le Globe*, 2 April 1825: 'protestantism in literature and in the arts'.

29. Musset, *Lettres de Dupuis et Cotonet* (Charpentier, Paris, 1887), p. 193: 'a meaning easy to grasp, it was synonymous with absurd'.

30. Musset, *Dupuis et Cotonet*, p. 194: 'Romanticism was nothing other than the combination of the frivolous and the serious, the grotesque and the terrible, the farcical and the horrible, or, if you prefer other words, comedy and tragedy.'

31. Musset, *Dupuis et Cotonet*, p. 202: 'the classical was then only the imitation of Greek poetry and the romantic the imitation of German, English and Spanish poetry?'

32. Musset, *Dupuis et Cotonet*, p. 203: 'could it, we thought, be merely a matter of form? could this incomprehensible Romanticism refer to the break in the verse-line, about which there was so much fuss?'

33. Musset, *Dupuis et Cotonet*, p. 220: 'in the end, we believe that Romanticism is made up of all these adjectives used together, and of nothing else'.

34. Hugo, 1824 Preface to the *Odes et Ballades*, *Œuvres Complètes* (Hetzel & Quartin, Paris, n.d.), *Poésie*, 1 16: 'these sentries left by the Lord on the towers of Jerusalem, who will not rest by day or night'.

35. Wordsworth, *Michael*, lines 40–60.

THE HISTORICAL PERSPECTIVE

1. van Tieghem, *Le Romantisme dans la littérature européenne*, p. 247.

2. I. Berlin, *Some sources of Romanticism*. Six lectures delivered in Washington, broadcast B.B.C. Third Programme, Aug.–Sept. 1966.

3. M. Akenside, *Pleasures of Imagination*, book 1, line 120.

4. J. Macpherson, *The Poems of Ossian* (1784), 1 205.

5. E. Young, *Conjectures on Original Composition* (Manchester U.P., 1918), p. 7.

6. Young, *Conjectures*, p. 13.

7. L. Abercrombie, *Romanticism* (1926), p. 28 n.

8. Brockes, *Considerations on the moonlight of a pleasant spring evening*, *Earthly Joy in God*, reprinted in *Deutsche Literatur in Entwicklungsreihen: Das Weltbild der deutschen Aufklärung* (Leipzig, 1930), p. 245.
Hardly had the night begun to appear
Which promised the joy of cool after the burden of the day's heat,
When a new day seemed to dawn:

Out of the grey mist covering the horizon with crimson streaks
After the sultry atmosphere of the day
The full moon had just risen with a reddish gold shine,
And from its changing circle,
Which fills the night with shimmering light,
More grace flowed than shimmering light.

9. Goethe, *To the Moon.*

> Once more you fill the bushes and the valley
> Silently with a misty radiance,
> At last too you release
> My soul completely;
> Over my fields you spread
> Your gaze soothingly,
> Like the gentle eye of a friend
> Watching my destiny.

10. F. Strich, 'Europe and the Romantic movement', in *German Life and Letters,* ii (1948–9) 87.

11. F. Schlegel, in *Kritische Schriften*, p. 37 : 'a progressive universal poetry'.

12. Mme de Staël, *De l'Allemagne* (Oxford, 1906), p. 1 : 'For the past twenty years the French have been so preoccupied with political happenings that all literary matters have been in abeyance.'

13. Staël, *De l'Allemagne*, p. 171 : 'For some time people in France have been reading hardly anything other than memoirs and novels; it is not entirely out of frivolity that people have become less equal to serious reading, but because the happenings of the Revolution have accustomed them to attach importance solely to knowledge of events and men.'

14. W. F. Schirmer, *Kleine Schriften* (Tübingen, 1950), p. 173 : 'herald or interpreter'.

15. Staël, *De l'Allemagne*, p. 178 : 'the mannered style of writing'.

16. X. Marmier, Preface to a translation of Schiller's poems (1854), p. vi : 'a fairy-tale land, where men warble and sing like birds'.

17. Staël, *De l'Allemagne*, p. 33 : 'that which preceded Christianity and that which followed it'.

18. Nodier, *Débats*, 19 April 1817 : 'the head of the school of melancholy'.

19. Stokoe, *German influence in the English Romantic period*, app. v, pp. 180–7, lists German works translated into English, 1789–1803.

20. Keats, *Letters* (Oxford U.P., 1934), p. 72.

21. Nodier, *Débats*, 6 January 1816 : 'national controversy'.

22. Duvicquet, *Le Globe*, 6 December 1825 : 'the word "romantic" is used in France nowadays to denote any work contrary to the system current in France since Louis XIV'.

23. Desmarais, *Le Globe*, 29 October 1825 : 'the final bastion, the literary Bastille'.

24. Anon. *Le Globe*, 29 October 1825 : 'freedom', 'imitation only from nature', 'originality'.

25. Duvergier de Hauranne, *Le Globe*, 24 March 1825 : 'life, activity, surging forwards'.

26. Goethe, as reported by Eckermann, *Gespräche mit Goethe* (Insel-Verlag, 1955), p. 673, 6 March 1830 : 'What the French now regard as a new tendency in their literature is basically nothing but a reflection of what German literature has sought and achieved during the last fifty years.'

INDIVIDUALISM

1. Novalis, *Blütenstaub* 59, in *Werke* (Verlag Lambert Schneider, Heidelberg, 1953), I 323 : 'Only the individual is of interest, therefore all that is classical is not individual'.

2. Rousseau, *Confessions* (Garnier, Paris, 1879), p. 1 : 'I am undertaking a project without precedent and not liable to imitation. I want to show my fellow-men a man just as he is, true to nature; and this man will be myself. Myself alone. I feel my heart and I know men. I am not made like any of those I have come across. I venture to believe that I am not made like any other existing man. If I am not better, at least I am different.'

3. Rousseau, *Les Rêveries du Promeneur Solitaire* (Manchester U.P., 1942), p. 8 : 'the joy of communing with my soul'.

4. Rousseau, *Rêveries*, p. 52 : 'absorbed in myself'.

5. Rousseau, *Rêveries*, p. 11 : 'all my sustenance within myself'.

6. Rousseau, *Rêveries*, p. 3 : 'what am I in myself'.

7. Coleridge, *On Poesy or Art*, in *Biographia Literaria* (Oxford, 1907), II 259.

8. Fichte, opening words of the Introduction to the *Wissenschaftslehre* : 'Heed only yourself : turn your gaze away from all around you, and inwards on to yourself; this is the first demand that philosophy makes of its apprentice. Nothing outside of you matters, but solely you yourself.'

9. Coleridge, *Biog. Lit.* II 21–3.

10. Coleridge, *Biog. Lit.* II 33.

11. Coleridge, *Biog. Lit.* II 14.

12. F. Schlegel, *Ideen* 60, in *Kritische Schriften*, p. 93 : 'It is just his individuality that is the primary and eternal element in man. To make a cult of the formation and development of this individuality would be a kind of divine egotism.'

13. Novalis, *Blütenstaub* 30, in *Werke*, i 315 : 'It is the supreme task of human development to take possession of one's transcendental self, to be, as it were, the quintessential ego of one's ego.'

14. Novalis, *Blütenstaub* 18, in *Werke*, i 310 : 'It is inwards that the mysterious path leads.'

15. Schleiermacher, *Denkmale der inneren Entwicklung* (Leipzig, 1914), p. 107 : 'Friendship is an approach to individuality into infinity, and can therefore be shared and perfected likewise into infinity, and is only an approach to oneself.'

16. F. Schlegel, *Ideen* 43, in *Kritische Schriften*, p. 90 : 'What man is to the other creatures on earth, the artist is to man.'

17. F. Schlegel, *Ideen* 45, in *Kritische Schriften*, p. 91 : 'He who has his centre of gravity within himself is an artist.'

18. F. Schlegel, *Ideen* 44, in *Kritische Schriften*, p. 91 : 'Every artist is a mediator for all others.'

19. Novalis, *Blütenstaub* 35, in *Werke*, i 317 : 'We are engaged on a mission : we are called to fashion the world.'

20. F. Schlegel, in *Kritische Schriften*, p. 38 : 'alone is infinite, just as it alone is quite free, recognizing as its prime law that the poet's caprice brooks no law'.

21. A. W. Schlegel, *Über dramatische Kunst und Literatur*, ii 30 : 'an originality unheeding of classical models'.

22. H. A. Korff, *Geist der Goethezeit* (Leipzig, 1940), iii 311 : 'decisive swing . . . from the allegiance of modern poetry to the Ancient ideal of beauty to a confident self-assertion'.

23. Hugo, *Réponse à un acte d'accusation*, in *Les Contemplations*.
    'And over the batallions of Alexandrines, drawn up in
    formation,
    I blew a revolutionary wind.
    I put the red cap of liberty on to the old dictionary.'
    'Into battle, prose and verse! draw up in fighting order!'

24. P. Trahard, *Le Romantisme défini par 'Le Globe'* (1924), p. 100 : 'What is characteristic of the new doctrine, what distinguishes it above all from classicism, is its strong contempt for all ideas taken on trust, for theories learnt by heart, for traditions un- tested by reason; it is in fact a distrust of authority and an altogether seditious love of liberty.'

25. Trahard, *Le Romantisme défini par 'Le Globe'*, p. 11 : 'What is this Jerusalem that they want to conquer, who is this enemy

they are determined to fight? the enemy is routine, the Jerusalem is liberty.'

26. Trahard, *Le Romantisme défini par 'Le Globe'*, p. 18: 'To put it briefly, subjection to grammatical rules, independence in all else, this must be the two-fold motto of the romantic party.'

27. Hugo, Preface to *Hernani*, in *Théâtre Complet* (Édition Pléiade, Paris, 1963), I 1147: 'Romanticism, so often wrongly defined, is in the last resort – and this is its true definition, taking only its militant aspects into account – nothing but liberalism in literature.'

28. Hugo, Preface to *Cromwell*, in *Théâtre Complet*, I 444: 'opposed to the tyranny of systems, laws and rules'.

29. Trahard, *Le Romantisme défini par 'Le Globe'*, p. 24: 'In practice romanticism is a lively coalition of various interests, all with one common aim: to combat the rules, the rules dictated by convention.'

30. Deschamps, 'La guerre en temps de paix', appendix to *Préface des Études françaises et étrangères* (1925), p. 74: 'The essence of romanticism lies not so much in the period of literature from which the subject is drawn, as in the tendency of some writers to cast off the rules of art.'

31. Quoted by P. Moreau, *Le Classicisme des Romantiques* (1932), p. 164: 'All systems are false; only genius is true.'

32. Staël, *De la Littérature* (Geneva, 1959), p. 189: 'If asked which is better: a work with great defects and great beauty or a mediocre, correct work, I would answer without hesitation that any work with even a single ray of genius is preferable.'

33. Hugo, Preface to *Les Orientales*, in *Œuvres Complètes, Poésie*, II 3 and 5: 'the exact geography of the intellectual world', 'the roadmaps of art on which the frontiers of the possible and the impossible are marked in red and blue'.

34. Hugo, Preface to *Cromwell*, in *Théâtre Complet*, I 434: 'There are no rules or models; or rather, no other rules than the general laws of nature, that govern all art, and the special laws that arise with each work from the circumstances peculiar to each subject. . . . The poet, and this should be emphasized, must be guided only by nature, truth and inspiration.'

35. Vigny, *Lettre à Lord XX*, in *Théâtre Complet* (1858), p. 316: 'the disease that often afflicts our country'; 'the same ideas, the same expressions, the same sounds'.

36. Stendhal, *Racine et Shakespeare*, p. 10: 'a French habit, a deeply rooted habit'.

37. Stendhal, *Racine et Shakespeare*, p. 165.

38. Stendhal, *Racine et Shakespeare*, p. 45 : 'it needs courage to be a romantic because it involves taking risks'.
39. Deschamps, *Préface des Études françaises et étrangères*, p. 35 : 'the last fortress'.
40. Vigny, in *Théâtre Complet*, p. 314 : 'A simple question must be settled. It is this : "Will the French theatre admit a modern tragedy or not? – a tragedy that gives a broad picture of life, instead of one restricted by the final catastrophe of the plot; that is composed of characters, not parts, peaceful scenes without high drama amidst comic and tragic scenes; written in an informal language, in turn comic or tragic, and at times epic?" '
41. A. W. Schlegel, aphorism from *Athenäum*, in *Sämtliche Werke* (Böcking, n.d.), VIII 12.
42. Staël, *De la Littérature*, p. 207 : 'heroes portrayed with their weaknesses, virtues in all their inconsistency, the commonplace alongside the lofty'; 'from human life'; 'from an ideal of beauty'.
43. Vigny, in *Théâtre Complet*, p. 327 : 'conventional elegance'; 'more natural beauty'.
44. Vigny, in *Théâtre Complet*, p. 318 : 'First he will take a great expanse of time in his ample grasp and will make whole lives move within it; he will create man, not as a species, but as an individual; he will let his figures lead their own lives, and will only put into their hearts the seeds of passion that produce great events; then, when the hour has come, and only then, he will show destiny entangling its victims in inextricable knots. Whereupon, far from considering his characters too small for the space, he will groan and exclaim that they lack air and space, for art will be like life.'
45. Constant, *Réflexions sur la tragédie*, in *Œuvres* (Édition Pléiade, Paris, 1957), p. 958 : 'local colour is the foundation of truthfulness'.
46. Hugo, Preface to *Cromwell*, in *Théâtre Complet*, I 441 : 'a free, unrestricted, straightforward verse-form, that dares to speak without prudishness, to express itself without preciosity; that moves naturally and easily from comedy to tragedy, from the sublime to the grotesque'.
47. Vigny, in *Théâtre Complet*, p. 322 : 'in favour of the true, up-to-date word'.
48. Vigny, in *Théâtre Complet*, p. 314 : 'in art, as in life, will move from its customary simplicity to passionate exaltation'.
49. Vigny, in *Théâtre Complet*, p. 321 : 'A drama will never show anything other than characters come together to speak of their problems; they must therefore speak. . . . And does not every man, in the course of ordinary conversation, have favourite

phrases, recurrent terms derived from his upbringing, his profession, his interests? Does he not have a preference for certain comparisons and for a whole range of words in daily use? Must every character then always avail himself of the same words, the same images that others use too? No, he must be precise or diffuse, careless or pedantic, lavish or sparing of embellishment according to his character, his age and his inclinations.'

50. Deschamps, *Préface des Études françaises et étrangères*, p. 51: 'that the crux of the matter is not the actual division of the scenes and acts, the sudden transitions from a forest to a castle or from one province to another, but the individualized portrayal of characters, the constant replacement of narrative by action, the spontaneity of the language, the poetic coloration, and a style that is wholly modern'.

51. Hugo, Preface to *Cromwell*, in *Théâtre Complet*, I 265: 'not the beautiful, but the typical'.

52. Hugo, Preface to *Cromwell*, in *Théâtre Complet*, I 191: 'The modern muse will realize that not everything in the world is beautiful, that the ugly exists beside the beautiful, the distorted along with the graceful, the grotesque as a counterbalance to the sublime, the evil with the good, shade with light. She will begin to do like nature, to mingle in her creations – without, however, fusing – shade and light, the grotesque and the sublime.'

53. F. Schlegel, in *Kritische Schriften*, p. 41: 'From the romantic point of view the most curious sorts of poetry, even the eccentric and the monstrous, are of value as preliminary exercises to universality, provided there is in them some grain of originality.'

54. F. Schlegel, in *Kritische Schriften*, p. 37: 'Romantic poetry is a progressive universal poetry. It is destined not merely to reunite the separate genres of poetry and to link poetry to philosophy and rhetoric. It would and should also mingle and fuse poetry and prose, genius and criticism, artistic poetry and natural poetry, make poetry lively and sociable, and life and society poetic, poeticize wit, fill and saturate the forms of art with worthwhile subject matter. It embraces all that is poetic from the most stupendously complex aesthetic systems down to the sigh, the kiss uttered in artless song by the child creating its own poetry.'

55. A. W. Schlegel, *Über dramatische Kunst und Literatur*, III 14: 'Ancient art and poetry aim at a sharp division of the disparate, the romantic has a liking for perfect fusion; all the opposites: nature and art, poetry and prose, gravity and jest, recollection

and presentiment, the spiritual and the sensuous, the earthly and the divine, life and death, are inextricably mingled.'

56. Tieck and Wackenroder, *Phantasien über die Kunst*, in *Deutsche National-Literatur* 145 (Berlin), p. 91 : 'I am of the opinion that all things can and must exist side by side, and that there is no more narrow-minded defamation of the sublimity of art than to draw premature, sharp dividing lines between its various spheres.'

57. Novalis, *Blütenstaub* 58, in *Werke*, I 322 : 'the confused'; 'the well-ordered'.

58. Novalis, *Heinrich von Ofterdingen*, in *Werke*, I 181 : 'The world becomes a dream, the dream becomes a world.'

59. C. H. Herford, *The Age of Wordsworth* (1914), p. xxviii.

60. Marginal note to F. Schlegel's *Ideen*, 51 : 'Do not animals, plants, stones, stars and breezes also belong with mankind, which is merely a central meeting point of countless varied threads? Can mankind be understood divorced from nature, and is it so very different from other manifestations of nature?'

61. Keats, *Sonnet*, published in 1817.

62. Wordsworth, *London, 1802*.

63. Wordsworth, *To a Distant Friend*.

64. Coleridge, *Frost at Midnight*.

65. Coleridge, *Hymn before Sunrise, in the Vale of Chamouni*.

66. Wordsworth, *Ode on Intimations of Immortality*.

67. Coleridge, *To Nature*.

68. Cf. Abrams, 'The Correspondent Breeze : A Romantic Metaphor', in *English Romantic Poets*, pp. 37–54.

69. Rousseau, *Œuvres Complètes* (Édition Pléiade, Paris, 1959), II 78 : 'It is a general experience common to all men, though not all are aware of it, that high up in the mountains, where the air is pure and rarified, one is conscious of a greater ease in breathing, a greater sense of physical lightness, a greater mental serenity, an attenuation of pleasure and of passion. Up there, in keeping with the sights around us, our thoughts assume a certain vague, sublime grandiosity, a certain vague, voluptuous charm, quite devoid of harsh sensuality. It is as if all low, earthly feelings were left behind us as we rise above the human level, and as we draw nigh to the ethereal realms, the soul absorbs something of their eternal purity.'

70. Coleridge, to William Sotheby, 10 September 1802, in *Letters*, ed. E. L. Griggs (Oxford, 1956), II 460.

71. Shelley, *On Love*, in *Complete Works*, ed. R. Ingpen and W. E. Beck (1965), VI 202.

72. Shelley, *The Invitation.*
73. Shelley, *The Recollection.*
74. Shelley. *A Dream of the Unknown.*
75. Lamartine, *L'Isolement*, in *Premières Méditations* : 'rivers, rocks, forests'.
76. Lamartine, *L'Automne*, in *Premières Méditations* : 'earth, sun, valleys'.
77. Lamartine, *Au Rossignol*, in *Harmonies Poétiques.*
78. Coleridge, *Frost at Midnight.*
79. Blake, *Vision of the Last Judgement*, in *Poetry and Prose*, ed. G. Keynes (1946), p. 651.
80. Novalis, *Zueignung* (*Dedication*) to *Heinrich von Ofterdingen* : 'To gaze deep into the soul of the wide world.'
81. Schelling, *Werke* (1797), II 55 : 'Nature should be spirit made visible, spirit nature become invisible.'
82. Novalis, *Die Lehrlinge zu Saïs*, in *Werke*, I 254 : 'Hyacinth now ran as far as he could, through valleys and wildernesses, over hills and streams, towards the mysterious land. Everywhere he asked men and beasts after the holy goddess (Isis). Some laughed, some remained silent, no one told him anything. At first he passed through rough, wild regions, mist and cloud obscured his path, storms raged incessantly; then he came to vast sandy deserts of hot dust, and as he wandered on, he too changed, time seemed to grow longer and his inner restlessness subsided, he became gentler and the tumultuous impulses within him turned into a tranquil but strong sense of purpose that absorbed his whole being. It was as if many years had gone by. Now the country became more luxurious and varied once more, the air warm and blue, the path smoother, green bushes tempted him with their pleasant shade, but he did not understand their language, they did not appear to be speaking either, yet they filled his heart with green hues and a cool stillness. That sweet longing grew ever stronger within him, the leaves became ever more succulent, the birds and beasts ever more jubilant, the fruits more luscious, the sky bluer, the air warmer and his love more ardent, the time sped with increasing rapidity, as though he were approaching his goal.'
83. Novalis, *Heinrich von Ofterdingen*, in *Werke*, I 92 : 'a strange subterranean realm'.
84. Novalis, *Heinrich von Ofterdingen*, in *Werke*, I 90 : 'introverted dream world'.
85. Tieck, *Werke* (Bibliographisches Institut Leipzig, n.d.), II 57 : 'He came to regions where he had never been, the rocks grew

steeper, nothing was green, the bare mountains called him with angry cries and a desolate, moaning wind drove him on.'

86. Tieck, *Werke*, II 68 : 'the sighs and moans audible everywhere in nature to him who has ears to hear; a great wound heaves painfully on the plants, the foliage, the flowers and trees, they are the corpse of former marvellous worlds of stone, they show us an image of the most ghastly decay'.

87. Hoffmann, *Sämtliche Werke* (Rösl & Cie., Leipzig, 1924), v 232 : 'Not a tree, not a blade of grass grows in the bare shattered cleft, and jagged rock-formations tower above it all around in strange shapes, some like huge ossified beasts, some like colossal men. Down in the chasm stones and scoria – burned-out dross of metal – lie about in a chaos of destruction, and a narcotic sulphurous vapour always rises from it, as if the dregs of hell were being boiled and were poisoning all the green air of nature with their fumes. One might well believe that this was the spot where Dante descended and saw the Inferno in all its horror, with its pitiless tortures.'

88. Hoffmann, *Werke*, v 277 : 'the paths of an enchanted garden'.

89. Hoffmann, *Werke*, v 244 : 'He gazed at the Elysian fields of splendid metallic trees and plants that bore scintillating stones in place of fruit, blossom and flowers.'

90. Goethe, *Die Leiden des jungen Werthers*, in *Werke* (Bergland-Buch, Salzburg, 1949), I 417 : 'I could lead the best and happiest life, were I not a fool.'

91. Byron, *Childe Harold's Pilgrimage*, canto I, stanza lxxxiv.

92. Byron, *Childe Harold*, canto II, stanza xvi.

93. Chateaubriand, *René* (Oxford U.P., 1926), pp. 140–1 : 'I see a young man whose head is full of day-dreams, who is disgruntled with everything and is shunning his social obligations to yield to idle speculation. . . . What are you doing all alone in the depths of the forest, where you are wasting your time and neglecting your duties? Arrogant young man, who thought that man could suffice unto himself. . . .'

94. Byron, *Childe Harold*, canto II, stanza xvi.

95. Byron, *Childe Harold*, canto I, stanza ix.

96. Musset, *La Confession d'un Enfant du Siècle* (Conard, Paris, 1937), p. 337 : 'Oh unhappy creature! you could never know how to love!' 'That's as maybe, I can well believe it; but as God is my witness, I know how to suffer.'

97. Coleridge, *The Rime of the Ancient Mariner*, lines 282 ff.

98. Byron, *Childe Harold*, canto III, stanza xlii.

99. Chateaubriand, *René*, p. 101 : 'a tendency to melancholy'.

100. Byron, *Childe Harold*, canto i, stanza xxvii.
101. Byron, *Childe Harold*, canto i, stanza iv.
102. Chateaubriand, *René*, p. 120 : 'profound sense of tedium'.
103. Musset, *Enfant du Siècle*, p. 200: 'dreadful struggle of my youth with my sense of tedium'.
104. Musset, *Enfant du Siècle*, p. 14: 'unfathomable feeling of uneasiness'.
105. De Quincey, *The Confessions of an English Opium Eater* (Everyman's Library), p. 6.
106. Chateaubriand, *René*, p. 116 : 'unstable desires'.
107. Goethe, *Werther*, in *Werke*, i 393 : 'for you have seen nothing as inconstant, as unstable as this heart of mine. My dear friend! need I say this to you who have so often had to watch me shift from sorrow to debauchery, from sweet melancholy to destructive passion?'
108. Chateaubriand, *René*, p. 103 : 'I was impetuous by nature, of unstable character. At times noisy and exuberant, at others silent and sad.'
109. Musset, *Enfant du Siècle*, p. 72 : 'All these sufferings inspired a kind of frenzy in me; sometimes I wanted to do like the monks and to torture myself in order to subdue my sensuality; at other times I wanted to go out into the street, into the country, just anywhere, to fling myself at the feet of the first woman I saw and to swear eternal love to her.'
110. Byron, *Childe Harold*, canto i, stanza ii.
111. Byron, *Childe Harold*, canto i, stanza vi.
112. Musset, *Enfant du Siècle*, p. 275 : 'as soon as I ceased to scoff, I wept'.
113. Musset, *Enfant du Siècle*, p. 261 : 'truly at myself, face to face'.
114. Chateaubriand, *René*, p. 117: 'Alas! I am seeking I know not what, but the urge to seek does not leave me. Is it my fault if I come up against limits everywhere and if the finite is worthless to me?'
115. Novalis, *Blütenstaub* 1, in *Werke*, i 307 : 'We seek the infinite everywhere and always find only finite things.'
116. Rousseau, *Confessions*, p. 34: 'So I attained my sixteenth year, restless, dissatisfied with everything and with myself, without relish for my position, without the pleasures befitting my age, consumed by aimless longings, given to weeping and sighing without knowing wherefore, and fondly cherishing my daydreams for lack of anything equally absorbing.'
117. Young, *Night Thoughts*, in *Works* (1813), i 100.
118. Chateaubriand, *René*, p. 135 : 'I even found a sort of unexpected

satisfaction in the abundance of my grief, and with hidden joy I realized that grief is a sensation as ephemeral as pleasure.'

119. Musset, *Enfant du Siècle*, p. 86 : 'I burrowed into the depths of my heart to feel its pangs of torture.'

120. Young, *Night Thoughts*, in *Works*, I 283.

121. Young, *Night Thoughts*, in *Works*, I 286.

122. Chateaubriand, *René*, p. 137 : 'One enjoys anything out of the ordinary, even if it is a misfortune.'

123. Chateaubriand, *René*, p. 116 : 'the prey of his imagination'.

124. W. Rose, *From Goethe to Byron: the development of 'Weltschmerz' in German literature* (1924).

125. Cf. V. Rossel, *Histoire des relations littéraires entre la France et l'Allemagne* (1897), pp. 96–103.

126. Hugo, Preface to *Cromwell*, in *Théâtre Complet*, I 415 : 'Christianity brought melancholy into being.'

127. Byron, *Childe Harold*, Preface to canto IV.

128. Goethe, *Werther*, in *Werke*, I 395 : 'I turn inwards on to myself and I find a whole world! Again more in foreboding and sombre longing than in actual, vivid substance. Everything swims before me and I face the world with a dreamy smile.'

129. Goethe, *Werther*, in *Werke*, I 449 : 'Werther, you are a sick man.'

130. Goethe, *Werther*, in *Werke*, I 423 : 'my sickness'.

131. Goethe, *Werther*, in *Werke*, I 435 : 'I am unable to help myself.'

132. Goethe, *Werther*, in *Werke*, I 444 : 'I feel all too well that the fault is mine alone – not fault! – Suffiice it to say that within me is the source of all my misery and of all my former joys.'

133. Goethe, *Werther*, in *Werke*, I 457 : 'Oh why did you have to be born with this vehemence, this unquenchable passion that is in all you do?'

134. Chateaubriand, *René*, p. 103 : 'self-inflicted ills'.

135. Chateaubriand, *René*, p. 120 : 'For a while I wrestled with my affliction, but without gusto and without the will to conquer it.'

136. Goethe, *Werther*, in *Werke*, I 439 : 'As nature declines into autumn, autumn reigns within and about me. My leaves turn yellow and already the leaves of the trees round about have fallen.'

137. Chateaubriand, *René*, p. 118 : 'Autumn took me unawares in the midst of these doubts; I entered with delight into the season of storms. At times I would have liked to be one of those warriors roaming amongst the winds, the clouds, and the phantoms; at other times I envied the fate of even the shepherd I saw warming his hands at a little fire of brushwood that he had lit in a nook of

the woods. I listened to his doleful songs which reminded me that in every land man's spontaneous song is sad, even when expressing happiness. Our heart is an imperfect instrument, a lyre with missing strings, on which we have to render sounds of joy by the tunes associated with sorrow.'

138. Musset, *Enfant du Siècle*, p. 137 : 'it is my senses that are active; my heart plays no part'.

139. Musset, *Enfant du Siècle*, p. 163 : 'imprisoned in my solitude'.

140. Goethe, *Werther*, in *Werke*, I 472 : 'He died at mid-day. The official's presence and his activity quietened any commotion. At about eleven at night he let him be buried in the spot he had chosen. The old man followed the corpse and also his sons, Albert could not. There were fears for Lotte's life. Workmen bore him. No priest accompanied him.'

141. Byron, *Manfred*, I i 144.

142. Byron, *Don Juan*, canto IV, stanza iii.

143. Byron, *Don Juan*, canto XV, stanza xxii.

144. Byron, *Don Juan*, canto VII, stanza vi.

145. Byron, *Don Juan*, canto VII, stanza iv.

146. Byron, *Don Juan*, canto VII, stanzas ii and iii.

147. Byron, *Don Juan*, canto I, stanzas xciii and xciv.

148. Byron, *Don Juan*, canto II, stanza clxxi.

149. Byron, *Don Juan*, canto II, stanza clxxviii.

150. Byron, *Don Juan*, canto III, stanza viii.

IMAGINATION

1. Blake, *Vision of the Last Judgement*, in *Poetry and Prose*, p. 651.

2. Blake, *Vision of the Last Judgement*, in *Poetry and Prose*, p. 639.

3. Coleridge, *Biog. Lit.* I 202.

4. Wordsworth, *Preface to the 'Lyrical Ballads'*, in *Poetical Works*, ed. E. de Selincourt (Oxford, 1944), II 409.

5. Shelley, *Defence of Poetry*, in *Complete Works*, VII 136.

6. Shelley, *Defence of Poetry*, in *Complete Works*, VII 109.

7. Keats, to his brother George, 18 Sept. 1819, in *Letters*, p. 343.

8. Keats, to Benjamin Bailey, 22 Nov. 1817, in *Letters*, p. 48.

9. Byron, *Letters and Journals* (1901), V 554.

10. Shelley, *Defence of Poetry*, in *Complete Works*, VII 109.

11. Schleiermacher, *Über die Religion* (Deutsche Bibliothek, Berlin, n.d.), p. 94 : 'that imagination is the supreme and prime quality of man'.

12. F. Schlegel, in *Kritische Schriften*, p. 322 : 'In my opinion and

according to my usage, the romantic is that which presents a subjective theme in an imaginative form.'

13. Schelling, *System des transzendentalen Idealismus*, in *Werke* (Felix Meiner, Leipzig, n.d.), iii 628 : 'What we call nature is a poem that lies hidden in a mysterious, wondrous form. But the veil could be lifted if we were to recognize in it the Odyssey of the spirit which seeks, and yet also flees itself in a curiously paradoxical self-deception. Through the world of the senses, as through a faint haze, we catch a glimpse of the realm of the imagination, the aim of our aspirations, hidden like the meaning behind the words.'

14. Vigny, 'Réflexions sur la vérité dans l'art', foreword to *Cinq-Mars*, *Œuvres* (Edition Pléiade, Paris, 1948) ii 25 : 'primarily a creative force'.

15. Lamartine, *Première Préface des Méditations*, in *Œuvres* (Hachette, Paris, 1915), pp. 368–70 : 'life is life'; 'before and after the daily round of real work'; 'poetry is not life; it is a relaxation or a consolation derived from one's own voice.'

16. M. Gilman, *The Idea of Poetry in France* (Cambridge, Mass., 1955), p. 206.

17. Vigny, *Journal d'un Poète*, in *Œuvres*, ii 901 : 'Art is a selection from truth.'

18. Hugo, Preface to *Cromwell*, in *Théâtre Complet*, i 425 : 'the essence of drama is reality'.

19. H. Peyre, *Shelley et la France* (Cairo, 1935), p. 148 : 'very down-to-earth in its raptures, a very good boy'.

20. Soumet, *Les scrupules littéraires de Mme la Baronne de Staël*, in E. Eggli and P. Martino, *Le Débat romantique en France* (1933), i 219 : 'The French cannot be told too often that they are too cautious in crossing the fields of imagination; they are not idealistic enough in their approach to the fine arts; they want to reduce everything to precise imitation; but the gift for poetry, this luxuriance of the soul, sometimes has to scorn the beauty of real things in order to achieve that special sublimity that can arise only from its own inspiration.'

21. I. Babbitt, *Rousseau and Romanticism* (Boston, 1919), p. 61.

22. Baudelaire, *Salon de 1859*, in *Œuvres Complètes* (1955), ii 125 : 'the monsters of my phantasy'; 'the queen of faculties'.

23. Addison, *Spectator*, no. 4711.

24. Gray, *Correspondence with William Mason* (1853), pp. 146 and 46.

25. F. Schlegel, in *Kritische Schriften*, p. 310 : 'other than the hieroglyphic expression of outer nature transfigured by the imagination'.

26. Bodmer, *Von den poetischen Gemälden*, in W. Burkhard, *Schrift-werke deutscher Sprache* (Aarau, 1953), II 31 : 'the imagination is not merely the soul's treasury, where the senses store their pictures in safe-keeping for subsequent use; besides this it also has a region of its own which extends much further than the dominion of the senses . . . Imagination outstrips all the world's magicians : it not only places the real before our eyes in a vivid image and makes distant things present, but also, with a power more potent than that of magic, it draws that which does not exist out of the state of potentiality, gives it a sem-blance of reality and makes us see, hear and feel these new creations.'

27. Shelley, *Defence of Poetry*, in *Complete Works*, VII 134.

28. Shelley, *Defence of Poetry*, in *Complete Works*, VII 137.

29. Blake, *Vision of the Last Judgement*, in *Poetry and Prose*, p. 651.

30. Blake, *Annotations to Berkeley's 'Siris'*, in *Poetry and Prose*, p. 818.

31. Coleridge, *On Poesy and Art*, in *Biog. Lit.* II 258.

32. Korff, *Geist der Goethezeit*, III 278 : 'the creative imagination to a cardinal principle'.

33. A. W. Schlegel, *Über dramatische Kunst und Literatur*, I 24 : 'is the poetry of longing'; 'between recollection and foreboding'; 'the poetry of possession'.

34. Tieck, *Kritische Schriften* (Leipzig, 1848), I 49 : 'because his imagination creates everywhere the characters and happenings he desires; he transforms huts into palaces, windmills into giants, etc.'

35. Novalis, *Blütenstaub* 18, in *Werke*, I 310–11 : 'Imagination posits the world to come either up on high or down in the depths or in some psychic transmutation. We dream of journeys through the universe : is not the whole universe within us? We do not know the depths of the human spirit. It is inwards that the mysterious path leads. Within ourselves, or nowhere, is eternity to be found with its worlds, both past and future. The outer world is a world of shadows, it throws its shadow into the realm of light.'

36. A. W. Schlegel, *Über dramatische Kunst und Literatur*, I 23 : 'In Christianity everything has been reversed : the contemplation of the infinite has destroyed the finite; life has become a world of shadows and of darkness, and only yonder does the eternal day of true being dawn.'

37. Shelley, *Defence of Poetry*, in *Complete Works*, VII 107 and 109.

38. A. W. Schlegel, *Über dramatische Kunst und Literatur*, I 24–5 :

'The Greek ideal of humanity was a perfect concord and balance of all forces, natural harmony. The moderns, on the other hand, have become conscious of an inner dualism which precludes such an ideal; hence they strive in their poetry to reconcile and fuse insolubly the two worlds between which we are torn: the spiritual and the sensuous.'

39. Schleiermacher, *Denkmale der inneren Entwicklung*, p. 107: 'an approach to individuality into infinity, and can therefore be shared and perfected likewise into infinity, and is only an approach to oneself'.

40. B. Willey, 'Coleridge on Imagination and Fancy', in *Proceedings of the British Academy* (1946), p. 181.

41. Ritter, *Fragmente aus dem Nachlass eines jungen Physikers*, 631 (Heidelberg, 1810): 'He who perceives in the infinity of nature only *one* entity, *one* perfect poem in which every word, every syllable reiterates the harmony of the whole, he has indeed won the highest prize, the exclusive gift of love!'

42. Baader, *Vom Wärmestoff* (1786), p. 39: 'Love is the common factor that links all the creatures in the universe and holds them together. Call it what you will: gravity, attraction, cohesion, affinity, corrosion etc., all words which, to be sure, give no explanation; but how could they? – Suffice it to say that all matter has a tendency to unify (which is visible under and above our moon). Attraction, agglutination is, therefore, an un-contested fact, a phenomenon that perhaps admits of no further explanation, nor does it require such. Without affinity, no wholeness, no world is conceivable; our earth would for ever be a chaotic, dead wasteland, a mush without shape or form, truly an absurdity.'

43. Novalis, *Sämtliche Werke*, ed. P. Kluckhohn (Leipzig, 1928), VI 28: 'Poetry induces the deepest insight and interactivity, the truest communion of the finite with the infinite.'

44. Novalis, *Blütenstaub* 122, in *Werke*, I 344: 'Humanity is the common organ of the Gods. Poetry unites them, like us.'

45. Novalis, *Werke*, I 382: 'And all of a sudden the umbilical cord tore, the fetters of light – the earthly splendour vanished and with it my grief. My melancholy streamed away into a new unfathomable world – You, ecstasy of night, slumber of heaven came upon me.'

46. F. Schlegel, in *Kritische Schriften*, p. 37: 'not merely to reunite the separate genres of poetry and to link poetry to philosophy and rhetoric. It would and should also mingle and fuse poetry and prose, genius and criticism, artistic poetry and natural poetry,

make poetry lively and sociable, and life and society poetic'.

47. Schleiermacher, *Über die Religion*, p. 120 : 'art and its works'.
48. Tieck, *Phantasien über die Kunst*, p. 48 : 'Pictures fade, poems die away, – but it was not to verses and colours that they owed their existence. In its very presence art contains eternity and needs no future, for eternity is the sign of its perfection.'
49. Lamartine, *Des Destinées de la Poésie*, in *Œuvres*, p. 423 : 'the pieces of poetry that I have published are only garbled sketches, shattered fragments of the poem within my soul'.
50. K. Coburn, *Inquiring Spirit* (1951), p. 20.
51. Coleridge, *On the Principles of Genial Criticism*, in *Biog. Lit.* II 220–1.
52. Coleridge, *On the Principles of Genial Criticism*, in *Biog. Lit.* II 232.
53. A. W. Schlegel, *Über dramatische Kunst und Literatur*, III 8–9 : 'Form is mechanical if it is imposed from without as a fortuitous addition unrelated to the object's essence; as a soft mass, for instance, is presssed into some shape which it retains on hardening. Organic form, on the other hand, is innate; it evolves from the inner being and attains its final pre-destined shape with the seed's maturity. Such forms may be seen throughout nature, wherever living forces are active, from the crystallization of salts and minerals, through plants and flowers right up to the formation of the human face. In the fine arts too, as in nature, the greatest of artists, every genuine form is organic, i.e. determined by the work's content.'
54. H. C. Robinson, *Diary, Reminiscences and Correspondence* (1869), I 352.
55. J. Shawcross, Introduction to Coleridge's *Biog. Lit.* I lxxxviii–lxxxix.
56. Coleridge, *Biog. Lit.* I 101.
57. Coleridge, *Biog. Lit.* I 102.
58. *Letters of Charles Lamb* (1888), II 332.
59. Coleridge, Note headed 'Solger's *Erwin*', in K. Coburn, *Inquiring Spirit*, p. 99.
60. This term was coined by K. Coburn as the title of her edition of Coleridge's notes.
61. I. A. Richards, Preface to *Coleridge on Imagination* (1934).
62. Coleridge, 'Note on a sermon on the prevalence of infidelity and enthusiasm by Walter Birch', in K. Coburn, *Inquiring Spirit*, p. 103.
63. Coleridge, *Biog. Lit.* I 202.
64. M. Bowra, *The Romantic Imagination* (Oxford Paperback, 1961), p. 271.

65. Shelley, *Defence of Poetry*, in *Complete Works*, VII 123.
66. Blake, *Descriptive Catalogue*, in *Poetry and Prose*, p. 145.
67. Shelley, *Defence of Poetry*, in *Complete Works*, VII 111.
68. Shelley, *Defence of Poetry*, in *Complete Works*, VII 115.
69. Shelley, *Defence of Poetry*, in *Complete Works*, VII 117.
70. Shelley, *Defence of Poetry*, in *Complete Works*, VII 112.
71. Shelley, *Defence of Poetry*, in *Complete Works*, VII 116.
72. Shelley, *Defence of Poetry*, in *Complete Works*, VII 140.
73. Wordsworth, *Preface to the 'Lyrical Ballads'*, in *Poetical Works*, II 394.
74. Keats, *Letters*, p. 30.
75. Keats, *Letters*, p. 207.
76. Keats, *Letters*, p. 49.
77. Shelley, *Defence of Poetry*, in *Complete Works*, VII 137.
78. Coleridge, *On Poesy and Art*, in *Biog. Lit.* II 253.
79. A. W. Schlegel, *Über dramatische Kunst und Literatur*, III 15: 'closer to the secret of the universe'.
80. F. Schlegel, *Geschichte der alten und neuen Literatur*, p. 282: 'by raising the veil of mortality, it lets us glimpse the secret of the unseen world in the mirror of a penetrating imagination'.
81. Runge, *Hinterlassene Schriften* (1840), II 124: 'in every perfect work of art we are fully aware of our intimate relationship to the universe'.
82. Novalis, *Sämtliche Werke*, x 443: 'Feeling for poetry has much in common with feeling for the mystical. It is a feeling for the particular, the personal, the unknown, the mysterious, the revelatory, the fortuitous. It portrays what cannot be portrayed. It sees what cannot be seen, feels what cannot be felt. . . . The feeling for poetry is closely akin to the feeling for prophecy, to religious divination altogether.'
83. Schleiermacher, *Über die Religion*, p. 9: 'a true priest of the Highest in that he brings Him' (God); 'closer to those who are used to grasping only the finite and the trifling; he presents them with the heavenly and eternal as an object of pleasure and unity'.
84. Wackenroder, *Phantasien über die Kunst*, p. 70: 'the enchanted castle of art'.
85. Wackenroder, *Herzensergießungen eines kunstliebenden Kloster-bruders*, in *Deutsche Literatur in Entwicklungsreihen, Romantik*, III (Leipzig, 1931), p. 87: 'the divine sublimity of art'.
86. Wackenroder, *Phantasien über die Kunst*, p. 69: 'the profound, eternal holiness'.
87. Wackenroder, *Herzensergießungen*, p. 87: 'the divinity of art'.

88. Wackenroder, *Herzensergießungen*, p. 51: 'Now in my mind's eye I gaze mournfully at the consecrated field by your walls, Nürnberg; the graveyard that is the resting-place of Albrecht Dürer, who was once the glory of Germany, indeed of all Europe. Unheeded he rests there amid countless gravestones, each decorated with metal imagery, insignia of an ancient art, and between them grow tall sunflowers that turn the graveyard into a pleasant garden. There rest the forgotten remains of our old Albrecht Dürer who makes me proud to be a German.

   'Few have been granted the privilege, that heaven seems to have accorded me, of understanding the very soul of your pictures, of appreciating their particular character in such profundity. I look around and see few who have lingered before you with such real love and such ardent admiration as I.'

89. A. W. Schlegel, *Sämtliche Werke* (1846) I 263: 'interpreter of that divine revelation, the language of the Gods'.

90. F. Schlegel, in *Kritische Schriften*, p. 50: 'There is a type of poetry whose alpha and omega is the relationship of the ideal and the real, and which must, on the analogy of philosophical terminology, be called transcendental poetry. It begins as satire with the absolute distinction between ideal and real, is poised between the two in elegy, and finally achieves complete identity of the two in the idyll. But just as one would attach little importance to a transcendental philosophy that was not critical, that did not represent the act of producing as well as the product, and did not also contain within its system of transcendental thoughts a characterization of transcendental thinking: the same also holds true of this poetry which unites, in modern poets, transcendental notions and ideas for a poetic theory of the creative act with artistic contemplation and self-portrayal, such as is found in Pindar, in Greek lyrical fragments and ancient elegies and more recently in Goethe, and in each of its representations it should also represent itself, and always be at one and the same time poetry and poetry of poetry.'

91. Shelley, *Defence of Poetry*, in *Complete Works*, VII 131.

92. Hugo, *Odes et Ballades*, in *Œuvres Complètes, Poésie*, I 6: 'The domain of poetry is without bounds. Beneath the real world there is an ideal world, visible in all its splendour to those who have grown accustomed, through deep thought, to perceive in things more than just things.'

93. Hugo, Preface to *Cromwell*, in *Théâtre Complet*, I 437: 'the aim of art is well-nigh divine'.

94. Vigny, *Chatterton*, in *Œuvres*, I 888: 'he reads from the stars the path indicated by the Lord's finger'.

95. Lamartine, *Des Destinées de la Poésie*, in *Œuvres*, p. 387: 'It is the embodiment of the innermost stirrings of man's heart and of his loftiest thoughts, of the most grandiose sights in nature and of its most harmonious sounds! It is both feeling and experience, spirit and matter; and for this reason it is the perfect language, the supreme language that embraces all aspects of man, giving his mind ideas, his imagination pictures, and music to his ear.'

96. Lamartine, *Des Destinées de la Poésie*, in *Œuvres*, p. 420: 'strong unshakable belief that philosophies, religions and literatures were only more or less satisfactory expressions of our relationship to the infinite Being'.

97. Lamartine, *Des Destinées de la Poésie*, in *Œuvres*, p. 415: 'Besides this philosophical, rational, political and social function, the poetry of the future will have a new task to fulfil: it must follow the trends of the social set-up and of the press; it must turn towards the people and become popular.'

98. Coleridge, *Biog. Lit.* II 102.

99. Shelley, *Defence of Poetry*, in *Complete Works*, VII 137.

100. Tieck, in *Kritische Schriften*, I 38: 'this vast alchemical process that turned everything he touched into gold'.

101. Wordsworth, *Preface to the 'Lyrical Ballads'*, in *Poetical Works*, II 410.

102. Wordsworth, *Preface to the 'Lyrical Ballads'*, in *Poetical Works*, II 436.

103. Wordsworth, *Preface to the 'Lyrical Ballads'*, in *Poetical Works*, II 386.

104. Blake, *Poetry and Prose*, p. 821.

105. Blake, *Poetry and Prose*, p. 822.

106. H. C. Robinson, letter to Dorothy Wordsworth, Feb. 1826; in *Romantic Perspectives* (1964), p. 135.

107. Blake, *Poetry and Prose*, p. 623.

108. Blake, *Auguries of Innocence*.

109. Novalis, *Blütenstaub* 35, in *Werke*, I 317: 'We are engaged on a mission: we are called to fashion the world.'

110. Novalis, *Sämtliche Werke*, VI 100: 'the world must be romanticized'. 'By investing the commonplace with a lofty significance, the ordinary with a mysterious aspect, the familiar with the prestige of the strange, the finite with a semblance of infinity, I am romanticizing.'

111. Novalis, *Blütenstaub* 24, in *Werke*, I 313: 'his faculty for revelation'.

112. Novalis, *Werke*, I 327: 'And should not the future bring back the former state?'

113. Novalis, *Werke*, I 303 : 'It must come, the holy age of everlasting peace.'

114. F. Schlegel, *Geschichte der alten und neuen Literatur*, p. 335 : 'out of the pure light of external hope, as an imaginative vision transfigured by faith and love, like the rainbow after the storm . . . or the dawn out of darkness'.

115. Blake, *Vision of the Last Judgement*, in *Poetry and Prose*, p. 638.

116. Shelley, *Defence of Poetry*, in *Complete Works*, VII 136.

117. Shelley, Dedication of *The Cenci*, in *Complete Works*, II 67.

118. Shelley, *Defence of Poetry*, in *Complete Works*, VII 135.

119. Wordsworth, *The Excursion*, book III, lines 335–7.

120. 'Oh Poet, it is thus that great poets act.'

121. van Tieghem, *Le Romantisme dans la littérature européenne*, p. 483 : 'product of Romanticism'.

122. Tieck, *Die altdeutschen Minnelieder*, *Deutsche Literatur in Ent-wicklungsreihen, Romantik*, X (Leipzig, 1931), p. 88 : 'the real apogee of Romantic poetry. Love, religion, chivalry and magic are interwoven into one magnificent poem.'

123. *Hugo raconté par un témoin de sa vie* (Brussels, 1863), II 300 : 'the book has no historical pretensions'.

124. *Hugo raconté par un témoin de sa vie*, II 300 : 'that is not what matters in the book. Any worth it may have is as a work of imagination, fancy and fantasy'.

125. A. W. Schlegel, *Vorlesungen über schöne Kunst und Literatur* (1884), p. 91 : 'How can the infinite be made explicit and apparent? Only in images and symbols.'

126. A. W. Schlegel, *Über dramatische Kunst und Literatur*, I 25 : 'Sensuous impressions ought to be hallowed through a myster-ious interpenetration of lofty sentiments, while the spiritual should find in tangible forms a sensuous equivalent for its in-expressible perception of the infinite.'

127. A. W. Schlegel, *Vorlesungen über schöne Kunst und Literatur*, p. 91 : 'we either seek an external form for the spiritual, or we relate the external to something hidden within'; 'the creation of poetry (taking this phrase in the widest sense to refer to all the arts) is nothing other than a constant quest for symbols'.

128. A. W. Schlegel, *Vorlesungen über schöne Kunst und Literatur*, p. 90 : 'a symbolical representation of the infinite'.

129. Wackenroder, *Herzensergießungen*, p. 59 : 'hieroglyphics'.

130. Coleridge, *Biog. Lit.* II 259.

131. *Statesman's Manual; Political Tracts of Wordsworth, Coleridge and Shelley* (Cambridge U.P., 1953), p. 25.

132. *Statesman's Manual,* p. 24.
133. F. Kermode, *Romantic Image* (Routledge Paperback, 1961), p. 44.
134. Abrams, *English Romantic Poets,* pp. 37–54.
135. R. A. Foakes, *The Romantic Assertion* (1958), p. 46.
136. Coleridge, *Biog. Lit.* I 59.
137. Blake, *Descriptive Catalogue,* in *Poetry and Prose,* p. 630.
138. Blake, *Annotations to 'Poems' by Wordsworth,* in *Poetry and Prose,* p. 821.
139. Blake, *Descriptive Catalogue,* in *Poetry and Prose,* p. 607.
140. R. P. Warren, *Selected Essays* (New York, 1957), p. 262.
141. Byron, *Childe Harold,* canto III, stanza vii.

142.

> Oh your moving, sublime voice
> Is too pure for this lowly abode :
> The music that pervades you
> Is an inspiration that rises to God.
>
> Your warbling, your humming
> Is a melodious blend
> Of the sweetest sounds of nature
> And the softest sighs of heaven.
>
> Your voice, unaware of its own sound,
> Is the voice of the blue firmament,
> Of trees, of resonant caverns,
> Of the valley asleep in the shade.
>
> You muster the sounds gathered
> From the murmur of the waves,
> From the rustle of the leaves,
> From the whisper of the echoes,
>
> From the water dripping drop by drop
> Off the bare rock down into the pool,
> Reverberating in its grotto
> As it ripples the blue expanse,
>
> From the rapturous plaints
> That rise from the woods by night,
> From the muffled roll of the waves
> On the sand or in the reeds;

And from these sweet sounds, mingling
With the heavenly inspiration that is yours,
God made your voice, O Philomele,
And you your song of praise to the night.

143.   Oh mingle your voice with mine!
One ear listens to us both;
But your ethereal prayer
Can better rise to the waiting heavens.

144. Hugo, *Les deux îles*, in *Œuvres Poétiques* (Édition Pléiade, Paris, 1964), I 394.

This is the image of glory :
First a dazzling prism,
Then an expiatory mirror,
In which the purple looks like blood!

145. Hugo, *Œuvres Poétiques*, I 395.

Oh monument of revenge! ineradicable trophy!
Bronze, turning on your steadfast base,
You raise to heaven your glory and your inanity;
And of all that a colossal hand made,
You alone remain standing; – a triumphal ruin
   Of the giant's edifice!

Relic of the Great Empire and of the Great Army,
Column that resounds with high renown!
I love you : strangers admire you in fear.

146. Hugo, *Œuvres Poétiques*, I 480.

Look, – a meteor! it sparkles and fades away.
Many a great man too, stricken by hidden grief,
Shines awhile and goes into his grave.
The common herd ignores him and follows the crowd;
To the ploughman bent over his furrow at eventide,
   What matters a star that falls!

147. F. Schlegel, in *Kritische Schriften*, p. 38 : 'Romantic poetry is still in the process of evolution; this indeed is its very essence, that it is eternally evolving, never completed.'

148. Tieck, in *Kritische Schriften*, I 44 : 'The wondrous is now becoming ordinary and natural to us.'

149. Novalis, *Sämtliche Werke*, x 244 : 'Poetry is a representation of the soul – of the inner world in its totality.'

150.   The new world is dawning
        And it eclipses the brightest sun,
        From under the moss-grown ruins
        A wondrously strange future shimmers,
        And what was hitherto commonplace,
        Now seems quaint and marvellous.
        The realm of love is inaugurated,
        Fable starts to spin her yarn.
        Nature's creative game begins,
        In pursuit of potent phrases,
        And so the world's great soul
        Stirs and blossoms far and wide and on and on.
        Everything must intertwine,
        Each growing and maturing through the other;
        Every being is contained in them all,
        By coalescing with them
        And plunging eagerly into their depths,
        It renews its own essence
        And reaps countless new thoughts.
        The world becomes a dream, the dream becomes a world
        And what was thought past,
        Approaches anew from afar.
        Imagination shall have its way,
        To weave the threads at will,
        To throw a veil over some things, to reveal others,
        Till it wafts away in an enchanted cloud.

FEELING

1. van Tieghem, *Le Mouvement romantique* (1923), p. 139 : 'this complete change of sensibility and of its expression in the arts'.
2. Mary Wollstonecraft, *Caves of Fancy*, in *Posthumous Works* (1793).
3. Voltaire, letter to M. Desforges-Maillard, in F. Vial and L. Denise, *Idées et doctrines littéraires du XVIIIième siècle* (1909), p. 164 : 'I value poetry only in so far as it adorns reason.'
4. Vial and Denise, *Idées et doctrines littéraires du XVIIIième siècle*, p. 161 : 'a moderate enthusiasm within the bounds of reason'.

5. Goethe, *Werke*, I 626 : 'entirely feeling'.

6. Goethe, *Werke*, I 148 : 'fragments of a great confession'.

7. Novalis, *Sämtliche Werke*, VI 379 : 'the heart is the key to the world and to life'.

8. Goethe, *Werke*, I 437 : 'this heart, in which I take such pride, which is the sole source of all my strength, of all my joy and of all my misery'.

9. Rousseau, *Confessions*, p. 4 : 'I felt before I thought : that is man's lot.'

10. Rousseau, *La Nouvelle Héloïse* (Hachette, Paris, 1925), p. 172 : 'the heart begets true happiness'.

11. Coleridge, *The Friend*, section II, essay 11.

12. Coleridge, *Letters*, ed. H. Coleridge (1895), p. 428.

13. Coleridge, *Letters*, p. 450.

14. Coleridge, *Letters*, p. 210.

15. Coleridge, *Biog. Lit.* ch. IV.

16. Schleiermacher, *Über die Religion*, p. 37 : 'neither thought nor deed, but intuition and feeling'.

17. Hugo, 'Compte rendu d'*Éloa*', in Vial and Denise, *Idées et doctrines littéraires du XIXième siècle* (1918), p. 98 : 'It is not in fact from the springs of Hippocrene, from the Castalian fountains, nor indeed from the stream of Permessus that the poet draws his inspiration, but quite simply from his soul and his heart.'

18. Novalis, *Schriften*, ed. J. Minor (Jena, 1923), II 299 : 'an art that stirs the soul'.

19. Coleridge, *On the Principles of Genial Criticism*, in *Biog. Lit.* II 221.

20. Keats, to Benjamin Bailey, 22 Nov. 1817, in *Letters*, p. 49.

21. De Quincey, *To a Young Man whose education had been neglected*, letter III, in *Works*, ed. D. Masson (Edinburgh, 1889), x 48.

22. F. Schlegel, *Geschichte der alten und neuen Literatur*, p. 59 : 'is in fact fervour, the most sublime and beautiful feeling'.

23. Sénacour, *Obermann* (1840), pp. xx–xxi : 'These letters do not form a novel. They have no dramatic progression, no deliberate build-up of happenings, no definite conclusion, none of the traits that make a work interesting. There are descriptions, of a kind that lead to a better understanding of natural phenomena and to an insight into a much neglected field, the relationship of man to what is known as the sphere of the inanimate.'

24. E. Rickwood, in *From Blake to Byron* (1957), p. 24.

25. A. W. Schlegel, *Über dramatische Kunst und Literatur*, I 42 : 'The dramatist cannot enjoy the privilege of ecstatic dreams, he must keep to the most direct route to his goal.'

26. Herford, *The Age of Wordsworth*, p. 135.
27. van Tieghem, *Le Romantisme dans la littérature européenne*, p. 445.
28. Mary Shelley, 'Note on *The Cenci*', in Shelley, *Complete Works* II 165.
29. Shelley, *Complete Works*, II 157.
30. Shelley, *Complete Works*, II 72.
31. van Tieghem, *Le Romantisme dans la littérature européenne*, p. 464: 'the more lyrical and imaginative features of Romanticism'.
32. Hugo, *Œuvres Poétiques*, p. 713: 'the human heart is like the earth, you can sow, plant, cultivate whatever you please on its surface; it will nevertheless bring forth its natural vegetation, its wild flowers and fruits; no axe or probe will ever plumb its depths; and like the earth, so also the human heart will always remain unscathed; it is the foundation of art just as the earth is of nature'.
33. Wordsworth, *Preface to the 'Lyrical Ballads'*, in *Poetical Works*, II 387.
34. Wordsworth, *Preface to the 'Lyrical Ballads'*, in *Poetical Works*, II 400.
35. Wordsworth, *Preface to the 'Lyrical Ballads'*, in *Poetical Works*, II 394–5.
36. Wordsworth, *Preface to the 'Lyrical Ballads'*, in *Poetical Works*, II 388.
37. Wordsworth, *Preface to the 'Lyrical Ballads'*, in *Poetical Works*, II 388.
38. Wordsworth, *Preface to the 'Lyrical Ballads'*, in *Poetical Works*, II 393.
39. *Early Letters of William and Dorothy Wordsworth*, ed. E. de Selincourt (Oxford, 1935), p. 295.
40. Wordsworth, *Preface to the 'Lyrical Ballads'*, in *Poetical Works*, II 388–9.
41. See F. W. Bateson, *Wordsworth* (1954), ch. i.
42. Wordsworth, *Laodamia*, lines 73–75.
43. Keats, *Letters*, p. 117.
44. Keats, *Letters*, p. 102.
45. Keats, *Letters*, p. 53.
46. Keats, *Letters*, p. 52.
47. Byron, *Letters and Journals*, v 318.
48. F. A. Pottle, 'The Case of Shelley', in *English Romantic Poets*, p. 297.
49. Shelley, *To a Skylark*.
50. Lamartine, *Le Poète Mourant*, in *Premières Méditations*.

My lyre has often been bathed in tears;
But sobs are heavenly dew to us;
Beneath a cloudless sky the heart cannot mature.

51. Staël, *Œuvres Complètes* (1820), x 274: 'The poetry of the ancients is a purer form of art, that of the moderns makes us shed more tears.'

52. Chénier, *Élégies*, i 22: 'the heart alone creates poetry'.

53. *La Muse Française*, ii 145: 'a genius for feeling'.

54. Musset, 'Un mot sur l'art moderne', in *Œuvres Complètes* (1866) ix 129: 'art is feeling'.

55. Hugo, *Œuvres Complètes*, xvii 130: 'What in fact is a poet? A man who has strong feelings and who expresses them in impassioned words. Poetry is almost purely feeling.'

56. Vigny, *Journal d'un poète*, in *Œuvres*, ii 1121: 'The *objective* epic and dramatic poets like Homer, Shakespeare, Dante, Molière and Corneille are more forceful, dignified and sublime than the *subjective* elegiac poets like Petrarch who portray themselves and bewail their inner sorrows.'

57. Vigny, *Journal d'un Poète*, in *Œuvres*, ii 1127: 'The heart certainly exists as a moral factor. Its joys and sorrows are felt; but it is a dark room, and its light is the intellect.'

58. Lamartine, *Des Destinées de la Poésie*, in *Œuvres*, p. 379: 'revival of moral and poetic feeling'.

59. Chateaubriand, *Œuvres Complètes* (1836), xi 259: 'The great writers have put their experience into their works. It is only one's own heart that one can depict well, ascribing it to other people.'

60. Stendhal, *Pensées* (1931), ii 283: 'one cannot depict what one has not felt'.

61. 'all that is most inward in everything'.

62. 'this penetrating self-portrayal'.

63. Lamartine, Preface to *Méditations Poétiques* (Hachette, Paris, 1931), p. 11: 'I was expressing myself for myself.' 'It was not an art, it was to relieve my own heart, weary of its sobbing . . . These lines were a plaint, a cry from the soul.'

64. Lamartine, Preface to *Méditations Poétiques*, p. 16: 'regressions into myself, personal laments or ravings'.

65. Musset, *La Nuit de Décembre*: 'who was as like me as a brother'

66. Musset, *La Nuit de Mai*: 'My mouth remains silent / To listen to the voice of my heart.'

67. Musset, *La Nuit d'Août*: 'Your heart or you: which is the poet? / It is your heart.'

68. Musset, *Poésies: À mon ami Édouard B*: 'Oh belabour your heart, it is there that genius resides.'

69. Musset, *Namouna*, lines 37–40 :

> Be sure of this, – it is the heart that speaks and sighs
> When the hand writes, – it is the heart that melts;
> It is the heart that expands, opens and breathes,
> Like a blithe pilgrim at the top of a hill.'

70. Musset, *Chanson* : 'my faint heart'.

71.
> Nothing makes us as sublime as a sublime sorrow,
> But in your stricken state, do not believe, oh poet,
> That your voice should stay silent in this world.
> The most despairing songs are the most beautiful,
> And I know some immortal lines that are sheer sobs.'

72. Shelley, *To a Skylark*.
73. Vigny, *Chatterton*, in *Théâtre Complet*, p. 61 : 'Open your heart to display it on a shop-counter! If it is wounded, so much the better! it is worth more! even a little battered, it will fetch a higher price!'

74.
> It was as if heaven
> Had softly kissed the earth,
> So that in the radiance of her blossom
> She now had to dream of him.

75. R. Huch, *Die Blütezeit der Romantik* (Leipzig, 1913), p. 278 : 'the spiritual ability to fly'.
76. A. W. Schlegel, *Über dramatische Kunst und Literatur*, ii 61 : 'more or less delicate hints, interspersed in the representation, admitting its own exaggerated one-sidedness in the role allocated to imagination and feeling'.
77. 'Everywhere we seek the infinite and always find only finite things.'
78. Wordsworth, *Preface to the 'Lyrical Ballads'*, in *Poetical Works*, ii 386.
79. Wordsworth, *Preface to the 'Lyrical Ballads'*, in *Poetical Works*, ii 383.
80. Wordsworth, *Preface to the 'Lyrical Ballads'*, in *Poetical Works*, ii 386–7.
81. Herder, *Werke* (Bibliographisches Institut, Leipzig, n.d.), ii 39 : 'He who would still find in our midst traces of this soundness should certainly not seek it among scholars : artless children, women, people with common sense, they are the ones who are

the only and the best orators of our age – if eloquence is what I take it to mean.'

82. Wordsworth, *Preface to the 'Lyrical Ballads'*, in *Poetical Works*, II 386.

83. Wordsworth, *Preface to the 'Lyrical Ballads'*, in *Poetical Works*, II 383.

84. Wordsworth, *Preface to the 'Lyrical Ballads'*, in *Poetical Works*, II 398.

85. Blake, *Annotations to 'Poems' by Wordsworth*, in *Poetry and Prose*, p. 821.

86. Tennyson, *A Memoir by his son* (1897), II 505.

87. Coleridge, *Biog. Lit.* II 97.

88. Coleridge, 'My first acquaintance with the poets', in *Works*, ed. A. R. Waller (1902), XII 270.

89. Shelley, in *Complete Works*, II 73.

90. Coleridge, *Table Talk*, 31 May 1830.

91. Novalis, *Werke*, I 188: 'They had now come to an extensive clearing in the woods, where there were several crumbling towers behind deep ditches. Fresh foliage climbed up round the old walls like a youthful garland in an old grey head. Looking at the grey stones, the jagged cracks and the tall gruesome shapes, one gazed into the immeasurable expanse of time and saw the remotest happenings contracted into little shining moments. Thus heaven shows us infinite spaces clothed in dark blue, and the furthest hosts of its weighty colossal worlds in a sort of milky shimmer, as innocent as a child's cheek.'

92. Bowra, *The Romantic Imagination*, p. 59.

93. Keats, *Letters*, p. 83.

94.   Love reason; always let your writings
        Derive from it alone their lustre and their worth.

95. Musset, *Après une lecture*, stanza X: 'My first point is the need to be unreasonable.'

96. Staël, *De l'Allemagne*, p. 170: 'improvised rather than composed'.

97. Hugo, *Notre-Dame de Paris* (n.d.), I 9: 'gush forth in a single surge'.

98. 'Here are four books of poetry written just as they were felt, not arranged into any particular order or sequence such as underlies nature without its becoming apparent; genuine poems, devoid of pose, the testimony less of the poet than of the human being, the intimate, involuntary disclosure of his experiences day by day, pages from his inner life, prompted at times by sadness, at times by joy.'

99. Lamartine, First Preface to *Méditations*, p. 12 : 'To be moved is the real art.'

100. Chénier, *Élégies*, I 22.

101. Gilman, *The Idea of Poetry in France*, p. 165.

102. Hugo, *Odes*, book II, *À mes Odes*, section ii :

> Happy he who does not shun the gloom of oblivion!
> Happy he who knows not what doleful memories
>   The sound of a name may rouse!
>   And that fame lies uneasy,
>   And that the poet's prize
>   Is the prize of martyrdom.
>
> Happy the bird that soars and flutters
> Without fear of huntsman, storm or mishap!
>   Happy he who would nought venture!
>   Happy he who pursues what he should!
>   Happy he who lives only for the sake of living,
>   Who sings only for the sake of singing!

103. Lamartine, *Le Lac*, stanza XIII :

> Oh lake! silent rocks! grottoes! dark forest!
> You that are untouched or regenerated by time;
> Cherish, beauteous nature, of this night cherish
>   At least the memory.

104. Musset, *La Nuit d'Août*, lines 123–7 :

> Oh Muse! what matters life or death to me?
> I love, and I would grow pale; I love, and I would suffer;
> I love, and for one kiss I would gladly give my genius;
> I love, and I would feel on my emaciated cheek
> A stream of tears that never cease their flow.

105. Hugo, *Réponse à un acte d'accusation*, in *Les Contemplations* :

> Into battle, prose and verse! draw up in fighting order!
>
> And over the batallions of Alexandrines, drawn up in formation,
> I blew a revolutionary wind.
> I put the red cap of liberty on to the old dictionary.

106. P. Hazard, 'Les caractères nationaux du lyrisme romantique français', in *Quatre Études* (Oxford U.P., 1940), p. 84.

107. Hazard, in *Quatre Études*, p. 44.
108. Moreau, *Le Classicisme des Romantiques*, p. 191: 'latent prudence'.
109. F. Strich, 'Die Romantik als europäische Bewegung', in *Festschrift für H. Wölfflin* (Munich, 1924), p. 48.
110. Arnim, *Von Volksliedern*, in *Deutsche Literatur in Entwicklungsreihen, Romantik*, x 117–18 : 'Meanwhile the scholars cultivated a genteel language of their own, which for a long time excluded the people from all that was lofty and splendid, and which they must eventually either abandon or popularize, when they realize that their endeavours run counter to all true culture in trying to establish language as something permanent, because it must of necessity always remain pliable, ready to fit the thought that seeks expression; for only in this way is it renewed each day, without artificial aids. Because of this linguistic division and neglect of the people's superior poetic heritage the Germany of to-day by and large lacks folk-poetry, and only when it becomes less scholarly, or at least less specifically attached to book-learning, does folk-song come into being and reach us without being printed or written, winging through the air like a white crow.'
111. Korff, *Geist der Goethezeit*, iv 224–7.
112. *The Forsaken Maiden* :

> At dawn when the cocks crow,
> Before the stars fade,
> I have to stand at the hearth,
> I have to light the fire.
>
> The glow of the flames is lovely,
> The sparks fly up;
> I stare blankly at them,
> Sunk in sorrow.

113. *The Broken Ring* :

> There is a cool valley
> Where a mill-wheel turns.

114. Hazlitt, 'The Englishman', in *Selected Essays*, ed. G. Keynes (1930), p. 802.
115. Vigny, *Journal d'un Poète*, in *Œuvres*, ii 894 : 'Lamartine is a poet of limitless intoxication, devoid of form.'

CONCLUSION: PERSPECTIVE

1. R. Wellek, *History of Modern Criticism* (1955), 18.
2. I. Siciliano, *Il Romanticismo francese* (Florence, 1964), p. 34.
3. M. Moraud, *Le romantisme français en Angleterre* (1833), p. 7: 'noisy', 'spectacular', 'its pursuit of the exception, of the blatant contrast', 'its contempt for tradition, for conventions'.
4. C. Dédéyan, *Victor Hugo et l'Allemagne* (1964).
5. van Tieghem, *Le Mouvement romantique*, p. 51: 'at least the poets of the Gottingen group and above all those of the *Storm and Stress* between 1770 and 1780 must be called Romantics'.
6. H. N. Fairchild, 'The Romantic movement in England', in *Publications of the Modern Language Association of America*, LV (1940) 24.
7. Barzun, *Classic, Romantic and Modern*, pp. 137 and 14.
8. Baudelaire, *Salon de 1846*, in *Œuvres* (Édition Pléiade, Paris, 1961), p. 879: 'he who speaks of Romanticism speaks of modern art'.
9. Baudelaire, *Salon de 1859*, in *Œuvres Complètes*, II 125: 'what a mysterious faculty is this queen of all faculties'.
10. Baudelaire, *Salon de 1859*, in *Œuvres Complètes*, II 125: 'it is the synthesis'.
11. Baudelaire, *Salon de 1859*, in *Œuvres Complètes*, II 126: 'it creates a new world'.
12. Baudelaire, *Salon de 1859*, in *Œuvres Complètes*, II 126: 'it is intimately related to the infinite'.
13. 'Dreaming is a second life'.
14. Nerval, *Œuvres* (Édition Pléiade, Paris, 1952), I 363: 'the incursion of dream into real life'.
15. Coleridge, *On the Principles of Genial Criticism*, in *Biog. Lit.* II 221.

Bibliography

———◆━━◆◆◆ ❖ ◆◆◆◆━━◆———

In view of the vast amount that has been written about Romanticism, it is possible to give only a selective bibliography, concentrating on works that are either comparative in approach or in some way specially striking or challenging. A discriminating review of newer criticism in this field is contained in R. Wellek's 'Romanticism Re-examined', in *Concepts of Criticism* (Yale U.P., 1963). Though it is at times difficult to separate the 'general' from the 'comparative', under the former heading are listed those works that deal with Romanticism as a whole phenomenon, while the latter covers those that make specific juxtapositions.

GENERAL

L. ABERCROMBIE, *Romanticism* (1926).
A good starting-point; a sensible attempt to arrive at the broadest possible definition of the concept.

M. H. ABRAMS, *The Mirror and the Lamp* (Oxford U.P., 1953).
Brilliant analysis of the contrast between eighteenth-century mimetic and nineteenth-century expressive theories of art.

I. BABBITT, *Rousseau and Romanticism* (Boston, Mass., 1919).
Hardly about Rousseau; an eccentric and challenging disparagement of Romanticism.

F. BALDENSPERGER, ' "Romantique", ses analogues et ses équivalents : tableau synoptique de 1650 à 1810', in *Harvard Studies and Notes in Philology*, XIX (1937).
A table of quotations illustrating the development of the word and the concept.

F. BALDENSPERGER, 'Pour une interprétation équitable du romantisme européen', in *Helicon*, I, no. 3 (1938).
Traces history of word back to 1667.

J. BARZUN, *Classic, Romantic and Modern* (1962).
A most provocative book that aims at a new definition of Romanticism, but chooses one so wide as to be fraught with danger.

J. B. HALSTED (ed.), *Romanticism: Problems of definition, explanation and evaluation* (Boston, Mass., 1965).
   Reprints in convenient form excerpts from Babbitt, Barzun, Lovejoy, Croce, Wellek, Foakes, etc.

A. O. LOVEJOY, 'On the discrimination of Romanticisms', in *Publications of the Modern Language Association of America*, XXIX (1924), reprinted in Lovejoy's *Essays in the History of Ideas* (Baltimore, 1948) and in *English Romantic Poets*, ed. M. H. Abrams (Oxford U.P., 1960).
   A crucial statement that is essential reading.

F. L. LUCAS, *The Decline and Fall of the Romantic Ideal* (Cambridge, 1936).
   Bizarre but stimulating.

M. PECKHAM, *Beyond the Tragic Vision* (New York, 1962).
   An ingenious re-interpretation of the nineteenth century as a period of reconstruction after the collapse of Enlightenment values.

M. PRAZ, *The Romantic Agony* (Oxford U.P., 1933).
   The decadent after-effects of Romanticism.

'ROMANTICISM: a symposium', in *Publications of the Modern Language Association of America*, LV (1940).
   A set of articles on Romanticism in England, France, Germany, Italy and Spain: the quickest introduction to the whole field.

H. G. SCHENK, *The Mind of the European Romantics* (1966).
   Sees Romanticism as spiritual dissonance and traces the conflict between unredeemed nihilism and Christian salvation in the minds of nineteenth-century Europeans by reference to their lives.

H. G. SCHENK, 'The Romantic movement in Europe', in *The Listener* (25 January 1957).
   Through the eyes of a social historian.

L. P. SMITH, 'Four Romantic Words', in *Words and Idioms* (1925).
   Most illuminating account of the history of 'romantic', 'originality', 'creation' and 'genius'.

F. STRICH, 'Europe and the Romantic movement', in *German Life & Letters*, II (1948).

A. K. THORLBY (ed.), *The Romantic Movement* (1966).
   A useful compilation of critical opinions covering a wide range of topics and standpoints.

R. Wellek, *A History of Modern Criticism* (1955), vol. I: *The Later Eighteenth Century*. vol. II: *The Romantic Age*.
Indispensable.

COMPARATIVE

F. Baldensperger, *Goethe en France* (1904).

F. Baldensperger, *Études d'histoire littéraire*. In vol. I (1907): 'Young et ses *Nuits* en France' and 'La *Léonore* de Bürger dans la littérature française'. In vol. II (1910): 'Esquisse d'une histoire de Shakespeare en France'.

G. Bonarius, *Zum magischen Realismus bei Keats und Novalis* (Giessen, 1950).

J. M. Carré, *Goethe en Angleterre* (1920).
Specially part I: 1780–1830.

J. M. Carré, *Les écrivains français et le mirage allemand* (1947).

L. Cazamian, 'Le romantisme en France et en Angleterre: quelques différences', in *Études Anglaises*, I (1937).
Difference between French Classical and English Elizabethan heritage.

C. Dédéyan, *Victor Hugo et l'Allemagne* (1964).

A. C. Dunstan, 'German influence on Coleridge', in *Modern Language Review*, XVII and XVIII (1922 and 1923).

E. Eggli, *Schiller et le romantisme français* (1927).

E. Estève, *Byron et le romantisme français* (1929).

L. A. Fouret, 'Romantisme français et romantisme allemand', in *Mercure de France* (1927).

H. E. Holthusen, 'Das klassisch-romantische Deutschlandsbild in Frankreich, England und Amerika', in *Merkur* (July 1959).

V. Klemperer, 'Romantik und französische Romantik', in *Idealistische Neuphilologie* (1922).

J. Körner, *Die Botschaft der deutschen Romantik an Europa* (Augsburg, 1929).
Somewhat misleading title; concerns the reception of A. W. Schlegel's *Vorlesungen* outside Germany.

E. C. Mason, *Deutsche und englische Romantik* (Göttingen 1959).
Essays on various aspects of the relationship between German and English Romanticism; full of interesting suggestions.

M. Moraud, *Le romantisme français en Angleterre* (1883).

H. OPPEL, 'Englische und deutsche Romantik', in *Die Neueren Sprachen*, x (1956).

H. PEYRE, *Shelley et la France* (Cairo, 1935).
Specially part II.

L. REYNAUD, *L'influence allemande en France au XVIIIième et au XIXième siècle* (1922).
A collection of data.

L. REYNAUD, *Le romantisme des origines anglo-germaniques* (1926).
Traces infiltration of English and German ideas into France.

V. ROSSEL, *Histoire des relations littéraires entre la France et l'Allemagne* (1897).
Catalogue of articles, translations and contacts.

W. F. SCHIRMER, *Der Einfluss der deutschen Literatur auf die englische im 19. Jahrhundert* (Halle, 1947).

M. A. SMITH, *L'influence des Lakistes sur les romantiques français* (1920).

F. W. STOKOE, *German influence in the English Romantic period* (Cambridge, 1926).
Contains much solid information.

F. STRICH, 'Die Romantik als europäische Bewegung', in *Festschrift für Heinrich Wölfflin* (Munich, 1924).
Thoughtful and thought-provoking.

J. TEXTE, *Études de littérature européenne* (1898).
Specially 'Wordsworth et la poésie lakiste en France' and 'L'influence allemande dans le romantisme français'.

P. VAN TIEGHEM, *Le romantisme dans la littérature européenne* (1948).
The standard work; a sweeping survey of Romanticism in European literature, arranged according to themes and genres and seeking to synthesize similarities; written from the French point of view; vast, though at times inaccurate bibliography.

P. VAN TIEGHEM, 'Essai sur le romantisme européen', *Bibliothèque universelle et Revue de Genève*, II (1929).
On the common features of European Romanticism.

P. VAN TIEGHEM, *Ossian en France* (1917).

P. VAN TIEGHEM, *Ossian et l'ossianisme dans la littérature européenne au XVIIIième siècle* (Groningen, 1920).

P. VAN TIEGHEM, *La poésie de la nuit et des tombeaux* (1921).

J. VOISINE, *Rousseau en Angleterre à l'époque romantique* (1956).

z

R. WELLEK, 'The concept of Romanticism in literary history', in *Comparative Literature*, I (1949), reprinted in *Concepts of Criticism* (Yale U.P., 1963).
  Emphasizes the unity of European Romanticism.

R. WELLEK, 'German and English Romanticism', in *Confrontations* (Princeton U.P., 1965).

L. A. WILLOUGHBY, 'Coleridge und Deutschland', in *Germanisch-Romanische Monatsschrift*, XXIV (1936).

ENGLISH ROMANTICISM

M. H. ABRAMS (ed.), *English Romantic Poets* (Oxford U.P., 1960).
  A collection of good essays.

J. V. BAKER, *The Sacred River* (Louisiana State U.P., 1957).
  A study of Coleridge's theory of imagination.

W. J. BATE, 'Coleridge on the function of art', in *Perspectives of Criticism*, ed. H. Levin (Cambridge, Mass., 1950).

F. W. BATESON, *Wordsworth: a Re-interpretation* (1954).

E. BERNBAUM, *Guide through the Romantic Revolt* (New York, 1949).
  A useful handbook with extensive bibliographies.

H. BLOOM, *Shelley's Mythmaking* (New Haven, 1959).

H. BLOOM, *The Visionary Company* (New York, 1961).

C. M. BOWRA, *The Romantic Imagination* (Oxford U.P., 1961).
  Stimulating essays on various poets and works.

R. A. FOAKES, *The Romantic Assertion* (1958).

B. FORD (ed.), *From Blake to Byron*, Pelican Guide to English Literature (1957).
  Good essays and bibliographies.

S. GARDNER, *Infinity on the Anvil* (Oxford, 1954).
  A sensitive study of Blake.

A. GÉRARD, *L'idée romantique de la poésie en Angleterre* (1958).
  A penetrating analysis based on a perceptive reading of Romantic poetry.

C. H. HERFORD, *The Age of Wordsworth* (1914).

G. HOUGH, *The Romantic Poets* (1953).
  A sound basic study.

F. KERMODE, *Romantic Image* (1957).
  A suggestive book, though more concerned with the later Romantic generation of Yeats than with that of Wordsworth.

G. W. KNIGHT, *The Starlit Dome* (Oxford, 1941).

J. L. LOWES, *The Road to Xanadu* (1930).

A. E. POWELL, *The Romantic Theory of Poetry* (1926).
An examination in the light of Croce's aesthetic, with flashes of brilliant insight.

I. A. RICHARDS, *Coleridge on Imagination* (1934).

A. RODWAY, *The Romantic Conflict* (1963).
Original sociological interpretation.

R. P. WARREN, 'A Poem of Pure Imagination', in *Selected Essays* (New York, 1957).
Subtle interpretation of *The Ancient Mariner*.

B. WILLEY, *Nineteenth Century Studies* (1949).
Specially section on Coleridge.

B. WILLEY, 'Coleridge on Imagination and Fancy', in *Proceedings of the British Academy* (1946).
Lucid exposition of the meaning and significance of the 'celebrated but useless' distinction.

L. A. WILLOUGHBY, 'English Romantic Criticism', in *Weltliteratur: Festgabe für F. Strich* (Bern, 1952).

FRENCH ROMANTICISM

J. B. BARRÈRE, *Hugo, l'homme et l'œuvre* (1952).

J. B. BARRÈRE, *La fantaisie de Victor Hugo* (1949–60).

R. BRAY, *Chronologie du Romantisme* (1932).
Day by day, blow by blow account of the emergence of the Romantic movement in France.

F. W. M. DRAPER, *The Rise and Fall of the French Romantic Drama* (1923).
A string of plots and events.

E. EGGLI and P. MARTINO, *Le Débat romantique en France* (1933).
An invaluable, well edited collection of manifestoes.

M. GILMAN, *The Idea of Poetry in France* (Cambridge, Mass., 1958).
Deals only with lyric poetry – from de la Motte to Baudelaire – but within that limit masterly.

P. HAZARD, 'Les caractères nationaux du lyrisme romantique français', in *Quatre Études* (Oxford U.P., 1940).

I. A. HENNING, '*L'Allemagne*' de Mme de Staël et la polémique romantique (1929).

A collection of contemporary opinions, from which some unwarranted conclusions are drawn.

P. LASSERRE, *Le Romantisme français* (1907).

G. LOTE, *En préface à 'Hernani'* (1930).

P. MOREAU, *Le Romantisme* (1932).

P. MOREAU, *Le Classicisme des Romantiques* (1932).
A tendentious book about the tyranny of Classicism over Romanticism in France.

I. SICILIANO, *Il Romanticismo francese* (Florence, 1964).

P. VAN TIEGHEM, *Le Romantisme français* (1951).
A good introduction.

P. VAN TIEGHEM and G. MICHAUD, *Le Romantisme* (1952).
Schematic but helpful.

P. TRAHARD, *Le Romantisme défini par 'Le Globe'* (1924).
Outlines with illustrations the shifts of opinion.

F. VIAL and L. DENISE, *Idées et doctrines littéraires du XVIIIième siècle* (1909).

F. VIAL and L. DENISE, *Idées et doctrines littéraires du XIXième siècle* (1918).

GERMAN ROMANTICISM

H. EICHNER, 'F. Schlegel's theory of Romantic poetry', in *Publications of the Modern Language Association of America*, LXXI (1956).

R. HAYM, *Die romantische Schule* (Berlin, 1870).
For long the accepted work on the subject; now rather dated.

B. HAYWOOD, *Novalis: the Veil of Imagery* (The Hague, 1959).

R. HUCH, *Die Blütezeit der Romantik* (Leipzig, 1913).

P. KLUCKHOHN, *Die deutsche Romantik* (Leipzig, 1924).
A precise, clear account.

P. KLUCKHOHN, *Das Ideengut der deutschen Romantik* (Tübingen, 1953).

H. A. KORFF, *Geist der Goethezeit* (Leipzig, 1949).
A monumental four-volume analysis of the whole age of Goethe, full of penetrating and illuminating criticism; unfortunately available only in German.

A. O. LOVEJOY, 'On the meaning of "romantic" in early German Romanticism', in *Modern Language Notes*, XXXI and XXXII (1916 and 1917).

G. R. MASON, *From Gottsched to Hebbel* (1961).
A useful introduction to this period.

K. Negus, *Hoffmann's Other World* (Pennsylvania U.P., 1965).
On Hoffmann's 'new mythology'.

P. Reiff, *Die Ästhetik der deutschen Frühromantik* (Illinois, 1946).
Detailed critical account of aesthetic theories.

W. Rose, *From Goethe to Byron: the development of 'Weltschmerz' in German literature* (1924).

W. F. Schirmer, *Kleine Schriften* (Tübingen, 1950).
Includes three good essays on A. W. Schlegel.

F. Strich, *Deutsche Klassik und Romantik* (Munich, 1924).
In the wake of Wölfflin's art criticism, a dialectical confrontation of Classicism as the embodiment of perfection and Romanticism of infinitude.

M. Thalmann, *Das Märchen und die Moderne* (Stuttgart, 1961).
Perceptive comments on Hoffmann.

R. Tymms, *Doubles in literary psychology* (Cambridge, 1949).

R. Tymms, *German Romantic Literature* (1955).

O. Walzel, *Deutsche Romantik* (Berlin, 1926).

L. A. Willoughby, *The Romantic movement in Germany* (Oxford, 1930).
A handy brief summary.

Index